KOVELS'
NEW DICTIONARY
OF MARKS

ALSO BY RALPH AND TERRY KOVEL

Books

Dictionary of Marks—Pottery and Porcelain
A Directory of American Silver, Pewter and Silver Plate
American Country Furniture 1780–1875
The Kovels' Collector's Guide to American Art Pottery
The Kovels' Organizer for Collectors
Kovels' Know Your Antiques
Kovels' Know Your Collectibles
The Kovels' Book of Antique Labels
The Kovels' Collectors' Source Book
Kovels' Antiques & Collectibles Fix-It Source Book
Kovels' Guide to Selling Your Antiques & Collectibles
Kovels' American Silver Marks 1650 to the Present

Price Guides

Kovels' Antiques & Collectibles Price List
The Kovels' Bottle Price List
The Kovels' Price Guide for Collector Plates, Figurines, Paperweights, and
    Other Limited Editions
The Kovels' Illustrated Price Guide to Royal Doulton
The Kovels' Illustrated Price Guide to Depression Glass and American
    Dinnerware
Kovels' Advertising Collectibles Price List

KOVELS'
NEW DICTIONARY
OF MARKS

Ralph & Terry Kovel

CROWN PUBLISHERS, INC.   NEW YORK

Grateful acknowledgment is given to the following companies, corporations, and individuals for use of information and for permission to use reproductions of their marks, their marking systems, or information from their publications in this book:

The Dyson Perrins Museum Trust, Worcester, England, for information on Royal Worcester porcelain; The Homer Laughlin China Company for permission to reproduce their dating system and certain marking information; The Hutchinson Publishing Group Limited and Clarkson N. Potter, Inc., for permission to reproduce material from *The Doulton Lambeth Wares* by Desmond Eyles (1975), *Royal Crown Derby* by John Twitchett F.R.S.A. and Betty Bailey F.R.S.A. (1976), and *Royal Worcester Porcelain* by Henry Sandon (1975); Millicent S. Mali for permission to reproduce a chart from her book *Quimper Faience*, privately printed, 1979; the Patent Office and the Public Record Office, London, for information on English registry marks; The Pfaltzgraff Company for information on their history and permission to use a reproduction of their current mark; Royal Doulton and the Royal Doulton Group for information on their history; Violette Steinke for permission to reproduce the chart on year code marks of Royal Delft plates, parts of which were published in an article entitled "Delving into Royal Delft," *The Plate Collector*, March 1984; and the Syracuse China Corporation for permission to reproduce their marking systems.

Grateful acknowledgment is made for use of material from
Dictionary of Marks—Pottery and Porcelain. Copyright 1953 by Crown
Publishers, Inc. Reprinted by permission of Crown Publishers, Inc.

CROWN is a trademark of Crown Publishers, Inc.
Manufactured in the United States of America
Library of Congress Cataloging-in-Publication Data
Kovel, Ralph M.
    Kovels' New dictionary of marks.
    Bibliography: p.
    Includes indexes.
    1. Pottery—Marks. 2. Porcelain—Marks. I. Kovel,
Terry H. II. Title. III. Title: New dictionary of
marks.
NK4215.K68 1985   738'.0275   85–15146
ISBN 0-517-55914-5

10 9

*Thirty-three years later, the thoughts are the
same, the presentation more elaborate.*

To   *and*

our mothers;

To   *and*

our fathers;

and, of course, To

ACKNOWLEDGMENTS

We have really been writing this book for more than thirty years. Ever since July 7, 1953, the day we saw our first copy of our first book, we have been keeping records of marks. Unfortunately we cannot thank the thousands of our readers who have·added to our files of information through all those years. Rather, the thanks are to those who helped us clear up mysteries during the last two years. Many companies sent information and we thank all of them by including correct entries in the book. Some companies spent hours checking out minor problems. This list includes Arklow Pottery, Chessell Pottery, Franciscan Ceramics, Haas Group, Keystone Pottery, Mayer China Co., Myott-Meakin (1982) Ltd., Noritake Co. Ltd., Pfaltzgraff Pottery, Rosenthal Glass & Porcelain AG, Royal Doulton Tableware Ltd., Royal Worcester Spode Ltd., Shenango China Co., Wedgwood Group, and West Highland Pottery. Many librarians helped and we thank all of them. Jackie Anderson of the Jenkintown Public Library spent days researching one missing company in her area and to her, as the representative of all hardworking librarians, we say a special thanks.

You have to work on a project like this to understand the trivial problems that can take days of research, and patient rechecking of facts. Our staff, including Harriet Goldner, Gay Hunter, Nancy Saada, Carol Chin, Janet London, Sandy Brady, and all the others, including Mike, Eleanor, John, Grace, Edie, Beth, Randy, and Debbie, helped make this book possible and accurate. Crown Publishers' experts, including Pamela Thomas, Milt Wackerow, and Ann Cahn, made it look even better. We thank all of them.

Research always builds on earlier research and this book would not have been possible without the help of the many authors who preceded us. A full bibliography is included at the back of the book so you, too, can learn from these talented authors.

Ralph Kovel
Terry Kovel
October 1985

CONTENTS

How to Use This Book: An Introduction x

THE MARKS

SOME ADDITIONAL INFORMATION

HOW TO USE THIS BOOK:
AN INTRODUCTION

Dictionary of Marks—Pottery and Porcelain, published in 1953, was our first book. It listed the marks, or backstamps, on ceramics by the shape of the mark, not by country, maker, or by many of the other ways that were available at the time. The book has been reprinted more than forty times and has been popular with collectors and museum researchers for thirty years. It is still in print and is available at most libraries and bookstores. The book has a special place in our lives because it was our first book and the start of our writing career. Now, forty-two books later, we have decided to write this sequel to our *Dictionary of Marks.* We have been gathering information and marks and filing them away for years.

Collectors today are interested in many types of pottery and porcelain. Some of the most popular collectibles were made during the 1950s, after our first book was written and published. This book is not a revision but a companion to *Dictionary of Marks.* About 10 percent of the marks in the new book appeared in the old book. That is because either we located more information, or the subject was of such interest that its omission would have been obvious, or because the marks were part of a company history and were needed to keep the dating information clear.

The first section of the book is a listing of marks that look like objects or designs, such as crowns, shields, birds, etc. The second section is an alphabetical list of marks that are initials and/or words. The arrangement of marks in each section is a bit capricious; we basically arranged them from simple to complex. We also assumed that the mark on your dish might be blurred, so we occasionally placed a mark by the outline, not by the letters of the name. We then made the index as complete as possible to give you clues about marks with words or symbols that may appear in a different section.

Each mark appears in a rectangle with a letter code, and is indexed by page number and by code letter. With each mark is the name of the factory, location, type of ceramic, how the mark was applied, date of mark. Sometimes we added the dates of the factory, current name of successor company, and occasionally the special name of the mark used by American collectors. We had many problems with the company names. Obviously, the original name of a German company was in German. When translated, several possible forms could have been used. In some cases, we did a comfortable translation. If the initials in the mark were directly connected to the foreign name, we may have used a more awkward translation. In a few cases we felt it was best to keep the foreign title.

The problem of dating a mark was relatively simple. We use "1895–1900" to mean the mark may have been used during those years. If we used a date such as "1895 +," we were not positive how long after 1895 the mark was in use. "Ca.1895" means we are only suggesting a general time period, and the date could have been used at any time during the years on either side of 1895.

The factory dates proved more difficult. Most of the time they are from the first year that any predecessor company worked until the last year any successor company worked, provided that the name or management was continuous. Two companies frequently merged into one and the mark was used for the new company. We then dated it back to the oldest company with a direct relationship to the mark. For example, the mythical company of "Ralph Ltd." was founded in 1820. This company bought "Terry and Son," a company started in 1840. If the new firm took the name "Great Pottery, Inc.," it would then be listed as dating from 1820. If "Terry and Son" had bought "Ralph Ltd.," the new company would be dated from 1840. The information was often sketchy and sometimes conflicting, so we often had to use our best judgment. The successor company, if it is still in business, is listed at the bottom of the mark caption.

The marks were chosen primarily so the book would be useful to the average collector. The majority of marks date after 1850. Some are current marks. (It may be disappointing, but it is important to know you do *not* own an antique.) Most of the marks listed are from the United States, England, Germany, and France. Some factories are represented by many marks because each one gives dating information. Some firms have only a single mark that was in use for many years.

We had so many special problems to untangle with dating marks, tracing factory histories, etc., that we decided to add a few special sections at the back of the book to help you. One section, "The Vocabulary of Marks," lists words that appear in marks that will help to date the mark. Another section shows some of the factory "family trees" we were able to trace. Still another lists all the marks we found that incorporated systemized dating backstamps.

Last, but not least, is the Selected Reading. In most cases, the title of the book indicates the content, but if not we have included a comment to help. These books, as well as actual ceramic pieces, clippings, interviews, and correspondence, were the main sources of our information. We list only 3,500 of the 20,000 marks that we were able to find in doing our research; the others probably appear in these books.

We welcome any corrections or comments. It is doubtful that we will revise this book thirty years from now, but we will keep the notes for future researchers.

THE
MARKS

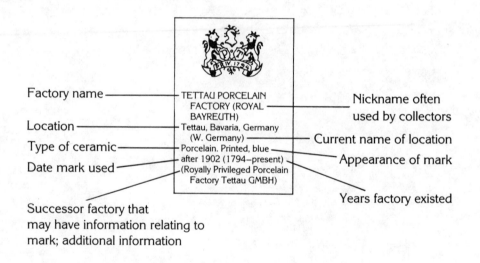

Factory name —————————— TETTAU PORCELAIN FACTORY (ROYAL BAYREUTH) ————— Nickname often used by collectors

Location —————————— Tettau, Bavaria, Germany (W. Germany) ————— Current name of location

Type of ceramic —————————— Porcelain. Printed, blue ————— Appearance of mark

Date mark used —————————— after 1902 (1794–present) (Royally Privileged Porcelain Factory Tettau GMBH) ————— Years factory existed

Successor factory that may have information relating to mark; additional information

A ANCHOR	**B** SAMSON & CO. Paris, France Porcelain 1885+ (1873–1957+)	**C** VILLEROY & BOCH Mettlach, Saar, Germany (W. Germany) Earthenware. Impressed ca.1836–ca.1850 (1813–present) (various names, owners & locations)	**D** ROOKWOOD POTTERY CO. Cincinnati, OH, U.S.A. Art pottery. Stamped or relief before 1883 (1880–1967) (Names, molds purchased by Arthur J. Townley, Michigan Center, MI,1982)
E ANCHOR PORCELAIN CO. LTD. Longton, Staffordshire, England Porcelain. Impressed or printed 1901–1915 (1901–1918)	**F** ARMAND MARSEILLE Köppelsdorf, Thuringia, Germany (E. Germany) Dolls' heads, porcelain ca.1910+ (1865–1919+) (By 1965 Electroceramics Works Sonneberg VEB)	**G** ANCHOR POTTERY CO. Trenton, NJ, U.S.A. Dinner & toilet sets. Printed ca.1895 (1893–1927)	**H** ERNST BOHNE SONS Rudolstadt, Thuringia, Germany (E. Germany) Decorative porcelain. Impressed 1878–ca.1920 (1854– ca.1920)
I BRITISH ANCHOR POTTERY CO. LTD. Longton, Staffordshire, England Earthenware. Printed or impressed 1884–1913 (1884–1964+)	**J** HUBBE BROTHERS Haldensleben, Prussia, Germany (E. Germany) White & decorated artistic & utility ware 1882–1898(1875–ca.1898)	**K** GEORG MLADENK & CO. Vidin, Bulgaria Pottery ca.1920 (1900+)	**L** MOSER BROTHERS BRITANNIA PORCELAIN WORKS Mayerhofen, Bohemia (Dvory, Czechoslovakia) Hard paste porcelain ca.1898–1925 (1898– ca.1925)
M MOLLER & DIPPE Unterkoditz, Thuringia, Germany (E. Germany) Porcelain ca.1883–ca.1931 (1846– 1931+)	**N** PORSGRUND PORCELAIN FACTORY Porsgrunn, Norway Hard paste porcelain 1948–1954 (1885– present)	**O** FR. BOHME PORCELAIN FACTORY Sorau, Brandenburg, Germany (E. Germany) Table & decorative porcelain ca.1894–1918 (1894– 1918)	**P** ROYAL FABRIQUE FONTEBASSO Treviso, Venezia, Italy Soft paste porcelain 1873+ (1860–1873+)

A

OSCAR SCHALLER & CO.
Schwarzenbach-Saale,
 Bavaria, Germany (W.
 Germany)
Porcelain
1882–ca.1918 (1882–
 present)
(Winterling Group)

B

C. TIELSCH & CO.
Altwasser, Silesia, Germany
 (Walbrzych, Poland)
Porcelain. Blue underglaze
ca.1875–ca.1918 (1845–
 present)
(Hutschenreuther AG)

C

SAUER & ROLOFF
 EARTHENWARE
 FACTORY
Haldensleben, Prussia,
 Germany (E. Germany)
Earthenware & porcelain
1905 + (ca.1905–1908 +)

D

THOMAS MADDOCK &
 SONS
Trenton, NJ, U.S.A.
Earthenware, sanitary ware
(1882–1929 +)

E

VERNON
Fismes, Marne, France
Stoneware, porcelain.
 Green
1840 +

F

W. DAVENPORT & CO.
Longport, Staffordshire,
 England
Porcelain & earthenware.
 Impressed
ca.1800–ca.1860 (ca.
 1793–1887)

G

A. FARINI
Faenza, Italy
Majolica
(1850–1878)

H

FRIEDRICH
 GOLDSCHEIDER
 VIENNA
 MANUFACTORY
Vienna, Austria
Porcelain
1885 + (1885–present)
(various names)

I

GIUSEPPE CARLO
 GALVANI
Pordenone, Italy
Creamware
1823–1845 (ca.1823–
 ca.1883)

J

GUSTAFSBERG
Gustafsberg, Sweden
Faience, semiporcelain,
 earthenware
1910–1940 (1786–
 present)

K

GUSTAFSBERG
Gustafsberg, Sweden
Faience, semiporcelain,
 earthenware
1935–1939 (1825–
 present)

L

GUSTAFSBERG
Gustafsberg, Sweden
Faience, semiporcelain,
 earthenware, various
 dates
1910–1940 (1825–
 present)

M

KARLSKRONA
 PORCELAIN FACTORY
 AB
Karlskrona, Sweden
Porcelain
1924–1933 (1918–
 present)

N

LENINGRAD STATE
 FACTORY
Leningrad, U.S.S.R.
Porcelain
(before 1917–present)

O

A. LANTERNIER & CO.
Limoges, France
Hard paste porcelain, dolls'
 heads
1855 + (1855–1980 +)

P

HERCULANEUM POTTERY
Liverpool, Lancashire,
 England
Earthenware & porcelain.
 Impressed or printed
ca.1796–1833 (ca.1793–
 1841)

A

MAFRA & SON
Caldas da Rainha, Portugal
Imitation Palissy ware.
Impressed
1853 +

B

PORSGRUND PORCELAIN
FACTORY
Porsgrunn, Norway
Porcelain
Current (1885–present)

C

NEW CHELSEA
PORCELAIN CO. (LTD.)
Longton, Staffordshire,
England
China. Printed
ca.1919 + (1912–1961)
Variations in mark

D

NEW CHELSEA
PORCELAIN CO. (LTD.)
Longton, Staffordshire,
England
China. Printed
ca.1943 + (1912–1961)
Variations in mark

E

W. DAVENPORT & CO.
Longport, Staffordshire,
England
Porcelain, earthenware.
Impressed
ca.1805–1820 (ca.1793-
1887)

F

GUSTAFSBERG
Gustafsberg, Sweden
Faience, semiporcelain,
earthenware
1970 + (1825–present)

G

GUSTAFSBERG
Gustafsberg, Sweden
Faience, semiporcelain,
earthenware
Variations from 1932 +
(1825–present)

H

GUSTAFSBERG
Gustafsberg, Sweden
Faience, semiporcelain,
earthenware
1930–ca.1940 (1825–
present)

I

GUSTAFSBERG
Gustafsberg, Sweden
Faience, semiporcelain,
earthenware
1839–1860 (1825–
present)

J

GUSTAFSBERG
Gustafsberg, Sweden
Faience, semiporcelain,
earthenware
1860–1890 (1825–
present)

K

BRITISH ANCHOR
POTTERY CO. LTD.
Longton, Staffordshire,
England
Earthenware. Printed or
impressed
1945 + (1884–1964 +)

L

FURNIVALS, LTD.
Cobridge, Staffordshire,
England
Earthenware
1890–1910 (1890–
1964 +)

M

ANCHOR PORCELAIN CO.
LTD.
Longton, Staffordshire,
England
Porcelain. Printed
1915–1918 (1901–1918)

N

SAMPSON BRIDGWOOD
& SON
Longton, Staffordshire,
England
Earthenware. Printed
1912 + (ca.1805–present)

O

GUSTAFSBERG
Gustafsberg, Sweden
Faience, semiporcelain,
earthenware
1885–ca.1890 (1825–
present)

P

SAMPSON BRIDGWOOD
& SON
Longton, Staffordshire,
England
Earthenware. Printed
1910 + (ca.1805–present)

A

SAMPSON BRIDGWOOD
& SON
Longton, Staffordshire,
England
Earthenware, porcelain
1885 (ca.1805–present)

B

FURNIVALS, LTD.
Cobridge, Staffordshire,
England
Earthenware
(1890–1964+)

C

ANCHOR POTTERY CO.
Trenton, NJ, U.S.A.
Semiporcelain
1908+ (1893–1927)

D

GUSTAFSBERG
Gustafsberg, Sweden
Faience, semiporcelain,
earthenware
1890–1910 (1825–
present)

E

W. DAVENPORT & CO.
Longport, Staffordshire,
England
Earthenware, porcelain.
Printed blue underglaze
ca.1860–1870 (ca.1793–
1887)

F

W. DAVENPORT & CO.
Longport, Staffordshire,
England
Earthenware, porcelain
1860–1887 (ca.1793–
1887)

G

W. DAVENPORT & CO.
Longport, Staffordshire,
England
Earthenware, porcelain
ca.1805–1820 (ca.1793–
1887)

H

CROWN
CORONA
G.H & CO
ENGLAND

GATER, HALL & CO./
BARRATT'S OF
STAFFORDSHIRE LTD.
Tunstall & Burslem,
Staffordshire, England
Earthenware. Printed
1936–1943+ (1895–
present)

I

GUSTAFSBERG
Gustafsberg, Sweden
Faience, semiporcelain,
earthenware
1895–1930 (1825–
present)

J

SAMPSON BRIDGWOOD
& SON
Longton, Staffordshire,
England
Earthenware. Printed
1950+ (ca.1805–present)

K

ANIMALS, FISH & INSECTS

L

BELLEEK
WILLETS

WILLETS
MANUFACTURING CO.
Trenton, NJ, U.S.A.
Belleek-type wares. Red,
brown, black, green, or
blue
1879–1912+ (1879–
1962)

M

NAUTILUS PORCELAIN
CO.
Glasgow, Scotland
China, parian. Printed
1896–1913 (1896–1913)

N

MANGRUM
HOLBROOK
SAN FRANCISCO

D. E. McNICOL POTTERY
CO.
East Liverpool, OH, &
Clarksburg, WV, U.S.A.
Yellowware, Rockingham,
white ironstone. Quality
stamp
ca.1935–ca.1950 (1892–
1954)

O

DEDHAM POTTERY
Dedham, MA, U.S.A.
Crackleware, stoneware.
Impressed
1895–1932 (1895–1943)

P

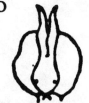

DEDHAM POTTERY
Dedham, MA, U.S.A.
Crackleware, stoneware.
Blue, imprinted
1896–1943 (1895–1943)

A

EDGE, MALKIN & CO.
Burslem, Staffordshire, England
Earthenware. Printed
ca.1873–1903 (1871–1903)

B

DAVID McBIRNEY & CO.
(BELLEEK POTTERY CO.)
Belleek, Co. Fermanagh, Ireland
Parian, porcelain.
Impressed or relief
1863–1891 (1863–present)

C

DAVID McBIRNEY & CO.
(BELLEEK POTTERY CO.)
Belleek, Co. Fermanagh, Ireland
Parian, porcelain. Printed, black
1891–1926 (1863–present)

D

DAVID McBIRNEY & CO.
(BELLEEK POTTERY CO.)
Belleek, Co. Fermanagh, Ireland
Parian, porcelain. Printed, black
1927–1941 (1863–present)

E

DAVID McBIRNEY & CO.
(BELLEEK POTTERY CO.)
Belleek, Co. Fermanagh, Ireland
Parian, porcelain. Printed, green
1946–1955 (1863–present)

F

DAVID McBIRNEY & CO.
(BELLEEK POTTERY CO.)
Belleek, Co. Fermanagh, Ireland
Parian, porcelain. Printed, green
1956–1965 (1863–present)

G

WEDGWOOD & CO.
Tunstall, Staffordshire, England
Earthenware, stone china. Printed
1862–1890 (1860–present)
(member of Wedgwood Group)

H

ENOCH WEDGWOOD LTD.
Hanley & Stoke, Staffordshire, England
Earthenware
Current (1965–present)
(member of Wedgwood Group)

I

E. HUGHES & CO.
Fenton, Staffordshire, England
China. Printed
ca.1908–1912 (1889–1953)

J

ENOCH WEDGWOOD LTD.
Hanley & Stoke, Staffordshire, England
Earthenware
Current (1965–present)
(member of Wedgwood Group)

K

HOLLINSHEAD & KIRKHAM
Tunstall, Staffordshire, England
Earthenware. Printed
1900–1924 (ca.1870–present)
(Johnson Brothers, member of Wedgwood Group)

L

BWTHYN POTTERY
Barmouth, Wales
Studio pottery. Impressed or printed
1956+ (1956+)

M

H. M. WILLIAMSON & SONS
Longton, Staffordshire, England
Porcelain. Printed
ca.1908+ (ca.1879–1941)

N

ONONDAGA POTTERY CO.
Syracuse, NY, U.S.A.
White granite, semivitreous ware, tableware
1893–1895 (1871–present)
(Syracuse China Co.)

O

ONONDAGA POTTERY CO.
Syracuse, NY, U.S.A.
White granite, semivitreous ware, tableware
1890–1903 (1871–present)
(Syracuse China Co.)

P

SOCIETÀ CERAMICA RICHARD
Milan, Italy
Porcelain, faience, earthenware
1883 (1735–present)
(Richard-Ginori)

A

SOCIETÀ CERAMICA
RICHARD
Milan, Italy
Porcelain, faience,
earthenware
1883 (1735–present)
(Richard-Ginori)

B

ROYAL DRAGON NIPPON
Japan
Porcelain
1890–1921

C

VODREY & BROTHERS
POTTERY CO.
East Liverpool, OH, U.S.A.
Dinnerware, semivitreous
ware, tableware
1896–ca.1920 (ca.1857–
1928)

D

C. C. THOMPSON
POTTERY CO.
East Liverpool, OH, U.S.A.
Ironstone, dinnerware
1890–ca. 1910 (1868–
1938)

E

P. DONATH SILESIAN
PORCELAIN FACTORY
Tiefenfurth, Silesia,
Germany (Parowa,
Poland)
Porcelain
ca.1910–1916 (ca.1890–
1916)

F

ROCKINGHAM WORKS
Swinton, Yorkshire,
England
Earthenware, porcelain.
Printed
ca.1826–1830 (ca.1745–
1842)

G

TAYLOR, SMITH &
TAYLOR
East Liverpool, OH, U.S.A.
Semivitreous, vitreous ware
1901–ca.1930 (1901–
present)
(Anchor Hocking)

H

EDWARD MARSHALL
BOEHM
Trenton, NJ, U.S.A.
Nonlimited sculptures
1958–1970 (1950–
present)

I

EDWARD MARSHALL
BOEHM
Trenton, NJ, U.S.A.
Porcelain
1952–1954 (1950–
present)

J

GEORGE HOBSON
Burslem, Staffordshire,
England
Earthenware. Printed or
impressed
1901–1923 (1901–1923)

K

EDWARD MARSHALL
BOEHM
Trenton, NJ, U.S.A.
Nonlimited sculptures
1971 (1950–present)

L

EDWARD MARSHALL
BOEHM
Trenton, NJ, U.S.A.
Nonlimited sculptures
1971 (1950–present)

M

GEORGE WADE & SON
LTD.
Burslem, Staffordshire,
England
Porcelain, earthenware.
Printed
ca.1936+ (1922–present)

N

WILHELM KUTSCHER &
CO. SCHWARZENBERG
PORCELAIN FACTORY
Schwarzenberg, Saxony,
Germany (E. Germany)
Decorative porcelain
1908–1931 (1908–1931)

O

C. M. HUTSCHEN-
REUTHER PORCELAIN
FACTORY
Hohenberg, Bavaria,
Germany (W. Germany)
Porcelain
ca.1925–ca.1941 (1814–
present)
(Hutschenreuther AG)

P

HARKER POTTERY CO.
East Liverpool, OH, U.S.A.
Stoneware, dinnerware
ca.1950 (1890–1972)

A

EDWIN M. KNOWLES
CHINA CO.
East Liverpool, OH, &
Chester, WV, U.S.A.
Vitreous & semivitreous
ware
ca.1957–1963 (1900–
1963)

B

BOCH FRÈRES
La Louvière, Belgium
Pottery
after 1914 (1841–present)

C

BRUNT, BLOOR, MARTIN
& CO.
East Liverpool, OH, U.S.A.
Ironstone, dinnerware
1875–1882 (1875–1882)

D

WALLACE & CHETWYND
POTTERY CO.
East Liverpool, OH, U.S.A.
Ironstone
1882–1901 (1882–1901)

E

WALLACE & CHETWYND
POTTERY CO.
East Liverpool, OH, U.S.A.
Semivitreous ware
ca.1896 (1882–1901)

F

WILLIAM ADAMS & SONS,
LTD.
Tunstall, Staffordshire,
England
Earthenware, basalt, jasper,
parian. Printed
1879–1891 + (1769–
present)
(Member of Wedgwood
Group)

G

HERTEL, JACOB & CO.
GMBH
Rehau, Bavaria, Germany
(W. Germany)
Porcelain
1969 + (1906–1969 +)

H

SCHONWALD PORCELAIN
FACTORY
Schonwald, Bavaria,
Germany (W. Germany)
Hard paste porcelain
ca.1898–1927 (1898–
present)
(Hutschenreuther AG)

I

SUSIE COOPER POTTERY
(LTD.)
Burslem, Staffordshire,
England
Earthenware, china. Printed
ca.1932 (ca.1930–1964 +)

J

KNOWLES, TAYLOR &
KNOWLES
East Liverpool, OH, U.S.A.
Ironstone
1878–1885 (1870–1929)

K

BUFFALO POTTERY CO.
Buffalo, NY, U.S.A.
Semivitreous & vitreous
ware. Stamped
1907–1940s (year stamp
varies) (1901–present)
(Buffalo China, Inc.)

L

BUFFALO POTTERY CO.
Buffalo, NY, U.S.A.
Deldare ware
1909–1925 (year stamp
varies) (1901–present)
(Buffalo China, Inc.)

M

BUFFALO POTTERY CO.
Buffalo, NY, U.S.A.
Deldare ware
1911–1925 (year stamp
varies) (1901–present)
(Buffalo China, Inc.)

N

ROBLIN ART POTTERY
San Francisco, CA, U.S.A.
Faience, red clay, porcelain.
Impressed
(1899–1906)

O

SCHWARZBURG
WORKSHOP FOR
PORCELAIN ART
Unterweissbach, Thuringia,
Germany (E. Germany)
Porcelain. Impressed
1908–ca.1938 (1908–
present)
(Oldest Volkstedt Porcelain
Factory)

P

EARTHENWARE WORKS
AG
Breslau, Silesia (Wroclaw,
Poland)
Earthenware, technical &
sanitary porcelain
ca.1937–1945 (1915–
1945)

A

STEUBENVILLE POTTERY
CO.
Steubenville, OH, U.S.A.
Dinnerware
1920–1930s (1879–
ca.1960)

B

FELL & THROPP CO.
Trenton, NJ, U.S.A.
White granite
ca.1900 (ca.1879–1901)

C

BAVARIA

MARKTSCHWABEN
CERAMICS FACTORY
Marktschwaben, Bavaria,
Germany
Porcelain
ca.1929–1937 (ca.1829–
1937)

D

MADDOCK

JOHN MADDOCK & SONS
(LTD.)
Burslem, Staffordshire,
England
Earthenware, ironstone.
Importer's mark
Current (1842–present)
(Maddock Hotel Ware
Division of Royal Stafford
China Ltd.)

E

THOMAS MORRIS
Longton, Staffordshire,
England
Porcelain. Printed
ca.1892 + (1892–1941)

F

PALISSY POTTERY LTD.
Longton, Staffordshire,
England
Earthenware
ca.1948 + (1946–present)
(Subsidiary of Royal
Worcester Spode Ltd.)

G

MANUEL ALVAREZ &
HIJOS, SA
Vigo, Spain
Porcelain
1927 +

H

BOHEMIA CERAMIC
WORKS AG
Neurohlau, Bohemia (Nova
Role, Czechoslovakia)
Porcelain
1931–1945 (1921–1945)

I

E. BRAIN & CO. LTD.
Fenton, Staffordshire,
England
Porcelain. Printed
1945–1963 (1903–
present)
(member of Wedgwood
Group)

J

BARKER

POTTERY

SAMUEL BARKER & SON
Nr. Rotherham, Yorkshire,
England
Earthenware. Printed or
impressed
ca.1834 + (1834–1893)

K

DON

POTTERY

DON POTTERY
Swinton, Yorkshire,
England
Earthenware. Impressed or
printed
1820–1834 (1790–1893)

L

BEVERLY

McNICOL CHINA

D. E. McNICOL POTTERY
CO.
Clarksburg, WV, & East
Liverpool, OH, U.S.A.
Vitreous ware
ca.1935–ca.1950 (1892–
1954)

M

FRANCIS MORLEY (& CO.)
Hanley, Staffordshire,
England
Earthenware, ironstone.
Impressed or printed
1845–1858 (1845–1858)

N

MORITZ FISCHER
Herend, Hungary
Hard paste porcelain
1897–1900 (1839–
1948 +)

O

W. F. MURRAY & CO.
Rutherglen, Glasgow,
Scotland
Pottery. Impressed or
printed
ca.1890 + (1870–1898)

P

J. DIMMOCK & CO.
Hanley, Staffordshire,
England
Earthenware. Printed
ca.1878–1904 (1862–
1904)

A

WILLIAM H. LOCKITT
Hanley, Staffordshire,
England
Earthenware. Printed
1913–1919 (1901–1919)

B

EGERSUND POTTERY
FACTORY
Egersund, Norway
Porcelain
1850+ (1847–present)
(Porsgrund Porcelain
Factory)

C

REDFERN & DRAKEFORD
Longton, Staffordshire,
England
Porcelain. Printed or
impressed
1892–1909 (1892–1933)

D

WILLIAM HUDSON
Longton, Staffordshire,
England
Porcelain. Printed
1936–1941+ (ca.1889–
present)
(Hudson & Middleton)

E

HAWLEY, BROS./
NORTHFIELD HAWLET
POTTERY CO. LTD.
Rotherham, Yorkshire,
England
Earthenware. Printed or
impressed
1898–1919 (1868–1919)

F

PICKARD, INC.
Chicago, IL, U.S.A.
Porcelain & porcelain
decorating
1938–present (1893–
present)

G

TETTAU PORCELAIN
FACTORY (ROYAL
BAYREUTH)
Tettau, Bavaria, Germany
(W. Germany)
Porcelain. Blue or green
ca.1968–present (1794–
present)
(Royally Privileged Porcelain
Factory Tettau GMBH)

H

US ZONE

TETTAU PORCELAIN
FACTORY (ROYAL
BAYREUTH)
Tettau, Bavaria, Germany
(W. Germany)
Porcelain
1946–1949 (1794–
present)
(Royally Privileged Porcelain
Factory Tettau GMBH)

I

TETTAU PORCELAIN
FACTORY (ROYAL
BAYREUTH)
Tettau, Bavaria, Germany
(W. Germany)
Porcelain. Printed blue
after 1957+ (1794–
present)
(Royally Privileged Porcelain
Factory Tettau GMBH)

J

TETTAU PORCELAIN
FACTORY (ROYAL
BAYREUTH)
Tettau, Bavaria, Germany
(W. Germany)
Porcelain
1946–1949 (1794–
present)
(Royally Privileged Porcelain
Factory Tettau GMBH)

K

S.C. RICHARD

SOCIETÀ CERAMICA
RICHARD
Milan, Italy
Porcelain, faience
current (1735–present)
(Richard-Ginori)

L

TETTAU PORCELAIN

SONTAG & SONS (ROYAL
BAYREUTH)
Tettau, Bavaria, Germany
(W. Germany)
Porcelain. Green or blue
underglaze
ca.1887–1902 (1794–
present)
(Royally Privileged Porcelain
Factory Tettau GMBH)

M

Königl. pr.Tettau

ROYALLY PRIVILEGED
PORCELAIN FACTORY
TETTAU (ROYAL
BAYREUTH)
Tettau, Bavaria, Germany
(W. Germany)
Porcelain. Green
underglaze, gold, blue,
red overglaze
1968–present (1794–present)

N

S. FIELDING & CO.
Stoke, Staffordshire,
England
Earthenware, majolica.
Printed
ca.1891–1913 (1879–
1964+)

O

DOULTON & CO.
Burslem, Staffordshire, &
Lambeth, London,
England
Earthenware, stoneware,
porcelain. Printed or
impressed
1922–1956 (1853–present)
(Royal Doulton Tableware
Ltd.)

P

DOULTON & CO.
Burslem, Staffordshire, &
Lambeth, London
Earthenware, stoneware,
porcelain. Printed
1922–1927 (1853–
present)
(Royal Doulton Tableware
Ltd.)

A

DOULTON & CO.
Burslem, Staffordshire, &
 Lambeth, London,
 England
Earthenware, stoneware,
 porcelain. Printed or
 impressed
1902–present (variations)
 (1853–present)
(Royal Doulton Tableware
 Ltd.)

B

THOMAS POOLE
Longton, Staffordshire,
 England
China, earthenware. Printed
1912+ (1880–present)
(Royal Stafford China Ltd.)

C

JOHN MADDOCK & SONS
 LTD
Burslem, Staffordshire,
 England
Earthenware, ironstone.
 Printed
ca.1896+ (ca.1839–present)
(Maddock Hotel Ware,
 Division of Royal Stafford
 China Ltd.)

D

EAST END POTTERY CO.
East Liverpool, OH, U.S.A.
Ironstone, semivitreous
 ware
1894–1901, 1903–1907
 (1894–1901, 1903–
 1907)

E

WILLIAM RIDGWAY (&
 CO.)
Hanley, Staffordshire,
 England
Earthenware. Printed
ca.1834–1854 (ca.1830–
 present)
(Royal Doulton Tableware
 Ltd.)

F

W. MOORCROFT (LTD.)
Burslem, Staffordshire,
 England
Earthenware. Paper label
ca.1930–1949 (1913–
 present)

G

WORCESTER PORCELAIN
Worcester, England
Hard paste porcelain
1820–1840 (ca.1751–
 present)
(Royal Worcester Spode
 Ltd.)

H

CHARLES MEAKIN
Hanley, Staffordshire,
 England
Earthenware. Printed
1883–1889 (1883–1889)

I

CRESCENT POTTERY
Trenton, NJ, U.S.A.
Semigranite dinnerware
1899–1902 (1881–
 1902+)

J

EAST TRENTON
 POTTERY CO.
Trenton, NJ, U.S.A.
White granite, ironstone
1888–ca.1905 (1888–
 ca.1905)

K

BAREUTHER & CO.
 PORCELAIN FACTORY
 WALDSASSEN AG
Waldsassen, Bavaria,
 Germany (W. Germany)
Porcelain
ca.1969+ (1866–present)

L

CHARLES MEIGH & SON
Hanley, Staffordshire,
 England
Earthenware. Printed or
 impressed
1851–1861 (1851–1861)

M

PARAGON CHINA (CO.)
 LTD.
Longton, Staffordshire,
 England
Porcelain. Printed
ca.1932+ (1920–present)
(Royal Doulton Tableware
 Ltd.)

N

PARAGON CHINA (CO.)
 LTD.
Longton, Staffordshire,
 England
Porcelain. Printed
ca.1957+ (1920–present)
(Royal Doulton Tableware
 Ltd.)

O

SWILLINGTON BRIDGE
Yorkshire, England
Ironstone, earthenware.
 Printed
ca.1820–ca.1850

P

FRANCIS MORLEY (& CO.)
Hanley, Staffordshire,
 England
Ironstone
ca.1845–1858 (1845–
 1858)

A

JACKSON VITRIFIED
  CHINA CO.
Falls Creek, PA, U.S.A.
Pottery
ca.1939–ca.1960 (1917–
  present)
(Jackson China Co.)

B

ROUSE & TURNER
Jersey City, NJ, U.S.A.
White pottery
ca.1855–ca.1880
  (ca.1855–ca.1892)

C

R. DAVIES & CO.
Gateshead, England
Ornamental tiles
(1831–1844)

D

THOMAS FURNIVAL &
  SONS
Cobridge, Staffordshire,
  England
Earthenware. Printed
ca.1818–1890 (1871–
  1964 +)

E

THOMAS, JOHN &
  JOSEPH MAYER
Burslem, Staffordshire,
  England
Earthenware, china, parian.
  Printed
1843–1855 (1843–1855)

F

NATIONAL CHINA CO.
East Liverpool & Salineville,
  OH, U.S.A.
Ironstone, semiporcelain
1911–ca.1924 (1899–
  1929)

G

WILLIAM ADAMS & SONS
  LTD.
Tunstall & Stoke,
  Staffordshire, England
Earthenware, basalt, jasper,
  parian. Printed
ca.1950 + (1769–present)
(member of Wedgwood
  Group)

H

MORLEY & ASHWORTH
Hanley, Staffordshire,
  England
Earthenware, ironstone.
  Printed
1859–1862 (1859–1862)

I

G. L. ASHWORTH & BROS.
Hanley, Staffordshire,
  England
Earthenware, ironstone.
  Printed
1862 + (1784–present)
(member of Wedgwood
  Group)

J

AMERICAN CROCKERY
  CO.
Trenton, NJ, U.S.A.
White granite
ca.1890 (1876–ca.1900)

K

WILLIAM ADAMS & SONS
  LTD.
Tunstall & Stoke,
  Staffordshire, England
Earthenware, basalt, jasper,
  parian. Printed
1896–1914 (1769–
  present)
(member of Wedgwood
  Group)

L

EMPIRE POTTERY
Trenton, NJ, U.S.A.
Pottery
1863–ca.1884 (1863–
  ca.1918)

M

HENRY MEAKIN
Cobridge, Staffordshire,
  England
Earthenware. Printed
1873–1876 (1873–1876)

N

PROSPECT HILL
  POTTERY
Trenton, NJ, U.S.A.
Semiporcelain & white
  granite
ca.1880 + (1880–ca.1895)

O

J. & G. MEAKIN (LTD.)
Hanley, Staffordshire,
  England
Earthenware, ironstone.
  Printed
ca.1890 + (1851–present)
(member of Wedgwood
  Group)

P

GLASGOW POTTERY CO.
  (JOHN MOSES & CO.)
Trenton, NJ, U.S.A.
White granite
ca.1895 (1859–1906)

A CROWN POTTERY CO. Evansville, IN, U.S.A. Whiteware, ironstone, semiporcelain. ca.1891 (1891–1962)	**B**  BLAKENEY POTTERY LTD. Stoke, Staffordshire, England Earthenware. Printed, blue 1968 + (1968–present)	**C** EXTRA QUALITY AMERICAN CHINA CO. Toronto, OH, U.S.A. Semiporcelain, white granite (1894–1910)	**D** PEORIA POTTERY CO. Peoria, IL, U.S.A. Stoneware, ironstone, white granite. 1888–1890 (1873–1902)
E WILLIAM BRUNT POTTERY CO. East Liverpool, OH, U.S.A. Ironstone 1894 (1848–1911) (various names)	**F** W Y S WILLIAM YOUNG & SONS Trenton, NJ, U.S.A. Earthenware 1853–1857 (1853–1857)	**G** ALFRED MEAKIN.LTD ALFRED MEAKIN (LTD.) Tunstall, Staffordshire, England Earthenware ca.1897 + (1873–present) (Myott-Meakin Ltd.)	**H**  A.J.WILKINSON LTD ARTHUR J. WILKINSON Burslem, Staffordshire, England Earthenware, ironstone. Printed ca.1896 + (1885–1964 +)
I JOHNSON·BROS ENGLAND JOHNSON BROS. LTD. Hanley & Tunstall, Staffordshire, England Earthenware, ironstone. Impressed or printed 1883–1913 (1883– present) (member of Wedgwood Group)	**J**  MELLOR TAYLOR & C° ENGLAND MELLOR, TAYLOR & CO. Burslem, Staffordshire, England Earthenware. Printed or impressed 1880–1904 (1880–1904)	**K** STEUBENVILLE POTTERY CO. Steubenville, OH, U.S.A. Semiporcelain, porcelain, white granite ca.1900 + (1879–ca.1960)	**L** EAST END POTTERY CO. East Liverpool, OH, U.S.A. Ironstone, semivitreous ware 1894–1901, 1903–1907 (1894–1901, 1903– 1907)
M  WARRANTED ☆ WHEELING POTTERY CO. Wheeling, WV, U.S.A. White granite 1880–1886 (1879– ca.1910)	**N** ROYAL PATENT IRONSTONE T&R BOOTE T. & R. BOOTE, LTD. Burslem, Staffordshire, England Earthenware, parian. ca.1900 (1842–1964 +)	**O**  ROYAL . PATENT . IRONSTONE. TURNER.GODDARD&C° TURNER, GODDARD & CO. Tunstall, Staffordshire, England Earthenware 1867–1874 (1867–1874)	**P**  PIONEER POTTERY CO. Wellsville, OH, U.S.A. Ironstone 1884–ca.1891 (1884– 1900)

A

ETRURIA POTTERY
(OTT & BREWER)
Trenton, NJ, U.S.A.
White granite
ca.1863+ (1863–1894)

B

PINDER, BOURNE & CO.
Burslem, Staffordshire,
England
Earthenware
1862–1882 (1862–
present)
(Royal Doulton Tableware
Ltd.)

C

NEW YORK CITY
POTTERY
New York, NY, U.S.A.
White granite
1871 (1853–1888)

D

F. B. BEERBOWER & CO.
Elizabeth, NJ, U.S.A.
Stoneware
(1816–ca.1902)

E

JACOB & THOMAS
FURNIVAL
Hanley, Staffordshire,
England
Earthenware. Printed
ca.1843 (ca.1843–1964+)

F

RIDGWAY & MORLEY
Hanley, Staffordshire,
England
Earthenware. Printed
1842–1844 (1842–1844)

G

STEUBENVILLE POTTERY
CO.
Steubenville, OH, U.S.A.
White granite, "Canton"
china
ca.1879–1904+ (1879–
ca.1960)

H

VODREY & BROTHERS
POTTERY CO.
East Liverpool, OH, U.S.A.
Ironstone
1876–1896 (ca.1857–
1928)

I

ANCHOR POTTERY
Trenton, NJ, U.S.A.
Dinnerware
1894–ca.1898 (1893–
1927)

J

VODREY & BROTHERS
POTTERY CO.
East Liverpool, OH, U.S.A.
Ironstone
1876–1896 (ca.1857–
1928)

K

WOOD & SON(S) (LTD.)
Burslem, Staffordshire,
England
Earthenware, ironstone.
ca.1910+ (1865–present)

L

RIDGWAYS
(BEDFORD WORKS) LTD.
Hanley, Staffordshire,
England
Earthenware
ca.1930+ (1920–present)
(Royal Doulton Tableware
Ltd.)

M

JOSEF RIEBER & CO.
PORCELAIN FACTORY
AG
Mitterteich, Bavaria,
Germany (W. Germany)
Porcelain
ca.1964+ (1918–ca.1978)

N

TETTAU PORCELAIN
FACTORY (ROYAL
BAYREUTH)
Tettau, Bavaria, Germany
(W. Germany)
Porcelain. Printed, green
ca.1919 (1794–present)
(Royally Privileged Porcelain
Factory Tettau GMBH)

O

TETTAU PORCELAIN
FACTORY (ROYAL
BAYREUTH)
Tettau, Bavaria, Germany
(W. Germany)
Porcelain. Printed, blue
after 1902 (1794–present)
(Royally Privileged Porcelain
Factory Tettau GMBH)

P

ROYALLY PRIVILEGED
PORCELAIN FACTORY
TETTAU GMBH (ROYAL
BAYREUTH)
Tettau, Bavaria, Germany
(W. Germany)
Porcelain
1972+ (1794–present)

A

PARAGON CHINA (CO.)
Longton, Staffordshire,
England
Porcelain. Printed
ca.1939–1949 (1920–
present)
(Royal Doulton Tableware
Ltd.)

B

POUNTNEY & CO. (LTD.)
Bristol, Gloucestershire,
England
Earthenware. Printed
ca.1889 + (1849–1964 +)

C

EAST LIVERPOOL
POTTERY CO.
East Liverpool, OH, U.S.A.
Ironstone
1894–1896 (1894–1901)

D

CHESTER POTTERY
Phoenixville, PA, U.S.A.
Semigranite ware. Printed
black
1895–1896 (1894–1897)

E

MAYER CHINA CO.
Beaver Falls, PA, U.S.A.
White granite, semivitreous
ware
ca.1904 + (1881–present)

F

FURNIVALS LTD.
Cobridge, Staffordshire,
England
Earthenware
ca.1910–1913 (1890–
1964 +)

G

GOODWIN POTTERY CO.
East Liverpool, OH, U.S.A.
Ironstone
1893–ca.1906 (1844–
1853, 1863–1865, 1872–
1913)

H

THOMAS HUGHES & SON
(LTD.)
Burslem, Staffordshire,
England
Earthenware, china. Printed
1910–1930 (1895–
present)
(Arthur Wood & Son, Ltd.)

I

HICKS & MEIGH
Hanley, Staffordshire,
England
Earthenware, ironstone
ca.1806–1822 (1806–
1822)

J

JOHN RIDGWAY (& CO.)
Hanley, Staffordshire,
England
Porcelain, earthenware
ca.1841 + (ca.1830–
present)
(Royal Doulton Tableware
Ltd.)

K

PEORIA POTTERY CO.
Peoria, IL, U.S.A.
Stoneware, whiteware
1888–1890 (1873–1902)

L

BROCKMAN POTTERY
CO.
Cincinnati, OH, U.S.A.
Porcelain, white granite
(1888–1912)

M

ISAAC DAVIS (PROSPECT
HILL POTTERY)
Trenton, NJ, U.S.A.
Semiporcelain, white
granite
1876 + (ca.1875–ca.1895)
(Prospect Hill Pottery from
1880)

N

ISAAC DAVIS (PROSPECT
HILL POTTERY)
Trenton, NJ, U.S.A.
Semiporcelain, white
granite
ca.1879 + (ca.1875–
ca.1895)
(Prospect Hill Pottery from
1880)

O

TEMPEST, BROCKMAN &
CO.
Cincinnati, OH, U.S.A.
Porcelain, white granite
1881 + (1862–1888)

P

WILLETS
MANUFACTURING CO.
Trenton, NJ, U.S.A.
White granite,
semiporcelain, porcelain
ca.1879–1884 (1879–
1962)

A

ETRURIA POTTERY (OTT & BREWER)
Trenton, NJ, U.S.A.
White granite
ca.1863+ (1863–1894)

B

GLASGOW POTTERY (JOHN MOSES & CO.)
Trenton, NJ, U.S.A.
White granite
ca.1895–1904+ (1859–1906)

C

EAST TRENTON POTTERY CO.
Trenton, NJ, U.S.A.
White granite
ca.1888–1905+ (ca.1888–ca.1905)

D

FELL & THROPP CO.
Trenton, NJ, U.S.A.
White granite
ca.1900 (ca.1879–1901)

E

COOK POTTERY CO.
Trenton, NJ, U.S.A.
White granite
ca.1893–ca.1926 (1894–1929)

F

NYON
Nyon, Switzerland
Porcelain, pottery. Blue underglaze.
(ca.1780–1860)

G

JULIUS HERING & SON
Koppelsdorf, Thuringia, Germany (E. Germany)
Electrotechnical porcelain
ca.1908–1945 (1908–1945+)
(United Porcelain Works Koppelsdorf VEB)

H

PFLUGER BROTHERS & CO.
Nyon, Switzerland
Porcelain
1800+ (1800–present)

I

CARL THIEME SAXONIAN PORCELAIN FACTORY
Potschappel, Saxony, Germany (E. Germany)
Porcelain
ca.1876–1888 (1872–present)
(Saxonian Porcelain Manufactory Dresden VEB)

J

JOHN DAN
Wivenhoe, Essex, England
Studio-type pottery. Incised
1953+ (1953–1964+)

K

SLAMA & CO.
Vienna, Austria
Porcelain decorating & distributing
1959+ (1868–present)

L

MERRIMAC POTTERY CO.
Newburyport, MA, U.S.A.
Art pottery. Impressed
1902–1908 (1902–1908)

M

KINJO NIPPON
Japan
Porcelain
before 1921

N

POOLE POTTERY LTD.
Poole, Dorset, England
Earthenware. Printed
1972+ (1963–present)

O

CARTER, STABLER & ADAMS (LTD.)/POOLE POTTERY LTD.
Poole, Dorset, England
Earthenware. Printed, variations in wording
1952 to present (1921–present)

P

POOLE POTTERY LTD.
Poole, Dorset, England
Earthenware. Printed, variations in border-shape
1973+ (1963–present)

A

CARTER, STABLER &
ADAMS (LTD.)/POOLE
POTTERY LTD.)
Poole, Dorset, England
Earthenware. Printed,
variations in border-
shape to 1973
1956–1966 (1921–
present)

B

QUIMPER

FAÏENCERIE DE LA
GRANDE MAISON
(HUBAUDIÈRE)
Quimper, France
Faience
1939 (1773–present)
(Société Nouvelle des
Faïenceries de Quimper
HB Henriot)

C

WANNOPEE POTTERY
CO.
New Milford, CT, U.S.A.
Art pottery. Impressed,
relief, or gold paper label
(1892–1903)

D

F & R

FORD & RILEY
Burslem, Staffordshire,
England
Earthenware. Printed
1882–1893 (1882–
1964 +)

E

W.T. COPELAND & SONS

W. T. COPELAND (&
SONS LTD.)
Stoke, Staffordshire,
England
Earthenware. Printed
1867–1890 (1847–
present)
(Royal Worcester Spode
Ltd.)

F

LOSANTI (MARY LOUISE
MCLAUGHLIN)
Cincinnati, OH, U.S.A.
Porcelain. Incised
(1876–1939)

G

R L
—
L

RAYMOND LAPORTE
Limoges, France
Porcelain, faience
(1883–1897)

H

ARROWS

I

ALFRED BRUNO
SCHWARTZ PORCELAIN
& FIRE-CLAY FACTORY
BERLIN
Berlin, Germany
Porcelain, earthenware
ca.1891 + (1890 +)

J

MEISSEN

ERNST TEICHERT GMBH
Meissen, Saxony, Germany
(E. Germany)
Porcelain, tiles. Blue
underglaze.
1900 + (1872–1945 +)
(nationalized in 1945)

K

BK

BENEDIKT KNAUTE
Giesshubel, Bohemia
(Struzna, Czechoslovakia)
Porcelain. Blue underglaze,
impressed letters
1828–1830 (1815–1840)

L

Cr

JOHANN ANTON HLADIK
Giesshubel, Bohemia
(Struzna, Czechoslovakia)
Porcelain. Blue underglaze
1813–1815 (1813–1815)

M

UNGER, SCHNEIDER &
CO./CARL
SCHNEIDER'S HEIRS
Grafenthal, Thuringia,
Germany (E. Germany)
Porcelain
ca.1879–ca.1954 (1861–
ca.1972)
(after 1887, Carl
Schneider's Heirs)

N

UNGER, SCHNEIDER &
CO.
Grafenthal, Thuringia,
Germany (E. Germany)
Porcelain
ca.1861–ca.1887 (1861–
1887)

O

HARKER POTTERY CO.
East Liverpool, OH, U.S.A.
Semivitreous ware
1890–1930 (1890–1972)

P

HERMANN OHME
PORCELAIN
MANUFACTORY
Niedersalzbrunn, Silesia,
Germany (Szczawienko,
Poland)
Porcelain
1882 + (1882–ca.1930)

A  WILLIAM DE MORGAN London, England (mark of Cantagali Factory, Florence, Italy) Earthenware. Printed ca.1901 (ca.1872–1911)	**B** KALK PORCELAIN FACTORY Eisenberg, Thuringia, Germany (E. Germany) Porcelain 1904+ (1863–present) (Special Porcelain Eisenberg VEB)	**C** R. BLOCH PORCELAIN OF PARIS Paris, France Dinnerware, porcelain 1939+ (1829–1963+)	**D** CHRISTIAN FISCHER Zwickau, Saxony, Germany (E. Germany) Porcelain ca.1875–1929 (1845–1929+)
E EISENBERG SPECIAL PORCELAIN VEB Eisenberg, Thuringia, Germany (E. Germany) Porcelain 1972+ (1895–present)	**F** J. O. NILSON Hackefors, Sweden Hard paste porcelain 1929+	**G** KALK PORCELAIN FACTORY Eisenberg, Thuringia, Germany (E. Germany) Porcelain ca.1896+ (1863–present) (Special Porcelain Eisenberg VEB)	**H** R. BLOCH PORCELAIN OF PARIS Paris, France Porcelain, dinnerware 1954+ (1829–1963+)
I DENVER CHINA & POTTERY CO. Denver, CO, U.S.A. Art pottery (1901–1905)	**J** PEORIA POTTERY CO. Peoria, IL, U.S.A. Stoneware, ironstone 1889–1890 (1873–1902)	**K** LAVIOLETTE Limoges, France Porcelain 1896+ (1896–1905)	**L** MINTON Stoke, Staffordshire, England Porcelain, earthenware, majolica. Printed 1850+ (1793–present) (Royal Doulton Tableware Ltd.)
M FAÏENCERIE DE LA GRANDE MAISON (HUBAUDIÈRE) Quimper, France Faience 1958 (1773–present) (Société Nouvelle des Faïenceries de Quimper HB Henriot)	**N** HARKER POTTERY CO. East Liverpool, OH, U.S.A. Ironstone 1890–1904 (1890–1972)	**O**  HARKER POTTERY CO. East Liverpool, OH, U.S.A. Semivitreous ware c.1950 (1890–1972)	**P** HARKER POTTERY CO. East Liverpool, OH, U.S.A. Semivitreous ware ca.1890 (1890–1972)

A

HARKER POTTERY CO.
East Liverpool, OH, U.S.A.
White granite &
semiporcelain
1890–ca.1900 (1890–
1972)

B

BANNERS

C

McNICOL-SMITH CO./
McNICOL-CORNS
CHINA CO.
East Liverpool, OH, U.S.A.
Semivitreous ware, various
pattern names
1907–1928 (1889–1928)

D

POTTER'S CO-
OPERATIVE CO.
East Liverpool, OH, U.S.A.
Ironstone, various pattern
names
ca.1900 (1882–1925)

E

CARTWRIGHT BROS. CO.
East Liverpool, OH, U.S.A.
Ironstone, various pattern
names
ca.1905 (1880–1927)

F

VODREY & BROTHERS
POTTERY CO.
East Liverpool, OH, U.S.A.
Ironstone toiletware, various
pattern names
1896–1928 (ca. 1857–
1928)

G

POTTER'S CO-
OPERATIVE CO.
East Liverpool, OH, U.S.A.
Ironstone toiletware, various
pattern names
ca.1896 (1882–1925)

H

MINTON
Stoke, Staffordshire,
England
Porcelain, earthenware.
Printed, various pattern
names
ca.1830–1860 (1793–
present)
(Royal Doulton Tableware
Ltd.)

I

BUCKAU PORCELAIN
MANUFACTORY
Magdeburg-Buckau,
Prussia, Germany (E.
Germany)
Porcelain
1833+ (1833–ca.1940)

J

J. DIMMOCK & CO.
Hanley, Staffordshire,
England
Earthenware. Printed
ca.1878–1904 (1862–
1904)

K

F & SONS
BURSLEM

FORD & SONS (LTD.)
Burslem, Staffordshire,
England
Earthenware. Printed,
various pattern names
1893–1938 (ca.1893–
1964+)

L

GRENVILLE POTTERY
LTD.
Tunstall, Staffordshire,
England
Earthenware
1946–1964+ (1946–
1964+)

M

OHIO CHINA CO.
East Palestine, OH, U.S.A.
Porcelain, semiporcelain
(1886–1912)

N

BOISBERTRAND &
DORAT
Limoges, France
Porcelain
1929 (1903–ca.1938)
(1884–1896, Boisbertrand
& Theilloud; 1896–1903,
Boisbertrand, Theilloud
& Dorat)

O

LEON SAZERAT,
BLONDEAU & CO.
Limoges, France
Porcelain
1891+ (1884–1893+)

P

MORLEY & ASHWORTH
Hanley, Staffordshire,
England
Earthenware, ironstone.
Printed
1859–1862 (1859–1862)

A	B	C	D

HALL CHINA CO. East Liverpool, OH, U.S.A. Semivitreous ware, various pattern names 1903–1911 (1903– present)	ONONDAGA POTTERY CO. Syracuse, NY, U.S.A. Dinnerware prior to 1966 (1871– present) (Syracuse China Co.)	UNITED CHINA & GLASS CO. New Orleans, LA "Onion Meissen" pattern dinnerware 1953–present	ROOKWOOD POTTERY Cincinnati, OH, U.S.A. Art pottery. Stamped ca.1883 (1880–1967) (Name, molds purchased by Arthur J. Townley, Michigan Center, MI,1982)

E	F	G	H

ROOKWOOD POTTERY Cincinnati, OH, U.S.A. Garfield pitcher. Impressed 1881–1882 (1880–1967) (Name, molds purchased by Arthur J. Townley, Michigan City, MI, 1982)	RÖRSTRAND PORCELAIN FACTORY Lidkoping, Sweden Porcelain, various pattern names 1885+ (1726–present) (Rörstrand AB)	ROSEVILLE POTTERY CO. Zanesville, OH, U.S.A. Stoneware, art pottery after 1900 (1892–1954)	STERLING CHINA CO. East Liverpool, OH, U.S.A. Vitreous ware ca.1946–present (1917– present)

I	J	K	L

TAYLOR, SMITH & TAYLOR E. Liverpool, OH, U.S.A. Semivitreous ware 1928–ca.1945 (1901– present) (Anchor Hocking)	MAYER CHINA CO. Beaver Falls, PA, U.S.A. Ironstone. Underglaze ca.1881–1896 (1881– present)	THOMAS CHINA CO. Lisbon, OH, U.S.A. Semivitreous ware 1902–1905 (1900–1905)	UNITED STATES POTTERY Bennington, VT, U.S.A. Rockingham 1852–1858 (1793–1858)

M	N	O	P

VERNON KILNS Vernon, CA, U.S.A. Semivitreous ware, earthenware 1947–1956 (1912–1958)	WALLACE & CHETWYND POTTERY CO. East Liverpool, OH, U.S.A. Ironstone ca.1896 (1882–1901)	WILLIAM ADAMS & SONS LTD. Tunstall & Stoke, Staffordshire, England 1893–1917 (1769– present) (member of Wedgwood Group)	JAMES HADLEY & SONS LTD. Worcester, England Porcelain, earthenware, terra-cotta. Printed 1902–1905 (1896–1905)

A

JOSIAH SPODE
Stoke, Staffordshire,
England
Earthenware
ca.1830+ (ca.1762–
present)
(Royal Worcester Spode
Ltd.)

B

SWANSEA POTTERY
Swansea, Wales
Pottery. Printed
ca.1847–1850 (ca.1783–
1870)

C

THOMAS TILL & SONS
Burslem, Staffordshire,
England
Earthenware. Printed,
various pattern names
ca.1861 (ca.1850–1928)

D

MINTON
Stoke, Staffordshire,
England
Porcelain, earthenware.
Printed
ca.1882–1836 (1793–
present)
(Royal Doulton Tableware
Ltd.)

E

JACOB FERDINAND LENZ
Zell on Harmersbach,
Badenia, Germany (W.
Germany)
Earthenware, various
pattern names
ca.1820–1840 (1794–
present)
(various names & owners,
Georg Schmider United
Zell Ceramic Factories)

F

J. & M. P. BELL & CO.
Glasgow, Scotland
Earthenware, various
pattern names
ca.1850–1870 (1842–
1928)

G

ARABIA PORCELAIN
FACTORY
Helsingfors (Helsinki),
Finland
Porcelain, various pattern
names
(1874–present)
(Upsala-Ekeby Group)

H

BURFORD BROS.
East Liverpool, OH, U.S.A.
Ironstone toiletware
ca.1881–1904 (1879–
1904)

I

GUSTAFSBERG
Gustafsberg, Sweden
Porcelain
1880–1925 (1825–
present)

J

WEDGWOOD & CO.
Tunstall, Staffordshire,
England
Earthenware, ironstone
ca.1925+ (1860–present)
(member of Wedgwood
Group)

K

JOSIAH SPODE
Stoke, Staffordshire,
England
Earthenware. Printed
ca.1805–1833 (ca.1762–
present)
(Royal Worcester Spode
Ltd.)

L

ARABIA PORCELAIN
FACTORY
Helsingfors (Helsinki),
Finland
Porcelain
(1874–present)
(Upsala-Ekeby Group)

M

JOHN THOMSON
Glasgow, Scotland
Earthenware
ca.1816–1865 (ca.1816–
ca.1896)

N

McNICOL CHINA
MADE EXPRESSLY
FOR
SOUTHERN PACIFIC
S.S. LINES.
JAS. M. SHAW & CO.
N.Y.

D. E. McNICOL POTTERY
CO.
East Liverpool, OH, U.S.A.
Vitreous ware
ca.1935–1954 (1892–
1954)

O

BOOTHS & COLCLOUGHS
LTD.
Hanley, Staffordshire,
England
Bone china, earthenware.
Printed
1950–present (1948–
present)
(various names, now Royal
Doulton Tableware Ltd.)

P

WILLIAM ADAMS & SONS
LTD.
Tunstall & Stoke,
Staffordshire, England
Earthenware, basalt
ca.1819–1864 (ca.1769–
present)
(member of Wedgwood
Group)

A

G. L. ASHWORTH & BROS.
Hanley, Staffordshire,
England
Earthenware, ironstone.
Printed
1862–ca.1890 (1784–
present)
(member of Wedgwood
Group)

B

HOTOVEN
HARKER
THE OLDEST
POTTERY IN
AMERICA
COOKINGWARE

HARKER POTTERY CO.
East Liverpool, OH, U.S.A.
Semivitreous ware
1935–ca.1950 (1890–
1972)

C

DENBY

JOSEPH BOURNE & SON,
LTD.
Denby, Derbyshire,
England
Stoneware. Impressed or
printed
ca.1948–1964 + (ca.1809–
present)
(Denby Tableware)

D

TRADE MARK
BARKER BROS
LONGTON

BARKER BROS. LTD.
Longton, Staffordshire,
England
China, earthenware. Printed,
various pattern names
ca.1880 + (1876–1964 +)

E

TAYLOR, SMITH &
TAYLOR
East Liverpool, OH, U.S.A.
Semivitreous ware
ca.1920 (1901–present)
(Anchor Hocking)

F

EMPIRE WARE
STOKE-ON-TRENT
ENGLAND

EMPIRE PORCELAIN CO.
Stoke, Staffordshire,
England
Earthenware. Printed or
impressed
late 1940s–late 1950s
(1896–1964 +)

G

ENGLAND
FALCON WARE

THOMAS LAWRENCE
(LONGTON) LTD.
Longton, Staffordshire,
England
Earthenware. Printed or
impressed
1936 + (1892–1964 +)

H

WILLOW
MADEINENGLAND
JOHN STEVENTON
& SONS LTD
BURSLEM

JOHN STEVENTON &
SONS LTD.
Burslem, Staffordshire,
England
Earthenware
ca.1923–1936 (1923–
1964 +)

I

BARRATT'S OF
STAFFORDSHIRE LTD.
Burslem, Staffordshire,
England
Earthenware. Printed
1961–1964 + (1895–
present)

J

EMPIRE PORCELAIN CO.
Stoke, Staffordshire,
England
Earthenware. Printed
1896–1912 (1896–
1964 +)

K

UNDERGLAZE
J.&E. MAYER

MAYER CHINA CO.
Beaver Falls, PA, U.S.A.
Ironstone, various pattern
names
ca.1900 (1881–present)

L

HENRY MILLS
Hanley, Staffordshire,
England
Earthenware. Printed
ca.1892 (ca.1892)

M

PERCY

KARLSKRONA
PORCELAIN FACTORY
AB
Karlskrona, Sweden
Porcelain
1943–1960 (1918–
present)

N

GUSTAFSBERG
Gustafsberg, Sweden
Porcelain, various pattern
names
1908–1941 (1825–
present)

O

CARTWRIGHT BROS. CO.
East Liverpool, OH, U.S.A.
Semivitreous ware
ca.1918 (1880–1927)

P

THOMAS FURNIVAL &
SONS
Cobridge, Staffordshire,
England
Earthenware. Printed
ca.1871–1890 (1871–
1964 +)

A

KORNILOV
St. Petersburg, Russia
 (Leningrad, U.S.S.R.)
Porcelain
(1835–1917)

B

KUZNETSOV
Novo-Kharitonovo &
 various cities, U.S.S.R.
Porcelain
(1810+)

C

MERCER POTTERY CO.
Trenton, NJ, U.S.A.
Ironstone, semiporcelain
ca.1900+ (1868–ca.1937)

D

STEUBENVILLE POTTERY
 CO.
Steubenville, OH, U.S.A.
Dinnerware, semivitreous
 ware
(1879–ca.1960)

E

D.F. HAYNES & SON
 (CHESAPEAKE
 POTTERY)
Baltimore, MD, U.S.A.
Semiporcelain, majolica
1900+ (1881–1914)

F

LUDWIG WESSEL
Bonn, Rhineland, Germany
 (W. Germany)
Earthenware
ca.1905+ (1825–present)
(Wessel Ceramic Works
 AG)

G

PAUL RAUSCHERT KG
Steinwiesen, Bavaria,
 Germany (W. Germany)
Porcelain
1971–1981+ (1965–
 present)
(acquired firm of Porcelain
 Factory Edward Haerter)

H

FRENCH CHINA CO.
Sebring, OH, U.S.A.
Dinnerware
ca.1900+ (ca.1900–
 present)
(Royal China Co.)

I

LUDWIG WESSEL
Bonn, Rhineland, Germany
 (W. Germany)
Earthenware
ca.1905+ (1825–present)
(Wessel Ceramic Works
 AG)

J

SCHWANDORF POTTERY
 FACTORY
Schwandorf, Bavaria,
 Germany (W. Germany)
Porcelain, earthenware
ca.1970+ (1865–present)
(Hutschenreuther-Keramag
 GMBH)

K

MAYER CHINA CO.
Beaver Falls, PA, U.S.A.
Ironstone
ca.1881–1896 (1881–
 present)

L

GUSTAFSBERG
Gustafsberg, Sweden
Ironstone
1854–ca.1860 (1825–
 present)

M

RIDGWAY, MORLEY,
 WEAR & CO.
Hanley, Staffordshire,
 England
Earthenware. Printed,
 various pattern names
1836–1842 (1836–1844)

N

HINES BROS.
Fenton, Staffordshire,
 England
Earthenware. Printed
1886–1907 (1886–1907)

O

BIRDS

P

UNION PORCELAIN
 WORKS
Greenpoint, NY, U.S.A.
Hard paste porcelain.
 Impressed
1878 (1865–1904)

A

WHEELING POTTERY CO.
Wheeling, WV, U.S.A.
Earthenware, ironstone,
porcelain
1893+ (1879–ca.1910)

B

BERLIN PORCELAIN
MANUFACTORY
Teltow, Brandenburg,
Germany (E. Germany)
Porcelain
1904–ca.1911 (1904–
ca.1932)

C

BUCKAU PORCELAIN
MANUFACTORY
Magdeburg-Buckau,
Prussia, Germany (E.
Germany)
Porcelain. Blue underglaze
ca.1850 (1833–ca.1940)

D

C. TIELSCH & CO.
Altwasser, Silesia, Germany
(Walbrzych, Poland)
Porcelain. Blue underglaze
ca.1875–ca.1934 (1845–
present)
(Hutschenreuther AG)

E

C. M. HUTSCHEN-
REUTHER PORCELAIN
FACTORY
Arzberg, Bavaria, Germany
(W. Germany)
Porcelain. Green
underglaze
1948+ (1814–present)
(Hutschenreuther AG)

F

JOSEPH SCHACHTEL
Charlottenbrunn, Silesia,
Germany (Zofiowka,
Poland)
Hard paste porcelain
ca.1887–ca.1919 (1859–
1919)

G

KORNILOV
St. Petersburg, Russia
(Leningrad, U.S.S.R.)
Porcelain
(1853–1917)

H

ROYAL PORCELAIN
MANUFACTORY
Berlin, Germany
Porcelain. Blue
1844–1847 (1763–
present)
(State's Porcelain
Manufactory)

I

MORITZ ZDEKAUER
Altrohlau, Bohemia (Stara
Role, Czechoslovakia)
Porcelain. Green
underglaze
ca.1938–1945 (1884–
1945+)
(nationalized in 1945)

J

MORITZ ZDEKAUER
Altrohlau, Germany (Stara
Role, Czechoslovakia)
Porcelain. Green
underglaze
ca.1900 (1884–1945+)
(nationalized in 1945)

K

ALTROHLAU PORCELAIN
FACTORIES
Altrohlau, Bohemia (Stara
Role, Czechoslovakia)
Porcelain. Green
underglaze
ca.1918–1939 (1813–
1945+)
(nationalized in 1945)

L

F. A. SCHUMANN
Berlin, Germany
Porcelain. Blue underglaze
ca.1851–1869 (ca.1835–
ca.1869)

M

STRIEGAUER PORCELAIN
FACTORY
Stanowitz, Silesia, Germany
(Strzegnom, Poland)
Porcelain
(1873–ca.1927)

N

WALKER CHINA CO.
Bedford, OH, U.S.A.
Porcelain
(1923–present)

O

THOMAS FORESTER &
SONS (LTD.)
Longton, Staffordshire,
England
Porcelain, earthenware.
Printed
1912–1959 (1883–1959)

P

WILLIAM ADAMS & SONS
LTD.
Tunstall, Staffordshire,
England
Blue printed earthenware.
Printed
1804–1840 (1769–
present)
(member of Wedgwood
Group)

A

ADOLF PERSCH
Elbogen, Bohemia (Loket,
Czechoslovakia)
Hard paste porcelain
1902–1937 (1902–1937)

B

SOCIETÀ CERAMICA
ITALIANA
Laveno, Italy
Earthenware, various
pattern names
(1856–present)

C

ENOCH WOOD & SONS
Burslem, Staffordshire,
England
Pottery, porcelain.
Impressed
1818–1846 (1818–1846)

D

C. T.

C. TIELSCH & CO.
Altwasser, Silesia, Germany
(Walbrzych, Poland)
Porcelain. Blue underglaze
ca.1875–ca.1934 (1845–
present)
(Hutschenreuther AG)

E

CYBIS PORCELAINS

CYBIS PORCELAINS
Trenton, NJ, U.S.A.
Porcelain
(ca.1939–present)

F

JEAN HAVILAND
Limoges, France
Ceramics
1957+ (1957–present)

G

JAEGER & CO.
Marktredwitz, Bavaria,
Germany (W. Germany)
Porcelain. Green
underglaze
before 1979 (1898–
present)
(Jaeger Porcelain GMBH)

H

W. DAVENPORT & CO.
Longport, Staffordshire,
England
Earthenware
1820–1860 (ca.1793–
1887)

I

WOOD & SON(S) (LTD.)
Burslem & Stoke;
Staffordshire, England
Hotel ware, tableware
current (1865–present)

J

ROZENBURG
The Hague, Holland
Porcelain. Painted
1890–1914 (1885–
1914+)

K

C P P Co.

CRYSTAL PORCELAIN
POTTERY CO. LTD.
Cobridge, Staffordshire,
England
Porcelain
1882–1886 (1882–1886)

L

CHRISTIE & BEARDMORE
Fenton, Staffordshire,
England
Earthenware. Printed
1902–1903 (1902–1903)

M

HERCULANEUM POTTERY
Liverpool, Lancashire,
England
Earthenware, porcelain.
Printed, impressed
ca.1833–1836 (ca.1793–
1841)

N

A. B. JONES & SONS
(LTD.)
Longton, Staffordshire,
England
Porcelain, earthenware.
Printed
ca.1920 (1900–present)
(Royal Grafton Bone China)

O

ROOKWOOD POTTERY
Cincinnati, OH, U.S.A.
Pottery. Printed underglaze,
black
1880–1882 (1880–1967)
(Name, molds purchased
by Arthur J. Townley,
Michigan Center, MI,1982)

P

F. GROSVENOR (& SON)
Glasgow, Scotland
Earthenware, stoneware.
Printed
1879–1926 (ca.1869–
1926)

A

WANNOPEE POTTERY
CO.
New Milford, CT, U.S.A.
Ironstone
(1892–1903)

B

WILLIAM HENRY GOSS
(LTD.)
Stoke, Staffordshire,
England
Porcelain. Printed
1862–1930 (ca.1858–
1944)

C

EDWIN BENNETT
POTTERY CO.
Baltimore, MD, U.S.A.
Graniteware
1875 + (1856–1936)

D

NIPPON
Japan
Porcelain. Turquoise
ca.1891–ca.1921

E

TRENLE BLAKE CHINA
CO.
Ravenswood, WV, U.S.A.
Vitreous ware.
ca.1940–1966 (ca.1942–
1966)

F

EDWIN BENNETT
POTTERY CO.
Baltimore, MD, U.S.A.
Yellowware
ca.1886 (1856–1936)

G

HOMER LAUGHLIN CHINA
CO.
East Liverpool, OH, U.S.A.
Semivitreous dinnerware
ca.1935 (1877–present)

H

WELLSVILLE CHINA CO.
East Liverpool, OH, U.S.A.
Vitreous hotel ware.
ca.1955 (1902–1969)

I

HENNEBERG PORCELAIN
VEB
Ilmenau, Thuringia,
Germany (E. Germany)
Porcelain
1973–present (1973–
present)

J

RICHARD ECKERT & CO.
PORCELAIN FACTORY
VOLKSTEDT
Volkstedt, Thuringia,
Germany (E. Germany)
Porcelain
1895–1918 (1894–present)
(various names & owners,
now Oldest Volkstedt
Porcelain Factory)

K

BOULTON, MACHIN &
TENNANT
Tunstall, Staffordshire,
England
Earthenware. Printed,
impressed
1889–1899 (1889–1899)

L

ENGLAND

CHARLES FORD
Hanley, Staffordshire,
England
Porcelain. Printed,
impressed
ca.1900 (1874–1904)

M

T. RATHBONE & CO.
Tunstall, Staffordshire,
England
Earthenware
ca.1912 (1898–1923)

N

FORD & POINTON, LTD.
Hanley, Staffordshire,
England
Porcelain. Printed
ca.1920 (1917–1936)

O

BOULTON, MACHIN &
TENNANT
Tunstall, Staffordshire,
England
Earthenware. Printed,
impressed
1889–1899 (1889–1899)

P

AMERICAN ART-CERAMIC
CO.
Corona, NY, U.S.A.
Terra-cotta, pottery
(1901–ca.1909)

A

PODMORE, WALKER & CO.
Tunstall, Staffordshire, England
Earthenware. Printed, various pattern names
1834–1859 (1834–present)
(member of Wedgwood Group)

B

POTTER'S CO-OPERATIVE CO.
East Liverpool, OH, U.S.A.
Ironstone
ca.1892 (1882–1925)

C

GOODWIN POTTERY CO.
East Liverpool, OH, U.S.A.
Ironstone, earthenware
ca.1888–1893 (1844–1853, 1863–1865, 1872–1913)

D

UNION POTTERIES CO.
East Liverpool, OH, U.S.A.
Ironstone, earthenware
1898–1905 (1894–1905)

E

WILTSHAW & ROBINSON (LTD.)
Stoke, Staffordshire, England
Earthenware, porcelain
ca.1890 + (1890–present)
(Carlton Ware Ltd.)

F

NEW ENGLAND POTTERY CO.
Boston, MA, U.S.A.
Whiteware. Black beneath glaze
(1854–1914)

G

AMERICAN CROCKERY CO.
Trenton, NJ, U.S.A.
White granite. Printed in black
ca.1890 (1876–ca.1900)

H

EDWIN M. KNOWLES CHINA CO.
East Liverpool, OH, U.S.A.
Semivitreous dinnerware
1934 + (1900–1963)

I

POTTER'S CO-OPERATIVE CO.
East Liverpool, OH, U.S.A.
Ironstone, table & toilet ware
ca.1896 (1882–1925)

J

KNOWLES, TAYLOR & KNOWLES
East Liverpool, OH, U.S.A.
Ironstone tableware
ca.1880–ca.1890 (1870–1929)

K

GLASGOW POTTERY (JOHN MOSES & CO.)
Trenton, NJ, U.S.A.
White granite. Printed in black
1878 + (1859–1906)

L

HOMER LAUGHLIN CHINA CO.
East Liverpool, OH, U.S.A.
Semivitreous ware, art pottery
ca.1900 (1877–present)

M

HOMER LAUGHLIN CHINA CO.
East Liverpool, OH, U.S.A.
Ironstone
ca.1900 (1877–present)

N

EAST MORRISANIA CHINA WORKS
New York, NY, U.S.A.
White granite, earthenware
ca.1893 (ca.1893)

O

RED WING POTTERY
Red Wing, MN, U.S.A.
Pottery dinnerware
1935 + (1878–1967)

P

RED WING POTTERY
Red Wing, MN, U.S.A.
Pottery dinnerware
1935 + (1878–1967)

A  RED WING POTTERY Red Wing, MN, U.S.A. Pottery dinnerware 1967 (1878–1967)	**B** BYRDCLIFFE POTTERY Woodstock, NY, U.S.A. Art pottery. Impressed 1903–1928 (1903–1928)	**C** F. G.  VIENNA FRIEDRICH GOLDSCHEIDER VIENNA MANUFACTORY Vienna, Austria Porcelain. Printed, impressed ca.1885–ca.1897 (1885– present) (various names)	**D** MARQUE DE FABRIQUE C.F&P LIMOGES CHABROL FRÈRES & POIRER Limoges, France Hard paste porcelain ca.1929 (1917–ca.1933)
E DORIC CHINA Longton, Made in England DORIC CHINA Fenton & Longton, Staffordshire, England Porcelain. Printed 1926–1935 (1924–1935)	**F** STUBBS BROS. Fenton, Staffordshire, England Porcelain. Printed ca.1899–1904 (1899– 1904)	**G** BOWL & URN	**H** PORCELAIN FLES Delft, Holland Stoneware, faience (1653–present) (various names & owners)
I Delft D.C. COOK POTTERY CO. Trenton, NJ, U.S.A. Delft ca.1894 (1894–1929)	**J** ECW AMERICAN/EDGERTON ART CLAY WORKS Edgerton, WI, U.S.A. Art pottery 1902–1903 (1892–1899, 1902–1903)	**K** HPCo BURSLEM. ENGLAND GIBSON & SONS Burslem, Staffordshire, England Earthenware. Printed ca.1904–1909 (1885– 1972 +)	**L** MF ENGLAND MORLEY, FOX & CO. LTD. Fenton, Staffordshire, England Earthenware ca.1906 (1906–1944)
M M Z. MORITZ ZDEKAUER Altrohlau, Bohemia (Stara Role, Czechoslovakia) Porcelain 1884–ca.1909 (1884– 1945 +) (nationalized in 1945)	**N** NYMOLLE DENMARK STENTOJ NYMOLLE CERAMIC FACTORY Nymolle, Denmark Stoneware 1942 + (1936–1942 +)	**O** S.&G SCHMELZER & GERIKE Althaldensleben, Prussia, Germany (E. Germany) Earthenware ca.1886–ca.1931 (1863– ca.1931)	**P** W. AUSTRIA H. WEHINGER & CO. Horn, Bohemia (Hory, Czechoslovakia) Hard paste porcelain 1905–1918 (1905–1945)

A

JOSIAH WEDGWOOD &
SONS LTD.
Barlaston & Stoke,
Staffordshire, England
Bone china, earthenware
current (ca.1759–present)
(member of Wedgwood
Group)

B

AREQUIPA
CALIFORNIA

AREQUIPA POTTERY
Fairfax, CA, U.S.A.
Art pottery
(1911–1918)

C

AULT

WILLIAM AULT
Swadlincote, Staffordshire,
England
Earthenware. Printed
1887–1923 (1887–1923)

D

AMPHORA WORK
REISSNER
Turn-Teplitz, Bohemia
(Trnovany,
Czechoslovakia)
Pottery
1892–1905 (1892–1945+)
(various names,
nationalized in 1945)

E

MARK

BRUSH POTTERY
Roseville & Zanesville, OH,
U.S.A.
Art pottery
1927–1929 (1907–1908,
1925–present)

F

MORGAN BELLEEK
Canton, OH, U.S.A.
Porcelain
(1923–1934)

G

POPE-GOSSER
U.S.A.

POPE-GOSSER CHINA
CO.
Coshocton, OH, U.S.A.
Porcelain, dinnerware
(1902–1958)

H

EDWIN M. KNOWLES
CHINA CO.

EDWIN M. KNOWLES
CHINA CO.
East Liverpool, OH, U.S.A.
Semiporcelain
1900–1948 (1900–1963)

I

J. & M. P. BELL & CO.
Glasgow, Scotland
Earthenware, porcelain
(1842–1928)

J

WILLIAM RIDGWAY (& CO.)
Hanley, Staffordshire,
England
Earthenware. Printed,
various pattern names
ca.1830–1854 (ca.1830–
present)
(Royal Doulton Tableware
Ltd.)

K

RIDGWAYS
Hanley, Staffordshire,
England
Earthenware, various
pattern names
after 1891 (1879–present)
(Royal Doulton Tableware
Ltd.)

L

Bewley POTTERY
.MADE IN ENGLAND

BAILEY POTTERIES LTD.
Fenton, Staffordshire,
England
Earthenware. Printed
1935–1940 (1935–1940)

M

VITREOUS
J & E. MAYER.

MAYER CHINA CO.
Beaver Falls, PA, U.S.A.
Semivitreous ware
before 1964 (1881–
present)

N

WOOD'S
WARE
WOOD & SONS
ENGLAND

WOOD & SON(S) (LTD.)
Burslem, Stoke,
Staffordshire, England
Earthenware, ironstone.
Printed
ca.1917+ (1865–present)

O

FLORENTINE
CHILLICOTHE

FLORENTINE POTTERY
Chillicothe, OH, U.S.A.
Art pottery
(1900–1919)

P

HACKWOOD
Shelton & Hanley,
Staffordshire, England
Earthenware, creamware,
ironstone
ca.1830–1840 (ca. 1827–
1855)

A

BLUE JOHN POTTERY LTD.
Hanley, Staffordshire, England
Earthenware. Printed
1949+ (1939–1964+)

B

HYALYN COSCO
Hickory, NC, U.S.A.
Porcelain
(1940s–present)

C

WELLER POTTERY
Zanesville, OH, U.S.A.
Art pottery
ca.1925 (1882–1948)

D

WELLER POTTERY
Zanesville, OH, U.S.A.
Art pottery
late 1920s (1882–1948)

E

WELLER POTTERY
Zanesville, OH, U.S.A.
Art pottery
1920s (1882–1948)

F

TAYLOR, SMITH & TAYLOR
East Liverpool, OH, U.S.A.
Semivitreous tableware
ca.1925 (1901–present)
(Anchor Hocking)

G

POTTERY GUILD
New York, NY, U.S.A.
Dinnerware
(1937–1946)

H

VERNON KILNS
Vernon, CA, U.S.A.
Earthenware, semivitreous ware, various pattern names
1955 (1912–1958)

I

BAREUTHER & CO. PORCELAIN FACTORY WALDSASSEN AG
Waldsassen, Bavaria, Germany (W. Germany)
Porcelain
ca.1966+ (1866–present)

J

RUDOLSTADT PORCELAIN FACTORY
Rudolstadt, Thuringia, Germany (E. Germany)
Porcelain
1918–1932 (1882–1932)

K

GEORG SCHMIDER
Zell on Harmersbach, Badenia, Germany (W. Germany)
Earthenware
1907–1928 (1907–present)

L

SALEM CHINA CO.
Salem, OH, U.S.A.
Dinnerware
1940s+ (1898–1967)

M

STETSON CHINA CO.
Lincoln, IL, U.S.A.
Semiporcelain
(1919–1965)

N

BENNINGTON POTTERS, INC.
Bennington, VT, U.S.A.
Earthenware
(ca.1949–present)

O

BUILDING & TOWER

P

KERAMIA

SLAMA & CO.
Vienna, Austria
Porcelain decorating
1951–1981+ (1868–present)

A

JULIUS DRESSLER
Biela, Bohemia (Bela, Czechoslovakia)
Porcelain, earthenware
ca.1900–1945 (1888–ca.1945)

B

CRAEMER & HERON
PORCELAIN FACTORY
MENGERSREUTH
Mengersreuth, Thuringia, Germany (E. Germany)
Porcelain
ca.1908–1913 (1908–1913)

C

MADE IN
ZUID-HOLLAND

SOUTH HOLLAND
POTTERY
MANUFACTORY (ZUID)
Gouda, Holland
Porcelain, delft
(1897–present)

D

PLAZUID
GOUDA
HOLLAND

PLAZUID FACTORY
(GOUDA)
Gouda, Holland
Delft
ca.1920–ca.1930 (1749–1930+)

E

REINHOLD
SCHLEGELMILCH
PORCELAIN
FACTORIES (R.S. PRUSSIA)
Tillowitz, Silesia, Germany (Tulovice, Poland)
Porcelain
1898–1908 (1869–ca.1938)

F

W.HULME
NORTH R.S
RELIABLE
BURSLEM
ENGLAND
SEMI-PORCELAIN

WILLIAM HULME
Burslem, Staffordshire, England
Earthenware. Printed
1891–1936 (1891–1941)

G

LIMOGES
france

PORCELAINES LIMOGES
CASTEL
Limoges, France
Porcelain
1944–1973 (1944–1980+)

H

MANHATTAN
AMERICAN
LIMOGES
SEBRING-OHIO

LIMOGES CHINA CO.
East Liverpool, OH, U.S.A.
Semivitreous dinnerware
1935–1936 (1900–1955)
(American Limoges China Co.)

I

B&G
COPENHAGEN
DANISH CHINA WORKS

BING & GRONDAHL
Copenhagen, Denmark
Porcelain
1898+ (1853–present)

J.

B&G
KJØBENHAVN
DANISH CHINA WORKS
B & G

BING & GRONDAHL
Copenhagen, Denmark
Porcelain
1899+ (1853–present)

K

B&G
KJØBENHAVN
COPENHAGEN
B & G

BING & GRONDAHL
Copenhagen, Denmark
Porcelain
1914+ (1853–present)

L

B&G
KJØBENHAVN
DANMARK
B & G

BING & GRONDAHL
Copenhagen, Denmark
Porcelain
1948+ (1853–present)

M

B&G
KJØBENHAVN
DANMARK
B & G

BING & GRONDAHL
Copenhagen, Denmark
Porcelain
1915+ (1853–present)

N

B&G
KJØBENHAVN
DENMARK

BING & GRONDAHL
Copenhagen, Denmark
Porcelain
1962+ (1853–present)

O

B&G
KJØBENHAVN
MADE IN
DENMARK

BING & GRONDAHL
Copenhagen, Denmark
Porcelain
1952–1958 (1853–present)

P

B&G
KJØBENHAVN
MADE IN DENMARK
B & G

BING & GRONDAHL
Copenhagen, Denmark
Porcelain
1902+ (1853–present)

A  GIEN Gien, France Faience, majolica 1970 + (1864–present)	**B**  MERCER POTTERY CO. Trenton, NJ, U.S.A. Porcelain, white granite (1868–ca.1937)	**C** HARKER POTTERY CO. East Liverpool, OH, U.S.A. Semivitreous ware 1939–1947 (1890–1972)	**D** ARABIA PORCELAIN Helsingfors (Helsinki), Finland Porcelain, ceramics 1928–1932 (1874– present) (Upsala-Ekeby Group)
E ARABIA PORCELAIN Helsingfors (Helsinki), Finland Porcelain, ceramics 1917–1927 (1874– present) (Upsala-Ekeby Group)	**F** C. T. MALING & SONS Newcastle upon Tyne, Northumberland, England Earthenware. Printed 1890 + (1890–1963)	**G**  GIEN Gien, France Faience, majolica 1864 + (1864–present)	**H** SAMPSON HANCOCK (& SONS) Stoke, Staffordshire, England Earthenware. Printed, various pattern names 1906–1912 (1858–1937)
I  **HAVILAND** **CHINA** HAVILAND SA Limoges, France Porcelain 1958–present (1941– present)	**J**  C. T. MALING & SONS Newcastle upon Tyne, Northumberland, England Earthenware ca.1949–1963 (1890– 1963)	**K** THEODORE HAVILAND & CO. Limoges, France Porcelain, green 1892 + (1892–present) (Haviland SA)	**L** ARABIA PORCELAIN Helsingfors (Helsinki), Finland Porcelain, ceramics. Colored stamp 1932–1949 (1874–present) (Upsala-Ekeby Group)
M  PFALTZGRAFF CO. York, PA, U.S.A. Redware, stoneware current (1811–present)	**N** VILLEROY & BOCH Mettlach, Saar, Germany (W. Germany) Earthenware, soft paste porcelain. Variations in mark 1883–1930s (1813– present) (various names, owners, & locations)	**O** EDWARD BINGHAM Castle Hedingham, Essex, England Earthenware. Relief 1864–1901 (1864–1901)	**P**  ZSOLNAY Pecs, Hungary Lusterware, art pottery ca.1862 + (1862–present)

A

CHARLES JAMES MASON
& CO.
Lane Delph, Staffordshire,
England
Ironstone. Printed
1829–1945 (1829–1845)

B

RIDGWAY & MORLEY
Hanley, Staffordshire,
England
Ironstone. Printed
1842–1844 (1842–1844)

C

RÖRSTRAND PORCELAIN
FACTORY
Rörstrand, Sweden
Porcelain
1850 + (1726–present)
(Rörstrand AB)

D

T. G. GREEN & CO. (LTD.)
Nr. Burton-on-Trent,
Derbyshire, England
Cookware, oven-to-table
ware. Variations in
wording
ca.1930–present (ca.1864–
present)

E

T. G. GREEN & CO. (LTD.)
Nr. Burton-on-Trent,
Derbyshire, England
Earthenware, stoneware.
Printed
1888 + (ca.1864–present)

F

NORTH STAFFORDSHIRE
POTTERY CO. LTD.
Hanley, Staffordshire,
England
Willowware
(1940–present)
(Ridgway Potteries Group)

G

LOVATT'S POTTERIES,
LTD.
Langley Mill, Nr.
Nottingham, England
Stoneware, earthenware.
Printed, impressed
ca.1931–1962 (1895–
present)
(Denby Tableware)

H

FAÏENCERIE DE LA
GRANDE MAISON
(HUBAUDIÈRE)
Quimper, France
Pottery
1922 + (1773–present)
(Société Nouvelle des
Faïenceries de Quimper
HB Henriot)

I

E. & A. MULLER
PORCELAIN FACTORY
Schonwald, Bavaria,
Germany (W. Germany)
Porcelain
ca.1911–ca.1927
(1904–present)
(Porcelain Factory
Schonwald, branch of
Hutschenreuther AG)

J

LIMOGES CHINA CO.
East Liverpool, OH, U.S.A.
Semivitreous dinnerware
1945–ca.1950 (1900–
1955)
(after 1949, American
Limoges China Co.)

K

CASTLETON CHINA, INC.
New Castle, PA, U.S.A.
Porcelain
(1940–present)
(Anchor Hocking)

L

BANCROFT & BENNETT
Burslem, Staffordshire,
England
Earthenware. Printed
1946–1950 (1946–1950)

M

TAYLOR, SMITH &
TAYLOR
East Liverpool, OH, U.S.A.
Tableware
ca.1935 (1901–present)
(Anchor Hocking)

N

ERA ART POTTERY CO.
Stoke, Staffordshire,
England
Earthenware. Printed
1936 + (1930–1947)

O

SHENANGO CHINA CO.
New Castle, PA, U.S.A.
Porcelain
(1901–present)
(Anchor Hocking)

P

STEUBENVILLE POTTERY
CO.
Steubenville, OH, U.S.A.
Dinnerware
(1879–ca.1960)

A

VERNON KILNS
Vernon, CA, U.S.A.
Earthenware, semivitreous
ware
1930s (1912–1958)

B

INTERPACE
CORPORATION
Los Angeles, CA, U.S.A.
Franciscan ware
1974–1979 (1875–
present)
(various owners & names,
now member of
Wedgwood Group)

C

GLADDING, McBEAN &
CO.
Los Angeles, CA, U.S.A.
Franciscan ware
ca.1947–1953 (1875–
present)
(member of Wedgwood
Group)

D

ABBEYDALE NEW BONE
CHINA CO. LTD.
Duffield, Derbyshire,
England
Porcelain
1962+ (1962+)

E

MOSA PORCELAIN & TILE
FACTORY
Maastricht, Holland
Porcelain
(1883–present)

F

RYE POTTERY
Rye, Sussex, England
Pottery
current (1869–present)

G

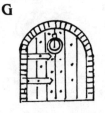

BARN POTTERY, LTD.
Paignton, Devon, England
Earthenware
1964+ (1964+)

H

JOSEPH BOURNE & SON
LTD.
Denby, Derbyshire,
England
Stoneware. Impressed,
printed
ca.1910 (ca.1809–present)
(Denby Tableware)

I

J

ROCKINGHAM WORKS
Swinton, Yorkshire,
England
Earthenware, stone china,
porcelain. Impressed,
printed, various pattern
names
ca.1745–1826+ (ca.1745–
1842)

K

ALKA-KUNST ALBOTH &
KAISER
Staffelstein, Bavaria,
Germany (W. Germany)
Porcelain
1927–1953 (1872–
present)
(Kaiser Porcelain)

L

ALLERTONS LTD.
Longton, Staffordshire,
England
Porcelain, earthenware,
lusterware. Printed
ca.1912+ (1859–1942)

M

PORCELAINIÈRE DE
LIMOGES
Limoges, France
Porcelain
1930–1962+ (1737–
present)

N

PALISSY POTTERY LTD.
Longton, Staffordshire,
England
Earthenware
current (1946–present)
(subsidiary of Royal
Worcester Spode Ltd.)

O

BURGESS & LEIGH
Burslem, Staffordshire,
England
Earthenware. Printed,
various pattern names
ca.1919 (1862–present)

P

BOCH FRÈRES
La Louvière, Belgium
Pottery
current (1841–present)

A

AUGUST NOWOTNY
Altrohlau, Bohemia (Stara
   Role, Czechoslovakia)
Faience, earthenware,
   porcelain. Blue
1838–1884 (1923–
   1945+)
(various names & owners)

B

BURGESS & LEIGH
Burslem, Staffordshire,
   England
Earthenware. Printed
1930+ (1862–present)

C

CHARLES COLLINSON &
   CO.
Burslem, Staffordshire,
   England
Earthenware. Printed
1851–1873 (1851–1873)

D

W. DAVENPORT & CO.
Longport, Staffordshire,
   England
Creamware, porcelain,
   ironstone. Printed
1820–1860 (ca.1793–
   1887)

E

CHARLES MEIGH & SON
Hanley, Staffordshire,
   England
Earthenware. Printed,
   various pattern names
1851–1861 (1851–1861)

F

COPELAND & GARRETT
Stoke, Staffordshire,
   England
Porcelain, earthenware,
   parian. Printed in gold
1833–1847 (1833–
   present)
(Royal Worcester Spode
   Ltd.)

G

EDGE, MALKIN & CO.
Burslem, Staffordshire,
   England
Earthenware. Printed
ca.1871–1880 (1871–
   1903)

H

GUSTAFSBERG
Gustafsberg, Sweden
Semiporcelain, faience,
   earthenware
1860–1905 (1825–
   present)

I

CO-OPERATIVE
   WHOLESALE SOCIETY
   LTD.
Longton, Staffordshire,
   England
Earthenware. Printed
1946+ (1946–1964+)

J

W. DAVENPORT & CO.
Longport, Staffordshire,
   England
Earthenware, creamware,
   porcelain, ironstone
ca.1840–ca.1867(ca.1793-
   1887)

K

PICKARD CHINA CO.
Chicago, IL, U.S.A.
Porcelain
(1893–present)
(Pickard, Inc.)

L

M. GREEN & CO.
Fenton, Staffordshire,
   England
Porcelain, earthenware.
   Printed
1859–1876 (1859–1876)

M

GUSTAFSBERG
Gustafsberg, Sweden
Semiporcelain, faience,
   earthenware. Printed
1860–1880 (1825–
   present)

N

SPODE
Stoke, Staffordshire,
   England
Porcelain, earthenware,
ca.1830 (ca.1762–present)
(Royal Worcester Spode
   Ltd.)

O

GUSTAFSBERG
Gustafsberg, Sweden
Semiporcelain, faience,
   earthenware
ca.1840 (1825–present)

P

HAYNES, BENNETT & CO.
   (CHESAPEAKE
   POTTERY)
Baltimore, MD, U.S.A.
Faience, semiporcelain,
   majolica, parian. Printed
1881–ca.1895 (1881–
   1914)

A

W. ADAMS & SONS LTD.
Tunstall & Stoke,
  Staffordshire, England
Ironstone
ca.1850+ (1769–present)
(member of Wedgwood
  Group)

B

J. & M. P. BELL & CO.
Glasgow, Scotland
Earthenware, parian
before 1869 (1842–1928)

C

JABEZ BLACKHURST
Tunstall, Staffordshire,
  England
Earthenware. Printed,
  various pattern names
1872–1883 (1872–1883)

D

J. & M. P. BELL & CO.
Glasgow, Scotland
Earthenware, parian
before 1896 (1842–1928)

E

COALPORT PORCELAIN
  WORKS
Coalport, Shropshire,
  England
Porcelain. Printed
1830–1850 (ca. 1795–
  present)
(member of Wedgwood
  Group)

F

UNION LIMOUSINE
Limoges, France
Porcelain
1950–1975 (1908–
  1979+)

G

LIPPERT & HAAS
Schlaggenwald, Bohemia
  (Horni Slavko,
  Czechoslovakia)
Porcelain
ca.1808 (ca.1808–1945+)

H

MORLEY & ASHWORTH
Hanley, Staffordshire,
  England
Earthenware, ironstone.
  Printed, various pattern
  names
ca.1862 (1859–1862)

I

MINTON
Stoke, Staffordshire,
  England
Porcelain, earthenware,
  parian, majolica. Printed,
  various pattern names
ca.1841–1873 (1793–
  present)
(Royal Doulton Tableware
  Ltd.)

J

MINTON
Stoke, Staffordshire,
  England
Porcelain, earthenware,
  parian, majolica. Printed
ca.1836–1841 (1793–
  present)
(Royal Doulton Tableware
  Ltd.)

K

VILLEROY & BOCH
Mettlach, Saar, Germany
  (W. Germany)
Earthenware. Blue or black,
  stamped
ca.1890 (1813–present)
(various names, owners, &
  locations)

L

MINTON
Stoke, Staffordshire,
  England
Porcelain, earthenware,
  parian, majolica. Printed
1830+ (1793–present)
(Royal Doulton Tableware
  Ltd.)

M

MINTON
Stoke, Staffordshire,
  England
Porcelain, earthenware,
  parian, majolica. Printed
ca.1841–1873 (1793–
  present)
(Royal Doulton Tableware
  Ltd.)

N

GUSTAFSBERG
Gustafsberg, Sweden
Semiporcelain, faience,
  earthenware
ca.1860 (1825–present)

O

PICKARD CHINA CO.
Chicago, IL, U.S.A.
Porcelain
1919–1922 (1893–
  present)
(Pickard, Inc.)

P

ERDMANN
  SCHLEGELMILCH
Suhl, Thuringia, Germany
  (W. Germany)
Porcelain
ca.1902–1938 (1881–
  1938)

A

READ & CLEMENTSON
Hanley, Staffordshire,
England
Earthenware. Printed,
various pattern names
1833–1835 (1833–1835)

B

RIDGWAY, MORLEY,
WEAR & CO.
Hanley, Staffordshire,
England
Earthenware. Printed
1836–1842 (1836–1844)

C

RÖRSTRAND PORCELAIN
FACTORY
Lidkoping, Sweden
Faience, porcelain. Blue
underglaze
1852 + (1726–present)
(Rörstrand AB)

D

WALK PORCELAIN
"ROSE"
Aschaffenburg, Bavaria,
Germany (W. Germany)
Dresser sets
1974–present (1974–
present)

E

L. DE LA RIVA & CO.
Sargadelos, Spain
Earthenware
1845–1862 (1804–1875)

F

G. L. A. & BROS.
Hanley, Staffordshire,
England
Earthenware, ironstone
(1862–1957 +)

G

EDWIN BENNETT
POTTERY CO.
Baltimore, MD, U.S.A.
Semigranite
1892 + (1856–1936)

H

RÖRSTRAND PORCELAIN
FACTORY
Lidkoping, Sweden
Porcelain, faience
1912 (1726–present)
(Rörstrand AB)

I

RIDGWAY & MORLEY
Hanley, Staffordshire,
England
Earthenware. Printed
1842–1844 (1842–1844)

J

SWINNERTONS LTD.
Hanley, Staffordshire,
England
Earthenware. Printed
ca.1946 + (1906–1964 +)

K

ANTHONY SHAW & CO.
Tunstall, Staffordshire,
England
Dinnerware
1851 + (1851–1900)

L

UTZCHNEIDER & CO.
Sarreguemines, France
Pottery
1915 + (ca.1770–present)

M

WILLIAM ADAMS & SONS
LTD.
Tunstall & Stoke,
Staffordshire, England
Earthenware, basalt, jasper,
parian. Printed
1819–1864 (1769–present)
(member of Wedgwood
Group)

N

EAST LIVERPOOL
POTTERY CO.
East Liverpool, OH, U.S.A.
Semivitreous dinnerware
1896–1901 (1894–1901)

O

WARWICK CHINA CO.
Wheeling, WV, U.S.A.
Porcelain
(1887–1951)

P

WEDGWOOD & CO.
Tunstall, Staffordshire,
England
Earthenware, ironstone.
Printed
ca.1925 + (1860–present)
(member of Wedgwood
Group)

A

W. S. GEORGE CO.
Kittanig, PA, U.S.A.
Dinnerware
1932 + (1880–1959)

B

HOMER LAUGHLIN CHINA CO.
East Liverpool, OH, U.S.A.
Ironstone dinnerware
ca.1965 (1877–present)

C

ROYAL CHINA CO.
Sebring, OH, U.S.A.
Semivitreous dinnerware
1951–ca.1960 (1933–present)

D

HOMER LAUGHLIN CHINA CO.
East Liverpool, OH, U.S.A.
Semivitreous tableware
ca.1953 (1877–present)

E

DOULTON & CO.
Burslem, Staffordshire, England
Earthenware, stoneware
ca.1900 (1853–present)
(Royal Doulton Tableware Ltd.)

F

EDWIN M. KNOWLES CHINA CO.
East Liverpool, OH, U.S.A.
Semivitreous dinnerware
ca.1935 (1900–1963)

G

HOMER LAUGHLIN CHINA CO.
East Liverpool, OH, U.S.A.
Semivitreous dinnerware
ca.1939 (1877–present)

H

HOMER LAUGHLIN CHINA CO.
East Liverpool, OH, U.S.A.
Semivitreous dinnerware
ca.1954 (1877–present)

I

HOMER LAUGHLIN CHINA CO.
East Liverpool, OH, U.S.A.
Semivitreous dinnerware
ca.1940–1946 (1877–present)

J

STETSON CHINA CO.
Chicago, IL, U.S.A.
Porcelain, dinnerware, various pattern names
(1919–1965)

K

SYRACUSE CHINA CORP.
Syracuse, NY, U.S.A.
Porcelain
(1871–present)
(various names & owners)

L

SYRACUSE CHINA CORP.
Syracuse, NY, U.S.A.
Porcelain
(1871–present)
(various names & owners)

M

GONDER CERAMIC ART CO.
Zanesville, OH, U.S.A.
Pottery
(1941–1957)

N

SYRACUSE CHINA CORP.
Syracuse, NY, U.S.A.
Porcelain
(1871–present)
(various names & owners)

O

McNICOL-SMITH CO.
East Liverpool, OH, U.S.A.
Ironstone tableware
ca.1901 (1889–1907)

P

TAYLOR, SMITH & TAYLOR
East Liverpool, OH, U.S.A.
Semivitreous tableware
ca.1963–ca.1968 (1901–present)
(Anchor Hocking)

A

HARKER POTTERY CO.
East Liverpool, OH, U.S.A.
Semivitreous dinnerware
1960–1972 (1890–1972)

B

HOMER LAUGHLIN CHINA
CO.
East Liverpool, OH, U.S.A.
Semivitreous dinnerware
1950–ca.1960 (1877–
present)

C

CIRCLE— OVAL

D

CYBIS PORCELAINS
Trenton, NJ, U.S.A.
Porcelain
1947–1951 (ca.1939–
present)

E

HOMER LAUGHLIN CHINA
CO.
East Liverpool, OH, U.S.A.
Semivitreous dinnerware
ca.1936 (1877–present)

F

GATER, HALL & CO
Burslem, Staffordshire,
England
Earthenware. Printed
1914+ (1895–present)
(Barratt's of Staffordshire
Ltd.)

G

HARKER POTTERY CO.
East Liverpool, OH, U.S.A.
Semivitreous dinnerware
ca.1960–1972 (1890–
1972)

H

WILLIAM DE MORGAN
Fulham, London, England
Earthenware, tiles, vases
1888–1897 (ca.1872–
1911)

I

ZSOLNAY
Pecs, Hungary
Lusterware, art pottery.
Printed
(1862–present)

J

CHELSEA POTTERY
London, England
Earthenware. Impressed,
incised
1952+ (1952–present)

K

C. M. HUTSCHEN-
REUTHER PORCELAIN
FACTORY
Hohenberg, Bavaria,
Germany (W. Germany)
Hard paste porcelain
1857–1899 (1814–
present)
(Hutschenreuther AG)

L

HOCHST PORCELAIN
MANUFACTORY GMBH
Hochst, Hesse, Germany
(W. Germany)
Table & decorative
porcelain. Blue
underglaze
1965–present (1965–
present)

M

BERNARD LEACH, C.B.E.
St. Ives, Cornwall, England
Pottery. Impressed
ca.1921+ (1921–1964+)

N

ROYAL COPENHAGEN
PORCELAIN FACTORY
LTD.
Copenhagen, Denmark
Matte porcelain
1929–1950 (1775–
present)

O

NORTH STAFFORDSHIRE
POTTERY CO. LTD.
Cobridge, Staffordshire,
England
Earthenware
1944+ (1940–present)
(Ridgway Potteries Group)

P

KERR & BINNS
(WORCESTER
PORCELAINS)
Worcester, England
Porcelain, earthenware,
parian. Printed, impressed
ca.1852–1862
(ca.1751–present)
(Royal Worcester Spode
Ltd.)

A 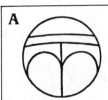 MICHAEL AMBROSE CARDEW Wenford Bridge, Cornwall, England Studio pottery, stoneware. Impressed ca.1939–1942, 1949–present (1926–present)	**B**  ROBINEAU POTTERY Syracuse, NY, U.S.A. Art pottery (1901–1928)	**C** ETRURIA POTTERY (OTT & BREWER) Trenton, NJ, U.S.A. Semiporcelain (1863–1894)	**D** C. L. & H. A. POILLON POTTERY Woodridge, NJ, U.S.A. Pottery (1901–1928)
E LEGRAND & CO. Limoges, France Porcelain (1924–1962 +)	**F** HEUBACH BROS. Lichte, Thuringia, Germany (E. Germany) Porcelain, dolls' heads, dolls, figurines 1882 + (1882–present) (various names & owners, now United Decorative Porcelain Works Lichte VEB)	**G** MOSAIC TILE CO. Zanesville, OH, U.S.A. Tile. Stamped (1894–1967)	**H** PEORIA POTTERY CO. Peoria, IL, U.S.A. Cream-colored ware 1890–1899 (1873–1902)
I STEUBENVILLE POTTERY CO. Steubenville, OH, U.S.A. Pottery ca.1960 (1879–ca.1960)	**J** LOW ART TILE WORKS Chelsea, MA, U.S.A. Tile. Arthur Osborne's mark ca.1877–ca.1893 (1877–1907)	**K** HALL CHINA CO. East Liverpool, OH, U.S.A. Vitrified ware 1973–present (1903–present)	**L** VAN BRIGGLE POTTERY Colorado Springs, CO, U.S.A. Pottery. Incised, date changed yearly 1900–1920 (1900–present)
M AMSTELHOEK Omwal, Holland Pottery. Printed (ca.1894–1912)	**N** ANDRE METTHEY Vallauris, France Stoneware, earthenware. Incised. ca.1901 (1901–1909 +)	**O** ARITA TABLETOP CO. Anaheim, CA, U.S.A. Porcelain, stoneware (1976–present)	**P** AMERICAN ENCAUSTIC TILING CO. Zanesville, OH, U.S.A. Tile (1875–1935)

A AULT & TUNNICLIFFE LTD. Swadlincote, Staffordshire, England Earthenware. Printed, impressed 1923–1937 (1923–1937)	**B** A. VIGNAUD Limoges, France Porcelain (1911–1980+) (part of Bernardaud in 1970)	**C** AVON ART POTTERY LTD. Longton, Staffordshire, England Earthenware. Printed, impressed 1930–1939 (1930–1969)	**D**  PAUL A. STRAUB New York, NY, U.S.A. Ceramics. Importer's mark 1948–1970 (1915–1970)
E  BEAVER FALLS ART TILE CO. Beaver Falls, PA, U.S.A. Tile (1886–1930)	**F** ROYAL PORCELAIN MANUFACTURY/ STATE'S PORCELAIN MANUFACTURY Berlin, Germany Earthenware. Black 1882–present (1763–present)	**G** INTERNATIONAL POTTERY CO. Trenton, NJ, U.S.A. Hotel ware, toiletware, semiporcelain. Underglaze, impressed (1860–1940+)	**H**  JULES MORLENT Bayeaux, France Porcelain 1878+ (1812–1951)
I  PISGAH FOREST POTTERY Arden, NC, U.S.A. Pottery, various dates 1920–1961 (1901–present)	**J** CASTLETON CHINA, INC. New Castle, PA, U.S.A. Porcelain, dinnerware (1940–present) (Anchor Hocking)	**K** ROSENTHAL GLASS & PORCELAIN AG Selb, Bavaria, Germany (W. Germany) Porcelain, earthenware. Green underglaze current (1879–present)	**L** COLCLOUGH CHINA LTD./ BOOTHS & COLCLOUGHS LTD. Longton, Staffordshire, England Bone china. Printed 1939–1954 (1937–present) (Royal Doulton Tableware Ltd.)
M DOULTON & CO. Lambeth, London, England Earthenware. Impressed, also without word "crown" 1891–1910 (1853–present) (Royal Doulton Tableware Ltd.)	**N**  D. E. McNICOL POTTERY CO. East Liverpool, OH, U.S.A. Semivitreous dinnerware ca.1905 (1892–1954)	**O** DESERT SANDS POTTERY Boulder City, NV, U.S.A. Pottery before 1962 (ca.1940–1978+)	**P** WILLIAM DE MORGAN Fulham, London, England Earthenware, tiles, vases. Impressed 1898–1907 (ca. 1872–1911)

A

HALL CHINA CO.
East Liverpool, OH, U.S.A.
Vitrified hotel ware
1981 + (1903–present)

B

DOULTON & CO.
Lambeth, London, England
Earthenware
ca.1873–ca.1914 (1853–
  present)
(Royal Doulton Tableware
  Ltd.)

C

A. E. HULL POTTERY CO.
Crooksville, OH, U.S.A.
Shulton's Old Spice
  Containers
1937–1944 (1905–1950,
  1952–present)
(Hull Pottery)

D

EDWIN BENNETT
  POTTERY CO.
Baltimore, MD, U.S.A.
Stoneware
1880 + (1856–1936)

E

FRIEDRICH KAESTNER
  PORCELAIN FACTORY
  GMBH
Oberhohndorf, Saxony,
  Germany (E. Germany)
Hard paste porcelain
(1883–1972)

F

HALL CHINA CO.
East Liverpool, OH, U.S.A.
Vitrified dinnerware
1938–ca.1953 (1903–
  present)

G

JULES-JOSEPH-HENRI
  BRIANCHON & GILLET
Paris, France
Porcelain. Black or brown
1864 + (1864 +)

H

GÉRARD, DUFRAISSEIX &
  ABBOT (G.D.A.)
Limoges, France
Porcelain
1937–1952 + (1902–
  present)

I

JOSEF BOCK PORCELAIN
  MANUFACTORY
  VIENNA
Vienna, Austria
Porcelain. Impressed,
  printed
after 1893–ca.1933 (1879–
  1960)

J

GIESSHUBEL
468

FRANZ LEHNERT
Giesshubel, Bohemia
  (Struzna, Czechoslovakia)
Porcelain. Impressed
1840–1946 (1840–1946)

K

GLASGOW POTTERY
  (JOHN MOSES & CO.)
Trenton, NJ, U.S.A.
Semiporcelain, white
  granite
1884 + (1859–1906)

L

W. H. GRINDLEY & CO.
  (LTD.)
Tunstall, Staffordshire,
  England
Earthenware, ironstone.
  Printed
ca.1914–1925 (1880–
  present)

M

A. E. HULL POTTERY CO.
Crooksville, OH, U.S.A.
Kitchenware. Impressed
1910–1935 (1905–1950,
  1952–present)
(Hull Pottery)

N

HALL CHINA CO.
East Liverpool, OH, U.S.A.
Dinnerware, yellowware,
  whiteware
ca.1930–ca.1972 (1903–
  present)

O

HALL CHINA CO.
East Liverpool, OH, U.S.A.
Dinnerware, yellowware,
  whiteware
ca.1916–ca.1930 (1903–
  present)

P

NORITAKE
Nagoya, Japan
Porcelain. Blue
1906 + (1904–present)

A

HARKER, TAYLOR & CO.
East Liverpool, OH, U.S.A.
Rockingham ware.
Embossed, impressed
1846–1851 (1846–1972)
(various names)

B

HAVILAND & CO.
Limoges, France
Porcelain. Green
1886+ (1864–present)
(Haviland SA)

C

HOGANAS CERAMICS
Hoganas, Sweden
Ceramics
1976+ (1797–1976+)

D

HOMER LAUGHLIN CHINA
CO.
East Liverpool, OH, U.S.A.
Semivitreous hotel ware.
Printed
ca.1901–ca.1915 (1877–
present)

E

MADE IN U. S. A.

UNIVERSAL POTTERIES,
INC.
Cambridge, OH, U.S.A.
Semiporcelain, earthenware
1934–1956 (1934–1956)

F

L. HUTSCHENREUTHER
PORCELAIN FACTORY
Selb, Bavaria, Germany (W.
Germany)
Porcelain
1887+ (1857–present)
(Hutschenreuther AG)

G

NILOAK POTTERY
Benton, AR, U.S.A.
Cast pottery
ca.1930–1942 (1909–
1944)

H

D. E. McNICOL POTTERY
CO.
East Liverpool, OH, U.S.A.
Semivitreous ware
ca.1905 (1892–1954)

I

IDEN POTTERY
Rye, Sussex, England
Earthenware, stoneware.
Printed
current (1961–present)

J

AMPHORA WORK
REISSNER
Turn-Teplitz, Bohemia
(Trnovany,
Czechoslovakia)
Pottery
1903–1918 (1892–1945+)
(various names,
nationalized in 1945)

K

JACKSON VITRIFIED
CHINA CO.
Falls Creek, PA, U.S.A.
Vitrified porcelain
1930s (1917–present)
(Jackson China Co.)

L

SEBRING POTTERY CO.
East Liverpool, OH, U.S.A.
Semivitreous ware
ca.1920–ca.1935 (1887–
1948)

M

J. B. WOOD & CO.
Longton, Staffordshire,
England
Earthenware. Printed,
impressed
1910–1926 (1897–1926)

N

JOHN S. MADDOCK (LTD.)
Burslem, Staffordshire,
England
Willowware
(1842–present)
(Maddock Hotel Ware
Division of Royal Stafford
China Ltd.)

O

CINCINNATI ART
POTTERY
Cincinnati, OH, U.S.A.
Pottery
1879–1886 (1879–1891)

P

DOULTON & CO.
Lambeth, London, England
Earthenware. Impressed,
printed
ca.1873–ca.1914 (1853–
present)
(Royal Doulton Tableware
Ltd.)

A

PILKINGTON'S TILES LTD.
Clifton Junction,
    Lancashire, England
Earthenware, tiles. Stamped
ca.1972 (1893–present)

B

LOVATT & LOVATT
Langley Mill, Nottingham,
    England
Earthenware, stoneware.
    Printed, impressed
ca.1900+ (1895–1964+)

C

BOURNE & LEIGH (LTD.)
Burslem, Staffordshire
    England
Earthenware
1930+ (1892–1941)

D

CHAUFFRIASSE &
    ROUGERIE
Limoges, France
Porcelain
1929+ (ca.1926–ca.1934)

E

LEGRAND & CO.
Limoges, France
Porcelain
(1924–1962+)

F

ANDRÉ PRÉVOT
Limoges, France
Porcelain
(1952–1979+)

G

MANUFACTURE
NOUVELLE DE
PORCELAINE
Limoges, France
Porcelain
(1960–1978+)

H

LONGWY FAIENCE CO.
Longwy, France
Pottery
1878+ (1798–present)

I

WELLER POTTERY
Zanesville, OH, U.S.A.
Art pottery
(1882–1948)

J

MARTIAL REDON & CO.
Limoges, France
Porcelain
1890+ (1882–1896)

K

ALTON TOWERS
    HANDCRAFT POTTERY
    (STAFFS.) LTD.
Alton Towers, Stoke,
    Staffordshire, England
Earthenware. Printed,
    impressed
(1953–1964+)

L

RYE POTTERY LTD.
Rye, Sussex, England
Pottery. Printed, impressed
1955–1956 (1869–
    present)

M

HOMER LAUGHLIN CHINA
    CO.
East Liverpool, OH, U.S.A.
Semivitreous ware
ca.1955 (1877–present)

N

MINTON
Stoke, Staffordshire,
    England
Porcelain, earthenware,
    majolica, parian. Printed
ca.1871–1875 (1793–
    present)
(Royal Doulton Tableware
    Ltd.)

O

MARBLEHEAD POTTERY
Marblehead, MA, U.S.A.
Pottery
before 1908–1936 (1904–
    1936)

P

MERKELBACH & WICK
Grenzhausen, Palatinate,
    Germany (W. Germany)
Stoneware, steins
1872–1921 (1872–
    present)
(Wick Works AG)

A

NATIONAL CHINA CO.
East Liverpool, OH, U.S.A.
Hotel ware
1911–ca.1924 (1899–
1929)

B

NEW CASTLE POTTERY
New Castle, PA, U.S.A.
Hotel ware, dinnerware
(1901–1905)

C

NEW DEVON POTTERY
LTD.
Newton Abbot, Devon,
England
Earthenware. Printed
1957 + (1957–present)

D

NORITAKE
Noritake, Nagoya, Japan
Porcelain. Underglaze
transfer in pink
1945–1952 (1904–
present)

E

NORMAN ROCKWELL
MUSEUM
Lincolnwood, IL, U.S.A.
Collector plates
current (1976–present)

F

ROSEVILLE POTTERY CO.
Zanesville, OH, U.S.A.
Art pottery, dinnerware.
Impressed
1914 + (1892–1954)

G

NATIONAL CHINA CO.
East Liverpool, OH, U.S.A.
Semivitreous dinnerware
1911–ca.1923 (1899–
1929)

H

PEWABIC POTTERY
Detroit, MI, U.S.A.
Art pottery
(1903–present)

I

PIONEER POTTERY CO.
East Liverpool, OH, U.S.A.
Semivitreous novelties,
tableware
1935–1958 (1935–
present)

J

PIONEER POTTERY CO.
Wellsville, OH, U.S.A.
Porcelain
1884–ca.1890 (1884–
1900)

K

PORSGRUND PORCELAIN
FACTORY
Porsgrunn, Norway
Porcelain
1911–1937 (1885–
present)

L

SCHONWALD PORCELAIN
FACTORY
Arzberg, Bavaria, Germany
(W. Germany)
Porcelain. Green underglaze
1920–1927 (1890–present)
(Porcelain Factory Arzberg)

M

HARKER POTTERY CO.
East Liverpool, OH, U.S.A.
Pottery, semivitreous
dinnerware. Stamped
ca.1965 (1890–1972)

N

RONDELEUX FILS AÎNÉ &
CIE
Vierzon, France
Porcelain
1914 (1902–1981 +)

O

AMERICAN ART CHINA
Trenton, NJ, U.S.A.
Ceramic
(1891–ca.1900)

P

THOMAS RECKNAGEL
Alexandrinenthal, Bavaria,
Germany (W. Germany)
Porcelain, figurines
1896–1934 (1886–1934)

A

PAUL REVERE POTTERY
Boston, MA, U.S.A.
Pottery
(1906–1942)

B

RICHARD MUTZ
Berlin, Germany
Art pottery. Stamped
ca.1905

C

REINHOLD MERKELBACH
Hohr-Grenzhausen,
  Palatinate, Germany (W.
  Germany)
Stoneware. Impressed
ca.1910 (1845–present)

D

ROYAL ALLER VALE &
  WATCOMBE POTTERY
  CO.
Torquay, Devon, England
Earthenware. Printed,
  impressed
ca.1958–1962 (ca.1901–
  1962)

E

WORCESTER ROYAL
  PORCELAIN CO. LTD.
Worcester, England
Bone china
current (1862–present)
(Royal Worcester Spode
  Ltd.)

F

ROSEVILLE POTTERY CO.
Zanesville, OH, U.S.A.
Art pottery, dinnerware.
  Impressed
ca.1905 (1892–1954)

G

RYE POTTERY
Rye, Sussex, England
Pottery. Printed, impressed
ca.1955–1956, current
  (1869–present)

H

F. A. SCHUMANN
Berlin, Germany
Porcelain. Blue underglaze
1851–1869 (ca.1835–
  ca.1869)

I

L. B. BEERBOWER & CO.
Elizabeth, NJ, U.S.A.
Stoneware, yellowware,
  ironstone
(1816–ca.1902)

J

HOMER LAUGHLIN CHINA
  CO.
East Liverpool, OH, U.S.A.
Semivitreous ware, various
  pattern names
ca.1901–ca.1915 (1877–
  present)

K

SHENANGO CHINA CO.
New Castle, PA, U.S.A.
Semiporcelain, vitrified
  china
(1901–present)
(Anchor Hocking)

L

J. J. SCHARVOGEL
Munich, Bavaria, Germany
  (W. Germany)
Porcelain, earthenware
  figurines. Impressed
1898–ca.1913 (1898–
  1923)

M

COALPORT PORCELAIN
  WORKS
Coalport, Shropshire,
  England
Porcelain. Printed
ca.1820 (ca.1795–present)
(member of Wedgwood
  Group)

N

SYLVAN POTTERY LTD.
Hanley, Staffordshire,
  England
Earthenware. Printed
ca.1946–1948
(1946–present)

O

GUSTAFSBERG
Gustafsberg, Sweden
Semiporcelain, faience,
  earthenware
1921–1940 (1825–
  present)

P

KNOWLES, TAYLOR &
  KNOWLES
East Liverpool, OH, U.S.A.
White granite, stone china
ca.1854 (1870–1929)

A

ERDMANN
SCHLEGELMILCH
PORCELAIN FACTORY
Suhl, Thuringia, Germany
(E. Germany)
Porcelain
1896–ca.1938 (1881–
1938)

B

SHORTER & SON
Stoke, Staffordshire,
England
Earthenware. Printed
ca.1940+ (1905–1964+)
(Crown Devon Group)

C

SYLVAN POTTERY LTD.
Hanley, Staffordshire,
England
Earthenware. Printed
ca.1946+ (1946–present)

D

ROYAL WINTON
Stoke, Staffordshire,
England
Earthenware
current (1886–present)

E

THÉODORE DECK
Paris, France
Terra-cotta, studio pottery.
Impressed
ca.1880 (1859–1891)

F

ROSENTHAL GLASS &
PORCELAIN AG
Selb, Bavaria, Germany (W.
Germany)
Porcelain
1978+ (1879–present)

G

ROSENTHAL GLASS &
PORCELAIN AG
Selb, Bavaria, Germany (W.
Germany)
Porcelain, earthenware
1962–present (1879–
present)

H

UNIVERSITY CITY
POTTERY
University City, MO, U.S.A.
Art pottery. Impressed,
printed
(1910–1915)

I

STERLING CHINA CO.
East Liverpool, OH, U.S.A.
Vitreous institutional ware
1951–1976 (1917–
present)

J

VILLEROY & BOCH
Mettlach, Saar, Germany
(W. Germany)
Earthenware, porcelain.
Stamped
ca.1880–1900 (1813–
present)
(various names, owners &
locations)

K

UTILITY PORCELAIN VEB
Grafenthal, Thuringia,
Germany (E. Germany)
Porcelain
ca.1972–present (1891–
present)

L

VILLEROY & BOCH
Mettlach, Saar, Germany
(W. Germany)
Earthenware, tiles
1928–1945 (1813–
present)
(various names, owners &
locations)

M

WADE, HEATH & CO. LTD.
Burslem & Stoke,
Staffordshire, England
Earthenware
current (1927–present)

N

WELLSVILLE CHINA CO.
East Liverpool, OH, U.S.A.
Ovenware, various pattern
names
ca.1940–ca.1950 (1902–
1969)

O

VIENNA ART CERAMIC
WORKSHOP
Vienna, Austria
Earthenware, porcelain,
figurines
(1908–1940)

P

WHEATLEY POTTERY CO.
Cincinnati, OH, U.S.A.
Artware pottery. Paper label
(1903–1936)

A WALRICH POTTERY Berkeley, CA, U.S.A. Studio pottery, tile, figurines. Raised disc (1922–ca.1930)	**B**  LIMOGES CHINA CO. East Liverpool, OH, U.S.A. Semivitreous dinnerware, various pattern names 1927–1932 (1900–1955) (American Limoges China Co.)	**C**  BETH BLIK Tollesbury, Essex, England Functional pottery (1963–1964 +)	**D** MISS MARGARET LEACH Aylburton, Gloucestershire, England Studio pottery. Impressed 1951–1956 (1946–1956)
E BANKO POTTERY Tokyo, Japan Redware, pottery (1780–present)	**F**  WHEELING POTTERY CO. Wheeling, WV, U.S.A. Semiporcelain 1888–1893 (1879– ca.1910)	**G** AMERICAN CHINAWARE CORP. East Liverpool, OH, U.S.A. Semivitreous dinnerware. Printed 1929–1931 (1929–1931)	**H** KARL NEHMZOW PORCELAIN FACTORY ALTENKUNSTADT Altenkunstadt, Bavaria, Germany (W. Germany) Porcelain. Blue, black overglaze ca.1960–present (1933– present)
I  ANCHOR POTTERY Trenton, NJ, U.S.A. Ironstone 1898 + (1893–1927)	**J** ARC-EN-CIEL Zanesville, OH, U.S.A. Art pottery. Stamped ca.1903 (1903–1907)	**K** WEST HIGHLAND POTTERY CO. LTD. Dunoon, Argyll, Scotland Earthenware current (after 1964– present)	**L** WELLER POTTERY Zanesville, OH, U.S.A. Molded art pottery ca.1910 (1882–1948)
M AUGUSTE DELAHERCHE Armentieres, France Stoneware with Chinese- type glaze (1894–ca.1940)	**N** THE WICK CHINA CO. Kittanning, PA, U.S.A. Ironstone, decorated ware (1889–present)	**O** CHESAPEAKE POTTERY Baltimore, MD, U.S.A. Pottery. Stamped 1887–1890 (1881–1914)	**P** BOVEY POTTERY CO. LTD. Bovey Tracey, Devon, England Earthenware. Printed, impressed ca.1937–1949(1894–1957)

A

BRITANNIA POTTERY CO.
LTD.
St. Rollox, Glasgow,
Scotland
Earthenware. Printed
1920–1935 (1920–1935)

B

CHARLES L. DWENGER
New York, NY, U.S.A.
Porcelain importer
(ca.1895–1917+)

C

CARTER & CO. LTD.
Poole, Dorset, England
Earthenware, art pottery
(1873–present)
(Poole Pottery Ltd.)

D

ROBERT HAVILAND & C.
PARLON
Limoges, France
Porcelain
ca.1942 + (1870–present)
(various names)

E

TRENTON POTTERIES
CO.
Trenton, NJ, U.S.A.
Vitreous porcelain
1892 + (1892–1960)

F

COOK POTTERY CO.
Trenton, NJ, U.S.A.
Dewey commemorative jug.
Stamped
1899 (1894–1929)

G

WILLIAM DE MORGAN
London, England
Earthenware. Impressed
1898 + (ca.1872–1911)
(various locations)

H

DARTMOUTH POTTERY
LTD.
Dartmouth, Devon,
England
Earthenware. Printed
current (1947–present)

I

ROSEVILLE POTTERY CO.
Zanesville, OH, U.S.A.
Porcelain, stoneware.
Impressed
1915 + (1892–1954)

J

DUDSON, WILCOX & TILL
LTD.
Hanley, Staffordshire,
England
Earthenware. Printed,
impressed
1902–1926 (1902–1926)

K

PICKARD CHINA CO.
Chicago, IL, U.S.A.
Decorative porcelain
1893–1894 (1893–
present)
(Pickard, Inc.)

L

HARKER POTTERY CO.
East Liverpool, OH, U.S.A.
Semivitreous dinnerware
ca.1930–1935 (1890–
1972)

M

GRIFFEN, SMITH & HILL
Phoenixville, PA, U.S.A.
Majolica, earthenware.
Impressed
ca. 1878–1889 (1878–
1889)

N

DENBY TABLEWARE
Denby, England
Stoneware, porcelain
1974 + (1895–present)

O

WELLER POTTERY
Zanesville, OH, U.S.A.
Art pottery
ca.1904 (1882–1948)

P

CAMBRIDGE ART
POTTERY
Cambridge, OH, U.S.A.
Faience, dinnerware
ca.1904 (1895–1909)

A

HALL CHINA CO.
East Liverpool, OH, U.S.A.
Vitrified kitchenware
1933–1976 (1903–
present)

B

HAMPSHIRE POTTERY
(J. S. TAFT)
Keene, NH, U.S.A.
Majolica
(1871–1923)

C

OKURA ART CHINA
(NORITAKE CO.)
Nagoya, Japan
Porcelain. Printed, magenta
before 1921 (1904–
present)

D

PICKARD CHINA CO.
Chicago, IL, U.S.A.
Porcelain
1895–1898 (1893–
present)
(Pickard, Inc.)

E

VERNON KILNS
Vernon, CA, U.S.A.
Porcelain
ca.1950 (1912–1958)

F

HAVILAND & CO.
Limoges, France
Porcelain
1879–1889 (1864–
present)
(Haviland SA)

G

A. E. HULL POTTERY CO.
Crooksville, OH, U.S.A.
Kitchenware, art pottery
1920s (1905–1950, 1952–
present)
(Hull Pottery)

H

HARKER POTTERY CO.
East Liverpool, OH, U.S.A.
Semivitreous ware
ca.1959 (1890–1972)

I

ISLE OF WIGHT POTTERY
Whippingham, Isle of
Wight, England
Earthenware. Printed,
impressed
ca.1930–1940 (ca.1930–
1940)

J

JAMES MACINTYRE & CO.
(LTD.)
Burslem, Staffordshire,
England
Porcelain. Printed,
impressed
1894–1928 (ca.1860–
ca.1928)

K

ROYAL PORCELAIN
MANUFACTORY
Berlin, Germany
Porcelain. Printed blue
1849–1870 (1763–
present)
(State's Porcelain
Manufactory)

L

— — — — — —
Kokura, Japan
Porcelain
1921–1940

M

RAYNAUD & CO.
Limoges, France
Porcelain
(1911–present)

N

J. BOYER
Limoges, France
Decorated porcelain
(1919–ca.1938)

O

SAMPSON BRIDGWOOD
& SON
Longton, Staffordshire,
England
Earthenware, porcelain
1870 + (ca.1805–present)

P

LEWIS STRAUS & SONS
New York, NY, U.S.A.
Porcelain importers
ca.1895–1917

A

E. HUGHES & CO.
Fenton, Staffordshire,
England
Porcelain. Printed
1905–1912 (1889–1953)

B

NELSON McCOY
POTTERY
Roseville, OH, U.S.A.
Stoneware, earthenware
late 1940s–1966 (1848–
present)
(Lancaster Colony Corp.)

C

HONITON POTTERY LTD.
Honiton, Devon, England
Earthenware. Printed,
impressed
1956+ (1881–present)

D

ROYAL CHINA CO.
Sebring, OH, U.S.A.
Semivitreous dinnerware
ca.1940–1955 (1933–
present)

E

VODREY & BROTHERS
POTTERY CO.
East Liverpool, OH, U.S.A.
Ironstone ware. Stamped
1876–1896 (ca.1857–
1928)

F

PISGAH FOREST
POTTERY
Arden, NC, U.S.A.
Porcelain
1920–1961 (1901–present)

G

PORTMEIRION
POTTERIES LTD.
Stoke, Staffordshire,
England
Earthenware
1962+ (1962–present)

H

ROYAL CHINA CO.
Sebring, OH, U.S.A.
Semivitreous dinnerware
ca.1940–1955 (1933–
present)

I

SAMUEL JOHNSON LTD.
Burslem, Staffordshire,
England
Earthenware. Printed
ca.1916–1931 (1887–
1931)

J

SMITH-PHILLIPS CHINA
CO.
East Liverpool, OH, U.S.A.
Semivitreous hotel ware
ca.1910 (1901–1929)

K

STOCKTON ART
POTTERY
Stockton, CA, U.S.A.
Art pottery, dinnerware
(1895–1902)

L

BURFORD BROS.
East Liverpool, OH, U.S.A.
Semivitreous porcelain,
creamware, granite,
ironstone
ca.1895 (1879–1904)

M

HALL CHINA CO.
East Liverpool, OH, U.S.A.
Dinnerware, various pattern
names
1933–1976 (1903–
present)

N

HALL CHINA CO.
East Liverpool, OH, U.S.A.
Porcelain, dinnerware.
Stamped, for Jewel Tea
Co.
1933–1976 (1903–
present)

O

THE LONGPARK
POTTERY
Longpark, England
Terra-cotta. Impressed
1883–ca.1895 (ca.1883–
1957)

P

FRANKLIN MINT
Franklin Center, PA, U.S.A.
Porcelain
(1965–present)

A

WARRANTED
PLATINUM GOLD
ALLOY
Made in
America

SALEM CHINA CO.
Salem, OH, U.S.A.
Semiporcelain, dinnerware
1918+ (1898–1967)

B

UPSALA-EKEBY LTD.
Upsala, Sweden
Porcelain
1918+ (1886–1942)
(Karlskrona Porcelain
Factory AB)

C

UNIVERSAL POTTERIES,
INC.
Cambridge, OH, U.S.A.
Pottery. Printed
1934–1956 (1934–1956)

D

UNIVERSITY CITY
POTTERY
University City, MO, U.S.A.
Pottery. Impressed, printed
1914+ (1910–1915)

E

NORTH DAKOTA
SCHOOL OF MINES
Grand Forks, ND, U.S.A.
Art pottery. Stamped
factory mark with incised
name.
(1892–1963)

F

CRESCENT POTTERY
Trenton, NJ, U.S.A.
Sanitary earthenware, white
granite, cream-colored
ware
1900–1902 (1881–
1902+)

G

SAMPSON BRIDGWOOD
& SON
Longton, Staffordshire,
England
Earthenware. Printed
1961+ (ca.1805–present)

H

WALRICH POTTERY
Berkeley, CA, U.S.A.
Earthenware, porcelain
(1922–ca.1930)

I

WATCOMBE
POTTERY CO.
Torquay, Devon, England
Earthenware, terra-cotta.
Printed
1875–1901 (1870–1962)

J

F. WINKLE & CO.
Stoke, Staffordshire,
England
Earthenware. Printed,
impressed
1908–1925 (1890–1931)

K

ZSOLNAY
Pecs, Hungary
Lusterware, art pottery.
Printed
ca.1865 (1862–present)

L

GEORGE S. HARKER &
CO.
East Liverpool, OH, U.S.A.
Ironstone
1879–1890 (1840–1972)
(various names)

M

THOMAS POOLE
Longton, Staffordshire,
England
Porcelain. Printed
ca.1929–1940 (1880–
present)
(Royal Stafford China, Ltd.)

N

GREENWOOD POTTERY
Trenton, NJ, U.S.A.
Ironstone. Printed, purple
1886+ (1868–ca.1933)
(various names)

O

WEDGWOOD & CO.
Tunstall, Staffordshire,
England
Earthenware, stone china
ca.1890–1906 (1860–
present)
(member of Wedgwood
Group)

P

CRONIN CHINA CO.
Minerva, OH, U.S.A.
Porcelain. Backstamp
(1934–1956)

A

22 K. GOLD
U.S.A.

FRENCH SAXON CHINA
CO.
East Liverpool, OH, U.S.A.
Semivitreous dinnerware
ca.1940–ca.1958 (1935–
present)
(Royal China Co.)

B

ALLERTON'S LTD.
Longton, Staffordshire,
England
Porcelain, earthenware.
Printed
ca.1915–1929 (1859–
1942)

C

Hand Printed
LINCOLN, ILL.

STETSON CHINA CO.
Lincoln, IL, U.S.A.
Porcelain, dinnerware.
Backstamp
ca.1958 (1919–1965)

D

RAYNAUD & CO.
Limoges, France
Undecorated porcelain
1960–present (1911–
present)

E

AREQUIPA POTTERY
Fairfax, CA, U.S.A.
Art pottery
(1911–1918)

F

VERNON KILNS
Vernon, CA, U.S.A.
Earthenware, semivitreous
ware
1947+ (1912–1958)

G

BAUER POTTERY
Los Angeles, CA, U.S.A.
Ring pattern dinnerware
1932+ (1905–ca.1958)

H

EDWIN BENNETT
POTTERY CO.
Baltimore, MD, U.S.A.
Earthenware, parian, bone
china, yellowware,
various dates
ca.1873–1885 (1856–1936)

I

JOHN BESWICK (LTD.)
Longton, Staffordshire,
England
Earthenware, porcelain
1946+ (1936–present)
(Royal Doulton Tableware
Ltd.)

J

BILTONS TABLEWARE,
LTD.
Stoke, Staffordshire,
England
Earthenware
current (1900–present)

K

BRITISH ART POTTERY
CO. (FENTON) LTD.
Fenton, Staffordshire,
England
Porcelain. Printed,
impressed
1920–1926 (1920–1926)

L

WILLIAM COENRAD
BROUWER
Gouda, Holland
Porcelain. Impressed
1898–1901 (ca.1898–
1933)

M

BURGESS & LEIGH
Burslem, Staffordshire,
England
Earthenware. Printed
1930+ (1862–present)

N

CARTWRIGHT BROS. CO.
East Liverpool, OH, U.S.A.
Ironstone dinnerware
1896–1927 (1880–1927)

O

CASTLETON CHINA, INC.
New Castle, PA, U.S.A.
Dinnerware
ca. 1968-1979 (1940–
present)
(Anchor Hocking)

P

SALEM CHINA CO.
Salem, OH, U.S.A.
Semiporcelain. Backstamp
1940s (1898–1967)

A  ROSENTHAL GLASS & PORCELAIN AG Selb, Germany (W. Germany) Porcelain. Green underglaze current (1879–present)	**B**  ARNHEMSCHE FAIENCE FACTORY Gouda, Holland Delft 1923–1930 (1923–1930+)	**C**  CONTINENTAL KILNS East Liverpool, OH, U.S.A. Semivitreous dinnerware 1944–1954 (1944–1954)	**D**  BING & GRONDAHL Copenhagen, Denmark Porcelain 1970+ (1853–present)
E  COPELAND & GARRETT Stoke, Staffordshire, England Porcelain, earthenware, parian. Printed 1833+ (1833–present) (Royal Worcester Spode Ltd.)	**F** COPELAND & GARRETT Stoke, Staffordshire, England Porcelain, earthenware, parian. Printed 1833+ (1833–present) (Royal Worcester Spode Ltd.)	**G** VERNON KILNS Vernon, CA, U.S.A. Earthenware, semivitreous ware ca.1935–1939 (1912–1958)	**H** CREIL & MONTEREAU Creil, France Faience, stoneware, soft paste porcelain. Sepia 1879+ (1819–1895)
I DALTON POTTERY Dalton, OH, U.S.A. Art pottery, hotel ware. Impressed 1920s (1842–1950+)	**J** JEAN POUYAT Limoges, France Porcelain (1842–present) (Guérin-Pouyat-Élite)	**K** DOULTON & CO. Lambeth, London, England Earthenware, stoneware. Impressed 1877–1880 (1853–present) (Royal Doulton Tableware Ltd.)	**L** GUSTAFSBERG Gustafsberg, Sweden Semiporcelain, faience, earthenware 1931+ (1825–present)
M FLINTRIDGE CHINA CO. Pasadena, CA, U.S.A. Porcelain dinnerware (1945–present)	**N** CHARLES AHRENFELDT Limoges, France Undercoated porcelain 1896–1969 (1859–1969)	**O**  GLADDING, McBEAN & CO. Los Angeles, CA, U.S.A. Franciscan ware 1939–1947 (1875–present) (member of Wedgwood Group)	**P** FRANZ ANTON MEHLEM EARTHENWARE FACTORY Bonn, Rhineland, Germany (W. Germany) Earthenware, porcelain. Printed blue or brown 1887–1920 (1836–1920)

A

GLOBE POTTERY CO. LTD.
Cobridge, Staffordshire, England
Earthenware. Printed
1930–1934 (1914–1964+)
(various names & owners)

B

FRIEDRICH GOLDSCHEIDER VIENNA MANUFACTORY
Vienna, Austria
Porcelain
1885–ca.1907 (1885–present)
(various names)

C

GRUEBY FAIENCE CO.
Boston, MA, U.S.A.
Semiporcelain, covered with opaque enamel.
Impressed
1910+ (1897–1911)

D

CROWN CHINA CRAFTS LTD.
Stoke, Staffordshire, England
Porcelain, earthenware.
Printed
1946–1958 (1946–1958)

E

— — — — —
Japan
Hand-painted porcelain.
Printed turquoise
1890–1921

F

TAKITO
Japan
Porcelain
(1880–ca.1948)

G

CANONSBURG POTTERY CO.
Canonsburg, PA, U.S.A.
Porcelain dinnerware.
Backstamp
1900–1909 (1900–1978)

H

SOUTHERN POTTERIES, INC.
Erwin, TN, U.S.A.
Porcelain. Hand-painted
1950s (1917–1957)

I

HAND PAINTED
UNDER GLAZE
VERNON KILNS
CALIF.
MADE IN U.S.A.

VERNON KILNS
Vernon, CA, U.S.A.
Earthenware, semivitreous ware
ca.1942–1947 (1912–1958)

J

VERNON KILNS
Vernon, CA, U.S.A.
Earthenware, semivitreous ware
1950–1954 (1912–1958)

K

VERNON KILNS
Vernon, CA, U.S.A.
Earthenware, semivitreous ware
ca.1953 (1912–1958)

L

HARKER POTTERY
East Liverpool, OH, U.S.A.
Semivitreous dinnerware
ca.1948–ca.1955 (1890–1972)

M

H. AYNSLEY & CO. (LTD.)
Longton, Staffordshire, England
Earthenware. Printed, impressed
1946–1954 (1873–present)
(subsidiary of Waterford)

N

HOMER LAUGHLIN CHINA CO.
East Liverpool, OH, U.S.A.
Porcelain dinnerware
ca.1965 (1877–present)

O

HUTSCHENREUTHER AG
Selb, Bavaria, Germany (W. Germany)
Porcelain. Green underglaze
1974–present (1969–present)

P

JOHANN HAVILAND
Waldershof, Bavaria, Germany (W. Germany)
Porcelain
(1907–present)
(various names, now Rosenthal Glass & Porcelain AG)

A

J. POUYAT
Limoges, France
Porcelain. Green
underglaze
(1842–present)
(Guérin-Pouyat-Élite)

B

JUSTIN THARAUD & SON/
PADEN CITY POTTERY
CO.
New York, NY, U.S.A.
Distributor, pottery
1948–1953

C

EDWIN M. KNOWLES
Newell, WV, U.S.A.
Collector plates
1974–present (1974–
present)

D

BLOCK CHINA CO.
New York, NY, U.S.A.
Distributors of ironstone by
Hall China Co.
1960s (ca.1930–present)

E

ROSENTHAL GLASS &
PORCELAIN AG
Selb, Bavaria, Germany (W.
Germany)
Porcelain, earthenware.
Green underglaze, blue
or gold overglaze
1969–present (1879–
present)
(name reestablished by
Bradford Exchange,
Chicago, IL)

F

LONGPARK POTTERY CO.
(LTD.)
Torquay, Devon, England
Earthenware. Impressed
ca.1920 (1883–1957)

G

WADE ULSTER LTD.
Portadown, Co. Armagh,
Northern Ireland
Earthenware, Irish porcelain
current (1953–present)

H

LIMOGES-TURGOT
Limoges, France
Collector plates. Printed
current (1770–present)

I

BOCH & BUSCHMANN
Mettlach, Saar, Germany
(W. Germany)
Earthenware. Impressed
ca. 1813–1825 (1813–
present)
(Villeroy & Boch)

J

EGERSUND POTTERY
FACTORY
Egersund, Norway
Faience
1954+ (1847–present)
(Porsgrund Porcelain
Factory)

K

NORTON POTTERY
Bennington, VT, U.S.A.
Stoneware, brown-glazed
pottery. Impressed.
1845–1847 (1793–1858)

L

ETRURIA POTTERY
(OTT & BREWER)
Trenton, NJ, U.S.A.
Belleek ware
ca.1885 (1863–1894)

M

NITTO
Japan
Porcelain. Blue
before 1921 (1890–1921)

N

UNIVERSAL POTTERIES,
INC.
Cambridge, OH, U.S.A.
Dinnerware, ovenware.
Backstamp
1934–1956 (1934–1956)

O

UNIVERSAL POTTERIES,
INC.
Cambridge, OH, U.S.A.
Dinnerware, ovenware.
Backstamp.
1934–1956 (1934–1956)

P

C. J. MASON
Liverpool, England
Ironstone. Impressed
ca.1813–1815 (1813–
1848)
(under various names,
marks sold to the
Wedgwood Group)

A	B	C	D

HAGA POTTERY Purmerend, Holland Art pottery. Printed ca.1900 (1897–1907+)	RED WING POTTERY Red Wing, MN, U.S.A. Stoneware. Stamped ca.1930+ (1878–1967)	RHEAD POTTERY Santa Barbara, CA, U.S.A. Art pottery. Impressed (1913–1917)	RIDGEWOOD CHINA Southampton, PA, U.S.A. Porcelain (1948–1971)
E	F	G	H
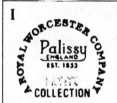			
ROSEVILLE POTTERY CO. Zanesville, OH, U.S.A. Stoneware, art pottery. Stamped 1939–1953 (1892–1954)	ROYAL CHINA CO. Sebring, OH, U.S.A. Porcelain dinnerware (1933–present)	WADE, HEATH & CO. LTD. Burslem, Staffordshire, England Earthenware. Printed, impressed ca.1953 (1927–present)	GRIMWADES LTD. Stoke, Staffordshire, England Earthenware, majolica. Printed 1934–1950 (1900– present) (Royal Winton Pottery)
I	J	K	L

ROYAL WORCESTER SPODE LTD. Worcester, England Porcelain, pottery, various pattern names 1970+ (ca. 1751–present)	RYE POTTERY Rye, Sussex, England Pottery 1947–1953 (1869– present)	SEBRING POTTERY CO. East Liverpool, OH, U.S.A. Porcelain, ironstone, toiletware. ca.1895 (1887–1948)	MERCER POTTERY CO. Trenton, NJ, U.S.A. Semiporcelain, table & toilet services (1868–ca.1937)
M	N	O	P

SOCIÉTÉ CÉRAMIQUE Maastricht, Holland Porcelain 1887+ (1863–1887+)	JOSIAH SPODE Stoke, Staffordshire, England Earthenware, porcelain, stone china ca.1821 (ca.1762–present) (Royal Worcester Spode Ltd.)	STERLING CHINA CO. East Liverpool, OH, U.S.A. Vitreous hotel & table ware ca.1949 (1917–present)	TAYLOR, SMITH & TAYLOR East Liverpool, OH, U.S.A. Ovenware ca.1957 (1901–present) (Anchor Hocking)

A

TAYLOR, SMITH &
  TAYLOR
East Liverpool, OH, U.S.A.
Ironstone tableware
ca.1970 (1901–present)
(Anchor Hocking)

B

TAYLOR, SMITH &
  TAYLOR
East Liverpool, OH, U.S.A.
Ironstone tableware
ca.1970 (1901–present)
(Anchor Hocking)

C

E.J.D. BODLEY
Burslem, Staffordshire,
  England
Porcelain, earthenware.
  Printed, impressed
1875–1892 (1875–1892)

D

VERNON KILNS
Vernon, CA, U.S.A.
Earthenware, semivitreous
  ware
1930s (1912–1958)

E

UNION PORCELAINIÈRE
Limoges, France
Undecorated porcelain
1928–1940 (?–1948+)

F

KARLSKRONA
  PORCELAIN FACTORY
  AB
Upsala, Sweden
Porcelain
1961–1970s (1918–
  present)

G

VERNON KILNS
Vernon, CA, U.S.A.
Earthenware, semivitreous
  ware, various pattern
  names
1947+ (1912–1958)

H

METLOX POTTERIES
Manhattan Beach, CA,
  U.S.A.
Dinnerware
1958–1978+ (1935–
  present)

I

VILLEROY & BOCH
Mettlach, Saar, Germany
  (W. Germany)
Porcelain, pottery. Incised
ca.1880–1883 (1813–
  present)
(various names, owners, &
  locations)

J

JOACHIM LANGLOIS
Bayeux, France
Porcelain. Blue or red
  underglaze
1830–1849 (1810–1849)

K

JOSIAH WEDGWOOD &
  SONS LTD.
Barlaston & Stoke,
  Staffordshire, England
Pottery, creamware. Printed
ca.1940–present (ca.1759–
  present)
(member of Wedgwood
  Group)

L

WEST END POTTERY CO.
East Liverpool, OH, U.S.A.
Semivitreous tableware
1928–1938 (1893–1938)

M

PAUL DACHSEL
Turn, Bohemia, Austria
  (Trnovany,
  Czechoslovakia)
Art pottery
ca.1904 (1904–1980+)

N

CHESAPEAKE POTTERY
Baltimore, MD, U.S.A.
Parian, vitreous ware.
  Backstamp
1887–1890 (1881–1914)

O

WALTON POTTERY CO.
  LTD.
Nr. Chesterfield, Derbyshire,
  England
Salt-glazed stoneware.
  Incised, impressed
1946–1956 (1946–1956)

P

CLIFTON ART POTTERY
Newark, NJ, U.S.A.
Crystalline glaze, Indian
  ware. Incised
1905–1911 (1905–1911)

A CANONSBURG POTTERY CO. Canonsburg, PA, U.S.A. Semiporcelain, ironstone (1900–1978)	**B** KENNETH QUICK St. Ives, Cornwall, England Studio pottery. Incised 1945+ (1945–1963)	**C** NELSON McCOY POTTERY Roseville, OH, U.S.A. Stoneware, earthenware, art pottery after 1930 (1848–present) (Lancaster Colony Corp.)	**D** PENDLEY POTTERY Tring, Hertfordshire, England Studio pottery, stoneware. Incised, printed ca.1949–1964+ (1949–1964+)
E GEORG SCHMIDER Zell on Harmersbach, Badenia, Germany (W. Germany) Earthenware, porcelain ca.1930–present (1907–present)	**F** HARKER POTTERY CO. East Liverpool, OH, U.S.A. Semivitreous dinner & oven ware. 1940–ca.1948 (1890–1972)	**G** HALL CHINA CO. East Liverpool, OH, U.S.A. Vitrified hotel ware ca.1960–present (1903–present)	**H** STETSON CHINA CO. Lincoln, IL, U.S.A. Whiteware 1960s (1919–1965)
I HOMER LAUGHLIN CHINA CO. East Liverpool, OH, U.S.A. Semivitreous dinnerware ca.1940 (1877–present)	**J** WILLIAM DE MORGAN Chelsea & Fulham, London, England Earthenware, tiles ca.1872–1875 (ca. 1872–1911)	**K** WELLER POTTERY Zanesville, OH, U.S.A. Pottery. Ink stamp 1920+ (1882–1948)	**L** JULIEN BALLEROY & CO. Limoges, France Porcelain 1914+
M ALTROHLAU PORCELAIN FACTORIES Altrohlau, Bohemia (Stara Role, Czechoslovakia) Porcelain. Green underglaze 1918–1939 (1813–1945+) (nationalized in 1945)	**N** CHARLES AHRENFELDT Limoges, France Porcelain 1891+ (1859–1969)	**O** MINTON Stoke, Staffordshire, England Porcelain, earthenware, parian, majolica. Printed ca.1822–1836 (1793–present) (Royal Doulton Tableware Ltd.)	**P** RÖRSTRAND PORCELAIN FACTORY Lidkoping, Sweden Porcelain, faience ca.1850 (1726–present) (Rörstrand AB)

A

F. & R. PRATT & CO.
Fenton, Staffordshire,
England
Earthenware, terra-cotta
before 1840 (ca. 1818–
present)
(member of Wedgwood
Group)

B

ETRURIA POTTERY
(OTT & BREWER)
Trenton, NJ, U.S.A.
Porcelain, semiporcelain
ca.1866 (1863–1894)

C

MALKIN, WALKER &
HULSE
Longton, Staffordshire,
England
Earthenware. Printed
1858–1864 (1858–1864)

D

TAYLOR, SMITH &
TAYLOR
East Liverpool, OH, U.S.A.
Semivitreous tableware
ca.1938–ca.1945 (1901–
present)
(Anchor Hocking)

E

COCKSON & HARDING
Shelton, Staffordshire,
England
Earthenware. Printed,
impressed, various
pattern names
(1856–1862)

F

D. F. HAYNES & CO.
(CHESAPEAKE
POTTERY CO.)
Baltimore, MD, U.S.A.
Porcelain, earthenware
ca.1881 (1881–1914)

G

W. DAVENPORT & CO.
Longport, Staffordshire,
England
Porcelain, ironstone
1830–1880 (ca.1793–
1887)

H

VODREY & BROTHERS
POTTERY CO.
East Liverpool, OH, U.S.A.
Ironstone
ca.1896 (ca.1857–1928)

I

NEW ENGLAND POTTERY
CO.
Boston, MA, U.S.A.
Yellow, cream-colored, &
whiteware, semiporcelain
ca.1880 (1854–1914)

J

JOHN & RICHARD RILEY
Burslem, Staffordshire,
England
Earthenware. Printed,
impressed
1802–1828 (1802–1828)

K

CHESAPEAKE POTTERY
Baltimore, MD, U.S.A.
Semiporcelain, majolica,
parian, porcelain
(1881–1914)
(various names)

L

TORQUAY TERRA-COTTA
CO.
Torquay, Devon, England
Terra-cotta
(1875–1940)
(various names)

M

VICTORIA PORCELAIN
FACTORY
Altrohlau, Bohemia (Stara
Role, Czechoslovakia)
Porcelain, earthenware.
Blue overglaze,
underglaze
1891–1918 (1883–1945)

N

J. & M. P. BELL & CO.
Glasgow, Scotland
Earthenware, parian.
Printed
ca.1881–1928 (1842–
1928)

O

JOHN WEDGE WOOD
Burslem & Tunstall,
Staffordshire, England
Earthenware, printed,
various pattern names
(1841–1860)

P

PODMORE, WALKER & CO.
Tunstall, Staffordshire,
England
Earthenware. Printed
1849–1859 (1834– present)
(member of Wedgwood
Group)

A

A. G. RICHARDSON & CO. LTD.
Tunstall, Staffordshire, England
Earthenware. Printed
1916–1970+ (1915–present)

B

A. B. & R. P. DANIELL
London, England
Porcelain for London dealer John Rose. Printed
1860–ca.1917 (ca.1825–1917)

C

AUGUST NOWOTNY
Altrohlau, Bohemia (Stara Role, Czechoslovakia)
Porcelain
1838–1884 (1823–1945+)
(various names & owners)

D

MINTON
Stoke, Staffordshire, England
Porcelain, earthenware, parian, majolica. Printed
ca.1841–1873 (1793–present)
(Royal Doulton Tableware Ltd.)

E

KORNILOV
St. Petersburg, Russia (Leningrad, U.S.S.R.)
Porcelain
1835–1917 (1835–1917)

F

CHARLES HOBSON (& SON)
Burslem, Staffordshire, England
Earthenware
ca.1880 (1865–1880)

G

W. DAVENPORT & CO.
Longport, Staffordshire, England
Earthenware, creamware, porcelain, ironstone
ca.1840–1867 (ca.1793–1887)

H

SAMUEL BARKER & SON
Nr. Rotherham, Yorkshire, England
Earthenware. Printed
ca.1851–1893 (1834–1893)

I

EGERSUND POTTERY FACTORY
Egersund, Norway
Faience
1870+ (1847–present)
(Porsgrund Porcelain Factory)

J

EGERSUND POTTERY FACTORY
Egersund, Norway
Faience
1865+ (1847–present)
(Porsgrund Porcelain Factory)

K

FORD & RILEY
Burslem, Staffordshire, England
Earthenware. Printed
(1882–1964+)

L

BENEDIKT BROS.
Meierhoxen, Bohemia (Dvory, Czechoslovakia)
Porcelain
1883–1925 (1897–1945+)

M

ARABIA PORCELAIN FACTORY
Helsingfors (Helsinki), Finland
Porcelain, stoneware
(1874–present)
(Upsala-Ekeby Group)

N

HEATH & BLACKHURST
Burslem, Staffordshire, England
Earthenware. Printed
1859–1877 (1859–1877)

O

PIONEER POTTERY CO.
Wellsville, OH, U.S.A.
Ironstone toiletware
1884–ca.1890 (1884–1900)

P

LOCKER & CO.
Derby, England
Porcelain
ca.1849–1859 (ca.1750–present)
(Royal Doulton Tableware Ltd.)

A MINTON Stoke, Staffordshire, England Porcelain, earthenware, parian, majolica. Printed ca.1851 (1793–present) (Royal Doulton Tableware Ltd.)	**B** PINDER, BOURNE & CO. Burslem, Staffordshire, England Earthenware 1862–1882 (1862– present) (Royal Doulton Tableware Ltd.)	**C** G. L. ASHWORTH & BROS. Hanley, Staffordshire, England Earthenware, ironstone ca.1870 (1784–present) (member of Wedgwood Group)	**D** RALPH MALKIN Fenton, Staffordshire, England Earthenware. Printed 1863–1881 (1863–1881)
E THOMAS C. WILD Longton, Staffordshire, England Porcelain. Printed 1905–1907 (1905– present) (various names, now Royal Doulton Tableware Ltd.)	**F** RATHBONE SMITH & CO. Tunstall, Staffordshire, England Earthenware. Printed 1883–1897 (1883–1897)	**G** ISAAC THOMAS & JAMES EMBERTON Tunstall, Staffordshire, England Earthenware. Printed 1869–1882 (1869–1882)	**H** THOMAS NICHOLSON & CO. Castleford, Yorkshire, England Earthenware. Printed ca.1854–1871 (ca.1854– 1871)
I THOMAS WOOD & SONS Burslem, Staffordshire, England Earthenware. Printed 1896–1897 (1896–1897)	**J** W. & R. MEIGH Stoke, Staffordshire, England Earthenware. Printed 1894–1899 (1894–1899)	**K** WALLACE & CHETWYND POTTERY CO. East Liverpool, OH, U.S.A. Ironstone ware 1882–1901 (1882–1901)	**L** WALLACE & CHETWYND POTTERY CO. East Liverpool, OH, U.S.A. Ironstone ware, various pattern names 1882–1901 (1882–1901)
M WATCOMBE POTTERY CO. Torquay, Devon, England Terra-cotta, Earthenware. Transfer-printed, impressed ca. 1875–1901 (1870–1962)	**N** VIKING POTTERY CO. Cobridge, Staffordshire, England Porcelain, earthenware. Printed 1950+ (1950–1964+)	**O**  ROBERT HERON (& SON) Sinclairtown, Kirkcaldy, Scotland Earthenware, Wemyss ware, Rockingham. Printed 1920–1929 (1820–1929)	**P** JOSEPH HOLDCROFT Longton, Staffordshire, England Earthenware, majolica, parian. Printed 1890–1939 (1865–1939)

A

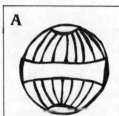

D. E. McNICOL POTTERY CO.
East Liverpool, OH, U.S.A.
Semivitreous ware
1897–ca.1915 (1892–1954)

B

Artists of the World

ARTISTS OF THE WORLD (DE GRAZIA)
Scottsdale, AZ, U.S.A.
Collector plates
1977–present (1977–present)

C

ALFRED MEAKIN (LTD.)
Tunstall, Staffordshire, England
Earthenware. Impressed, printed
ca.1875–1897 (1873–present)
(Myott-Meakin Ltd.)

D

R. J. ERNST ENTERPRISES
Escondido, CA, U.S.A.
Collector plates
1976–present (1976–present)

E

MINTON
Stoke, Staffordshire, England
Porcelain, earthenware, parian. Printed
ca.1863–1872 (1793–present)
(Royal Doulton Tableware Ltd.)

F

GEORGE CLEWS & CO.
Tunstall, Staffordshire, England
Earthenware. Printed
1935 + (1906–1961)

G

GRIMWADES LTD.
Stoke, Staffordshire, England
Earthenware. Printed
ca.1930 + (1900–present)
(Royal Winton Pottery)

H

J. GOODWIN STODDARD & CO.
Longton, Staffordshire, England
Porcelain. Printed
1936–1940 (1898–1940)

I

LOCKE & CO.
Worcester, England
Porcelain. Printed
ca.1895–1900 (1895–present)
(Royal Worcester Spode Ltd.)

J

SYRACUSE CHINA CORP.
Syracuse, NY, U.S.A.
Dinnerware
1893–1898 (1871–present)
(various names & owners)

K

ROYAL PORCELAIN GMBH
Kups, Bavaria, Germany (W. Germany)
Porcelain. Black
1972–present (1972–present)

L

ROYAL NISHIKI NIPPON
Japan
Porcelain. Olive green
(1890–1921)

M

UNIVERSAL POTTERIES, INC.
Cambridge, OH, U.S.A.
Semiporcelain, earthenware
(1934–1956)

N

WILLETS MANUFACTURING CO.
Trenton, NJ, U.S.A.
Belleek ware, pottery
(1879–1962)

O

BURGESS & LEIGH
Burslem, Staffordshire, England
Earthenware. Printed
1906–1912 (1862–present)

P

EDWIN BENNETT POTTERY CO.
Baltimore, MD, U.S.A.
Cream-colored ware
1884 + (1856–1936)

A

POTTER'S CO-
OPERATIVE CO.
East Liverpool, OH, U.S.A.
Ironstone
1890–ca.1900 (1882–
1925)

B

GLOBE POTTERY CO.
East Liverpool, U.S.A.
Semivitreous dinnerware
1888–1901, 1907–1912
(1881–1901, 1907–
1912)

C

E. HUGHES & CO.
Fenton, Staffordshire,
England
Porcelain. Printed
1914–1941 (1889–1953)

D

MERCER POTTERY CO.
Trenton, NJ, U.S.A.
Porcelain, white granite.
Impressed
(1868–ca.1937)

E

MOORE (BROS.)
Longton, Staffordshire,
England
Porcelain. Printed
ca.1891+ (1872–1905)

F

ETRURIA POTTERY
(OTT & BREWER)
Trenton, NJ, U.S.A.
Semiporcelain
(1863–1894)

G

THOMAS TILL & SONS
Burslem, Staffordshire,
England
Earthenware. Printed
ca.1919 (ca.1850–1928)

H

BURFORD BROS.
East Liverpool, OH, U.S.A.
Semivitreous dinnerware
ca.1900 (1879–1904)

I

WHEELING POTTERY CO.
Wheeling, WV, U.S.A.
Graniteware, pottery
(1879–ca.1910)

J

GREEN & CLAY
Longton, Staffordshire,
England
Earthenware. Printed,
impressed
(1888–1891)

K

W. H. GRINDLEY & CO.
LTD.
Tunstall, Staffordshire,
England
Earthenware, ironstone.
Printed, various pattern
names
ca.1891–1914 (1880–
present)

L

ARKINSTALL & SONS
(LTD.)
Stoke, Staffordshire,
England
Porcelain. Printed
(1904–1924)

M

WILLIAM ADAMS & SONS
LTD.
Tunstall & Stoke,
Staffordshire, England
Earthenware, basalt, jasper,
parian. Printed
ca. 1879–1891 (1769–
present)
(member of Wedgwood
Group)

N

EDWIN BENNETT
POTTERY CO.
Baltimore, MD, U.S.A.
Semiporcelain
1890+ (1856–1936)

O

H. M. WILLIAMSON &
SONS
Longton, Staffordshire,
England
Porcelain
ca.1903+ (ca.1879–1941)

P

WILLIAM BROWNFIELD (&
SONS)
Cobridge, Staffordshire,
England
Earthenware, porcelain.
Printed
1871–1891 (1850–1891)

A

ROYAL COPENHAGEN
  PORCELAIN FACTORY
  LTD.
Frederiksberg, Denmark
Porcelain, stoneware,
  faience
1870–1930 (1775–
  present)

B

AMPHORA WORK
  RIESSNER
Turn-Teplitz, Bohemia
  (Trnovany,
  Czechoslovakia)
Porcelain
ca.1905–ca.1945 (1892–
  1945+)
(various names,
  nationalized in 1945)

C

AMPHORA WORK
  RIESSNER
Turn-Teplitz, Bohemia
  (Trnovany,
  Czechoslovakia)
Porcelain
1892–1918 (1892–
  1945+)
(various names,
  nationalized in 1945)

D

ARZBERG PORCELAIN
  FACTORY
Arzberg, Bavaria, Germany
  (W. Germany)
Porcelain. Green
  underglaze
1974–present (1890–
  present)
(various names & owners,
  now Hutschenreuther
  AG)

E

ASHBY POTTER'S GUILD
Woodville, Derbyshire,
  England
Earthenware. Impressed
1909–1922 (1909–1922)

F

AVON ART POTTERY LTD.
Longton, Staffordshire,
  England
Earthenware. Printed
1947–1964+ (1930–
  1969)

G

BARKER POTTERY CO.
Chesterfield, Derbyshire,
  England
Stoneware. Printed,
  impressed
1928–1957 ((1887–1957))

H

BAUSCHER BROS.
  PORCELAIN FACTORY
  WEIDEN
Weiden, Bavaria, Germany
  (W. Germany)
Porcelain. Green underglaze
ca.1921–1939 (1881–
  present)

I

JOHN BESWICK (LTD.)
Longton, Staffordshire,
  England
Earthenware
1946+ (1936–present)
(Royal Doulton Tableware
  Ltd.)

J

HOWARD POTTERY CO.
Shelton, Staffordshire,
  England
Earthenware. Printed
1925–1964+ (1925–
  1964+)

K

CINCINNATI ART
  POTTERY
Cincinnati, OH, U.S.A.
Art pottery. Impressed.
1890–1891 (1879–1891)

L

CARTWRIGHT BROS. CO.
East Liverpool, OH, U.S.A.
Ironstone tableware
ca.1888 (1880–1927)

M

CHARLES GRAHAM
Brooklyn, NY, U.S.A.
Salt-glazed stoneware.
  Impressed
1880–ca.1900 (1880–
  ca.1900)

N

CHICAGO CRUCIBLE CO.
Chicago, IL, U.S.A.
Pottery
ca.1920 (ca.1920–ca.1932)

O

C. TIELSCH & CO.
Altwasser, Silesia, Germany
  (Walbrzych, Poland)
Porcelain. Green
  underglaze
ca.1887–ca.1918 (1845–
  present)
(Hutschenreuther AG)

P

HENRI D'ARCEAU-
  LIMOGES & SONS
Limoges, France
Porcelain collector plates
1973–1976 (1768–
  present)

A	B	C	D

		DOULTON & CO. Lambeth, London, England Pottery, porcelain. Impressed ca.1869–1872 (1853– present) (Royal Doulton Tableware Ltd.)	AMERICAN/EDGERTON ART CLAY WORKS Edgerton, WI, U.S.A. Art pottery 1895–1899 (1892–1899, 1902–1903)
WILLIAM DE MORGAN Fulham, England Earthenware, tiles, vases. 1888–1897 (ca. 1872– 1911)	DESERT SANDS POTTERY Boulder City, NV, U.S.A. Pottery. Stamped (ca.1940–1978+)		

E	F	G	H

B. BLOCH & CO. Eichwald, Bohemia (Dubi, Czechoslovakia) Porcelain, earthenware. Blue ca.1916–ca.1940 (1871– 1945)	WINTERLING PORCELAIN FACTORIES DISTRIBUTING COMPANY Windischeschenbach, Bavaria, Germany (W. Germany) Porcelain distributors. Green underglaze current (ca.1918–present) (Winterling Group)	E. BRAIN & CO. LTD. Fenton, Staffordshire, England Porcelain 1913+ (1903–present) (member of Wedgwood Group)	BAUSCHER BROS. PORCELAIN FACTORY WEIDEN Weiden, Bavaria, Germany (W. Germany) Porcelain. Printed ca.1900 (1881–present)

I	J	K	L
		GMB	
JAMES MACINTYRE & CO. (LTD.) Burslem, Staffordshire, England Faience 1890s–1913 (ca.1860– ca.1928)	SOCIETÀ CERAMICA RICHARD Milan, Italy Porcelain. Impressed 1884–1891 (1735– present) (Richard-Ginori)	GLADDING, McBEAN & CO. Los Angeles, CA, U.S.A. Franciscan dinnerware. Stamped after 1934 to before 1962 (1875–present) (member of Wedgwood Group)	HUTSCHENREUTHER AG Selb, Bavaria, Germany (W. Germany) Hard paste porcelain ca.1969–1981+ (1969– present)

M	N	O	P
L. HUTSCHENREUTHER PORCELAIN FACTORY Selb, Bavaria, Germany (W. Germany) Hard paste porcelain 1955–1969 (1857– present) (Hutschenreuther AG)	JACOB ZEIDLER & CO. Selb, Bavaria, Germany (W. Germany) Porcelain ca.1910–1917 (1866– 1917)	EDWIN M. KNOWLES CHINA CO. East Liverpool, OH, U.S.A. Semivitreous dinnerware 1959+ (1900–1963)	KRAUTHEIM & ADELBERG PORCELAIN FACTORY GMBH Selb, Bavaria, Germany (W. Germany) Porcelain ca.1922–1945 (1884– present)

A

LYMAN, FENTON & CO.
Bennington, VT, U.S.A.
Porcelain, Rockingham,
stoneware. Impressed
ca.1849 (1793–1858)

B

C. TEICHERT STOVE &
PORCELAIN FACTORY,
MEISSEN
Meissen, Saxony, Germany
(E. Germany)
Porcelain. Blue underglaze
1882–ca.1930 (1863–
1945)

C

BRUSH-McCOY POTTERY
CO.
Zanesville, OH, U.S.A.
Art pottery
1915–1925 (1911–
present)
(Brush Pottery)

D

NATIONAL CHINA CO.
East Liverpool & Salineville,
OH, U.S.A.
Semiporcelain
(1899–1929)

E

NAUTILUS PORCELAIN
CO.
Glasgow, Scotland
Porcelain, parian. Printed
1896–1913 (1896–1913)

F

BLOCH & CO.
Eichwald, Bohemia (Dubie,
Czechoslovakia)
Porcelain, earthenware.
Blue underglaze
ca. 1886–ca. 1940 (1871–
1940)

G

PORTMEIRION
POTTERIES LTD.
Stoke, Staffordshire,
England
Earthenware
(1962–present)

H

ADOLPHE PORQUIER
Quimper, France
Faience. Impressed
1840 + (1809–present)
(Société Nouvelle des
Faïenceries de Quimper
HB Henriot)

I

POXON CHINA CO./
VERNON POTTERIES
Vernon, CA, U.S.A.
Earthenware, semivitreous
ware
1912–1931 (1912–1958)

J

PETRUS REGOUT
Maastricht, Holland
Porcelain
ca.1870 (1836–1931 +)

K

ROBINSON &
LEADBETTER (LTD.)
Stoke, Staffordshire,
England
Parian. Impressed
ca.1885 + (1864–1924)

L

ROOKWOOD POTTERY
Cincinnati, OH, U.S.A.
Art pottery. Stamped
ca.1883 (1880–1967)
(name, molds purchased
by Arthur J. Townley,
Michigan Center, MI, 1982)

M

—————
Rubelles, France
Faience, earthenware.
Applied
ca.1836

N

RUSKIN POTTERY
Smethwick, Nr.
Birmingham, England
Earthenware. Impressed
ca.1904–1915 (1898–
1935)

O

STANFORD POTTERY
Sebring, OH, U.S.A.
Porcelain
(1945–1961)

P

STANGL POTTERY
Trenton, NJ, U.S.A.
Pottery. Stamped
ca.1972 (1805–1978)
(various names, Stangl
name first used in 1926)

A  EBELING & REUSS CO. Devon, PA, U.S.A. Importer ca.1972 (1866–present)	**B** TORQUAY TERRA COTTA C? LIMITED TORQUAY TERRA-COTTA CO. Torquay, Devon, England Terra-cotta. Printed, impressed 1875–ca.1890 (1875–1940) (various names)	**C**  COLCLOUGH CHINA LTD. Longton, Staffordshire, England Porcelain. Printed ca.1945–1948 (1937–present) (Royal Doulton Tableware Ltd.)	**D** MADE IN U.S.A VERNONWARE dishwasher and ovenproof VERNON KILNS Vernon, CA, U.S.A. Earthenware, semivitreous ware 1955–1958 (1912–1958)
E  WEIL CERAMIC CO. Los Angeles, CA, U.S.A. Porcelain. Underglaze ca.1950 + (ca.1948–ca.1954)	**F** JOSEF BOCK PORCELAIN MANUFACTORY VIENNA Vienna, Austria Porcelain. Impressed, printed 20th century (1879–1960)	**G** ALUMINITE FRUGIER LIMOGES·FRANCE RENÉ FRUGIER Limoges, France Porcelain cookware 1936–1952 + (1900–present) (Haviland SA)	**H** ANCIENNE MANUFACTURE IMPERIALE & ROYALE SUJETS RELIGIEUX MOUZIN LECAT & C? NIMY. MOUZIN LECAT & CO. Nimy-les-Mons, Belgium Religious subjects. Imprinted ca.1850 (ca.1850)
I  INTERNATIONAL POTTERY CO. (BURGESS & CAMPBELL) Trenton, NJ, U.S.A. Semiporcelain, white granite, various pattern names (1860–1940 +)	**J** CHARLES AHRENFELDT Limoges, France Porcelain after 1891 (1859–1969)	**K** CATALINA MADE IN U.S.A. POTTERY GLADDING, McBEAN & CO. Santa Catalina, CA, U.S.A. Pottery. Printed in ink 1937–1942 (1875–present) (member of Wedgwood Group)	**L**  COALPORT PORCELAIN WORKS Stoke, Staffordshire, England Porcelain ca.1946 + (ca.1795–present) (member of Wedgwood Group)
M  CUNNINGHAM & PICKETT Alliance, OH, U.S.A. Porcelain distributors (1938–1968)	**N** ERDMANN SCHLEGELMILCH Suhl, Thuringia, Germany (E. Germany) Porcelain. Green after 1891 (1881–1938)	**O** A. PILLIVUYT et FILS USINES DÉCY et LIMOGES FRANCE A. PILLIVUYT & SON Paris, France Porcelain 1913 + (1851–1963 +) (factories also in Foecy & Limoges)	**P**  HARKER POTTERY CO. East Liverpool, OH, U.S.A. Semivitreous ware ca.1944 (1890–1972)

A  MATT MORGAN POTTERY Cincinnati, OH, U.S.A. Art pottery. Impressed ca.1883 (1883)	**B** INTERNATIONAL POTTERY CO. Trenton, NJ, U.S.A. Semiporcelain tableware. Blue underglaze (1860–1940+)

C WHEELING POTTERY CO. Wheeling, WV, U.S.A. White granite 1880–1886 (1879– ca.1910)	**D**  GLASGOW POTTERY (JOHN MOSES & CO.) Trenton, NJ, U.S.A. Cream-colored ware, white granite, Rockingham, yellowware ca.1895+ (1859–1906)

E FINE CERAMICS COMPANY GMBH Siegburg, Rhineland, Germany (W. Germany) Porcelain, earthenware ca.1949 (1949+)	**F** BESWICK (LTD.) Stoke, Staffordshire, England Figurines current (1936–present) (Royal Doulton Tableware Ltd.)

G  BROWNFIELDS GUILD POTTERY SOCIETY LTD. Cobridge, Staffordshire, England Earthenware, porcelain. Printed 1891–1898 (1891–1900) (various names)	**H**  ———— Sèvres, France Hard paste porcelain. Imprinted, green, date varies, see page 249 1912–1916

I DELAWARE POTTERY CO. Trenton, NJ, U.S.A. Belleek porcelain, sanitary ware. Printed in black, impressed 1884–1892 (1884– ca.1918) (part of Trenton Potteries Co. after 1892)	**J** ERDMANN SCHLEGELMILCH PORCELAIN FACTORY (R. S. PRUSSIA) Suhl, Thuringia, Germany (E. Germany) Porcelain. Brown ca.1896–ca.1938 (1881– 1938)

K POHL BROS. PORCELAIN FACTORY Schmiedeberg, Germany (Kowary, Poland) Hard paste porcelain, electrotechnical porcelain 1871+ (1869–1945)	**L** JULIUS DRESSLER PORCELAIN FACTORY Biela, Bohemia (Bela, Czechoslovakia) Earthenware, porcelain ca.1900 (1888–ca.1945)

M  HARKER POTTERY East Liverpool, OH, U.S.A. Kitchenware, ovenware ca.1935 (1890–1972)	**N** LONGTON PORCELAIN CO. LTD. Longton, Staffordshire, England Porcelain. Printed 1892–1908 (1892–1908)

O ———— Sèvres, France Hard & soft paste porcelain. Painted blue or green, various dates, see page 249 1917–1920	**P** OEPIAG Pirkenhammer, Bohemia, (Brezova, Czechoslovakia) Porcelain 1918–1920 (1918–1945)

A OSCAR SCHLEGELMILCH Langewiesen, Thuringia, Germany (E. Germany) Hard paste porcelain ca.1904 + (1892–present) (Porcelain Combine Colditz VEB)	**B**  PIESAU PORCELAIN FACTORY VEB Piesau, Thuringia, Germany (E. Germany) Porcelain 1945–ca.1968 (1945– ca.1968)	**C** DUX PORCELAIN MANUFACTORY Dux, Bohemia (Duchcov, Czechoslovakia) Porcelain. Printed 1912–1918 (1860– present) (Duchcov Porcelain)	**D** AMEDEE LAMBERT Rouen, France Faience ca.1828–1830 (ca.1828– 1830)
E COLCLOUGH & CO./ STANLEY POTTERY LTD. Longton, Staffordshire, England Earthenware, china. Printed 1919–1931 (1887–1931)	**F** SZEILER STUDIO LTD. Hanley, Staffordshire, England Earthenware. Printed, impressed current (ca.1951–present)	**G** HALL CHINA CO. East Liverpool, OH, U.S.A. Semivitreous dinnerware 1903–1911 (1903– present)	**H** AKRON CHINA CO. Akron, OH, U.S.A. White granite, hotel ware (ca.1900–1908)
I  MADDOCK POTTERY Trenton, NJ, U.S.A. Porcelain ca.1904 + (1893–ca.1929)	**J** KNOWLES, TAYLOR & KNOWLES East Liverpool, OH, U.S.A. Semivitreous porcelain 1890–ca.1905 (1870– 1929)	**K**  CARTWRIGHT BROS. CO. East Liverpool, OH, U.S.A. Cream-colored tableware (1880–1927)	**L** VODREY & BROTHERS POTTERY CO. East Liverpool, OH, U.S.A. Ironstone 1876–1896 (ca.1857– 1928)
M BUFFALO POTTERY CO. Buffalo, NY, U.S.A. Semivitreous ware, semiporcelain. Stamped, year varies ca.1905 + (1901–present) (Buffalo China, Inc.)	**N** WILLIAM ADAMS & SONS LTD. Tunstall & Stoke, Staffordshire, England Earthenware, basalt, jasper, parian. Printed ca.1879 + (1769–present) (member of Wedgwood Group)	**O** CLEMENTSON BROS. LTD. Hanley, Staffordshire, England Earthenware. Printed 1870 + (1865–1916)	**P** EGERSUND POTTERY FACTORY Egersund, Norway Faience 1880 + (1847–present) (Porsgrund Porcelain Factory)

A

EGERSUND POTTERY
FACTORY
Egersund, Norway
Faience
1962 + (1847–present)
(Porsgrund Porcelain
Factory)

B

HOMER LAUGHLIN CHINA
CO.
East Liverpool, OH, U.S.A.
Earthenware, semivitreous
porcelain
ca.1907 (1877–present)

C

WHEELING POTTERY CO.
Wheeling, WV, U.S.A.
Whiteware, semiporcelain,
tiles
ca.1896 + (1879–ca.1910)

D

CHATRES-SUR-CHER
Chatres-sur-Cher, France
Porcelain
ca.1918 + (1918–1980 +)

E

RENÉ FRUGIER
Limoges, France
Porcelain
1952 + (1900–present)
(Haviland SA)

F

INTERNATIONAL
POTTERY
Trenton, NJ, U.S.A.
Semiporcelain, various
pattern names
ca.1870 (1860–1940 +)

G

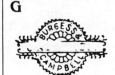

INTERNATIONAL
POTTERY
Trenton, NJ, U.S.A.
Semiporcelain, various
pattern names
ca.1904 (1860–1940 +)

H

F. WINKLE & CO.
Stoke, Staffordshire,
England
Earthenware. Printed
1890–1925 (1890–1931)

I

COLCLOUGH CHINA LTD./
BOOTHS &
COLCLOUGHS LTD.
Hanley, Staffordshire,
England
Bone china, earthenware.
Printed
1937–1954 (1937– present)
(Royal Doulton Tableware
Ltd.)

J

A. B. JONES & SONS
(LTD.)
Longton, Staffordshire,
England
Porcelain, earthenware.
Printed
1913 + (1900–present)
(Royal Grafton Bone China)

K

GRUNSTADT
EARTHENWARE
FACTORY
Grunstadt, Palatinate,
Germany (W. Germany)
Faience, earthenware
current (1799–present)

L

HANOVER POTTERY
Burslem, Staffordshire,
England
Earthenware. Printed
1953–1956 (1948–1956)

M

JACKSON VITRIFIED
CHINA CO.
Falls Creek, PA, U.S.A.
Dinnerware
1923–1946 (1917–
present)
(Jackson China Co.)

N

A. LANTERNIER & CO.
Limoges, France
Porcelain
ca.1970 + (1855–1980 +)

O

TAYLOR, SMITH &
TAYLOR
East Liverpool, OH, U.S.A.
Ironstone
ca. 1972 (1901–present)
(Anchor Hocking)

P

PADEN CITY POTTERY
CO.
Sisterville, WV, U.S.A.
Dinnerware
1930–1956 (1914–1963)

A

COALPORT PORCELAIN
WORKS
Coalport, Shropshire,
England
Porcelain. Printed
ca.1870–1880 (ca.1795–
present)
(member of Wedgwood
Group)

B

VILLEROY & BOCH
Mettlach, Saar, Germany
(W. Germany)
Earthenware, figurines, tiles
ca.1860 (1813–present)
(various names, owners &
locations)

C

VILLEROY & BOCH
Mettlach, Saar, Germany
(W. Germany)
Porcelain. Applied
1880–1883 (1813–
present)
(various names, owners, &
locations)

D

ROYAL COPENHAGEN
PORCELAIN FACTORY
LTD.
Copenhagen, Denmark
Porcelain, stoneware,
faience
1863–1920 (1775–
present)

E

COXON POTTERY
Wooster, OH, U.S.A.
Porcelain
(1926–ca.1930)

F

H. AYNSLEY & CO. (LTD.)
Longton, Staffordshire,
England
Earthenware. Printed,
impressed
1951+ (1873–present)
(subsidiary of Waterford)

G

ROSEVILLE POTTERY CO.
Zanesville, OH, U.S.A.
Dinnerware. Impressed,
various pattern names
ca.1904 (1892–1954)

H

PENNSYLVANIA MUSEUM
& SCHOOL OF
INDUSTRIAL ART
Philadelphia, PA, U.S.A.
Pottery. Green, yellow, blue
glaze
(1903–ca.1917)

I

W. S. GEORGE CO.
East Palestine, OH, U.S.A.
Semiporcelain, dinnerware
1950s (1880–1959)

J

HALL CHINA CO.
East Liverpool, OH, U.S.A.
Vitrified hotel ware
ca.1945 (1903–present)

K

STEUBENVILLE POTTERY
CO.
Steubenville, OH, U.S.A.
Pottery
ca.1905 (1879–ca.1960)

L

DAISON ART POTTERY

DAISON POTTERY
Torquay, Devon, England
Vases, figurines. Black,
stamped, underglaze
ca.1928–ca.1932 (ca.
1922–ca.1932)

M

MERCER POTTERY CO.
Trenton, NJ, U.S.A.
Ironstone, semivitreous,
semiporcelain
ca.1895–1905+ (1868–
ca.1937)

N

MORAVIAN POTTERY &
TILE WORKS
Doylestown, PA, U.S.A.
Tiles, pottery. Impressed
ca. 1904+ (1897–ca.
1963)

O

ROBERT HAVILAND & LE
TANNEUR
Limoges, France
Tableware
1929+ (1926–present)
(various names, now Robert
Haviland & C. Parlon)

P

UNION
PORCELAIN
WORKS
N.Y.

UNION PORCELAIN
WORKS
Greenpoint, NY, U.S.A.
Porcelain. Black printed
ca.1891 (1865–1904)

A

WILLIAM DE MORGAN
Chelsea, London, England
Earthenware
1872–1881 (ca. 1872–
1911)

B

ARC-EN-CIEL POTTERY
Zanesville, OH, U.S.A.
Jasperware
(1903–1907)

C

SALEM CHINA CO.
Salem, OH, U.S.A.
Porcelain, various pattern
names
ca.1940 + (1898–1967)

D

GALLUBA & HOFMANN
Ilmenau, Thuringia,
Germany (E. Germany)
Porcelain
1895–ca.1927 (1888–
1927)

E

WALDERSHOF
PORCELAIN FACTORY
Waldershof, Bavaria,
Germany (W. Germany)
Porcelain, Green
underglaze, green, red,
brown overglaze
1924–1938 (1907–present)
(Rosenthal Glass &
Porcelain AG)

F

PALISSY POTTERY LTD.
Longton & Stoke,
Staffordshire, England
Earthenware
current (1946–present)
(subsidiary of Royal
Worcester Spode Ltd.)

G

OSCAR SCHALLER & CO.
SUCCESSOR
Schwarzenbach, Bavaria,
Germany (E. Germany)
Porcelain
1918 + (1918–present)
(Winterling Group)

H

EAST PALESTINE
POTTERY CO.
East Palestine, OH, U.S.A.
Semiporcelain
(1884–1909)

I

ANCHOR POTTERY
Trenton, NJ, U.S.A.
Semiporcelain. Printed
(1893–1927)

J

BRITISH ANCHOR
POTTERY CO. LTD.
Longton, Staffordshire,
England
Earthenware. Printed,
impressed
1913–1940 (1884–
1964 +)

K

GIUSEPPE CARLO
GALVANI
Pordenone, Italy
Creamware
ca.1883 (ca.1823–ca.1883)

L

ALLERTONS LTD.
Longton, Staffordshire,
England
Porcelain, earthenware.
Printed
ca.1929–1942 (1859–
1942)

M

EDWARD MARSHALL
BOEHM
Trenton, NJ, U.S.A.
Porcelain, figurines
1951–1952 (1950–
present)

N

CHARLES REBOISSON
Limoges, France
Porcelain
(1942–1978 +)

O

CERAMIC ART CO.
Trenton, NJ, U.S.A.
Porcelain. Green
ca.1897 (1889–present)
(Lenox, Inc.)

P

CO-OPERATIVE
WHOLESALE SOCIETY
LTD.
Longton, Staffordshire,
England
Porcelain. Printed
ca.1950–1960s (1946–
1964 +)

A

CARL KNOLL
Fischern, Bohemia (Rybare, Czechoslovakia)
Pottery. Green underglaze
ca.1916–1918 (1848–1945)

B

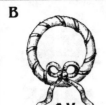

CHARLES MEIGH
Hanley, Staffordshire, England
Earthenware, stoneware.
Printed
(1835–1849)

C

COLONIAL CO.
East Liverpool, OH, U.S.A.
Semivitreous ware
(1903–1929)

D

TAYLOR, SMITH & TAYLOR
East Liverpool, OH, U.S.A.
Ironstone
ca.1965 (1901–1981)

E

DRESSEL, KISTER & CO.
Passau, Bavaria, Germany (W. Germany)
Porcelain
ca.1907–1922 (1840–1942)

F

POTTER'S CO-OPERATIVE CO.
East Liverpool, OH, U.S.A.
Ironstone
ca.1905 (1882–1925)

G

EMPIRE POTTERY
Trenton, NJ, U.S.A.
Pottery
ca.1892 (1863–ca.1918)

H

EGERSUND POTTERY-FACTORY
Egersund, Norway
Faience
1865 + (1847–present)
(Porsgrund Porcelain Factory)

I

GERARD, DUFRAISSEX & ABBOT (G.D.A.)
Limoges, France
Porcelain
1937–1976 + (1902–present)
(various names)

J

CERAMIC ART CO.
Trenton, NJ, U.S.A.
Porcelain. Lavender, green, brown, black, gold
ca.1896 (1889–present)
(Lenox, Inc.)

K

GOODWIN POTTERY CO.
East Liverpool, OH, U.S.A.
Semivitreous dinnerware
1893–ca.1906 (1844–1853, 1863–1865, 1872–1913)

L

HOMER LAUGHLIN CHINA CO.
East Liverpool, OH, U.S.A.
Semivitreous dinnerware
ca.1940–ca.1965 (1877–present)

M

KEYSTONE POTTERY COMPANY
Trenton, NJ, U.S.A.
Pottery
ca.1900 (1892–1935)

N

LENOX, INC.
Trenton, NJ, U.S.A.
Hard paste porcelain.
Green, blue, red, black, various wording
1906–present (1906–present)

O

LIMOGES CHINA CO.
Sebring, OH, U.S.A.
Semivitreous dinnerware
ca.1942 (1900–1955)
(American Limoges China Co.)

P

MORLEY & CO.
Wellsville, OH, U.S.A.
Ironstone
1879–1884 (1878–1891)

A

MANIFATTURA DI SIGNA
Florence, Italy
Porcelain
ca.1930 (ca.1930)

B

MITTERTEICH
PORCELAIN FACTORY
AG
Mitterteich, Bavaria,
Germany (W. Germany)
Porcelain. Gold & blue
overglaze, blue
underglaze
1918+ (1918–present)

C

MORIMURA BROS.
Tokyo, Japan
Porcelain
1910–1950 (1876–
present)
(Noritake Co.)

D

NORITAKE
Nagoya, Japan
Porcelain. Green, variations
in wording
ca.1911 + (1904–present)

E

NORITAKE
Nagoya, Japan
Porcelain
current (1904–present)

F

NORITAKE
Nagoya, Japan
Porcelain
ca.1953 + (1904–present)

G

NORITAKE
Nagoya, Japan
Porcelain, various pattern
names
current (1904–present)

H

NEW CHELSEA
PORCELAIN CO. LTD.
Longton, Staffordshire,
England
Porcelain
ca.1912 + (1912–1961)
(various names)

I

OSCAR & EDGAR
GUTHERZ MFS.
Altrohlau, Bohemia (Stara
Role, Czechoslovakia)
Porcelain. Green
1899–1918 (1889–1918)

J

PERLEE INC.
TRENTON BELEEK

PERLEE, INC.
Trenton, NJ, U.S.A.
Belleek-type porcelain
(ca.1920–1930)

K

POPE-GOSSER CHINA
CO.
Coshocton, OH, U.S.A.
Porcelain
ca.1950 (1902–1958)

L

JEAN POUYAT
Limoges, France
Porcelain
1890–1932 (1842–
present)
(Guérin-Pouyat-Élite)

M

PRICE & KENSINGTON
POTTERIES LTD.
Longport, Staffordshire,
England
Earthenware. Printed
1963–present (1962–
• present)

N

SHENANGO CHINA
New Castle, PA, U.S.A.
Reproduction States plates
1932 (1901–present)
(Anchor Hocking)

O

TAYLOR, SMITH &
TAYLOR
East Liverpool, OH, U.S.A.
Ironstone, tableware
ca.1972 (1901–present)
(Anchor Hocking)

P

RÖRSTRAND PORCELAIN
FACTORY
Rörstrand, Sweden
Porcelain, various pattern
names
1859 + (1726–present)
(Rörstrand AB)

A

EPIAG BRANCH
ALTROHLAU
Altrohlau, Bohemia (Stara
Role, Czechoslovakia)
Porcelain. Green
underglaze
1920–1939 (1920–
1945+)

B

SALISBURY CROWN
CHINA CO.
Longton, Staffordshire,
England
Bone china. Printed
ca.1952+ (ca.1927–
present)

C

ERDMANN
SCHLEGELMILCH (R. S.
PRUSSIA)
Suhl, Thuringia, Germany
(E. Germany)
Porcelain. Red star, green
wreath
1904+ (1881–1938)

D

REINHOLD
SCHLEGELMILCH (R. S.
GERMANY)
Tillowitz, Silesia, Germany
(Tulovice, Poland)
Porcelain. Printed, blue,
orange, red, green
after 1904 (1869–ca.1938)

E

REINHOLD
SCHLEGELMILCH (R. S.
TILLOWITZ)
Tillowitz, Silesia, Germany
(Tulovice, Poland)
Porcelain. Printed, green
1904+ (1869–ca.1938)

F

REINHOLD
SCHLEGELMILCH (R. S.
POLAND)
Tulovice, Poland
Porcelain. Red, gold, wreath
green
1919–1921 (1869–
ca.1938)

G

ERDMANN
SCHLEGELMILCH (R. S.
SUHL)
Suhl, Thuringia, Germany
(E. Germany)
Porcelain. Printed, red star,
green wreath
ca.1904 (1881–1938)

H

REINHOLD
SCHLEGELMILCH (R. S.
SILESIA)
Tillowitz, Silesia, Germany
(Tulovice, Poland)
Porcelain. Printed, green
after 1904–ca.1938 (1869–
ca.1938)

I

STADTILM PORCELAIN
FACTORY
Stadtilm, Thuringia,
Germany (E. Germany)
Porcelain
ca.1961–1972 (1894–
1972)
(Porcelainfinishing VEB)

J

CHARLES AMISON (& CO.
LTD.)
Longton, Staffordshire,
England
Porcelain. Printed
1951–1962 (1889–1962)

K

GLASGOW POTTERY
(JOHN MOSES & CO.)
Trenton, NJ, U.S.A.
White granite
1880+ (1859–1906)

L

STEUBENVILLE POTTERY
CO.
Steubenville, OH, U.S.A.
Pottery
ca.1904 (1879–ca.1960)

M

STEUBENVILLE POTTERY
CO.
Steubenville, OH, U.S.A.
White granite
ca.1900 (1879–ca.1960)

N

TAYLOR, SMITH &
TAYLOR
East Liverpool, OH, U.S.A.
Porcelain, various patterns
& wording
ca.1935–1981 (1901–
present)
(Anchor Hocking)

O

UNION CERAMIQUE
Limoges, France
Hard paste porcelain
(ca.1900–1950+)

P

UNION POTTERIES CO.
East Liverpool, OH, U.S.A.
Ironstone
1894–1905 (1894–1905)

A

SALEM CHINA CO.
Salem, OH, U.S.A.
Porcelain
ca.1940 (1898–1967)

B

VODREY & BROTHERS
POTTERY CO.
East Liverpool, OH, U.S.A.
Ironstone tableware
ca.1900 (ca. 1857–1928)

C

REICHENBACH
PORCELAINWORK VEB
Reichenbach, Thuringia,
Germany (E. Germany)
Porcelain
ca.1949–1968 (1900–
1968)
(various names, now
Porcelain Combine
Kahla VEB)

D

WEST END POTTERY CO.
East Liverpool, OH, U.S.A.
Semivitreous ware
ca.1933 (1893–1938)

E

W. & E. CORN
Longport, Staffordshire,
England
Earthenware. Printed
ca.1900–1904 (1864–
1904)

F

WHEELING POTTERY CO.
Wheeling, WV, U.S.A.
Cream-colored ware,
variations in wording
1894+ (1879–ca.1910)

G

W. H. GRINDLEY & CO.
LTD.
Tunstall, Staffordshire,
England
Earthenware, ironstone.
Printed
1925+ (1880–present)

H

E. & A. MÜLLER
PORCELAIN FACTORY
Schonwald, Bavaria,
Germany (W. Germany)
Porcelain
1909–1927 (1904–present)
(Porcelain Factory
Schonwald branch of
Hutschenreuther AG)

I

GEIJSBEEK POTTERY
Golden, CO, U.S.A.
Whiteware, various pattern
names
(1899–1904+)

J

WILLIAM ALSAGER
ADDERLEY/
ADDERLEYS LTD.
Longton, Staffordshire,
England
Porcelain, earthenware.
Printed
1876–1926 (1876–present)
(Royal Doulton Tableware
Ltd.)

K

GOODWIN POTTERY CO.
East Liverpool, OH, U.S.A.
Ironstone dinnerware
1885–ca.1897 (1844–
1853, 1863–1865, 1872–
1913)

L

DOULTON & CO.
Burslem, Staffordshire,
England
Earthenware, stoneware.
Printed, impressed,
variations in wording
ca.1882–1902 (1853–
present)
(Royal Doulton Tableware
Ltd.)

M

DOULTON & CO.
Lambeth, London, England
Earthenware, stoneware.
Impressed
ca.1880–1902 (1853–
present)
(Royal Doulton Tableware
Ltd.)

N

DOULTON & CO.
Burslem, Staffordshire,
England
Earthenware, porcelain.
Printed, impressed
ca.1912–1956 (1853–
present)
(Royal Doulton Tableware
Ltd.)

O

ROYAL
LANCASTRIAN
POTTERY
HAND MADE
IN ENGLAND

PILKINGTON'S TILES LTD.
Clifton Junction,
Lancashire, England
Earthenware, lusterware
1948–1957 (1893–
present)

P

HOMER LAUGHLIN CHINA
CO.
East Liverpool, OH, U.S.A.
Semivitreous dinnerware
ca.1934 (1877–present)

A

BRUSH POTTERY
Zanesville, OH, U.S.A.
Pottery
1930–1950s (1907–1908,
1925–present)

B

AVON ART POTTERY LTD.
Longton, Staffordshire,
England
Earthenware. Printed
1939–1947 (1930–1969)

C

VODREY & BROTHERS
POTTERY CO.
East Liverpool, OH, U.S.A.
Ironstone tableware
1876–1896 (ca.1857–
1928)

D

FRANKOMA POTTERY
Sapulpa, OK, U.S.A.
Pottery
1972+ (1936–present)

E

HOMER LAUGHLIN CHINA
CO.
East Liverpool, OH, U.S.A.
Semivitreous ovenware
1941–ca.1945 (1877–
present)

F

A. E. HULL POTTERY CO.
Crooksville, OH, U.S.A.
Pottery, kitchenware
1950s (1905–1950,1952–
present)
(Hull Pottery)

G

GRIMWADES LTD.
Stoke, Staffordshire,
England
Earthenware, majolica.
Printed
ca.1906+ (1900–present)
(Royal Winton Pottery)

H

VERNON KILNS
Vernon, CA, U.S.A.
Porcelain
1930s (1912–1958)

I

CHARLES W. McNAY &
SONS
Bo'ness, Scotland
Earthenware
ca.1946–1958 (1887–
1958)

J

DINKY ART CO.
Longton, Staffordshire,
England
Earthenware. Printed
1931–1947 (1931–1947)

K

GEORGE GRAINGER (&
CO.)
Worcester, England
Porcelain, parian,
semiporcelain. Printed
1850–1875 (ca.1839–
present)
(Royal Worcester Spode Ltd.)

L

GUSTAFSBERG
Gustafsberg, Sweden
Semiporcelain, faience,
earthenware, various
pattern names
1866–1892 (1825–present)

M

GREENWOOD POTTERY
Trenton, NJ, U.S.A.
Porcelain, earthenware
20th century (1868–
ca.1933)
(various names)

N

JAMES BROADHURST &
SONS, LTD.
Fenton, Staffordshire,
England
Earthenware. Printed
1957+ (1862–present)

O

PHILIP ROSENTHAL & CO.
AG
Selb, Bavaria, Germany (W.
Germany)
Porcelain, earthenware
1922+ (1879–present)
(various names, now
Rosenthal Glass &
Porcelain AG)

P

J. & M. P. BELL
Glasgow, Scotland
Earthenware, parian
before 1896 (1842–1928)

A

BOOTHS &
COLCLOUGHS LTD
Hanley, Staffordshire,
England
Bone china, earthenware.
Printed
1950–1954 (1948–
present)
(Royal Doulton Tableware
Ltd.)

B

MADE IN AMERICA

THÉODORE HAVILAND &
CO.
New York, NY, U.S.A.
Porcelain
1937–present (1892–
present)
(Haviland SA)

C

DEVONSHIRE POTTERIES
LTD.
Bovey Tracey, Devon,
England
Earthenware. Printed
1959+ (1947–present)

D

ELEKTRA PORCELAIN
CO. LTD.
Longton, Staffordshire,
England
Earthenware. Printed
ca.1940+ (1924–1940+)

E

LOCKHART & ARTHUR
Pollokshaws, Glasgow,
Scotland
Earthenware
(1855–1864)

F

J. FRYER & SON
Tunstall, Staffordshire,
England
Earthenware. Printed
ca.1945+ (1945–present)
(J. Fryer, Ltd.)

G

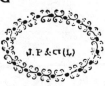

JOHN PRATT & CO. LTD.
Fenton, Staffordshire,
England
Earthenware. Printed,
various pattern names
1872–1878 (1872–1878)

H

JOHN & WILLIAM RIDGWAY
Hanley, Staffordshire,
England
Earthenware, porcelain.
Printed, impressed,
various pattern names
ca.1814–1830 (1814–
present)
(Royal Doulton Tableware
Ltd.)

I

LOCKHART & ARTHUR
Pollokshaws, Glasgow,
Scotland
Earthenware
(1855–1864)

J

MILLINGTON, ASTBURG &
POULSON
Trenton, NJ, U.S.A.
Whiteware
(1853–ca.1870)

K

MAYER & NEWBOLD
Lane End, Staffordshire,
England
Porcelain, earthenware.
Printed, painted
ca.1817–1833 (ca.1817–
1833)

L

MERCER POTTERY CO.
Trenton, NJ, U.S.A.
Ironstone
ca.1904 (1868–ca.1937)

M

FRIEDRICH SCHWAB
Gotha, Thuringia, Germany
(E. Germany)
Porcelain
1919–ca.1950 (1919–
1950)

N

VILLEROY & BOCH
Mettlach, Saar, Germany
(W. Germany)
Earthenware, porcelain.
Stamped
ca.1860+ (1813–present)

O

ARABIA PORCELAIN
FACTORY
Helsingfors (Helsinki),
Finland
Porcelain, stoneware,
various pattern names
(1874–present)
(Upsala-Ekeby Group)

P

WATHEN & LICHFIELD
Fenton, Staffordshire,
England
Earthenware. Printed
1862–1864 (1862–1864)

A

BURGESS & LEIGH
Burslem, Staffordshire,
England
Earthenware. Impressed,
printed
1862 + (1862–present)

B

CRESCENT

C

WORCESTER ROYAL
PORCELAIN CO. LTD.
Worcester, England
Bone china
current (1862–present)
(Royal Worcester Spode
Ltd.)

D

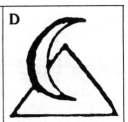

W. GOEBEL
Oeslau, Germany (W.
Germany)
Pottery
1890 + (1871–present)

E

SEBRING POTTERY CO.
East Liverpool & Sebring,
OH, U.S.A.
Semivitreous tableware
ca.1925–ca.1940 (1887–
1948)

F

GEORGE JONES (&
SONS LTD.)
Stoke, Staffordshire,
England
Porcelain, earthenware,
majolica. Printed,
impressed, various
pattern names
ca.1924–1951 (1861–
1951)

G

WILLIAM BRUNT SON &
CO.
East Liverpool, OH, U.S.A.
Ironstone
ca.1878–1892 (1848–
1911)
(various names)

H

ETRURIA POTTERY
(OTT & BREWER)
Trenton, NJ, U.S.A.
Belleek porcelain. Printed,
overglaze, red, brown
ca.1883 + (1863–1894)

I

ETRURIA POTTERY
(OTT & BREWER)
Trenton, NJ, U.S.A.
Belleek porcelain. Printed,
overglaze, red, brown
ca.1882 (1863–1894)

J

D. F. HAYNES & CO.
(CHESAPEAKE
POTTERY)
Baltimore, MD, U.S.A.
Semiporcelain
1882–1885 (1881–1914)

K

WILLIAM HULME
Cobridge, Staffordshire,
England
Earthenware. Printed
1948–1954 (1948–1954)

L

CROWN

M

PAULINE POTTERY
Chicago, IL, & Edgerton,
WI, U.S.A.
Decorated artware.
Impressed, variations in
wording
(1883–1893)

N

RICHARD KAMPF
PORCELAIN FACTORY
Grunlas, Bohemia (Loucky,
Czechoslovakia)
Porcelain
1939–1945 (1912–1945)

O

AMPHORA WORK
REISSNER
Turn-Teplitz, Bohemia
(Trnovany, Czechoslovakia)
Porcelain, earthenware,
figurines. Variations in
wording
1905–1910 (1892–1945 +)
(various names,
nationalized in 1945)

P

ROBINSON
RANSBOTTOM
POTTERY
Roseville, OH, U.S.A.
Stoneware
ca.1920–present (1900–
present)

A

ENOCH PLANT
Burslem, Staffordshire,
England
Earthenware. Printed,
Impressed
1895–1905 (1895–1905)

B

WORCESTER ROYAL
PORCELAIN CO. LTD.
Worcester, England
Porcelain, earthenware,
parian. Impressed
ca.1865–1880 (1862–
present)
(Royal Worcester Spode
Ltd.)

C

THOMAS POOLE
Longton, Staffordshire,
England
Porcelain, earthenware.
Impressed, printed
1880–1912 (1880–
present)
(crown mark used by other
factories)
(Royal Stafford China, Ltd.)

D

WILD BROS.
Longton, Staffordshire,
England
Porcelain. Printed,
impressed
1904 + (1904–1927)

E

OSCAR SCHLEGELMILCH
(R. S. PRUSSIA)
Langewiesen, Thuringia,
Germany (E. Germany)
Porcelain
1900 + (1892–present)
(Porcelain Combine Colditz
VEB)

F

ROYAL COPENHAGEN
PORCELAIN FACTORY
LTD.
Copenhagen, Denmark
Porcelain, stoneware,
faience
ca.1905 + (1775–present)

G

ROYAL COPENHAGEN
PORCELAIN FACTORY
LTD.
Copenhagen, Denmark
Porcelain, stoneware,
faience
1929–present (1775–
present)

H

WURTTEMBERG
PORCELAIN
MANUFACTORY
Schorndorf, Wurttemberg,
Germany (W. Germany)
Porcelain
1904–1939 (1904–1939)

I

SAMSON & CO.
Paris, France
Porcelain
ca.1885 + (1873–1957 +)

J

DERBY PORCELAIN
WORKS
Derby, England
Porcelain
1825–1830 (ca.1750–
present)
(Royal Doulton Tableware
Ltd.)

K

STATE'S PORCELAIN
MANUFACTORY
NYMPHENBURG
(ALBERT BAUML)
Nymphenburg, Bavaria,
Germany (W. Germany)
Porcelain. Blue underglaze
on reproductions of
Frankenthal, various dates
current (1747–present)
(various names & owners)

L

DERBY PORCELAIN
WORKS
Derby, England
Porcelain. Painted, date
letter in center
ca.1825–1848 (ca.1750–
present)
(Royal Doulton Tableware
Ltd.)

M

CROWN DERBY
PORCELAIN
Derby, England
Porcelain. Printed
ca.1878–1890 (ca.1750–
present
(Royal Doulton Tableware
Ltd.)

N

KAHLA PORCELAIN
FACTORY
Kahla, Thuringia, Germany
(E. Germany)
Porcelain
1938–1945 (1844–
present)
(Kahla Porcelain Combine
VEB)

O

DAVID MC BIRNEY & CO.
(BELLEEK POTTERY
CO.)
Belleek, Co. Fermanagh,
Ireland
Parian, porcelain. Printed,
impressed
1863–1880 (1863–
present)

P

PLANT BROTHERS
CROWN POTTERY
Longton, Staffordshire,
England
Porcelain. Printed
1898–1906 (ca.1889–
1906)

A

KAISER PORCELAIN
Staffelstein, Bavaria,
Germany (W. Germany)
Porcelain
1970–present (1872–
present)

B

RUSSIAN IMPERIAL
PORCELAIN FACTORY
St. Petersburg, Russia
(Leningrad, U.S.S.R.)
Porcelain
1801–1825 (1744–
1917+)

C

RUSSIAN IMPERIAL
PORCELAIN FACTORY
St. Petersburg, Russia
(Leningrad, U.S.S.R.)
Porcelain. Painted blue
1855–1881 (1744–
1917+)

D

A. B. JONES & SONS
(LTD.)
Longton, Staffordshire,
England
Porcelain, earthenware.
Printed
1900–1913 (1900–
present)
(Royal Grafton Bone China)

E

OLDEST VOLKSTEDT
PORCELAIN FACTORY
Volkstedt, Thuringia,
Germany (E. Germany)
Porcelain
1934+ (1760–present)
(various names & owners)

F

WAGNER & APEL
Lippelsdorf, Thuringia,
Germany (E. Germany)
Porcelain, figurines
ca.1954 (1877–present)
(Porcelain Figurines VEB)

G

BREMER & SCHMIDT
PORCELAIN FACTORY
Eisenberg, Thuringia,
Germany (E. Germany)
ca.1972 (1895–present)
(Special Porcelain
Eisenberg VEB)

H

WORCESTER
PORCELAINS
Worcester, England
Porcelain, earthenware,
parian. Impressed
ca.1807–1813 (ca.1751–
present)
(Royal Worcester Spode
Ltd.)

I

JULIUS GRIESBACH
PORCELAIN FACTORY
Coburg-Cortendorf,
Bavaria, Germany (W.
Germany)
Earthenware, figurines
1956–1973 (1890–
present)
(W. Goebel Cortendorf)

J

CERAMICA BRIANTEA
Milan, Italy
Utility ware
(1947+)

K

COLLINGWOOD &
GREATBATCH
Longton, Staffordshire,
England
Porcelain. Printed,
impressed
1870–1887 (1870–1887)

L

CARL SPITZ
Brux, Bohemia (Most,
Czechoslovakia)
Porcelain, earthenware,
faience
ca.1918–ca.1945 (1896–
ca.1945)

M

CHARLES WAINE
Longton, Staffordshire,
England
Porcelain. Printed
ca.1913–1920 (1891–
1920)

N

DERBY PORCELAIN
WORKS
Derby, England
Porcelain. Painted puce,
blue, black, & red
ca.1782–1825 (ca.1750–
present)
(Royal Doulton Tableware
Ltd.)

O

B. BLOCH & CO.
Eichwald, Bohemia (Dubi,
Czechoslovakia)
Porcelain, earthenware.
Blue, green
1923–1940 (1871–1945)

P

GROSSHERZOG'S
CERAMIC
MANUFACTORY
Darmstadt, Hesse, Germany
(W. Germany)
Figures, vases. Impressed
(1906–1913)

A

ERNEST WAHLISS
ALEXANDRA
PORCELAIN WORKS
Turn-Teplitz, Bohemia
(Trnovany,
Czechoslovakia)
Porcelain, figurines
1897–1906 (1894–1934)

B

FÜRSTENBERG
PORCELAIN
MANUFACTORY
Furstenberg, Brunswick,
Germany (W. Germany)
Porcelain. Blue, green
underglaze
ca.1922–present (1876–
present)
(various names & owners)

C

EMIL FISCHER
Budapest, Hungary
Porcelain
(1866–1980+)

D

WORCESTER
PORCELAINS
Worcester, England
Porcelain, earthenware,
parian. Impressed
ca.1813–1840 (ca.1751–
present)
(Royal Worcester Spode
Ltd.)

E

RUSSIAN IMPERIAL
PORCELAIN FACTORY
St. Petersburg, Russia
(Leningrad, U.S.S.R.)
Porcelain. Painted blue
1825–1855 (1744–
1917+)

F

GROSSHERZOG'S
CERAMIC
MANUFACTORY
Darmstadt, Hesse, Germany
(W. Germany)
Figures, vases. Impressed
(1906–1913)

G

J. UFFRECHT & CO.
Haldensleban, Prussia,
Germany (E. Germany)
Earthenware
1894–1924 (1855–1924)

H

RUDOLF KAMMER
Volkstedt, Thuringia,
Germany (E. Germany)
Porcelain, earthenware
1961–1972 (1953–
present)
(Decorative Porcelain
Rudolstadt VEB)

I

KENSINGTON FINE ART
POTTERY CO.
Hanley, Staffordshire,
England
Earthenware. Printed,
impressed
1892–1899 (1892–1899)

J

KRISTER PORCELAIN
MANUFACTORY
Waldenburg, Silesia,
Germany (Walbrzych,
Poland)
Porcelain, various names
1939–1945 (1831–
present)
(Rosenthal Glass &
Porcelain AG)

K

DRESSEL, KISTER & CO.
Passau, Bavaria, Germany
(W. Germany)
Porcelain, figurines. Blue
underglaze
1903–1904 (1840–1942)

L

BUEN RETIRO
Madrid, Spain
Porcelain. Red
1804–1808 (1760–1808)

M

PLAUE PORCELAIN
MANUFACTORY VEB
Plaue, Thuringia, Germany
(E. Germany)
Porcelain, figurines. Green,
blue
1974–present (1817–
present)
(various names & owners)

N

MÜLLER & CO.
Volkstedt, Thuringia,
Germany (E. Germany)
& Dromcolliher, Ireland
Porcelain, figurines. Irish
Dresden added after
1960
1907–present (1907–
present)

O

SOCIETÀ CERAMICA
RICHARD
Milan, Italy
Porcelain (see page 271)
1850–present (1735–
present)
(Richard-Ginori)

P

ERNST BOHNE SONS
Rudolstadt, Thuringia,
Germany (E. Germany)
Porcelain, figurines. Blue
underglaze, overglaze
1901–ca.1920 (1854–
ca.1920)

A

SANDIZELL PORCELAIN
FACTORY
Sandizell, Bavaria, Germany
(W. Germany)
Porcelain. Blue
1951–present (1951–
present)

B

ETRURIA POTTERY (OTT
& BREWER)
Trenton, NJ, U.S.A.
Parian, porcelain,
semiporcelain, variations
in wording
ca.1876 (1863–1894)

C

H. HUTSCHENREUTHER
Probstzella, Thuringia,
Germany (E. Germany)
Porcelain, figurines
ca.1886–ca.1945 (1886–
present)
(Porcelain Combine Kahla
VEB)

D

ROYAL PORCELAIN
MANUFACTORY
Ludwigsburg, Wurttemberg,
Germany (W. Germany)
Porcelain, figurines. Red,
gold overglaze
1806–1824 (1758–1824)

E

PHILIP ROSENTHAL & CO.
AG/ROSENTHAL
PORCELAIN AG
Kronach, Bavaria, Germany
(W. Germany)
Porcelain
1901–1956 (1879– present)
(various names, now
Rosenthal Glass &
Porcelain AG)

F

CROWN POTTERIES CO.
Evansville, IN, U.S.A.
Majolica, ironstone,
porcelain, semiporcelain
1904+ (1902–1962)

G

SOCIETÀ CERAMICA
RICHARD
Milan, Italy
Porcelain, faience
1875–1885 (1735–
present)
(Richard-Ginori)

H

RICHARD VERNON
WILDBLOOD
Longton, Staffordshire,
England
Porcelain. Printed
1887–1888 (1887–1888)

I

P. DONATH PORCELAIN
FACTORY/CARL HANS
TUPPACK
Tiefenfurth, Silesia,
Germany (Parowa,
Poland)
1896–1922 (ca.1890–
1935)

J

SITZENDORF PORCELAIN
MANUFACTORY
Sitzendorf, Thuringia,
Germany (E. Germany)
Porcelain, figurines,
earthenware. Blue
underglaze
ca.1902–ca.1972 (1845–
present)

K

EISENBERG SPECIAL
PORCELAIN VEB
Eisenberg, Thuringia,
Germany (E. Germany)
Earthenware, porcelain
1972–present (1895–
present)

L

STEVENSON &
HANCOCK
Derby, England
Porcelain, bisque. Painted
1861–1935 (ca.1859–
1935)
(once part of Derby
Porcelain Works)

M

SOMMER & MATSCHAK
Schlaggenwald, Bohemia
(Horne Slavkor,
Czechoslovakia)
Porcelain
(1904–1945)

N

THOMAS C. WILD & CO.
Longton, Staffordshire,
England
Porcelain
ca. 1896–1904 (1896–
present)
(various names, now Royal
Doulton Tableware Ltd.)

O

VISTA ALEGRE
Vista Alegre, Portugal
Hard paste porcelain
1830–present (1824–
present)

P

HEINRICH WINTERLING
PORCELAIN FACTORY
Marktleuthen, Bavaria,
Germany (W. Germany)
Porcelain
1934+ (1903–present)
(Winterling Group)

A

WALLENDORF
PORCELAIN FACTORY
VEB
Wallendorf, Thuringia,
Germany (E. Germany)
Porcelain
1964 + (1960–present)
(United Decorative
Porcelain Works Lichte
VEB)

B

WORCESTER
PORCELAINS
Worcester, England
Porcelain, earthenware,
parian. Printed,
impressed
ca.1862–1875 (ca.1751–
present)
(Royal Worcester Spode
Ltd.)

C

W. GOEBEL
Rodental, Bavaria, Germany
(W. Germany)
Figurines. Blue, black
underglaze, incised
1914–1920 (1871–
present)

D

W. GOEBEL
Rodental, Bavaria, Germany
(W. Germany)
Figurines. Blue, black
underglaze
1923–1949 (1871–
present)

E

WILDBLOOD & HEATH
Longton, Staffordshire,
England
Porcelain. Printed
ca.1889–1899 (1889–
1927)

F

ROYAL PORCELAIN
MANUFACTORY
Ludwigsburg, Wurttemberg,
Germany (W. Germany)
Porcelain. Gold overglaze
1816–1824 (1758–1824)

G

WURTTEMBERG
PORCELAIN
MANUFACTORY
Schorndorf, Wurttemberg,
Germany (W. Germany)
Porcelain, figurines
1904–1939 (1904–1939)

H

ROYAL PORCELAIN
MANUFACTORY
Berlin, Germany
Porcelain, figurines. Black,
green overglaze, various
dates
1890–1917 (1763–
present)
(State's Porcelain
Manufactory)

I

BOHEMIA CERAMIC
WORKS AG
Neurohlau, Bohemia (Nova
Role, Czechoslovakia)
Porcelain
1940–1945 (1921–1945)

J

CARL THIEME SAXONIAN
PORCELAIN FACTORY
Potschappel, Saxony,
Germany (E. Germany)
Porcelain, figurines
1902 + (1872–present)
(Saxonian Porcelain
Manufactory Dresden
VEB)

K

SCHNEIDER & CO.
Altrohlau, Bohemia (Stara
Role, Czechoslovakia)
Porcelain. Green, blue
1904–1945 (1904–1945)

L

G. L. ASHWORTH & BROS.
Hanley, Staffordshire,
England
Earthenware, ironstone.
Printed
1862–ca.1890 (1784–
present)
(member of Wedgwood
Group)

M

WILLIAM ADAMS & SONS
LTD.
Tunstall & Stoke,
Staffordshire, England
Earthenware, basalt, jasper,
parian. Printed
1914–1940 (1769–
present)
(member of Wedgwood
Group)

N

ADDERLEYS LTD.
Longton, Staffordshire,
England
Porcelain, earthenware.
Printed
1912–1926 (1906–
present)
(Royal Doulton Tableware
Ltd.)

O

ADDERLEYS LTD.
Longton, Staffordshire,
England
Porcelain, earthenware.
Printed
1912–1926 (1906–
present)
(Royal Doulton Tableware
Ltd.)

P

ADDERLEYS LTD.
Longton, Staffordshire,
England
Porcelain, earthenware
1950–1972 (1906–
present)
(Royal Doulton Tableware
Ltd.)

A

A. J. WILKINSON L?
ENGLAND

ARTHUR J. WILKINSON
Burslem, Staffordshire,
England
Earthenware, ironstone.
Printed
ca.1930+ (1885–1964+)

B

KAISER

KAISER PORCELAIN
Staffelstein, Bavaria,
Germany (W. Germany)
Porcelain, figurines. Blue
underglaze
1970–present (1872–
present)

C

Alboth & Kaiser
BAVARIA

ALKA-KUNST ALBOTH &
KAISER
Staffelstein, Bavaria,
Germany (W. Germany)
Porcelain, figurines
ca.1953–1970 (1872–
present)
(Kaiser Porcelain)

D

ALFRED MEAKIN L?
ENGLAND
ROYAL SEMI-PORCELAIN

ALFRED MEAKIN (LTD.)
Tunstall, Staffordshire,
England
Earthenware. Printed
ca.1891–1930 (1873–
present)
(Myott-Meakin Ltd.)

E

alka Kunst
BAVARIA

ALKA-KUNST ALBOTH &
KAISER
Staffelstein, Bavaria,
Germany (W. Germany)
Porcelain, figurines
ca.1953–1970 (1872–
present)
(Kaiser Porcelain)

F

ALLERTONS L?
ENGLAND
SEMI-PORCELAIN

ALLERTONS LTD.
Longton, Staffordshire,
England
Porcelain, earthenware,
luster decoration. Printed
1915–1929 (1859–1942)

G

Altenkunstadt
Bavaria

ROTHEMUND, HAGER &
CO.
Altenkunstadt, Bavaria,
Germany (W. Germany)
Porcelain
1919–1933 (1919–
present)
(Karl Nehmzow Porcelain
Factory)

H

ARABIA

ARABIA PORCELAIN
FACTORY
Helsingfors (Helsinki),
Finland
Porcelain, stoneware
1949–present (1874–
present)
(Upsala-Ekeby Group)

I

ASHWORTH BROS.
ROYAL STONE
CHINA

G. L. ASHWORTH & BROS.
Hanley, Staffordshire,
England
Earthenware, ironstone.
Printed
ca.1880+ (1784–present)
(member of Wedgwood
Group)

J

EST 1775
AYNSLEY
ENGLAND
Bone China

JOHN AYNSLEY & SONS
Longton, Staffordshire,
England
Porcelain. Printed
1891+ (1864–present)
(Waterford Glass Ltd.)

K

Bareuther

WALDSASSEN
PORCELAIN FACTORY
Waldsassen, Bavaria,
Germany (W. Germany)
Porcelain. Green
1960–ca.1970 (1866–
present)

L

Bareuther

WALDSASSEN
PORCELAIN FACTORY
Waldsassen, Bavaria,
Germany (W. Germany)
Porcelain. Green
1970–present (1866–
present)

M

Bavaria
Germany

OSCAR SCHALLER & CO.
SUCCESSOR
Kirchenlamitz, Bavaria,
Germany (W. Germany)
Porcelain
1921+ (1918–present)
(Winterling group)

N

BAY
KERAMIK
KRISTALL KERAMIK

EDWARD BAY
Ransbach, Rhineland,
Germany (W. Germany)
Stoneware, earthenware
1970–present (1933–
present)

O

"BBB"
ENGLAND

BOOTHS
Tunstall, Staffordshire,
England
Earthenware
1930+ (1891–present)
(Royal Doulton Tableware
Ltd.)

P

Bloor
Derby

DERBY PORCELAIN
WORKS
Derby, England
Porcelain
1811–1830 (ca.1750–
present)
(Royal Doulton Tableware
Ltd.)

A

DAREUTHER & CO.
PORCELAIN FACTORY
WALDSASSEN AG
Waldsassen, Bavaria,
Germany (W. Germany)
Porcelain
1971–present (1866–
present)

B

Colclough

COLCLOUGH CHINA LTD.
Longton, Staffordshire,
England
Porcelain
current (1937–present)
(Royal Doulton Tableware
Ltd.)

C

QueenAnne

ENGLAND

QUEEN ANNE
Stoke, Staffordshire,
England
current (ca.1964–present)
(Royal Doulton Tableware
Ltd.)

D

Royal Vale

COLCLOUGH CHINA LTD.
Longton, Staffordshire,
England
Porcelain
current (1937–present)
(Royal Doulton Tableware
Ltd.)

E

BOOTHS
Tunstall, Staffordshire,
England
Earthenware. Printed
ca.1906+ (1891–present)
(Royal Doulton Tableware
Ltd.)

F

**Branksome
China
England**

BRANKSOME CERAMICS/
E. BAGGALEY LTD.
Bournemouth, Hampshire,
England
Earthenware. Printed
1947–present (1945–
present)

G

BROWN-WESTHEAD,
MOORE & CO./
CAULDON LTD.
Hanley, Staffordshire,
England
Earthenware, porcelain.
Printed, impressed
1891–1920 (1862–
present)
(member of Wedgwood
Group)

H

*Chamberlain's
Worcester,
& 155,
New Bond Street,
London.
Royal Porcelain Manufactory.*

CHAMBERLAIN & CO.
Worcester, England
Porcelain. Printed
ca.1811–1840 (ca.1786–
present)
(Royal Worcester Spode
Ltd.)

I

CHARLES ALLERTON &
SONS
Longton, Staffordshire,
England
Porcelain, earthenware,
luster decoration
ca.1891–ca.1912 (1859–
1942)

J

CLARENCE

BRADLEYS
MADE IN
ENGLAND.

BRADLEYS
Longton, Staffordshire,
England
Porcelain. Printed
ca.1928–1941 (1922–
1941)

K

CLEMENTSON BROS.
LTD.
Hanley, Staffordshire,
England
Earthenware. Printed
1913–1916 (1865–1916)

L

WILDBLOOD, HEATH &
SONS
Longton, Staffordshire,
England
Porcelain. Printed
1899–1927 (1899–1927)

M

BONE **COALPORT** CHINA
MADE IN ENGLAND
EST.1750

COALPORT PORCELAIN
WORKS
Stoke, Staffordshire,
England
Porcelain
1960–present (ca.1795–
present)
(member of Wedgwood
Group)

N

**CONTINENTAL
CHINA**

ROSENTHAL GLASS &
PORCELAIN AG
Selb, Bavaria, Germany (W.
Germany)
Porcelain, earthenware,
figurines
1963+ (1879–present)

O

ROSENTHAL GLASS &
PORCELAIN AG
Selb, Bavaria, Germany (W.
Germany)
Porcelain. Import-export
mark for Block China,
NY, U.S.A.
current (1879–present)

P

COPELAND

W. T. COPELAND (&
SONS LTD.)
Stoke, Staffordshire,
England
Porcelain, parian,
earthenware. Printed
ca.1900 (1847–present)
(Royal Worcester Spode
Ltd.)

A

CORONA

GATER, HALL & CO./
BARRATT'S OF
STAFFORDSHIRE LTD.
Burslem, Staffordshire,
England
Earthenware
1914–1943 + (1895–
present)

B

HOMER LAUGHLIN CHINA
CO.
East Liverpool, OH, U.S.A.
Semivitreous dinnerware
ca.1935–ca.1941 (1877–
present)

C

SHENANGO CHINA CO.
New Castle, PA, U.S.A.
Semiporcelain, vitrified
ware, porcelain
1960 + (1901–present)
(Anchor Hocking)

D

CO-OPERATIVE
WHOLESALE SOCIETY
LTD.
Longton, Staffordshire,
England
Earthenware. Printed,
variations in wording
1950–1962 + (1946–
1964 +)

E

S. FIELDING & CO.
Stoke, Staffordshire,
England
Earthenware, majolica,
variations in wording
ca.1913–1930s (1879–
1964 +)

F

A. G. RICHARDSON & CO.
LTD.
Tunstall, Staffordshire,
England
Earthenware. Printed
ca.1925 + (1915–present)

G

GOVANCROFT
POTTERIES LTD.
Glasgow, Scotland
Earthenware, stoneware.
Printed, impressed
1913–1949 (1913–
1964 +)

H

CROWN POTTERIES CO.
Evansville, IN, U.S.A.
Majolica, ironstone,
semiporcelain, white
granite
ca.1950 (1902–1962)

I

J. DIMMOCK & CO.
Hanley, Staffordshire,
England
Earthenware. Printed
ca.1878–1904 (1862–
1904)

J

CROWN POTTERIES CO.
Evansville, IN, U.S.A.
Majolica, ironstone,
semiporcelain, white
granite
ca.1904 (1902–1962)

K

CROWN STAFFORDSHIRE
PORCELAIN CO. LTD.
Fenton, Staffordshire,
England
Porcelain. Printed,
variations in wording
ca.1906–ca.1930 + (1889–
present)
(member of Wedgwood
Group)

L

DUCHCOV PORCELAIN
Dux, Bohemia (Duchcov,
Czechoslovakia)
Porcelain, figurines
1947–present (1860–
present)
(Duchcovsky Porcelain,
Dux)

M

ROYAL COPENHAGEN
PORCELAIN FACTORY
LTD.
Copenhagen, Denmark
Porcelain, stoneware,
faience. Blue
1894–1900 (1775–
present)

N

W. DAVENPORT & CO.
Longport, Staffordshire,
England
Earthenware, creamware,
porcelain, ironstone.
Printed
ca.1870–1886 (ca.1793–
1887)

O

J. H. MIDDLETON (& CO.)/
HUDSON &
MIDDLETON LTD.
Longton, Staffordshire,
England
Porcelain
ca.1930–1941 + (1889–
present)

P

ROYAL COPENHAGEN
PORCELAIN FACTORY
LTD.
Copenhagen, Denmark
Porcelain, stoneware,
faience
ca.1922 (1775–present)

A

DERBY PORCELAIN
  WORKS
Derby, England
Porcelain. Printed red
ca.1830–1848 (ca.1750–
  present)
(Royal Doulton Tableware
  Ltd.)

B

DERBY CHINA

ROYAL CROWN DERBY
ENGLISH BONE CHINA

ROYAL CROWN DERBY
Derby, England
Porcelain
1964–1975 (1750–
  present)
(Royal Doulton Tableware
  Ltd.)

C

S. FIELDING & CO.
Stoke, Staffordshire,
  England
Earthenware, majolica.
  Printed
ca.1917–1930 (ca.1879–
  1964+)

D

JAEGER & CO.
Marktredwitz, Bavaria,
  Germany (W. Germany)
Porcelain. Variations in
  wording
1911+ (1898–present)
(Jaeger Porcelain GMBH)

E

COPENHAGEN
DENMARK

DAHL-JENSEN
  PORCELAIN
Copenhagen, Denmark
Porcelain. Printed blue
1928–present (1925–
  present)

F

KØBENHAVN

DAHL-JENSEN
  PORCELAIN
Copenhagen, Denmark
Porcelain
1925–1928 (1925–
  present)

G

————————
Dresden, Germany
Porcelain. Hand-drawn
  mark used by many
  decorators
1883–1893

H

DUNN BENNETT & CO.
  (LTD.)
Burslem, Staffordshire,
  England
Earthenware. Printed,
  variations in wording
1937–1964+ (1875–
  1964+)

I

DRESDEN
EARTHENWAREWORK
VEB
Dresden, Saxony, Germany
  (E. Germany)
Porcelain, earthenware
1956+ (1856–1965)

J

EDUARD HABERLANDER
  PORCELAIN FACTORY
Windischeschenbach,
  Bavaria, Germany
  (W. Germany)
Porcelain
ca. 1913–1928 (1913–
  present)
(Oscar Schaller & Co.
  Successor)

K

EMBASSY
MADDOCK
MADE IN
ENGLAND

JOHN MADDOCK & SONS
  LTD.
Burslem, Staffordshire,
  England
Earthenware, ironstone
ca.1935+ (1855–present)
(Maddock Hotel Ware
  Division of Royal Stafford
  China Ltd.)

L

Schönwald

E. & A. MÜLLER
  PORCELAIN FACTORY
Schonwald, Bavaria,
  Germany (W. Germany)
Porcelain
ca.1910–ca.1922 (1904–
  present)
(Porcelain Factory
  Schonwald, branch of
  Hutschenreuther AG)

M

ENGLAND

SAMUEL RADFORD (LTD.)
Fenton, Staffordshire,
  England
Porcelain. Printed
ca.1891+ (1879–1957)

N

ENGLAND
COALPORT
A.D. 1750.

COALPORT PORCELAIN
  WORKS
Coalport, Shropshire,
  England
Porcelain. Printed
ca.1891–ca.1920 (ca.
  1795–present)
(member of Wedgwood
  Group)

O

ENGLAND
THE PARAGON CHINA

STAR CHINA
Longton, Staffordshire,
  England
Porcelain. Printed
ca.1904–1919 (1900–
  present)
(various names, now Royal
  Doulton Tableware Ltd.)

P

Erbendorf
Bavaria

CHRISTIAN SELTMANN
Erbendorf, Bavaria,
  Germany (W. Germany)
Porcelain. Green
  underglaze
1940–ca.1955 (1923–
  present)
(operating in Weiden)

A

ERDMANN
SCHLEGELMILCH
Suhl, Thuringia, Germany
(E. Germany)
Porcelain. Green, blue
1891+ (1881–1938)

B

Eschenbach
BAVARIA

OSCAR SCHALLER & CO.
SUCCESSOR
Windischeschenbach,
Bavaria, Germany (W.
Germany)
Porcelain. Green underglaze
1945–present (1918–
present)
(Winterling Group)

C

E. SWASEY & CO.
Portland, ME, U.S.A.
Earthenware
(1886–ca.1891)

D

Eichwald

DR. WIDERA & CO.
PORCELAIN STOVE &
TILE FACTORY
EICHWALD
Eichwald, Bohemia (Dubi,
Czechoslavakia)
Porcelain, earthenware.
Blue, green
1940–1945 (1871–1945)

E

Eversberg
Bavaria-Germany

EVERSBERG PORCELAIN
FACTORY
Stockheim, Bavaria,
Germany (W. Germany)
Porcelain. Green
underglaze
1978–present (1978–
present)

F

FLORAL CHINA CO. LTD.
Longton, Staffordshire,
England
Porcelain floral ware.
Printed
ca.1946–1951 (1940–
1951)

G

THOMAS GREEN
Fenton, Staffordshire,
England
Porcelain, earthenware.
Printed
1847–1859 (1847-1859)

H

Flight&Barr

WORCESTER
PORCELAINS
Worcester, England
Porcelain. Blue
ca.1792–1807 (ca.1751–
present)
(Royal Worcester Spode
Ltd.)

I

FRANCIS MORLEY (& CO.)
Hanley, Staffordshire,
England
Earthenware, ironstone.
Printed, impressed
1845–1858 (1845–1858)

J

WILEMAN & CO.
Fenton & Longton,
Staffordshire, England
Porcelain, earthenware
ca.1892+ (1892–1925)
(Shellys Ltd.)

K

CAULDON POTTERIES
LTD.
Fenton, Staffordshire,
England
Reissues of F & R Pratt
designs. Printed
ca.1930+ (1920–present)
(member of Wedgwood
Group)

L

THOMAS FORESTER SON
& CO.
Fenton, Staffordshire,
England
Porcelain, earthenware.
Printed
1884–1888 (1884–1888)

M

KRAUTHEIM &
ADELBERG PORCELAIN
FACTORY GMBH
Selb, Bavaria, Germany (W.
Germany)
Porcelain. Export mark with
green overglaze
1945–present (1884–
present)

N

FRANK HAVILAND
LIMOGES

FRANK HAVILAND
Limoges, France
Porcelain
ca.1910–1924+ (1910–
1939)

O

Frankenthal

FRIEDRICH WILHELM
WESSEL
Frankenthal, Palatinate,
Germany (W. Germany)
Porcelain
1949–ca.1964 (1949–
ca.1964)

P

friedrichsburg
BAVARIA

JULIUS GRIESBACH
PORCELAIN FACTORY
Coburg-Cortendorf,
Bavaria, Germany (W.
Germany)
Earthenware, porcelain,
figurines
1935–1973 (1890–
present)
(W. Goebel Cortendorf)

A	B	C	D
GIBSON & SONS Burslem, Staffordshire, England Earthenware. Printed ca.1912+ (1885–1972+)	 TIRSCHENREUTH PORCELAIN FACTORY Tirschenreuth, Bavaria, Germany (W. Germany) Porcelain, figurines 1927+ (1838–present) (Hutschenreuther AG)	UNTERWEISSBACH PORCELAIN FACTORY VEB Unterweissbach, Thuringia, Germany (E. Germany) Porcelain, figurines 1956–ca.1962 (ca.1880–present) (various names & owners)	RAU PORCELAIN FACTORY Munich, Bavaria, Germany (W. Germany) Decorated porcelain. Overglaze 1945–ca.1978 (1946–present)
E	F	G	H
GIBSON & SONS Burslem, Staffordshire, England Earthenware ca.1930+ (1885–1972+)	GIBSON & SONS Burslem, Staffordshire, England Earthenware 1930–1972+ (1885–1972+)	 SOCIETÀ CERAMICA RICHARD Milan, Italy Majolica. Hand-drawn 1842–1860 (1735–present) (Richard-Ginori)	W. GOEBEL Rodental, Bavaria, Germany (W. Germany) Porcelain, figurines. Impressed blue, black underglaze 1937–1945 (1871–present)
I	J	K	L
GRAF & KRIPPNER Selb, Bavaria, Germany (W. Germany) Decorated porcelain 1906–ca.1929 (1906–present) (Villeroy & Boch)	SOCIETÀ CERAMICA RICHARD Milan, Italy Earthenware, porcelain, faience 1868–1881 (1735–present) (Richard-Ginori)	GRINDLEY HOTEL WARE CO. LTD. Tunstall, Staffordshire, England Earthenware. Printed 1908+ (1908–present) (Federated Potteries Ltd.)	HAMMERSLEY & CO. Longton, Staffordshire, England Porcelain. Impressed, printed 1887–1912 (1887–present) (Royal Worcester Spode Ltd.)
M	N	O	P
HERTEL, JACOB & CO. GMBH Rehau, Bavaria, Germany (W. Germany) Porcelain 1922–1969+ (1906–1969+)	HEINRICH & CO. Selb, Bavaria, Germany (W. Germany) Porcelain. Blue, green 1896–present (1896–present) (Villeroy & Boch)	HEINZL & CO. Granesau, Bohemia (Chranisov, Czechoslovakia) Mugs, cups, pots 1924–1939 (1924–1945)	HEINRICH & CO. Selb, Bavaria, Germany (W. Germany) Porcelain. Blue, green underglaze 1905–1907 (1896–present) (Villeroy & Boch)

A **HACKEFORS PORCELAIN AB** Linkoping, Sweden Porcelain 1957–present (1929–present) (Upsala-Ekeby Group)	**B**  **HAEGER POTTERIES** Dundee, IL, U.S.A. Tile, pottery, ironstone (1914–present)	**C**  **HAMMERSLEY & CO.** Longton, Staffordshire, England Porcelain. Printed 1912–1939 (1887–present) (Royal Worcester Spode Ltd.)	**D** **CROWN STAFFORDSHIRE PORCELAIN CO. LTD.** Fenton, Staffordshire, England Porcelain current (1889–present) (member of Wedgwood Group)
E **E. BAGGALEY LTD.** Bournemouth, Hampshire, England Earthenware current (1957–present)	**F**  **HARKER POTTERY CO.** East Liverpool, OH, U.S.A Semivitreous ware 1948–1963 (1890–1972)	**G** HEINRICH PORZELLAN **HEINRICH PORCELAIN** Selb, Bavaria, Germany (W. Germany) Porcelain. Blue, green underglaze 1976–present (1896–present) (Villeroy & Boch)	**H** **HEREND** Herend, Hungary Porcelain. Green 1891–1897 (1832–present)
I **HEINRICH PORCELAIN** Selb, Bavaria, Germany (W. Germany) Porcelain. Blue, green underglaze, blue, red, gold overglaze 1974–1976 (1896–present) (Villeroy & Boch)	**J** **HERCULANEUM POTTERY** Liverpool, Lancashire, England Earthenware, porcelain. Impressed, printed ca.1796–1833 (ca.1793–1841)	**K** **L. HUTSCHENREUTHER PORCELAIN FACTORY** Selb, Bavaria, Germany (W. Germany) Porcelain, figurines 1928–1943 (1857–present) (Hutschenreuther AG)	**L** HUTSCHENREUTHER ARZBERG BAVARIA · GERMANY **C. M. HUTSCHEN-REUTHER PORCELAIN FACTORY** Arzberg, Bavaria, Germany (W. Germany) Faience, earthenware, porcelain. Green underglaze 1963–present (1814–present) (Hutschenreuther AG)
M **C. M. HUTSCHENREUTHER** Arzberg, Bavaria, Germany (W. Germany) Faience, porcelain. Green underglaze ca.1928–ca.1963 (1814–present) (Hutschenreuther AG)	**N** WEDGWOOD & C°LD. ENGLAND. **WEDGWOOD & CO.** Tunstall, Staffordshire, England Earthenware, ironstone ca.1906+ (1860–present) (member of Wedgwood Group)	**O** IMPERIAL PSL **PFEIFFER & LOWENSTEIN** Schlackenwerth, Bohemia, (Ostrov, Czechoslovakia) Porcelain. Green underglaze 1914–1918 (1873–1941)	**P** IMPERIAL SEMI PORCELAIN MYOTT SON & C° ENGLAND **MYOTT, SON & CO.** Cobridge, Staffordshire, England Earthenware ca.1907+ (1875–present) (Myott-Meakin Ltd.)

A

LUDWIG WESSEL
Bonn, Rhineland, Germany
(W. Germany)
Faience, earthenware,
porcelain
1893+ (1825–present)
(Wessel Ceramic Works
AG)

B

SWILLINGTON BRIDGE
Swillington Bridge,
Yorkshire, England
Ironstone. Blue printed
ca.1820–ca.1850

C

J. & G. MEAKIN (LTD.)
Hanley, Staffordshire,
England
Earthenware, ironstone.
Printed
ca.1912+ (1851–present)
(member of Wedgwood
Group)

D

Bavana

J. KRONESTER
Schwarzenbach, Bavaria,
Germany (W. Germany)
Porcelain
ca.1972 (1905–present)

E

JACKSON & GOSLING
LTD.
Longton, Staffordshire,
England
Porcelain
ca.1912+ (1866–1964+)

F

Jäger

WILHELM JAGER
PORCELAIN FACTORY
Eisenberg, Thuringia,
Germany (E. Germany)
Porcelain
ca.1945–1960 (1868–
present)
(United Porcelainworks
Eisenberg VEB)

G

J. H. W.

LONGTON

J. H. WALTON
Longton, Staffordshire,
England
Porcelain. Printed,
impressed
1912–1921 (1912–1921)

H

JOHANN HAVILAND
BAVARIA
GERMANY

JOHANN HAVILAND
Waldershof, Bavaria,
Germany (W. Germany)
Porcelain. Green
underglaze
ca.1972 (1907–present)
(various names, now
Rosenthal Glass &
Porcelain AG)

I

BAVARIA
VOHENSTRAUSS
Johann Seltmann

JOHANN SELTMANN
Vohenstrauss, Bavaria,
Germany (W. Germany)
Porcelain. Green
underglaze
current (1901–present)

J

JOHN MADDOCK & SONS Lᵀᴰ
MADE IN ENGLAND

JOHN MADDOCK & SONS
LTD.
Burslem, Staffordshire,
England
Earthenware, ironstone.
Printed, variations in
wording
ca.1927+ (1855–present)
(Maddock Hotel Ware
Division of Royal Stafford
China Ltd.)

K

Johnson Bros.
England.

JOHNSON BROS. LTD.
Hanley, Staffordshire,
England
Earthenware, ironstone.
Printed
ca.1913+ (1883–present)
(member of Wedgwood
Group)

L

Kaestner Saxonia

FRIEDRICH KAESTNER
Oberhohndorf, Saxony,
Germany (E. Germany)
Porcelain. Green
underglaze
1928–ca.1972 (1883–
1972)

M

KELLER & GUÉRIN
Luneville, France
Faience
ca.1880 (ca.1788–1890+)

N

KARLSBAD
Knoll

CARL KNOLL PORCELAIN
FACTORY KARLSBAD
Fischern, Bohemia (Rybare,
Czechoslovakia)
Porcelain
ca.1910–1945 (1848–
1945)

O

kerakron
Melitta

FRISIA VAREL PORCELAIN
FACTORY
Frisia, Germany (W.
Germany)
Porcelain, stoneware,
earthenware
1971–present (1953–
present)

P

KOKUS
CHINA

SEBRING POTTERY CO.
East Liverpool & Sebring,
OH, U.S.A.
Ironstone
ca.1905 (1887–1948)

A

KONIGSZELT PORCELAIN
FACTORY
Konigszelt, Silesia,
Germany (Jaworzyna
Slaska, Poland)
Porcelain
1922–1928 (1863–
present)
(Hutschenreuther AG)

B

THURINGIAN PORCELAIN
WORKS VEB
Konigsee, Thuringia,
Germany (E. Germany)
Porcelain
1960–1968 (1892–
present)
(Kahla Porcelain Combine
VEB)

C

KONINKLYK FACTORY
(GOUDA)
Gouda, Holland
Delft blue & white utility
ware
1914+ (19th century–
present)

D

KONSTANZ PORCELAIN
MANUFACTORY GMBH
Konstanz, Badenia,
Germany (W. Germany)
Decorated porcelain
1929–1935 (1929–1935)

E

KLAUS & PETER MULLER
Hohr-Grenzhausen,
Palatinate, Germany (W.
Germany)
Porcelain, figurines
1958–present (1950–
present)
(Peter Muller)

F

R. M. KRAUSE
Schweidnitz, Silesia,
Germany (Swidnica,
Poland)
Decorated porcelain.
Overglaze
ca.1929 (1882–1929+)

G

KRAUTHEIM &
ADELBERG PORCELAIN
FACTORY GMBH
Selb, Bavaria, Germany (W.
Germany)
Decorated porcelain
(1884–present)

H

STOCKHARDT &
SCHMIDT-ECKERT
PORCELAIN FACTORY
KRONACH
Kronach, Bavaria, Germany
(W. Germany)
Porcelain
1912–present (1912–
present)

I

J. KRONESTER
Schwarzenbach, Bavaria,
Germany (W. Germany)
Porcelain. Green
underglaze
1969–present (1905–
present)

J

JOSEF KUBA
Wiesau, Bavaria, Germany
(W. Germany)
Porcelain. Overglaze
1947–present (1947–
present)

K

H. LANGE PORCELAIN
FACTORY
Krummennaab, Bavaria,
Germany (W. Germany)
Porcelain
1936–1939 (1879–
present)
(various names & owners,
now Christian Seltmann
GMBH)

L

LIMBACH PORCELAIN
FACTORY AG
Limbach, Thuringia,
Germany (E. Germany)
Porcelain, figurines. Green,
blue
1919–1944 (1882–1944)

M

CHASTAGNER
Limoges, France
Porcelain
1950+ (ca.1946–1980+)

N

PORCELAIN FIGURINES
VEB
Lippelsdorf, Thuringia,
Germany (E. Germany)
Porcelain, figurines
1974–present (1877–
present)

O

KEELING & CO.
Burslem, Staffordshire,
England
Earthenware. Printed
ca.1912–1936 (1886–
1936)

P

SPECHTSBRUNN
PORCELAIN FACTORY
Spechtsbrunn, Thuringia,
Germany (E. Germany)
Porcelain, figurines
1930–ca.1954 (1911–
present)

A

LUDWIGSBURG
PORCELAIN FACTORY
GMBH
Ludwigsburg, Wurttemberg,
Germany (W. Germany)
Porcelain, figurines. Blue
underglaze
1948–present (1918–
present)
(various names & owners)

B

HAAS & CZJZEK
Schlaggenwald, Bohemia
(Horni Slavkov,
Czechoslovakia)
Porcelain. Green
underglaze
1918–1939 (1867–
1945+)

C

G. M. & C. J. MASON/G. L.
ASHWORTH & BROS.
Hanley, Staffordshire,
England
Earthenware, ironstone.
Printed, variations in
wording
ca.1820 (1813–present)
(member of Wedgwood
Group)

D

MINTON
Stoke, Staffordshire,
England
Porcelain, earthenware.
Printed
ca.1860–1870 (1793–
present)
(Royal Doulton Tableware
Ltd.)

E

MAYER & SHERRATT
Longton, Staffordshire,
England
Porcelain. Printed
1921+ (1906–1941)

F

KLAUS & PETER MULLER
Hohr-Grenzhausen,
Palatinate, Germany (W.
Germany)
Porcelain, figurines
1957–present (1950–
present)
(Peter Muller)

G

BRITISH ANCHOR
POTTERY CO. LTD.
Longton, Staffordshire,
England
Earthenware. Printed,
impressed
1954+ (1884–1964+)

H

PAUL MULLER
PORCELAIN FACTORY
Selb, Bavaria, Germany
(W. Germany)
Porcelain
ca.1890–1917 (1890–
ca.1957)

I

MYOTT, SON & CO.
Cobridge, Staffordshire,
England
Earthenware
ca.1936+ (1875–present)
(Myott-Meakin Ltd.)

J

MORITZ ZDEKAUER
Altrohlau, Bohemia (Stara
Role, Czechoslovakia)
Faience, earthenware,
porcelain. Green
underglaze, overglaze
1884–1909 (1884–
1945+)
(nationalized in 1945)

K

NEW WHARF POTTERY
CO.
Burslem, Staffordshire,
England
Earthenware. Printed
ca.1890–1894 (1878–
1894)

L

NEWPORT POTTERY CO.
Burslem, Staffordshire,
England
Earthenware. Printed
ca.1920+ (1920–present)
(member of Wedgwood
Group)

M

TIRSCHENREUTH
PORCELAIN FACTORY
Tirschenreuth, Bavaria,
Germany (W. Germany)
Porcelain
ca.1900–ca.1927 (1838–
present)
(Hutschenreuther AG)

N

SAMPSON HANCOCK (&
SONS)
Stoke, Staffordshire,
England
Earthenware. Printed
1906–1912 (1858–1937)

O

TRIPTIS AG
Triptis, Thuringia, Germany
(E. Germany)
Porcelain
1931–ca.1945 (1881–
present)
(Kahla Porcelain Combine
VEB)

P

LENOX, INC.
Trenton, NJ, U.S.A.
Dinnerware, porcelain
current (1906–present)

A

REID & CO.
Longton, Staffordshire,
England
Porcelain. Printed
ca.1913–1922 (1913–
1946)

B

PAUL A. STRAUB & CO.
New York, NY, U.S.A.
Porcelain importer's mark
for L. Hutschenreuther
1948–1970 (1915–1970)

C

CREIDLITZ PORCELAIN
FACTORY
Creidlitz, Bavaria, Germany
(W. Germany)
Porcelain
ca.1908+ (1903–present)

D

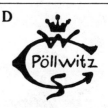

POLLWITZ PORCELAIN
FACTORY
Pollwitz, Thuringia,
Germany (E. Germany)
Porcelain
ca.1920–1938 (1920–
1938)

E

CARL THIEME SAXONIAN
PORCELAIN FACTORY
Potschappel, Saxony,
Germany (E. Germany)
Porcelain
ca.1955 (1872–present)
(Saxonian Porcelain
Manufactory Dresden
VEB)

F

BARKER BROS. LTD.
Longton, Staffordshire,
England
Porcelain, earthenware
1937+ (1876–1964+)

G

TIRSCHENREUTH
PORCELAIN FACTORY
Tirschenreuth, Bavaria,
Germany (W. Germany)
Porcelain. Green
underglaze
1947+ (1838–present)
(Hutschenreuther AG)

H

ROSINA CHINA CO.
Longton, Staffordshire,
England
Porcelain, various pattern
names
current (1941–present)

I

SAMUEL RADFORD (LTD.)
Fenton, Staffordshire,
England
Bone china. Printed
1928+ (1879–1957)

J

JOSEF RIEBER & CO.
PORCELAIN FACTORY
AG
Mitterteich, Bavaria,
Germany (W. Germany)
Porcelain
ca.1945–ca.1976 (1918–
ca.1978)

K

ROSENTHAL GLASS &
PORCELAIN AG
Selb, Bavaria, Germany (W.
Germany)
Porcelain
current (1879–present)

L

F. A. REINECKE
Eisenberg, Thuringia,
Germany (E. Germany)
Earthenware, porcelain.
Green underglaze
1927–1960 (1796–1972+)
(United Porcelainworks
Eisenberg VEB)

M

MUHLBACH PORCELAIN
FACTORY
Bruchmuhlbach, Palatinate,
Germany (W. Germany)
Earthenware
1951–ca.1970 (1951–
present)
(Winterling Group)

N

ROBERT HANKE
PORCELAIN FACTORY
Ladowitz, Bohemia
(Ledvice,
Czechoslovakia)
Porcelain. Red overglaze
ca.1882–1914 (1882–
1945)

O

RIDGWAY POTTERIES
LTD.
Stoke, Staffordshire,
England
Earthenware
ca.1960 (1955–present)
(Royal Doulton Tableware
Ltd.)

P

RIDGWAY POTTERIES
LTD.
Stoke, Staffordshire,
England
Earthenware
ca.1962 (1955–present)
(Royal Doulton Tableware
Ltd.)

A

RICHARD KLEMM
Dresden, Saxony, Germany
(E. Germany)
Decorated porcelain. Blue
overglaze
1886–1916 (1869–1916)

B

RÖRSTRAND AB
Lidkoping, Sweden
Porcelain, faience
current (1726–present)

C

PHILIP ROSENTHAL & CO.
AG/ROSENTHAL
PORCELAIN AG
Selb, Bavaria, Germany (W.
Germany)
Porcelain, earthenware.
Variations in wording
1907–1956 (1879–
present)
(Rosenthal Glass &
Porcelain AG)

D

Rosenthal
GERMANY

ROSENTHAL PORCELAIN
AG
Selb, Bavaria, Germany (W.
Germany)
Porcelain, earthenware
1953–present (1879–
present)
(Rosenthal Glass &
Porcelain AG)

E

ROSINA CHINA CO.
Longton, Staffordshire,
England
Porcelain
ca.1946+ (1941–present)

F

THOMAS C. WILD & SONS
(ROYAL ALBERT LTD.)
Longton, Staffordshire,
England
Porcelain. Printed
current (1917–present)
(various names, now Royal
Doulton Tableware Ltd.)

G

KERAFINA
Marktredwitz, Bavaria,
Germany (W. Germany)
Porcelain. Overglaze
1950–1958 (1950–
present)

H

CAULDON POTTERIES
LTD.
Stoke, Staffordshire,
England
Porcelain, earthenware.
Printed
1950–1962 (1920–
present)
(member of Wedgwood
Group)

I

Royal-Ironstone
MADE IN U.S.A.
•DETERGENT-PROOF,
•OVEN-PROOF
•DISHWASHER-SAFE
•UNDERGLAZE

ROYAL CHINA CO.
Sebring, OH, U.S.A.
Ironstone
ca.1968 (1933–present)

J

ROYAL
SEBRING OHIO
WARRANTED
22-K GOLD

ROYAL CHINA CO.
Sebring, OH, U.S.A.
Semivitreous dinnerware
1934–ca.1960 (1933–
present)

K

ROYAL CHINA
UNDERGLAZE
MADE IN U.S.A.

ROYAL CHINA CO.
Sebring, OH, U.S.A.
Semivitreous ware
ca.1950–ca.1960 (1933–
present)

L

ROYAL CORONA WARE
S.HANCOCK & SONS
STOKE-ON-TRENT
ENGLAND

SAMPSON HANCOCK (&
SONS)
Stoke, Staffordshire,
England
Earthenware. Printed
1912–1937 (1858–1937)

M

DERBY PORCELAIN
WORKS
Derby, England
Porcelain. Printed
ca.1890–1940 (1750–
present)
(Royal Doulton Tableware
Ltd.)

N

Royal Dresdner Art
Carlsbhmn Dreg

SCHUMANN CHINA CORP.
New York, NY, U.S.A.
Porcelain importer's mark
1931–ca.1941 (ca.1918–
ca.1941)

O

MUHLBACH PORCELAIN
FACTORY
Bruchmuhlbach, Palatinate,
Germany (W. Germany)
Porcelain, earthenware
1951–ca.1970 (1951–
present)
(Winterling Group)

P

GÉRARD, DUFRAISSEX &
ABBOT (G.D.A.)
Limoges, France
Porcelain
current (1902–present)
(various names)

A

KERAFINA
Marktredwitz, Bavaria,
Germany (W. Germany)
Porcelain. Overglaze
1950–present (1950–
present)

B

ALFRED COLLEY & CO.
LTD.
Tunstall, Staffordshire,
England
Earthenware. Printed,
impressed
1909–1914 (1909–1914)

C

JOHNSON BROS. LTD.
Hanley & Tunstall,
Staffordshire, England
Earthenware, ironstone.
Printed
ca.1900 + (1883–present)
(member of Wedgwood
Group)

D

WOOD & SON(S) (LTD.)
Burslem, Staffordshire,
England
Earthenware, ironstone.
Printed
1891–1907 (1865–
present)

E

THOMAS POOLE
Longton, Staffordshire,
England
Porcelain, earthenware.
Printed
1912 + (1880–present)
(Royal Stafford China Ltd.)

F

ARTHUR J. WILKINSON
Burslem, Staffordshire,
England
Earthenware, ironstone.
Printed, various pattern
names
ca.1907 (1885–1964 +)

G

GRIMWADES LTD.
Stoke, Staffordshire,
England
Earthenware, majolica
current (1900–present)
(Royal Winton Pottery)

H

ROZENBURG
The Hague, Holland
Porcelain
ca.1885–ca.1919 (1885–
1914 +)

I

K. STEINMANN
Tiefenfurth, Silesia,
Germany (Parowa,
Poland)
Porcelain
ca.1900–1938 (1868–
1938)

J

JAMES SADLER & SONS
(LTD.)
Burslem, Staffordshire,
England
Earthenware, teapots.
Printed
ca.1947–present (ca.1899–
present)

K

SEBRING POTTERY CO.
East Liverpool & Sebring,
OH, U.S.A.
Semivitreous table & toilet
ware
ca.1900 (1887–1948)

L

CHRISTIAN SELTMANN
Erbendorf, Bavaria,
Germany (W. Germany)
Porcelain. Green
underglaze
1946–1975 (1923–
present)
(operating in Weiden)

M

GEORGE C. MURPHY
POTTERY CO.
East Liverpool, OH, U.S.A.
Semivitreous ware,
ironstone
1897–1904 (1897–1901,
1903–1904)

N

SOHO POTTERY
Tunstall, Staffordshire,
England
Earthenware. Printed
ca.1901–1906 (1901–
present)
(Simpsons [Potters] Ltd.)

O

K. STEINMANN
Tiefenfurth, Silesia,
Germany (Parowa,
Poland)
Porcelain
ca.1896–1938 (1868–
1938)

P

K. STEINMANN
Tiefenfurth, Silesia,
Germany (Parowa,
Poland)
Porcelain
1914–1932 (1868–1938)

A

STAFFORDSHIRE
FINE BONE CHINA
OF
ARTHUR BOWKER
MADE IN ENGLAND

ARTHUR BOWKER
Fenton, Staffordshire,
England
Porcelain. Printed
1950–1958 (1948–1958)

B

CROWN STAFFORDSHIRE
PORCELAIN CO. LTD.
Fenton, Staffordshire,
England
Porcelain. Printed
1906+ (1889–present)
(member of Wedgwood
Group)

C

CARL HANS TUPPACK
Tiefenfurth, Silesia,
Germany (Parowa,
Poland)
Porcelain
1922–1935 (1919–1935)

D

STANLEY
FINE BONE CHINA
ENGLAND
EST · 1878

CHARLES AMISON (& CO.
LTD.)
Longton, Staffordshire,
England
Porcelain. Printed
1953–1962 (1889–1962)

E

STOKE POTTERY

GRIMWADES LTD.
Stoke, Staffordshire,
England
Earthenware, majolica, jet.
Printed
ca.1900+ (1900–present)
(Royal Winton Pottery)

F

STONE
CHINA
N°2

HICKS, MEIGH &
JOHNSON
Shelton, Staffordshire,
England
Earthenware, ironstone.
Printed
(1822–1835)

G

TAYLOR & KENT
LONGTON
ENGLAND

TAYLOR & KENT
Longton, Staffordshire,
England
Porcelain. Printed
ca.1912+ (1862–1964+)

H

TK
Thun
CZECHOSLOVAKIA

COUNT THUN'S
PORCELAIN FACTORY/
DUCHCOV PORCELAIN
Klosterle, Bohemia
(Klasterec, Czechoslovakia)
Porcelain, figurines. Green,
blue underglaze
1918–1939 & 1947–
present (1803–present)
(Duchcovsky Porcelain, Dux)

I

TRADE MARK.

R.H.&S.L.PLANT.

R. H. & S. L. PLANT (LTD.)
Longton, Staffordshire,
England
Porcelain. Printed
ca.1898+ (ca.1898–
present)
(Wedgwood-Royal Tuscan
Division)

J

TRENLE ROYAL

UNDERGLAZE **BLUE**

TRENLE CHINA CO.
East Liverpool, OH, U.S.A.
Semivitreous ware
1909–1917 (1909–
ca.1942)

K

TUSCAN
FINE ENGLISH
BONE CHINA
MADE IN
ENGLAND

R. H. & S. L. PLANT (LTD.)
Longton, Staffordshire,
England
Porcelain. Printed, various
pattern names
ca.1947–present (ca.1898–
present)
(Wedgwood-Royal Tuscan
Division)

L

UNTER
WEISS
BACH

UNTERWEISSBACH
PORCELAIN FACTORY
VEB
Unterweissbach, Thuringia,
Germany (E. Germany)
Porcelain, figurines
1959–present (ca.1880–
present)
(various names & owners)

M

VALE CHINA
MADE IN ENGLAND.
H.J.COLCLOUGH
LONGTON.

H. J. COLCLOUGH
Longton, Staffordshire,
England
Porcelain, earthenware.
Printed
1928–1937 (1897–
present)
(Royal Doulton Tableware
Ltd.)

N

VICTORIA
CHINA
CZECHOSLOVAKIA

SCHMIDT & CO.
PORCELAIN FACTORY
(VICTORIA)
Altrohlau, Bohemia (Stara
Role, Czechoslovakia)
Porcelain, earthenware.
Green, blue
1918–1939 (1882–1945)

O

Volkstedt

BEYER & BOCK
Volkstedt, Thuringia,
Germany (E. Germany)
Porcelain, figurines
ca.1931–present (1853–
1960+)
(nationalized in 1960)

P

W.Adams & Sons
England

WILLIAM ADAMS & SONS
LTD.
Tunstall & Stoke,
Staffordshire, England
Earthenware, basalt, jasper,
parian. Printed
1950+ (1769–present)
(member of Wedgwood
Group)

A  J. H. COPE & CO. Longton, Staffordshire, England Porcelain. Printed ca.1906+ (1887–1947)	**B** W. H. GRINDLEY & CO. LTD. Tunstall, Staffordshire, England Earthenware, ironstone. Printed ca.1925 (1880–present)	**C** *Winterling* WINTERLING FINE CERAMICS Bruchmuhlbach, Palatinate, Germany (W. Germany) Earthenware ca.1970–present (ca.1970–present) (Winterling Group)	**D**  WOOD & SON(S) (LTD.) Burslem, Staffordshire, England Earthenware, ironstone. Printed ca.1930+ (1865–present)
E # CROWN & CIRCLE OR OVAL	**F** C. M. HUTSCHEN- REUTHER PORCELAIN FACTORY Selb, Bavaria, Germany (W. Germany) Porcelain 1950–1963 (1814– present) (Hutschenreuther AG)	**G** T. W. BARLOW & SON Longton, Staffordshire, England Earthenware. Printed, impressed 1928–1936 (1882–1940)	**H** ROYAL COPENHAGEN PORCELAIN FACTORY LTD. Copenhagen, Denmark Porcelain. Blue ca.1892 (1775–present)
I EAST END POTTERY CO. (EAST END CHINA CO.) East Liverpool, OH, U.S.A. Semivitreous ware 1894–1908 (1894–1901, 1903–1907)	**J** GOVANCROFT POTTERIES LTD. Glasgow, Scotland Earthenware, stoneware. Printed 1949+ (1913–1964+)	**K** C. M. HUTSCHEN- REUTHER PORCELAIN FACTORY Arzberg, Bavaria, Germany (W. Germany) Porcelain. Green underglaze ca.1918–ca.1945 (1814– present) (Hutschenreuther AG)	**L** KAHLA PORCELAIN FACTORY VEB Kahla, Thuringia, Germany (E. Germany) Porcelain ca.1957–1964 (1954– present) (Kahla Porcelain Combine VEB)
M KARLSKRONA PORCELAIN FACTORY AB Karlskrona, Sweden Porcelain 1918–1942 (1918– present)	**N** METZLER & ORTLOFF Ilmenau, Thuringia, Germany (E. Germany) Porcelain ca.1970+ (1875–present) (Art Porcelain VEB)	**O**  – – – – – – – Japan Porcelain. Stamped, green, blue before 1921 (1891–1921)	**P** MINTON Stoke, Staffordshire, England Porcelain, earthenware. Printed 1862–1871 (1793–present) (Royal Doulton Tableware Ltd.)

A

SOCIETÀ CERAMICA
RICHARD
Milan, Italy
Porcelain, faience
current (1735–present)
(Richard-Ginori)

B

INTERNATIONAL
POTTERY CO.
Trenton, NJ, U.S.A.
White granite, porcelain.
Stamped
1903 + (1860–1940 +)

C

ROYAL COPENHAGEN
PORCELAIN FACTORY,
LTD.
Copenhagen, Denmark
Porcelain. Printed blue
1889 + (1775–present)

D

HOCHST PORCELAIN
MANUFACTORY
Hochst, Hesse, Germany
(W. Germany)
Porcelain. Blue underglaze,
copy of 18th-century
Hochst mark
1947–1964 (1947– present)
(Hochst Porcelain
Manufactory GMBH)

E

FASOLD & STAUCH
Bock-Wallendorf,
Thuringia, Germany (E.
Germany)
Porcelain. Blue
ca.1972 (1903–1972)
and
C.C. PUHLMANN & SON
Darmstadt, Hesse, Germany
(E. Germany)
Porcelain
ca.1977 (ca.1970–ca.1977)

F

WORCESTER ROYAL
PORCELAIN CO. LTD.
Worcester, England
Porcelain
1862–1875 (see date letter
table, page 254) (1862–
present)
(Royal Worcester Spode
Ltd.)

G

WORCESTER ROYAL
PORCELAIN CO. LTD.
Worcester, England
Porcelain
1876–1891 (see date letter
table, page 254, words
"Royal Worcester" added
1891) (1862–present)
(Royal Worcester Spode
Ltd.)

H

C. M. HUTSCHEN-
REUTHER PORCELAIN
FACTORY
Hohenberg, Bavaria,
Germany (W. Germany)
Porcelain
ca.1889 (1814–present)
(Hutschenreuther AG)

I

ADDERLEYS LTD.
Longton, Staffordshire,
England
Porcelain, earthenware.
Printed
1947–1950 (1906–
present)
(Royal Doulton Tableware
Ltd.)

J

TIRSCHENREUTH
PORCELAIN FACTORY
Tirschenreuth, Bavaria,
Germany (W. Germany)
Porcelain
ca.1970 (1838–present)
(Hutschenreuther AG)

K

BISHOP & STONIER
Hanley, Staffordshire,
England
Porcelain, earthenware.
Printed
1899–1936 (1876–1939)

L

BOOTHS
Tunstall, Staffordshire,
England
Earthenware. Printed
1891–1906 (1891–
present)
(Royal Doulton Tableware
Ltd.)

M

BROWN-WESTHEAD,
MOORE & CO.
Hanley, Staffordshire,
England
Earthenware, porcelain.
Printed
1862 + (1862–present)
(various names & owners,
now member of
Wedgwood Group)

N

GEO. BORGFELDT & CO.
New York, NY, U.S.A.
Importer
1936–ca.1976 (1881–
ca.1976)

O

LANCASTER & SONS/
LANCASTER &
SANDLAND LTD.
Hanley, Staffordshire,
England
Earthenware Printed
ca.1935–1964 + (1900–
1964 +)

P

A. G. RICHARDSON & CO.
LTD.
Tunstall & Ferrybridge,
Staffordshire, England
Earthenware. Printed
1916–1972 + (1915–
present)

A

DOULTON & CO.
Burslem, Staffordshire,
   England
Earthenware, porcelain.
   Printed, impressed
1885–1902 (England
   added after 1891) (1853–
   present)
(Royal Doulton Tableware
   Ltd.)

B

FRAUREUTH PORCELAIN
   FACTORY AG
Fraureuth, Saxony,
   Germany (E. Germany)
Porcelain. Blue, green
   underglaze
ca.1898–1935 (ca.1898–
   1935)

C

J. & G. MEAKIN (LTD.)
Hanley, Staffordshire,
   England
Earthenware, ironstone.
   Printed
ca.1890+ (1851–present)
(member of Wedgwood
   Group)

D

JOHN MADDOCK & SONS
   LTD.
Burslem, Staffordshire,
   England
Earthenware, ironstone
ca.1945+ (1855–present)
(Maddock Hotel Ware
   Division of Royal Stafford
   China Ltd.)

E

KIRKLAND & CO.
Tunstall, Staffordshire,
   England
Earthenware. Printed
ca.1938+ (1892–1964+)

F

KPM

ROYAL PORCELAIN
   MANUFACTORY/
   STATE'S PORCELAIN
   MANUFACTORY (KPM)
Berlin, Germany
Porcelain
1832–present (1763–
   present)

G

WANNOPEE POTTERY
   CO.
New Milford, CT, U.S.A.
Porcelain
ca.1900 (1892–1903)

H

KNOWLES, TAYLOR &
   KNOWLES
East Liverpool, OH, U.S.A.
Lotus ware. Printed
1891–ca.1898 (1870–
   1929)

I

KNOWLES, TAYLOR &
   KNOWLES
East Liverpool, OH, U.S.A.
Lotus ware. Printed
1891–ca.1898 (1870–
   1929)

J

MYOTT, SON & CO.
Cobridge/Hanley,
   Staffordshire, England
Earthenware
ca.1930+ (1875–present)
(Myott-Meakin Ltd.)

K

J. FRYER & SON
Tunstall, Staffordshire,
   England
Earthenware. Printed
1954–present (1945–
   present)
(J. Fryer Ltd.)

L

DRESDEN PORCELAIN
   CO.
Longton, Staffordshire,
   England
Porcelain. Printed
1896–1903 (1896–
   1904+)

M

KALK PORCELAIN
   FACTORY
Eisenberg, Thuringia,
   Germany (E. Germany)
Porcelain
ca.1900–present (1863–
   present)
(Special Porcelain
   Eisenberg VEB)

N

W. & E. CORN
Longport, Staffordshire,
   England
Earthenware. Printed
ca.1900–1904 (1864–
   1904)

O

ERDMANN
   SCHLEGELMILCH
Suhl, Thuringia, Germany
   (E. Germany)
Porcelain. Green
ca.1938 (1881–1938)

P

SAMUEL RADFORD (LTD.)
Fenton, Staffordshire,
   England
Porcelain. Printed
ca.1880+ (1879–1957)

A

L. HUTSCHENREUTHER
PORCELAIN FACTORY
Selb, Bavaria, Germany
(W. Germany)
Porcelain. Green underglaze
before 1945 (1857–present)
(Hutschenreuther AG)

B

ROYAL KINRAN CROWN
NIPPON
Japan
Porcelain. Blue, gold, green
(1890–1921)

C

GLASGOW POTTERY
(JOHN MOSES & CO.)
Trenton, NJ, U.S.A.
Toilet & table ware
ca.1900 (1859–1906)

D

CHRISTIAN SELTMANN
PORCELAIN FACTORY
Weiden, Bavaria, Germany
(W. Germany)
Porcelain. Green
underglaze
1954 + (1911–present)

E

FRAUREUTH PORCELAIN
FACTORY AG
Fraureuth, Saxony,
Germany (E. Germany)
Porcelain
ca.1898–ca.1928 (ca.
1898–1935)

F

PFEIFFER &
LOWENSTEIN
Schlackenwerth, Bohemia
(Ostrov, Czechoslovakia)
Porcelain
ca.1914–1918 (1873–
· 1941)

G

THOMAS & CO.
PORCELAIN FACTORY
Sophienthal, Bavaria,
Germany (W. Germany)
Porcelain. Printed,
variations in wording
1937–1957 (1920–present)
(Rosenthal Glass &
Porcelain AG)

H

S. W. DEAN
Burslem, Staffordshire,
England
Earthenware. Printed
1904–1910 (1904–1910)

I

TAYLOR, TUNNICLIFFE &
CO.
Hanley, Staffordshire,
England
Earthenware, porcelain.
Printed
ca.1875–1898 (1868–
1964 +)

J

TIRSCHENREUTH
PORCELAIN FACTORY
Tirschenreuth, Bavaria,
Germany (W. Germany)
Porcelain. Green underglaze
1969–present (1838–
present)
(Hutschenreuther AG)

K

W. & E. CORN
Longport, Staffordshire,
England
Earthenware. Printed
ca.1900–1904 (1864–
1904)

L

SIPIAGIN
Moscow, U.S.S.R.
Porcelain
(1820–1875 +)

M

WILLIAM ADAMS & SONS
LTD.
Tunstall & Stoke,
Staffordshire, England
Earthenware
current (1769–present)
(member of Wedgwood
Group)

N

WILLIAM ADAMS & SONS
LTD.
Tunstall & Stoke,
Staffordshire, England
Earthenware. Impressed
1810–1825 (1769–
present)
(member of Wedgwood
Group)

O

DERBY PORCELAIN
WORKS
Derby, England
Porcelain. Printed
ca.1820–1840 (ca.1750–
present)
(Royal Doulton Tableware
Ltd.)

P

LONGWY FAIENCE CO.
Longwy, France
Art pottery
after 1875 (1798–present)

A

JOHN MADDOCK & SONS LTD.
Burslem, Staffordshire, England
Earthenware, ironstone. Printed
1880–1896 (1855– present)
(Maddock Hotel Ware Division of Royal Stafford China Ltd.)

B

LONGWY FAIENCE CO.
Longwy, France
Art pottery
1890s (1798–present)

C

THOMAS CONE LTD.
Longton, Staffordshire, England
Earthenware
current (1892–present)
(Staffordshire Potteries)

D

GUSTAFSBERG
Gustafsberg, Sweden
Semiporcelain, faience, earthenware
ca.1910 (1825–present)

E

JAMES & RALPH CLEWS
Cobridge, Staffordshire, England
Earthenware. Impressed
ca.1818–1834 (1818–1834)

F

ANDREW STEVENSON
Cobridge, Staffordshire, England
Earthenware. Impressed
ca.1816–1830 (ca.1816–1830)

G

TRENLE CHINA CO.
East Liverpool, OH, U.S.A.
Semivitreous ware
1909–1917 (1909–ca.1942)

H

WILLIAM ADAMS & SONS LTD.
Tunstall & Stoke, Staffordshire, England
Ironstone. Printed, various pattern names
ca.1879–ca.1900 + (1769–present)
(member of Wedgwood Group)

I

ADDERLEYS LTD.
Longton, Staffordshire, England
Porcelain, earthenware. Printed
1912–1926 (1906–present)
(Royal Doulton Tableware Ltd.)

J

ALFRED FENTON & SONS
Hanley, Staffordshire, England
Porcelain, earthenware. Impressed, printed
1887–1901 (1887–1901)

K

A. G. HARLEY JONES
Fenton, Staffordshire, England
Earthenware, porcelain. Printed
ca.1923–1934 (1907–1934)

L

BLAIRS LTD.
Longton, Staffordshire, England
Porcelain. Printed
1914–1930 (1880–1930)

M

OSCAR SCHALLER & CO./ OSCAR SCHALLER & CO. SUCCESSOR
Schwarzenbache-Saale, Bavaria, Germany (W. Germany)
Porcelain
ca.1915 + (1882–present)
(Winterling Group)

N

CHARLES ALLERTON & SONS
Longton, Staffordshire, England
Porcelain, earthenware. Printed
ca.1890 + (1859–1942)

O

EMIL FISCHER
Budapest, Hungary
Porcelain
ca.1870 + (1866–1980 +)

P

BURGESS BROS.
Longton, Staffordshire, England
Earthenware. Printed
1922–1939 (1922–1939)

A

ENGLAND

BURSLEM POTTERY CO.
LTD.
Burslem, Staffordshire,
England
Earthenware. Printed
1894–1933 (1894–1933)

B

BROWN-WESTHEAD,
MOORE & CO.
Hanley, Staffordshire,
England
Earthenware, porcelain.
Printed, various patterns
1869–1904 (1862–present)
(various names & owners,
now member of
Wedgwood Group)

C

CARL KNOLL PORCELAIN
FACTORY KARLSBAD
Fischern, Bohemia (Rybare,
Czechoslovakia)
Porcelain. Impressed blue,
green
ca.1900+ (1848–1945)

D

BIRKS, RAWLINS & CO.
Stoke, Staffordshire,
England
Porcelain. Printed, year
varies
1900+ (1900–1933)

E

CLINCHFIELD POTTERY/
SOUTHERN
POTTERIES, INC.
Erwin, TN, U.S.A.
Dinnerware
ca.1920–1930 (1917–
1957)

F

THOMAS MORRIS
Longton, Staffordshire,
England
Porcelain. Printed
ca.1912+ (1892–1941)

G

WILLIAM ADAMS & SONS
LTD.
Tunstall & Stoke,
Staffordshire, England
Earthenware. Printed
ca.1879–ca.1900+ (1769–
present)
(member of Wedgwood
Group)

H

W. DAVENPORT & CO.
Longport, Staffordshire,
England
Porcelain
ca.1830–1840 (ca.1793–
1887)

I

KELLER & GUÉRIN
Luneville, France
Porcelain
1889+ (ca.1788–1890+)

J

UNWIN, HOLMES &
WORTHINGTON
Hanley, Staffordshire,
England
Earthenware. Printed,
various pattern names
ca.1865–1868 (ca.1865–
1868)

K

DURA PORCELAIN CO.
LTD.
Hanley, Staffordshire,
England
Porcelain. Printed
1919–1921 (1919–1921)

L

WILHELM & REINHOLD
BORDOLO BROTHERS
Grunstadt, Palatinate,
Germany (W. Germany)
Earthenware
ca.1887+ (1812–
ca.1900+)

M

F. HANCOCK & CO.
Stoke, Staffordshire,
England
Earthenware. Printed
1899–1900 (1899–1900)

N

FREDERICK MALKIN
Burslem, Staffordshire,
England
Earthenware. Printed
ca.1900–1905 (1891–
1905)

O

JAMES SMITH
Stoke, Staffordshire,
England
Porcelain, earthenware.
Printed
ca.1898–1922 (1898–
1924)

P

VILLEROY & BOCH
Mettlach, Saar, Germany
(W. Germany)
Earthenware. Stamped
blue, violet
ca.1855–ca.1870 (1813–
present)
(various names, owners, &
locations)

A

J. & G. MEAKIN (LTD.)
Hanley, Staffordshire,
England
Earthenware, ironstone.
Printed
ca.1890 + (1851–present)
(member of Wedgwood
Group)

B

J. & G. MEAKIN (LTD.)
Hanley, Staffordshire,
England
Earthenware, ironstone.
Printed
ca.1907 + (1851–present)
(member of Wedgwood
Group)

C

JOHN MEIR & SON
Tunstall, Staffordshire,
England
Earthenware. Printed,
impressed, various
pattern names
1837–1897 (1837–1897)

D

JOHN HEATH DAVIS
Hanley, Staffordshire,
England
Earthenware. Printed
ca.1881–1891 (1881–
1891)

E

THOMAS G. BOOTH
Tunstall, Staffordshire,
England
Earthenware. Printed
1876–1883 (1876–
present)
(Royal Doulton Tableware
Ltd.)

F

KALK PORCELAIN
FACTORY
Eisenberg, Thuringia,
Germany (E. Germany)
Porcelain
1900 + (1863–present)
(Special Porcelain
Eisenberg VEB)

G

PODMORE CHINA CO.
Hanley, Staffordshire,
England
Porcelain. Printed
1921–1941 (1921–1941)

H

FAIENCE
MANUFACTURING CO.
Greenpoint, NY, U.S.A.
Art pottery, majolica.
Printed
ca.1890 + (1880–1892)

I

RALPH HAMMERSLEY (&
SON)
Burslem, Staffordshire,
England
Earthenware
1868 + (1860–1905)

J

RIDGWAYS
Hanley, Staffordshire,
England
Earthenware. Printed
ca.1912 (1879–present)
(Royal Doulton Tableware
Ltd.)

K

ROPER & MEREDITH
Longton, Staffordshire,
England
Earthenware. Printed
1913–1924 (1913–1924)

L

JOHN RIDGWAY (& CO.)
Shelton, Hanley,
Staffordshire, England
Earthenware, porcelain,
various pattern names
1841 + (ca.1830–present)
(Royal Doulton Tableware
Ltd.)

M

WILLIAM ADAMS & SONS
LTD.
Tunstall & Stoke,
Staffordshire, England
Ironstone. Printed, various
pattern names
1879–ca.1900 + (1769–
present)
(member of Wedgwood
Group)

N

THE SPHINX (PETRUS
REGOUT)
Maastricht, Holland
Faience
1891 + (1836–1931 +)

O

STEVENSON, SHARP &
CO.
Derby, England
Porcelain
ca.1859 (1859–1863)

P

BIRKS, RAWLINS & CO.
Stoke, Staffordshire,
England
Porcelain. Printed
ca.1917 + (1900–1933)

A

WILLIAM HUDSON
Longton, Staffordshire,
England
Porcelain. Printed
1892–1912 (1889–
present)
(Hudson & Middleton)

B

T. RATHBONE & CO.
Tunstall, Staffordshire,
England
Earthenware. Various
pattern names
ca.1898 (1898–1923)

C

UPPER HANLEY POTTERY
CO.
Hanley & Cobridge,
Staffordshire, England
Earthenware. Printed,
variations in wording
1895–1910 (1895–1910)

D

W. H. ROBINSON
Longton, Staffordshire,
England
Porcelain. Printed
1901–1904 (1901–1904)

E

WILTON & ROBINSON/
CARLTON WARE LTD.
Stoke, Staffordshire,
England
Earthenware
ca.1894 (1890–present)

F

WEDGWOOD & CO.
Tunstall, Staffordshire,
England
Earthenware, stoneware.
Printed, various pattern
names
ca.1908+ (1860–present)
(member of Wedgwood
Group)

G

YNYSMEDW POTTERY
Swansea, Wales
Ironstone
ca.1840–1870+ (1840–
1870+)

H

GLOBE POTTERY CO.
East Liverpool, OH, U.S.A.
Semivitreous ware
ca.1900 (1881–1901,
1907–1912)

I

JAMES KENT (LTD.)
Longton, Staffordshire,
England
Porcelain, earthenware.
Printed
ca.1913+ (1897–present)

J

MINTON
Stoke, Staffordshire,
England
Porcelain, earthenware
ca.1873+ (1793–present)
(Royal Doulton Tableware
Ltd.)

K

E. HUGHES & CO./
HUGHES (FENTON)
LTD.
Fenton, Staffordshire,
England
Porcelain. Printed
1912–1941 (1889–1953)

L

W. H. GRINDLEY & CO.
LTD.
Tunstall, Staffordshire,
England
Earthenware, ironstone.
Printed
1925+ (1880–present)

M

JAMES KENT (LTD.)
Longton, Staffordshire,
England
Porcelain, earthenware.
Printed
ca.1910 (1897–present)

N

JAMES KENT (LTD.)
Longton, Staffordshire,
England
Earthenware
current (1897–present)

O

WILD & ADAMS (LTD.)
Longton, Staffordshire,
England
Earthenware
ca.1909+ (1909–1927)

P

GRIMWADES LTD.
Stoke, Staffordshire,
England
Earthenware. Various
pattern names
ca.1906+ (1900–present)
(Royal Winton Pottery)

A

GLOBE POTTERY CO.
LTD.
Cobridge, Staffordshire,
England
Earthenware. Printed
1917+ (1914–1964+)
(various names & owners)

B

W.T.H. SMITH (LTD.)
Longport, Staffordshire,
England
Earthenware. Printed
1898–1905 (1898–1905)

C

JOHN MORTLOCK
London, England
Retailer
ca.1885 (1746–1930)

D

BARRATT'S OF
STAFFORDSHIRE LTD.
Burslem, Staffordshire,
England
Earthenware. Printed
1945+ (1895–present)

E

MINTON
Stoke, Staffordshire,
England
Porcelain, earthenware.
Printed
ca.1912–1950 (1793–
present)
(Royal Doulton Tableware
Ltd.)

F

PEARL POTTERY CO.
Hanley, Staffordshire,
England
Earthenware. Printed
1912+ (1894–1936)

G

CLEMENTSON BROS.
LTD.
Hanley, Staffordshire,
England
Earthenware. Printed
1901–1913 (1865–1916)

H

ALFRED MEAKIN (LTD.)
Tunstall, Staffordshire,
England
Earthenware
ca.1907+ (1873–present)
(Myott-Meakin Ltd.)

I

HAMMERSLEY & CO.
Longton, Staffordshire,
England
Porcelain. Printed
current (1887–present)
(Royal Worcester Spode
Ltd.)

J

CLASSIC ROSE
COLLECTION
ROSENTHAL GROUP
GERMANY
ROSENTHAL GLASS &
PORCELAIN AG
Selb, Bavaria, Germany (W.
Germany)
Porcelain, earthenware.
Green underglaze
1969–1981+ (1879–
present)

K

CHELSEA ART POTTERY
H&G
BURSLEM ENGLAND
HOLLINSHEAD &
GRIFFITHS
Burslem, Staffordshire,
England
Earthenware. Printed
1890–1909 (1890–1909)

L

BONE CHINA
Colclough
MADE IN ENGLAND
A PRODUCT OF
RIDGWAY POTTERIES LTD
RIDGWAY POTTERIES
LTD.
Stoke, Staffordshire,
England
Earthenware
ca.1962 (1955–present)
(Royal Doulton Tableware
Ltd.)

M

COPELAND & GARRETT
Stoke, Staffordshire,
England
Porcelain, earthenware
1833–1847 (1833–
present)
(Royal Worcester Spode
Ltd.)

N

CROWN
DORSET
CROWN DORSET
POTTERY
Poole, Dorset, England
Pottery. Impressed
ca.1920–1937 (ca.1900–
1937)

O

F. & R. PRATT & CO.
Fenton, Staffordshire,
England
Earthenware. Printed
ca.1847–1860 (ca.1818–
present)
(member of Wedgwood
Group)

P

FINE BONE CHINA
CROWN
EST. 1801
STAFFORDSHIRE
ENGLAND
CROWN STAFFORDSHIRE
PORCELAIN CO. LTD.
Fenton, Staffordshire,
England
Porcelain. Printed
ca.1930–present (1889–
present)
(member of Wedgwood
Group)

A

HAMMERSLEY & CO.
Longton, Staffordshire,
England
Porcelain. Printed
1939–1964 + (1887–
present)
(Royal Worcester Spode
Ltd.)

B

HUTSCHENREUTHER AG
Selb, Bavaria, Germany (W.
Germany)
Porcelain
ca.1976–present (1969–
present)

C

SVEND JENSEN
Ringsted, Denmark
Limited edition plates
1973 + (1970–present)
(Desiree Denmark)

D

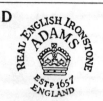

WILLIAM ADAMS & SONS
LTD.
Tunstall & Stoke,
Staffordshire, England
Earthenware, basalt. Printed
1962 + (1769–present)
(member of Wedgwood
Group)

E

ROYAL COPENHAGEN
PORCELAIN FACTORY,
LTD.
Copenhagen, Denmark
Porcelain. Green
1897–1922 (1775–
present)

F

ROYAL COPENHAGEN
PORCELAIN FACTORY,
LTD.
Copenhagen, Denmark
Porcelain. Green
1922–present (1775–
present)

G

ROYAL CROWN DERBY
Derby, England
Porcelain
1975 + (1750–present)
(Royal Doulton Tableware
Ltd.)

H

HUDSON & MIDDLETON
LTD.
Longton, Staffordshire,
England
Porcelain
current (1941–present)

I

KIRKLAND & CO.
Etruria, Staffordshire,
England
Earthenware. Printed
1892 + (1892–1964 +)

J

CHAPMANS LONGTON
LTD.
Longton, Staffordshire,
England
Porcelain. Printed
1930–1949 (1916–
1964 +)

K

CHARLES AMISON (& CO.
LTD.)
Longton, Staffordshire,
England
Porcelain. Printed
1930–1941 (1889–1962)

L

KARLSKRONA
PORCELAIN FACTORY
AB
Karlskrona, Sweden
Porcelain. Variations in
wording
1933–1968 (1918–1968)

M

ALKA-KUNST ALBOTH &
KAISER
Staffelstein, Bavaria,
Germany (W. Germany)
Porcelain
1927–ca.1953 (1872–
present)
(Kaiser Porcelain)

N

BING & GRONDAHL
Copenhagen, Denmark
Porcelain
current (1853–present)

O

COPELAND & GARRETT
Stoke, Staffordshire,
England
Porcelain, parian,
earthenware
1833–1846 (1833–
present)
(Royal Worcester Spode
Ltd.)

P

FORD & SONS (LTD.)/
FORD & SONS
(CROWNFORD) LTD.
Burslem, Staffordshire,
England
Earthenware. Printed
1930s (ca.1893–1964 +)

A LINDNER PORCELAIN FACTORY KG Kups, Bavaria, Germany (W. Germany) Porcelain 1970–present (1932–present)	**B** **ENGLAND** MOORE (BROS.) Longton, Staffordshire, England Porcelain. Printed 1902–1905 (1872–1905)	**C** OSCAR SCHLEGELMILCH PORCELAIN FACTORY Langewiesen, Thuringia, Germany (E. Germany) Porcelain. Blue, gold, green ca.1950–ca.1972 (1892–present) (subsidiary of Porcelain Combine Colditz VEB)	**D**  ALFRED MEAKIN (LTD.) Tunstall, Staffordshire, England Earthenware ca.1891+ (1873–present) (Myott-Meakin Ltd.)
E FORD & SONS (CROWNFORD) LTD. Burslem, Staffordshire, England Earthenware. Printed ca.1961–1964+ (ca.1938–1964+)	**F** **WARRANTED** EDWIN BENNETT POTTERY CO. Baltimore, MD, U.S.A. Semiporcelain 1897–1904+ (1856–1936)	**G** **DUCHESS** **BONE CHINA** *Made in England* A. T. FINNEY & SONS (LTD.) Longton, Staffordshire, England Porcelain 1961–present (1947–present)	**H** **ENGLAND.** A. G. HARLEY JONES Fenton, Staffordshire, England Earthenware, porcelain. Printed ca.1907+ (1907–1934)
I  GEO. BORGFELDT & CO. New York, NY, U.S.A. Importer ca.1978 (1881–ca.1976)	**J** MALING POTTERY Newcastle upon Tyne, Northumberland, England Willowware. Printed ca.1930 (1762–1963)	**K** CROWN STAFFORDSHIRE PORCELAIN CO. LTD. Fenton, Staffordshire, England Porcelain. Printed 1889–1912 (1889–present) (member of Wedgwood Group)	**L** VON SCHIERHOLZ'S PORCELAIN MANUFACTORY PLAUE GMBH Plaue, Thuringia, Germany (E. Germany) Porcelain ca.1967–1972 (1900–present) (Porcelain Manufactory Plaue VEB)
M IMPERIAL FACTORY, ALEXANDER II St. Petersburg, Russia (Leningrad, U.S.S.R.) Porcelain. Blue (1855–1881)	**N** T. & R. BOOTE, LTD. Burslem, Staffordshire, England Earthenware. Printed 1890–1906 (1842–1964+)	**O** G. L. ASHWORTH & BROS. Hanley, Staffordshire, England Earthenware, ironstone. Printed, various pattern names 1862–ca.1890 (1784–present) (member of Wedgwood Group)	**P** COPELAND W. T. COPELAND (& SONS LTD.) Stoke, Staffordshire, England Porcelain, parian, earthenware 1850–1867 (1847–present) (Royal Worcester Spode Ltd.)

A

COPELAND & GARRETT
Stoke, Staffordshire,
England
Porcelain, parian,
earthenware. Printed
ca.1833–1847 (1833–
present)
(Royal Worcester Spode
Ltd.)

B

STERLING CHINA CO.
Wellsville, OH, U.S.A.
Porcelain
current (1917–present)
(Scammell China Co.
purchased by Sterling in
1954)

C

J. & M. P. BELL
Glasgow, Scotland
Earthenware, parian.
Printed
ca.1850–1870 (1842–
1928)

D

L. HUTSCHENREUTHER
PORCELAIN FACTORY
Selb, Bavaria, Germany (W.
Germany)
Porcelain
ca.1956 + (1857–present)
(Hutschenreuther AG)

E

MINTON
Stoke, Staffordshire,
England
Porcelain. Printed
ca.1951–present (1793–
present)
(Royal Doulton Tableware
Ltd.)

F

KALK PORCELAIN
FACTORY
Eisenberg, Thuringia,
Germany (E. Germany)
Porcelain. Green underglaze
ca.1945–1972 (1863–
present)
(Special Porcelain
Eisenberg VEB)

G

PORCELAIN UNION
UNITED PORCELAIN
FACTORIES AG
Klosterle, Bohemia
(Klasterec,
Czechoslovakia)
Porcelain
1921–1927 (1921–1927)

H

CROWN & SHIELD

I

VIENNA PORCELAIN
FACTORY AUGARTEN
AG (ROYAL VIENNA)
Vienna, Austria
Porcelain
1923–1981 + (1922–
present)

J

ROYAL PORCELAIN
MANUFACTORY
NYMPHENBURG
Nymphenburg, Bavaria,
Germany (W. Germany)
Porcelain. Blue underglaze
1890–1895 (1747–present)
(State's Porcelain
Manufactory
Nymphenburg Albert
Bauml)

K

GEYER, KOERBITZ & CO.
Eisenberg, Thuringia,
Germany (E. Germany)
Earthenware
1882–1904 (1882–1904)

L

SPRINGER & CO.
Elbogen, Bohemia (Loket,
Czechoslovakia)
Porcelain. Blue, green
underglaze, impressed
ca.1891–1918 (1815–
1945)
(various names & owners)

M

VON SCHIERHOLZ'S
PORCELAIN
MANUFACTORY PLAUE
GMBH
Plaue, Thuringia, Germany
(E. Germany)
Porcelain. Blue, green
underglaze
ca.1907 + (1900–present)
(Porcelain Manufactory
Plaue VEB)

N

MORITZ FISCHER
Herend, Hungary
Porcelain. Blue enamel
1900–1934 (1839–
1948 +)

O

GEROLD & CO. NEW
PORCELAIN FACTORY
TETTAU/GEROLD &
CO. PORCELAIN
FACTORY
Tettau, Bavaria, Germany
(W. Germany)
Porcelain
1948–1981 + (1937–
present)

P

GRAND DUCAL MAJOLICA
MANUFACTORY/
STATE'S MAJOLICA
MANUFACTORY
Karlsruhe, Badenia,
Germany (W. Germany)
Earthenware, porcelain,
majolica. Printed,
impressed
1901 + (1901–present)

A

BROS. METZEL
PORCELAIN FACTORY
KONITZ
Konitz, Thuringia, Germany
(E. Germany)
Porcelain
ca.1909–ca.1945 (1909–
present)
(United Porcelainworks
Kahla-Konitz VEB)

B

LUDWIG WESSEL
Bonn, Rhineland, Germany
(W. Germany)
Porcelain
ca.1887–1907 (1825–
present)
(Wessel Ceramic Works
AG)

C

OLDEST VOLKSTEDT
PORCELAIN FACTORY
Volkstedt, Thuringia,
Germany (E. Germany)
Porcelain. Blue underglaze,
overglaze
ca.1915–1981 + (1760–
present)
(various names & owners)

D

ERNST WAHLISS
ALEXANDRA
PORCELAIN WORKS
Turn-Teplitz, Bohemia
(Trnovany,
Czechoslovakia)
Porcelain
ca.1905–ca.1921 (1894–
1934)

E

ARABIA PORCELAIN
FACTORY
Helsingfors (Helsinki),
Finland
Porcelain, stoneware.
Stamped
1890–1910 (1874–present)
(Upsala-Ekeby Group)

F

ANTON LANG
Budau, Bohemia (Budov,
Czechoslovakia)
Porcelain. Impressed
1860–1880 (1860–1880)
(1825–1860, Franz Lang)

G

BEYER & BOCK
Volkstedt, Thuringia,
Germany (E. Germany)
Porcelain. Impressed, green
underglaze, overglaze
ca.1905–ca.1931 (1853–
1960 +)
(nationalized in 1960)

H

FISCHER, BRUCE & CO.
Philadelphia, PA, U.S.A.
Importer
1933–1940, 1949–present
(1933–present)

I

BOHEMIA CERAMIC
WORKS AG
Neurohlau, Bohemia (Nova
Role, Czechoslovakia)
Porcelain
ca.1937–1945 (1921–
1945)

J

B. BLOCH & CO.
Eichwald, Bohemia (Dubi,
Czechoslovakia)
Porcelain. Blue, green
underglaze
ca.1915–ca.1920 (1871–
1945)

K

PORTMEIRION
POTTERIES LTD.
Stoke, Staffordshire,
England
Earthenware
current (1962–present)

L

FISCHER & CO.
PORCELAIN FACTORY
& DECORATING SHOP
GMBH
Oeslau, Bavaria, Germany
(W. Germany)
1950–ca.1975 (1950–
present)
(W. Goebel Porcelain
Factory)

M

C. M. HUTSCHEN-
REUTHER PORCELAIN
FACTORY
Hohenberg, Bavaria,
Germany (W. Germany)
Porcelain
ca.1904 + (1814–present)
(Hutschenreuther AG)

N

SAXONIAN PORCELAIN
FACTORY
Potschappel, Saxony,
Germany (E. Germany)
Porcelain
ca.1913 + (1872–1972)
(various names)

O

NEW ENGLAND POTTERY
CO.
Boston, MA, U.S.A.
Semiporcelain. Red
overglaze
1889–1895 (1854–1914)

P

EBELING & REUSS CO.
Devon, PA, U.S.A.
Importer
1955–present (1866–
present)

A

ERNST WAHLISS
ALEXANDRA
PORCELAIN WORKS
Turn-Teplitz, Bohemia
(Trnovany,
Czechoslovakia)
Porcelain
ca.1899–ca.1918 (1894–
1934)
(various names)

B

HUTSCHENREUTHER AG
Selb, Bavaria, Germany (W.
Germany)
Porcelain
ca.1975+ (1969–present)

C

SCHMIDT & CO.
PORCELAIN FACTORY
(VICTORIA)
Altohlau, Bohemia (Stara
Role, Czechoslovakia)
Porcelain
ca.1904–ca.1945 (1883–
1945)

D

GLORIA ANTON WEIDL
PORCELAIN
MANUFACTORY
Bayreuth, Bavaria, Germany
(W. Germany)
Porcelain. Blue overglaze
1947–1981+ (1947–
present)

E

GOSSE
Bayeux, France
Porcelain. Blue
1849–1878 (1849–1878)
(various names)

F

HEBER & CO. PORCELAIN
FACTORY
Neustadt, Bavaria, Germany
(W. Germany)
Porcelain
1900–1922 (1900–1922)

G

JAMES KENT (LTD.)
Longton, Staffordshire,
England
Porcelain, earthenware
ca.1901+ (1897–present)

H

KRAUTHEIM &
ADELBERG PORCELAIN
FACTORY GMBH
Selb, Bavaria, Germany (W.
Germany)
Porcelain. Printed
ca.1912–ca.1930+ (1884–
present)

I

SCHONWALD PORCELAIN
FACTORY
Schonwald, Bavaria,
Germany (W. Germany)
Porcelain
1911–1927 (1898–
present)
(Hutschenreuther AG)

J

PAUL MULLER
PORCELAIN FACTORY
Selb, Bavaria, Germany (W.
Germany)
Porcelain
1920–1928 (1890–
ca.1957)

K

ROYAL PORCELAIN GMBH
Kups, Bavaria, Germany
(W. Germany)
Porcelain
1972–1981+ (1972–
present)

L

LIMOGES-CASTEL
Limoges, France
Porcelain
1979+ (1944–1980+)

M

SCHAFER & VATER
PORCELAIN FACTORY
Rudolstadt, Thuringia,
Germany (E. Germany)
Porcelain
ca.1896–ca.1962 (1890–
ca.1962)

N

ROYAL FABRIQUE
FONTEBASSO
Treviso, Venezia, Italy
Ceramics
ca.1860+ (1860–1873+)

O

ROBERT HANKE
PORCELAIN FACTORY
Ladowitz, Bohemia
(Ledvice,
Czechoslovakia)
Porcelain. Red overglaze
ca.1900–ca.1918 (1882–
1945)

P

A. B. JONES & SONS
(LTD.)
Longton, Staffordshire,
England
Porcelain, earthenware.
Printed
ca.1957–present (1900–
present)
(Royal Grafton Bone China)

A

A. B. JONES & SONS
(LTD.)
Longton, Staffordshire,
England
Porcelain, earthenware.
Printed
ca.1949 + (1900–present)
(Royal Grafton Bone China)

B

NEW YORK &
RUDOLSTADT
POTTERY
Rudolstadt, Thuringia,
Germany (E. Germany)
Ceramics
ca.1887–ca.1918 (1882–
1918)

C

PALISSY POTTERY LTD.
Longton, Staffordshire,
England
Bone china
current (1946–present)
(Royal Worcester Spode
Ltd.)

D

NEW YORK &
RUDOLSTADT
POTTERY (ROYAL
RUDOLSTADT)
Rudolstadt, Thuringia,
Germany (E. Germany)
Porcelain
ca.1900–ca.1918 (1882–
1918)

E

ERDMANN
SCHLEGELMILCH
PORCELAIN FACTORY
Suhl, Thuringia, Germany
(E. Germany)
Porcelain. Printed, green
1881–ca.1925 (1881–
1938)

F

E. & A. MÜLLER
PORCELAIN FACTORY
Schwarza-Saale, Thuringia,
Germany (W. Germany)
Porcelain
ca.1895 + (1890–ca.1945)

G

COUNT THUN'S
PORCELAIN FACTORY
Klosterle, Bohemia
(Klasterec,
Czechoslovakia)
Porcelain. Green underglaze
1895–ca.1945 (1803–
present)
(Duchcovsky Porcelain, Dux)

H

WARDLE & CO. (LTD.)
Hanley, Staffordshire,
England
Earthenware, parian.
Printed
ca.1890–1935 (1871–
1935)

I

W. WOOD & CO.
Burslem, Staffordshire,
England
Earthenware. Printed
1915–1932 (1873–1932)

J

GEORG SCHMIDER
UNITED CERAMIC
FACTORIES ZELL
Zell on Harmersbach,
Badenia, Germany (W.
Germany)
Earthenware, porcelain
ca.1924 (1907–present)

K

ARABIA PORCELAIN
FACTORY
Helsingfors (Helsinki),
Finland
Porcelain, stoneware.
Export stamp
1880–1910 (1874– present)
(Upsala-Ekeby Group)

L

ARABIA PORCELAIN
FACTORY
Helsingfors (Helsinki),
Finland
Porcelain, stoneware. Color
stamp
1893–1907 (1874–
present)
(Upsala-Ekeby Group)

M

ARABIA PORCELAIN
FACTORY
Helsingfors (Helsinki),
Finland
Porcelain, stoneware. Color
stamp
1878–1910 (1874–
present)
(Upsala-Ekeby Group)

N

ARABIA PORCELAIN
FACTORY
Helsingfors (Helsinki),
Finland
Porcelain, stoneware. Color
stamp
1890–1910 (1874–
present)
(Upsala-Ekeby Group)

O

BAREUTHER & CO.
PORCELAIN FACTORY
WALDSASSEN AG
Waldsassen, Bavaria,
Germany (W. Germany)
Porcelain
ca.1966–1981 + (1866–
present)

P

FRANZ NEUKIRCHNER
PORCELAIN
MANUFACTORY
Marktredwitz, Bavaria,
Germany (W. Germany)
Porcelain
1916–1977 (1916–1981 +)

A

ARZBERG PORCELAIN
FACTORY
Arzberg, Bavaria, Germany
(W. Germany)
Porcelain. Green underglaze
1927–1981 + (1890–
present)
(various names & owners,
now Hutschenreuther AG)

B

BAREUTHER & CO.
PORCELAIN FACTORY
WALDSASSEN AG
Waldsassen, Bavaria,
Germany (W. Germany)
Porcelain
ca.1931–ca.1950 (1866–
present)

C

BOCH FRÈRES
Hainault, Belgium &
Septfontaines,
Luxembourg
Art pottery, domestic ware.
Printed, impressed
before 1891 (1841–
present)

D

SAMUEL KEELING & CO.
Hanley, Staffordshire,
England
Earthenware. Printed,
various pattern names
1840–1850 (1840–1850)

E

BOOTHS
Tunstall, Staffordshire,
England
Earthenware. Printed
1912 + (1891–present)
(Royal Doulton Tableware
Ltd.)

F

UTZCHNEIDER
Sarreguemines, France
Porcelain, faience. Printed
ca.1965 (ca.1770–present)

G

LONGWY FAIENCE CO.
Longwy, France
Art pottery, faience
ca.1920–1940 (1798–
present)

H

SPRINGER & CO.
Elbogen, Bohemia (Loket,
Czechoslovakia)
Porcelain. Green, blue
underglaze
ca.1910–1920 (1815–
1945)
(various names & owners)

I

SCHONWALD PORCELAIN
FACTORY/E. & A.
MULLER PORCELAIN
FACTORY
Schonwald, Bavaria,
Germany (W. Germany)
ca.1911–ca.1945 (1898–
present)
(under various names, now
Hutschenreuther AG)

J

MADDOCK & SEDDON/
JOHN MADDOCK
Burslem, Staffordshire,
England
Earthenware. Printed
ca.1839–1855 (ca.1839–
present)
(Maddock Hotel Ware
Division of Royal Stafford
China Ltd.)

K

GIBSON & SONS
Burslem, Staffordshire,
England
Earthenware
ca.1930 + (1885–1972 +)

L

W. H. GRINDLEY & CO.
LTD.
Tunstall, Staffordshire,
England
Earthenware, ironstone.
Printed
ca.1954–1960 + (1880–
present)

M

C. M. HUTSCHEN-
REUTHER PORCELAIN
FACTORY
Hohenberg, Bavaria,
Germany (W. Germany)
Porcelain. Green, black
1914 + (1814–present)
(Hutschenreuther AG)

N

ILMENAU PORCELAIN
FACTORY AG
Ilmenau, Thuringia,
Germany (E. Germany)
Porcelain. Green underglaze
1929–ca.1938 (1777–
present)
(various names & owners,
now Henneberg
Porcelain VEB)

O

ILMENAU PORCELAIN
FACTORY AG
Ilmenau, Thuringia,
Germany (E. Germany)
Porcelain
ca.1934–1973 (1777–
present
(various names & owners,
now Henneberg
Porcelain VEB)

P

LUDWIG WESSEL
Bonn, Rhineland, Germany
(W. Germany)
Porcelain, earthenware
ca.1893 + (1825–present)
(Wessel Ceramic Works
AG)

A

KELLER & GUÉRIN
Luneville, France
Faience, art pottery
1891 + (ca.1788–1890 +)

B

EDMUND KRUGER
PORCELAIN FACTORY
Blankenhain, Thuringia,
Germany (E. Germany)
Porcelain
ca.1900–1937 (1847–
1937)

C

HINRICHS & CO.
New York, NY, U.S.A.
Porcelain importers
ca.1880–1891

D

LONGWY FAIENCE CO.
Longwy, France
Art pottery, faience
after 1891 (1798–present)

E

MADDOCK POTTERY CO.
Trenton, NJ, U.S.A.
White granite
ca.1904 (1893–ca.1929)

F

JAMES KENT (LTD.)
Longton, Staffordshire,
England
Porcelain, earthenware
ca.1897–1901 (1897–
present)

G

LUDWIGSBURG
PORCELAIN
MANUFACTORY GMBH
Ludwigsburg, Wurttemberg,
Germany (W. Germany)
Porcelain. Blue underglaze
1948–1981 + (1918–
present)
(various names & owners)

H

PILLIVUYT & CO.
Foecy, France
Porcelain. Green
1850–1883 (1830–
present)

I

MERCER POTTERY CO.
Trenton, NJ, U.S.A.
Semiporcelain,
semivitreous ware.
Printed
ca.1902 (1868–ca.1937)

J

MYOTT, SON & CO.
Stoke Staffordshire,
England
Earthenware. Printed
ca.1898–1902 (1875–
present)
(Myott-Meakin Ltd.)

K

SOCIETÀ CERAMICA
RICHARD
Milan, Italy
Porcelain. Printed
ca.1920 (1735–present)
(Richard-Ginori)

L

ROYAL PORCELAIN
MANUFACTORY
NYMPHENBURG/
STATE'S PORCELAIN
MANUFACTORY
NYMPHENBURG
(ALBERT BAUML)
Nymphenburg, Bavaria,
Germany (W. Germany)
Porcelain
ca.1895 + (1747–present)
(various names & owners)

M

SOCIETÀ CERAMICA
RICHARD
Milan, Italy
Porcelain, faience
1880 + (1735–present)
(Richard-Ginori)

N

LICHTENSTERN BROS.
Wilhelmsburg, Austria
Earthenware
1890–1910 (1795–present)
(various names & owners,
now Ospag Austrian
Sanitary Ceramic &
Porcelain Industry AG)

O

RÖRSTRAND PORCELAIN
FACTORY
Rörstrand, Sweden
Faience, porcelain.
Impressed
1878 + (1726–present)
(Rörstrand AB)

P

EBELING & REUSS CO.
Devon, PA. U.S.A.
Importer
current (1866–present)

A

LAUGHLIN BROS.
East Liverpool, OH, U.S.A.
Ironstone
1873–1877 (ca.1870–
present)

B

ARNO FISCHER
PORCELAIN FACTORY
Ilmenau, Thuringia,
Germany (E. Germany)
Porcelain
ca.1907–1952 (1907–
present)
(Ilmenau Decorative &
Promotional Porcelain
Factory VEB)

C

BAVARIA
TIRSCHENREUTH
TIRSCHENREUTH
PORCELAIN FACTORY
Tirschenreuth, Bavaria,
Germany (W. Germany)
Porcelain
ca.1903–1981+ (1838–
present)
(Hutschenreuther AG)

D

R. H. PLANT & CO.
Longton, Staffordshire,
England
Porcelain. Printed
1898–1906 (1881–
present)
(Wedgwood, Royal Tuscan
Division)

E

RIDGWAYS (BEDFORD
WORKS) LTD.
Stoke, Staffordshire,
England
Earthenware
ca.1950 (1920–present)
(Royal Doulton Tableware
Ltd.)

F

FRANZ ANTON MEHLEM
EARTHENWARE
FACTORY
Bonn, Rhineland, Germany
(W. Germany)
Earthenware, porcelain.
Variations in wording
1888–ca.1920 (1836–1920)

G

OSCAR SCHALLER & CO.
SUCCESSOR
Windischeschenbach,
Bavaria, Germany (W.
Germany)
Porcelain
1950–1981+ (1918–
present)
(Winterling Group)

H

H. J. COLCLOUGH
Longton, Staffordshire,
England
Porcelain, earthenware.
Printed
1908–1928 (1897– present)
(Royal Doulton Tableware
Ltd.)

I

C. M. HUTSCHEN-
REUTHER PORCELAIN
FACTORY
Hohenberg, Bavaria,
Germany (W. Germany)
Porcelain. Export mark
1946–1981+ (1814–
present)
(Hutschenreuther AG)

J

SAMPSON BRIDGEWOOD
& SON
Longton, Staffordshire,
England
Earthenware, porcelain.
Printed
ca.1853+ (ca.1805–
present)

K

CARL SCHUMANN
PORCELAIN FACTORY
Arzberg, Bavaria, Germany
(W. Germany)
Porcelain
current (1881–present)

L

HENRY ALCOCK & CO.
(LTD.)
Cobridge, Staffordshire,
England
Earthenware. Printed
1880–1910 (1861–1910)

M

NIDERVILLER FAIENCE
FACTORY
Niderviller, France
Faience, porcelain
20th century (ca.1754–
present)

N

T. & R. BOOTE LTD.
Burslem, Staffordshire,
England
Earthenware, parian, tiles.
Printed
1890–1906 (1842–
1964+)

O

TAYLOR, SMITH & TAYLOR
Chester, WV, U.S.A.
Semivitreous ware
ca.1960 (1901–present)
(Anchor Hocking)

P

THOMAS HUGHES & SON
(LTD.)
Burslem, Staffordshire,
England
Earthenware, porcelain.
Printed
1930–1935 (1895–
present)
(Arthur Wood & Son Ltd.)

A VON SCHIERHOLZ'S PORCELAIN MANUFACTORY PLAUE GMBH Plaue, Thuringia, Germany (E. Germany) Porcelain. Blue, green underglaze 1907 + (1900–present) (Porcelain Manufactory Plaue VEB)	**B** WACHTERSBACH EARTHENWARE FACTORY Schlierbach, Hesse, Germany (W. Germany) Earthenware, figurines. Black, blue, green, variations in wording 1914–present (1832–present)	**C** **Wahliss** ERNST WAHLISS ALEXANDRA PORCELAIN WORKS Turn-Teplitz, Bohemia (Trnovany, Czechoslovakia) Porcelain, faience 1903–ca.1921 (1894–1934)	**D**  ARTHUR J. WILKINSON Burslem, Staffordshire, England Earthenware, ironstone ca.1891 + (1885–1964 +)
E ZEH, SCHERZER & CO. Rehau, Bavaria, Germany (W. Germany) Porcelain 1899–ca.1909 (1880–present)	**F** KARL SCHAAFF Zell on Harmersbach, Badenia, Germany (W. Germany) Earthenware 1880–1909 (1794–present) (various names & owners, now Georg Schmider United Zell Ceramic Factories)	**G**  P. H. LEONARD New York, NY, U.S.A. Porcelain importer 1890–ca.1908 (1890–ca.1910)	**H** # FLEUR DE LIS & PRINCE OF WALES FEATHERS
I RHEAD ŞANTA BARBARA RHEAD POTTERY Santa Barbara, CA, U.S.A. Art pottery ca.1913–1917 (1913–1917)	**J** CERALENE Paris, France Porcelain current (1960–present)	**K**  SÈVRES CHINA CO. East Liverpool, OH, U.S.A. Semivitreous ware after 1900 (1900–1908)	**L** FRENCH CHINA CO. East Liverpool, OH, U.S.A. Semivitreous ware 1916–1929 (ca.1900–present) (Royal China Co.)
M LOWESBY POTTERY Lowesby, England Earthenware. Impressed ca.1835–1840 (ca.1835–1840)	**N** BARKER BROS. LTD. Longton, Staffordshire, England Porcelain, earthenware. Printed 1912–1930 (1876–1964 +)	**O** SÈVRES CHINA CO. East Liverpool, OH, U.S.A. Semivitreous ware. Printed, variations in wording 1900–1908 (1900–1908)	**P** HOMER LAUGHLIN CHINA CO. East Liverpool, OH, U.S.A. Hotel ware ca.1970 (1877–present)

A

TRADE MARK COPYRIGHTED
**WARRANTED
22-K GOLD
GOLD CREST**

ROYAL CHINA CO.
Sebring, OH, U.S.A.
Semivitreous dinnerware
1934–1960 (1933–
present)

B

OSPAG AUSTRIAN
SANITARY CERAMIC &
PORCELAIN INDUSTRY
AG
Wilhelmsburg, Austria
1959–present (1945–
present)

C

C. TIELSCH & CO.
Altwasser, Silesia, Germany
(Walbrzych, Poland)
Hard paste porcelain
ca.1895–ca.1918 (1845–
present)
(Hutschenreuther AG)

D

HAMMERSLEY & ASBURY
Longton, Staffordshire,
England
Earthenware
1872–1875 (1872–1875)

E

Cᴴ H.C.
TRADE MARK

COOK POTTERY CO.
Trenton, NJ, U.S.A.
Belleek
ca.1900 (1894–1929)

F

JOHN EDWARDS (& CO.)
Fenton, Staffordshire,
England
Porcelain, earthenware.
Printed
ca.1880–1900 (1847–
1900)

G

D. J. EVANS & CO.
Swansea, Wales
Earthenware. Printed
1862–1870 (1862–1870)

H

MINTON
Stoke, Staffordshire,
England
Porcelain, earthenware.
Printed
ca.1878 (1793–present)
(Royal Doulton Tableware
Ltd.)

I

SPODE
Stoke, Staffordshire,
England
Porcelain
ca.1806 (ca.1762–present)
(Royal Worcester Spode
Ltd.)

J

EDWARD ASBURY & CO.
Longton, Staffordshire,
England
Porcelain, earthenware.
Printed
1875–1925 (1875–1925)

K

JOSEPH SCHACHTEL
Charlottenbrunn, Silesia,
Germany (Zofiowka,
Poland)
Porcelain
ca.1896–ca.1919 (1859–
1919)

L

FLOWER & TREE

M

JACOB SCHOLL
Tylersport, PA, U.S.A.
Earthenware. Impressed
ca.1830 (ca.1830)

N

NEW ENGLAND POTTERY
CO.
Boston, MA, U.S.A.
Creamware
1887+ (1854–1914)

O

ROYAL KINRAN CROWN
NIPPON
Japan
Porcelain. Blue, gold
(1890–1921)

P

WILLIAM DE MORGAN
Chelsea, London, England
Earthenware
1888+ (ca.1872–1911)

A

PLASTOGRAPHIC CO.
Vienna, Austria & Radowitz,
   Bohemia (Ledvice,
   Czechoslovakia)
Porcelain
before 1899–ca.1903
   (before 1899–ca.1903)

B

"CHERRY BLOSSOM"
Japan
Porcelain. Blue, green,
   magenta
before 1921

C

"R. C." NORITAKE
Japan
Porcelain. Hand-painted,
   green, blue
1906 +

D

BURGESS & LEIGH
Burslem, Staffordshire,
   England
Earthenware. Printed
1930s (1862–present)

E

ROYAL KAGA NIPPON
("PLUM BLOSSOM")
Japan
Porcelain. Blue
1890–1921

F

SCHIRNDING PORCELAIN
   FACTORY
Schirnding, Bavaria,
   Germany (W. Germany)
Porcelain. Underglaze
1974–present (1909–
   present)

G

OSCAR SCHLEGELMILCH
Langewiesen, Thuringia,
   Germany (E. Germany)
Porcelain
after 1892 (1892–present)
   (Porcelain Combine Colditz
   VEB)

H

MERKELSGRUN
   PORCELAIN FACTORY
Merkelsgrun, Bohemia,
   (Merklin, Czechoslovakia)
Porcelain
1918–1939 (1912–1945)

I

RETSCH & CO.
Wunsiedel, Bavaria,
   Germany (W. Germany)
Porcelain
1950 + (1884–present)

J

CARL THIEME SAXONIAN
   PORCELAIN FACTORY
Potschappel, Saxony,
   Germany (E. Germany)
Porcelain
ca.1913 + (1872–present)
   (Saxonian Porcelain
   Manufactory Dresden
   VEB)

K

GRAND DUCAL MAJOLICA
   MANUFACTORY
Karlsruhe, Badenia,
   Germany (W. Germany)
Majolica
1904–1927 (1901–
   present)

L

BURROUGHS &
   MOUNTFORD CO.
Trenton, NJ, U.S.A.
Creamware
1879 + (1879–1882)

M

SCHIRNDING PORCELAIN
   FACTORY
Schirnding, Bavaria,
   Germany (W. Germany)
Porcelain
1948–1974 (1909–
   present)

N

CHIKUSA
Japan
Porcelain. Green
ca.1890–1921

O

WILLIAM DE MORGAN
Chelsea, (London),
   England
Earthenware. Painted,
   impressed
1888–1897 (ca.1872–
   1911)

P

EMPIRE PORCELAIN CO.
Stoke, Staffordshire.
   England
Earthenware. Printed,
   impressed
1940s–1950s (1896–
   1964 +)

A

CAMPBELLFIELD
  POTTERY CO. (LTD.)
Glasgow, Scotland
Earthenware. Printed
ca.1884–ca.1905 (1850–
  1905)

B

A. W. BUCHAN & CO.
Portobello, Nr. Edinburgh,
  Scotland
Stoneware. Printed
1949 + (1867–present)

C

ALFRED STELLMACHER
IMPERIAL & ROYAL
PORCELAIN FACTORY/
ERNST WAHLISS
ALEXANDRA
PORCELAIN WORKS
Turn-Teplitz, Bohemia
  (Trnovany,
  Czechoslovakia)
Porcelain
after 1859–1897 (1859–
  1934)

D

ERNST WAHLISS
ALEXANDRA
PORCELAIN WORKS
Turn-Teplitz, Bohemia
  (Trnovany,
  Czechoslovakia)
Porcelain
ca.1894–ca.1921 (1894–
  1934)

E

PILKINGTON'S TILE &
  POTTERY CO. LTD.
Clifton Junction,
  Lancashire, England
Earthenware. Impressed
ca.1914–1938 (1893–
  present)
(Pilkington's Tiles Ltd.)

F

AUGUSTE DELAHERCHE
Armentieres, France
Stoneware. Painted
ca.1900 (1894–ca.1940)

G

ARTE DELLA CERAMICA
Florence, Italy
Porcelain. Painted
1896–1906 (1896–1906)

H

JAEGER & CO.
Marktredwitz, Bavaria,
  Germany (W. Germany)
Hard paste porcelain. Green
  underglaze
ca.1902 (1898–present)
(Jaeger Porcelain GMBH)

I

CO-OPERATIVE
WHOLESALE SOCIETY
LTD.
Longton, Staffordshire,
  England
Porcelain. Printed
1950s–1960s (1946–
  1964 +)

J

ROCKINGHAM WORKS
Swinton, Yorkshire,
  England
Earthenware
(ca.1745–1842)

K

PHILIP ROSENTHAL & CO.
Selb, Bavaria, Germany (W.
  Germany)
Porcelain. Printed
ca.1900 (1879–present)
(Rosenthal Glass &
  Porcelain AG)

L

— — — — — — —
Japan
Porcelain. Green, orange
1890–1921

M

NORITAKE
Nagoya, Japan
Porcelain
1945–1952 (1904–
  present)

N

GOTTHELF GREINER/
  G. GREINER'S SONS
Limbach, Thuringia,
  Germany (E. Germany)
Porcelain. Blue underglaze;
  purple, green, gold, black
  overglaze
1787–ca.1850 (1772–
  ca.1850)

O

ANNABURG
EARTHENWARE
FACTORY
Annaburg, Prussia,
  Germany (E. Germany)
Earthenware
before 1924–1945 (before
  1924–present)
(Earthenware Factory
  Annaburg VEB)

P

LIMBACH PORCELAIN
FACTORY AG
Limbach, Thuringia,
  Germany (E. Germany)
Porcelain. Blue
ca.1887–ca.1919 (1882–
  1944)

A

LEY & WEIDERMANN
Haldensleben, Prussia,
  Germany (E. Germany)
Earthenware
after 1882 (1882–ca.1959)

B

MERKELSGRUN
  PORCELAIN FACTORY
Merkelsgrun, Bohemia
  (Merklin, Czechoslovakia)
Porcelain. Green
  underglaze
1912–1918 (1912–1945)

C

BRUX PORCELAIN
  MANUFACTORY
Brux, Bohemia (Most,
  Czechoslovakia)
Porcelain
1924–1939 (1924–1945)

D

MAYER CHINA CO.
Beaver Falls, PA, U.S.A.
Ironstone, semiporcelain.
  Printed, underglaze
ca.1881–1896 (1881–
  present)

E

CHELSEA KERAMIC ART
  WORKS
Chelsea, MA, U.S.A.
Art pottery. Impressed
1891–1895 (1866–1940)

F

SEBASTIAN SCHMIDT/
  EBERHARD SUHR
Schmiedefeld & Rudolstadt,
  Thuringia, Germany (E.
  Germany)
Porcelain
ca.1892–ca.1906 (1857–
  1906 +)

G

ROSE VALLEY POTTERY
Rose Valley, PA, U.S.A.
Art Pottery
1901–1905 (1901–1905)

H

ARKLOW POTTERY LTD.
Arklow, Co. Wicklow,
  Ireland
Earthenware
current (1934–present)

I

JOHN MADDOCK & SONS
Trenton, NJ, U.S.A.
Earthenware
ca.1904 + (1894–1929)

J

COOK POTTERY CO.
Trenton, NJ, U.S.A.
Ironstone, semiporcelain
ca.1894 (1894–1929)

K

KENTON HILLS
  PORCELAIN
Erlanger, KY, U.S.A.
Art pottery. Impressed
1939–1940 (1939–1942)

L

KENTON HILLS
  PORCELAIN
Erlanger, KY, U.S.A.
Art pottery
ca.1940 (1939–1942)

M

LLADRÓ
Tabernes Blanques,
  Valencia, Spain
Porcelain
1965 + (1951–present)

N

MITTERTEICH
  PORCELAIN FACTORY
  AG
Mitterteich, Bavaria,
  Germany (W. Germany)
Hard paste porcelain
1918 + (1918–present)

O

COLUMBIAN ART
  POTTERY CO.
Trenton, NJ, U.S.A.
Belleek. Printed
ca.1895 (1893–ca.1902)

P

CARL THIEME SAXONIAN
  PORCELAIN FACTORY
Potschappel, Saxony,
  Germany (E. Germany)
Porcelain
ca.1913 + (1872–present)
(Saxonian Porcelain
  Manufactory Dresden
  VEB)

A

MORIMURA BROS.
Tokyo, Japan
Porcelain. Green, blue,
    magenta
1891+ (1876–present)
(Noritake Co.)

B

J. W. MUNLIEFF
Utrecht, Holland
Ceramics. Painted
ca.1896 (1856–1906)

C

WESTERN STONEWARE
    CO.
Monmouth, IL, U.S.A.
Stoneware
ca.1930+ (1906–1975)

D

HEINRICH & CO.
Selb, Bavaria, Germany
    (W. Germany)
1904+ (1896–present)
(Villeroy & Boch)

E

JEAN POUYAT
Limoges, France
Porcelain
1905+ (1842–present)
(Guérin-Pouyat-Élite)

F

C. G. SCHIERHOLZ & SON/
VON SCHIERHOLZ'S
    PORCELAIN
    MANUFACTORY
Plaue, Thuringia, Germany
    (E. Germany)
Porcelain. Green, blue
    underglaze
ca.1907–1927 (1817–
    present)
(Porcelain Manufactory
    Plaue VEB)

G

PEWABIC POTTERY
Detroit, MI, U.S.A.
Art pottery. Impressed
ca.1900 (1903–present)

H

HOMER LAUGHLIN CHINA
    CO.
East Liverpool, OH, U.S.A.
Semivitreous ware
ca.1960 (1877–present)

I

CAMBRIDGE ART
    POTTERY
Cambridge, OH, U.S.A.
Brown glazed ware
ca.1895+ (1895–1909)

J

DUX PORCELAIN
    MANUFACTORY
Dux, Bohemia (Duchcov,
    Czechoslovakia)
Porcelain
after 1912 (1860–present)
(Duchcov Porcelain)

K

HERMANN VOIGT
    PORCELAIN FACTORY
Schaala, Thuringia,
    Germany (E. Germany)
Porcelain
ca.1880–1938 (1872–
    1938)

L

L. A. BERKS & CO.
Stoke, Staffordshire,
    England
Porcelain, earthenware.
    Printed
1896–1900 (1896–1900)

M

BIRKS, RAWLINS & CO.
Stoke, Staffordshire,
    England
Porcelain. Printed
1900+ (1900–1933)

N

HERMANN VOIGT
    PORCELAIN FACTORY
Schaala, Thuringia,
    Germany (E. Germany)
Hard & soft paste porcelain
ca.1880–1938 (1872–
    1938)

O

BAUER POTTERY
Los Angeles, CA, U.S.A.
Dinnerware. Imprinted, blue
ca.1930+ (1905–ca.1958)

P

LIMOGES CHINA CO.
Sebring, OH, U.S.A.
Semivitreous dinnerware
1927–1932 (1900–
    ca.1955)
(American Limoges China
    Co.)

A

SAUER & ROLOFF
Haldensleben, Prussia,
   Germany (E. Germany)
Porcelain, earthenware
ca.1908 (ca.1905–1908 +)

B

AREQUIPA POTTERY
Fairfax, CA, U.S.A.
Art pottery. Painted, incised,
   impressed
ca.1915 (1911–1918)

C

ASHTEAD POTTERS LTD.
Ashtead, Surrey, England
Earthenware. Printed
1926–1936 (1926–1936)

D

DEMEULDRE
   ESTABLISHMENT
   S.P.R.L.
Etterbek, Brussels, Belgium
Porcelain
1920–1930 (1832–
   present)
(various names & owners)

E

DEMEULDRE
   ESTABLISHMENT
   S.P.R.L.
Etterbek, Brussels, Belgium
Porcelain
current (1832–present)
(various names & owners)

F

DEMEULDRE
   ESTABLISHMENT
   S.P.R.L.
Etterbek, Brussels, Belgium
Porcelain
current (1832–present)
(various names & owners)

G

VERNON KILNS
Vernon, CA, U.S.A.
Metlox dinnerware
ca.1956 + (1912–1958)

H

G. L. ASHWORTH & BROS.
Hanley, Staffordshire,
   England
Earthenware, ironstone
1957–1964 + (1784–
   present)
(member of Wedgwood
   Group)

I

ORANGE TREE POTTERY
Durham, England
Studio-type pottery.
Impressed, printed
1952–1964 + (1952–
   1964 +)

J

River Shore, Ltd.®

RIVER SHORE, LTD.
Caledonia, MI, U.S.A.
Limited editions
current (1975–present)

K

SYRACUSE CHINA CORP.
Syracuse, NY, U.S.A.
Vitreous ware
ca.1930 + (1871–present)
(various names & owners)

L

GLADDING, McBEAN &
   CO.
Los Angeles, CA, U.S.A.
Tropico pottery
1923 + (1875–present)
(member of Wedgwood
   Group)

M

C. T. MALING & SONS
Newcastle upon Tyne,
   Northumberland,
   England
Earthenware. Printed
ca.1870 (ca.1859–1963)

N

W. DAVENPORT & CO.
Longport, Staffordshire,
   England
Earthenware. Printed
1820–1860 (ca.1793–
   1887)

O

VERNON KILNS
Vernon, CA, U.S.A.
Metlox dinnerware
ca.1950 (1912–1958)

P

AUMA PORCELAIN WORK
   VEB
Auma, Thuringia, Germany
   (E. Germany)
Porcelain
1955–1972 (1909–
   present)
(various names, now
   Combine Ceramic Works
   Hermsdorf VEB)

A

STERLING CHINA CO.
East Liverpool, OH, U.S.A.
Semivitreous ware
ca.1945–ca.1955 (1917–present)

B

THURINGIAN
PORCELAINWORKS
GEHREN VEB
Gehren, Thuringia,
Germany (E. Germany)
Porcelain
1947–1969 (1884–present)
(Henneberg Porcelain VEB)

C

UNITED STATES
CERAMIC CO.
Hapboro, PA, U.S.A.
Porcelain
1964 + (1964–1968)

D

HAAS & CZJZEK
Schlaggenwald, Bohemia
(Horni Slavkov,
Czechoslovakia)
Porcelain. Green
after 1918–ca.1945 (1867–1945 +)

E

J. SCHNABEL & SON
Dessendorf, Bohemia
(Desna, Czechoslovakia)
Porcelain
ca.1900–ca.1931 (1869–ca.1931)

F

VILLEROY & BOCH
Schramberg, Wurttemberg,
Germany (W. Germany)
Earthenware, majolica
ca.1895–1912 (1813–present)
(Schramberg location
operated 1883–1912;
various names, owners &
locations).

G

SCHONWALD PORCELAIN
FACTORY
Schonwald, Bavaria,
Germany (W. Germany)
Porcelain. Green
underglaze
ca.1968–present (1898–present)
(Hutschenreuther AG)

H

HAAS & CZJZEK
Chodau, Bohemia (Chodov,
Czechoslovakia)
Porcelain
1905 + (1867–1945 +)

I

HAAS & CZJZEK
Chodau, Bohemia (Chodov,
Czechoslovakia)
Porcelain
ca.1939–1945 (1867–1945 +)

J

WILHELM DIEBENER
Gotha, Thuringia, Germany
(E. Germany)
Earthenware
ca.1954–ca.1964
(ca.1939–ca.1964)

K

ALFRED MEAKIN (LTD.)
Tunstall, Staffordshire,
England
Willowware
ca.1920 (1873–present)
(Myott-Meakin Ltd.)

L

HEWITT & LEADBEATER/
HEWITT BROS.
Longton, Staffordshire,
England
Porcelain, parian. Printed
1907–ca.1926 (1907–1926 +)

M

ROYAL CHINA CO.
East Liverpool, OH, U.S.A.
Semivitreous dinnerware
1949–ca.1960 (1933–present)

N

FOREIGN ALPHABETS

O

SAMSON & CO.
Paris, France
Lowestoft reproductions
ca.1875 (1873–1957 +)

P

JULIUS ROTHER
Mitterteich, Bavaria,
Germany (W. Germany)
Porcelain
ca.1899–1918 (ca.1899–ca.1918)

A

MILES MASON
Lane Delph, Staffordshire,
England
Porcelain. Printed
ca.1800–1816 (ca.1792–
1816)

B

CARL HANS TUPPACK
Tiefenfurth, Silesia,
Germany (Parowa,
Poland)
Porcelain
ca.1926–1935 (1919–
1935)

C

WILTSHAW & ROBINSON
(LTD.)
Stoke, Staffordshire,
England
Earthenware, porcelain
ca.1914 (1890–present)
(Carlton Ware Ltd.)

D

TORII
Japan
Porcelain. Torquoise
1894–1921

E

RÖRSTRAND PORCELAIN
FACTORY
Lidkoping, Sweden
Hard paste porcelain
ca.1884 (1726–present)
(Rörstrand AB)

F

MILES MASON
Liverpool, England
Willow porcelain. Printed
ca.1800–1816 (ca.1792–
1816)

G

B. NASSONOFF FACTORY
Moscow, U.S.S.R.
Porcelain. Blue
1811–ca.1813

H

KIRIAKOFF FACTORY
Moscow, U.S.S.R.
Porcelain
1813–ca.1816

I

Γ

FRANCIS GARDNER
PORCELAIN FACTORY
Werbiliki, U.S.S.R.
Hard paste porcelain
ca.1815+ (1765–present)
(Kusnetzoff)

J

Ѓ

G. POPOFF FACTORY
Moscow, U.S.S.R.
Porcelain
ca.1815+ (1800–1872)

K

NOVYKI BROTHERS
FACTORY
Moscow, U.S.S.R.
Hard paste porcelain
ca.1820+ (1820–1840)

L

В.СИПЯГИНа

SIPIAGIN FACTORY
Moscow, U.S.S.R.
Porcelain
ca.1820+ (1820–1875+)

M

САФРОНОВА
С

A. T. SAFRONOFF
FACTORY
Moscow, U.S.S.R.
Porcelain
ca.1830+ (1830–ca.1840)

N

козловыхъ

KOZLOFF FACTORY
Moscow, U.S.S.R.
Porcelain
ca.1820–1856

O

ПЕТРА
ФОМИНА

P. T. FOMIN FACTORY
Moscow, U.S.S.R.
Porcelain
(1806–1883)

P

ПОПОВЫ

G. POPOFF FACTORY
Moscow, U.S.S.R.
Hard paste porcelain.
Painted
1830+ (1800–1872)

A	B	C	D
ГАРДНЕРЪ	**БРАТЬЕВЬ НОВЫХЬ**	**ВРАТЬЕВЪ Корниловыхъ**	**БРАТЬЕВЪ РАУКИННЫХЬ**
FRANCIS GARDNER PORCELAIN FACTORY Moscow, U.S.S.R. Hard paste porcelain. Painted before 1891 (1765– present) (Kusnetzoff)	NOVYKI BROTHERS FACTORY Moscow, U.S.S.R. Hard paste porcelain. ca.1820 + (1820–1840)	KORNILOV FACTORY St. Petersburg (Leningrad), Russia (U.S.S.R.) Hard paste porcelain. Printed (ca.1835–ca.1885)	RASCHKIN FACTORY Moscow, Russia (U.S.S.R.) Porcelain (1820–1870)

E	F	G	H
ΦΙΛΕΩ ΙΠΠΟΝ	**ЗАВОДА Б КУЗНЕЦОБЫХЪ**	**Ф Г ГУЛИНА**	**ФАБРИКИ Я.Г. РАПУНОВАНОВАГО**
JOHN PHILLIPS & CO. Newton Abbot, Devon, England Earthenware 1868–1887 (1868–1887)	KUSNETZOFF FACTORY Novocharitonova, Russia (U.S.S.R.) Porcelain. Printed after 1889 (1810–present)	FABRICA GOSPODINA GULINA Rjasan, Russia (U.S.S.R.) Hard paste porcelain, faience. Impressed ca.1830 + (1830–1850)	NOVYKI BROTHERS FACTORY Moscow, Russia (U.S.S.R.) Hard paste porcelain. ca.1830 (1820–1840)

I	J	K	L
КЕРФАК	**HUMANS & BODY PARTS**		
PETROGRAD STATE FACTORY Leningrad, U.S.S.R. Porcelain 1917–1924 (before 1917– present) (State Porcelain Factory M. W. Lomonossow Leningrad)		MONMOUTH POTTERY CO. Monmouth, IL, U.S.A. Stoneware ca.1890–ca.1906 (ca. 1890–1975)	WAGNER & APEL Lippelsdorf, Thuringia, Germany (E. Germany) Porcelain 20th century (1877– present) (Porcelain Figurines VEB)

M	N	O	P
WARWICK MADE IN U.S.A.			
WARWICK CHINA CO. Wheeling, WV, U.S.A. Porcelain, semiporcelain ca.1944 (1887–1951)	LIMOGES CHINA CO. East Liverpool, OH, U.S.A. Semivitreous dinnerware ca.1939 (1900–1955) (American Limoges China Co.)	LIMOGES CHINA CO. Sebring, OH, U.S.A. Semivitreous dinnerware 1933–1936 (1900–1955) (American Limoges China Co.)	J. H. WEATHERBY & SONS (LTD.) Hanley & Stoke, Staffordshire, England Earthenware current (1891–present)

A

HARKER POTTERY CO.
East Liverpool, OH, U.S.A.
Dinnerware
after 1935–1948 (1890–1972)

B

LONHUDA POTTERY
Steubenville, OH, U.S.A.
Art pottery. Impressed
1893+ (1892–ca.1894)

C

REGENCY CHINA LTD.
Longton, Staffordshire,
England
Porcelain
1953+ (1953–present)

D

HOODS LTD.
. Fenton, Staffordshire,
England
Earthenware
ca.1919–1942 (1919–1964+)

E

SALEM CHINA CO.
Salem, OH, U.S.A.
Dinnerware
1918+ (1898–1967)

F

RHEAD POTTERY
Santa Barbara, CA, U.S.A.
Art pottery
ca.1913–1917 (1913–1917)

G

GUERNSEY POTTERY
LTD.
Guernsey, Channel Islands,
England
Redware, studio pottery
1964+ (ca.1964–present)

H

SHENANGO CHINA CO.
New Castle, PA, U.S.A.
Vitreous ware
ca.1935+ (1901–present)
(Anchor Hocking)

I

PISGAH FOREST
POTTERY
Pisgah Forest, NC, U.S.A.
Art pottery, various dates
1920–1961 (1901–present)

J

SHENANGO CHINA CO.
New Castle, PA, U.S.A.
Vitreous ware. Variations in
wording
current (1901–present)
(Anchor Hocking)

K

CARL HANS TUPPACK
Tiefenfurth, Silesia,
Germany (Parowa,
Poland)
Porcelain. Blue
ca.1931–1935 (1919–1935)

L

WOOD & SON(S) (LTD.)
Burslem, Staffordshire,
England
Earthenware. Printed
ca.1931+ (1865–present)

M

ROCKINGHAM WORKS
Swinton, Yorkshire,
England
Stone china. Printed,
impressed
ca.1815–1842 (ca.1754–1842)

N

POWELL, BISHOP &
STONIER
Hanley, Staffordshire,
England
Porcelain, earthenware
1880+ (1878–1891)

O

PETRUS REGOUT
Maastricht, Holland
Earthenware
1929–1931+ (1836–1931+)

P

WILLIAM BAILEY & SONS
Longton, Staffordshire,
England
Earthenware. Printed
1912–1914 (1912–1914)

A

BRUSH-McCOY POTTERY
CO.
Zanesville, OH, U.S.A.
Art pottery
1915–1925 (1911–
present)
(Brush Pottery)

B

VERNON KILNS
Vernon, CA, U.S.A.
Dinnerware
ca.1956 + (1912–1958)

C

UNIVERSAL POTTERIES,
INC.
Cambridge, OH, U.S.A.
Semiporcelain, earthenware
ca.1947–1956 (1934–
1956)

D

UNIVERSAL POTTERIES,
INC.
Cambridge, OH, U.S.A.
Semiporcelain, earthenware
ca.1947–1956 (1934–
1956)

E

AMERICAN CHINAWARE
CORP.
East Liverpool, OH, U.S.A.
Dinnerware
ca.1929–1931 (1929–
1931)

F

LIMOGES CHINA CO.
East Liverpool, OH, U.S.A.
Semivitreous dinnerware
1935–1941 (1900–1955)
(American Limoges China
Co.)

G

DEVONSHIRE POTTERIES
LTD.
Bovey Tracey, Devon,
England
Earthenware. Printed
1947 + (1947–present)

H

FINE ARTS PORCELAIN
LTD.
London, England
Earthenware. Printed
1948–1952 (1948–1952)

I

NEW ENGLAND POTTERY
CO.
Boston, MA, U.S.A.
Ironstone
1878–1883 (1854–1914)

J

SOCIETÀ CERAMICA
RICHARD
Milan, Italy
Earthenware
current (1735–present)
(Richard-Ginori)

K

POUNTNEY & CO. (LTD.)
Bristol, Gloucestershire,
England
Earthenware
ca.1900 + (1849–1964 +)

L

BISHOP & STONIER
Hanley, Staffordshire,
England
Porcelain, earthenware.
Printed, impressed
1936–1939 (1876–1939)

M

D. E. McNICOL POTTERY
CO.
East Liverpool, OH, U.S.A.
Vitreous institutional ware
ca.1933–ca.1950 (1892–
1954)

N

L. LOURIOUX
Foecy, France
Porcelain
ca.1971 (1898–present)

O

CROWN STAFFORDSHIRE
PORCELAIN CO. LTD.
Fenton, Staffordshire,
England
Porcelain
ca.1930 + (1889–present)
(member of Wedgwood
Group)

P

SAXON CHINA CO.
East Liverpool, OH, U.S.A.
Semivitreous ware
ca.1920 (1911–1929)

A	**B**	**C**	**D**
 SILBERMANN BROS. Hausen, Bavaria, Germany (W. Germany) Porcelain. Green underglaze ca.1929–1938 (1802–present) (Kaiser-Porcelain)	 BILTONS (1912) LTD. Stoke, Staffordshire, England Earthenware. Printed 1912+ (1900–present) (Biltons Tableware Ltd.)	 PARIS BROS. Oberkoditz, Thuringia, Germany (E. Germany) Porcelain ca.1910–1953 (1881–present) (Porcelainwork Oberkoditz VEB)	 HOMER LAUGHLIN CHINA CO. East Liverpool, OH, U.S.A. Semivitreous tableware ca.1955 (1877–present)

E	**F**	**G**	**H**
 BUFFALO POTTERY CO. Buffalo, NY, U.S.A. Semiporcelain 1906+ (1901–present) (Buffalo China, Inc.)	 SIR JAMES DUKE & NEPHEWS Burslem, Staffordshire, England Porcelain, parian. Printed ca.1860–1863 (1860–1863)	 WADE POTTERIES LTD. Portadown, Co. Armagh, Northern Ireland Porcelain current (1947–present)	 PURBECK POTTERY LTD. Bournemouth, Dorset, England Stoneware. Printed current (1965–present)

I	**J**	**K**	**L**
RUDOLF & EUGEN HAIDINGER Elbogen, Bohemia (Loket, Czechoslovakia) Porcelain. Blue underglaze ca.1815–1873 (1815–1945) (various names & owners)	EPIAG Elbogen, Bohemia (Loket, Czechoslovakia) Porcelain. Green underglaze, variations in wording ca.1941–1945 (1920–1945+)	NEW ENGLAND POTTERY CO. Boston, MA, U.S.A. Semiporcelain. Black underglaze 1886–1888 (1854–1914)	LINES

M	**N**	**O**	**P**
ROYAL PORCELAIN MANUFACTORY/ STATE'S PORCELAIN MANUFACTORY (KPM) Berlin, Germany Hard paste porcelain. Blue underglaze 1870–present (1763–present)	KPM ROYAL PORCELAIN MANUFACTORY/ STATE'S PORCELAIN MANUFACTORY (KPM) Berlin, Germany Hard paste porcelain. Impressed ca.1825–present (1763–present)	ROYAL PORCELAIN MANUFACTORY/ STATE'S PORCELAIN MANUFACTORY (KPM) Berlin, Germany Hard paste porcelain. Blue underglaze 1882–present (1763–present)	ROYAL COPENHAGEN PORCELAIN FACTORY LTD. Fredericksberg, Denmark Porcelain, faience. Blue 1775–1820, 1850–1870 (1775–present)

A	B	C	D

ROYAL COPENHAGEN PORCELAIN FACTORY LTD. Fredericksberg, Denmark Faience. Blue 1870–1890 (1775– present)	HAAGSCHE PLATEELBAKKERY Rozenburg, Holland Porcelain 1908+ (ca.1883–ca.1915)	ROYAL COPENHAGEN PORCELAIN FACTORY LTD. Fredericksberg, Denmark Faience 1903–present (1775– present)	VANCE/AVON FAIENCE Tiltonville, OH, U.S.A. Art pottery ca.1902–1905 (ca.1900– ca.1905)

E	F	G	H
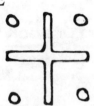			
VIENNA CERAMIC Vienna, Austria Ceramics. Impressed ca.1905+ (1905–1912)	SAMSON & CO. Paris, France Porcelain. Blue underglaze ca.1940 (1873–1957+)	SAMSON & CO. Paris, France Porcelain 1927+ (1873–1957+)	KARL ENS PORCELAIN FACTORY Volkstedt, Thuringia, Germany (E. Germany) Hard paste porcelain. Green underglaze 1919–1972 (1898– present) (Underglaze Porcelain Factory VEB)

I	J	K	L
KRANICHFELD PORCELAIN MANUFACTORY Kranichfeld, Saxony, Germany (E. Germany) Decorative porcelain, figurines 1903+ (1903+)	SORAU PORCELAIN FACTORY Sorau, Brandenburg, Germany (E. Germany) Porcelain ca.1898–1918 (1899– 1918)	CH. LEVY & CO. Charenton, France Porcelain. Blue ca.1876 (ca.1876–1881)	DRESSEL, KISTER & CO. Passau, Bavaria, Germany (W. Germany) Hard paste porcelain. Blue ca.1907–ca.1922 (1840– 1942)

M	N	O	P

C. G. SCHIERHOLZ & SON Plaue, Thuringia, Germany (E. Germany) Porcelain. Blue underglaze ca.1880–ca.1906 (1817– present) (Porcelain Manufactory Plaue VEB)	VOIGT BROS./ALFRED VOIGT Sitzendorf, Thuringia, Germany (E. Germany) Porcelain. Blue underglaze ca.1887–ca.1900 (1850– present) (Sitzendorf Porcelain Manufactory VEB)	SAMSON & CO. Paris, France Porcelain. Blue underglaze, overglaze ca.1940+ (1873–1957+)	ROYAL PORCELAIN MANUFACTORY/ STATE'S PORCELAIN MANUFACTORY (KPM) Meissen, Saxony, Germany (E. Germany) Porcelain. Blue underglaze, stamped (see page 270) ca.1860–1924 (1710– present) (State's Porcelain Manufactory Meissen VEB)

A

ROYAL PORCELAIN
MANUFACTORY
STATE'S PORCELAIN
MANUFACTORY (KPM)
Meissen, Saxony, Germany
(E. Germany)
Porcelain. Blue underglaze,
hand-painted
ca.1814–ca.1860 (1710–
present)
(State's Porcelain
Manufactory Meissen
VEB)

B

COALPORT PORCELAIN
WORKS
Coalport, Shropshire,
England
Porcelain
ca.1820–ca.1841(ca.1795–
present)
(member of Wedgwood
Group)

C

STATE'S PORCELAIN
MANUFACTORY (KPM)
Meissen, Saxony, Germany
(E. Germany)
Porcelain. Blue underglaze
1924–1934 (1710–
present)
(State's Porcelain
Manufactory Meissen
VEB)

D

JACOB PETIT
Fontainebleau, France
Porcelain
ca.1830–1842 (ca.1830–
1862)

E

ROYAL PORCELAIN
MANUFACTORY/
STATE'S PORCELAIN
MANUFACTORY (KPM)
Meissen, Saxony, Germany
(E. Germany)
Porcelain. Blue underglaze,
hand-painted
ca.1814–ca.1860 (1710–
present)
(State's Porcelain
Manufactory Meissen
VEB)

F

ERNST TEICHERT GMBH
Meissen, Saxony, Germany
(E. Germany)
Porcelain. Blue underglaze
after 1884 (1872–1945+)
(nationalized in 1945)

G

ACHILLE BLOCH
Paris, France
Porcelain. Blue underglaze,
overglaze
ca.1926+ (1887–present)
(various names, now
Porcelaine de Paris)

H

JOHN BEVINGTON
Hanley, Staffordshire,
England
Porcelain. Painted, blue
underglaze
1872–1892 (1872–1892)

I

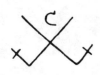

CH. LEVY & CO.
Charenton, France
Porcelain
1876+ (ca.1876–1881)

J

CHRISTOPHE WINDISCH
Brussels, Belgium
Porcelain
current (1832–present)
(Etablissements Demauldre
S.P.R.L., Manufacture de
Porcelaine de Bruxelles)

K

DKF

DORNHEIM KOCH &
FISCHER PORCELAIN &
POTTERY FACTORY
Grafenroda, Thuringia,
Germany (E. Germany)
ca.1880–ca.1938 (1880–
1938)

L

SCHOENAU BROS.
Huttensteinach, Thuringia,
Germany (E. Germany)
Porcelain
ca.1887–1920 (1865–
1920)

M

A. W. FR. KISTER
Scheibe-Alsbach,
Thuringia, Germany (E.
Germany)
Porcelain. Blue underglaze
ca.1875 (1838–present)
(Porcelain Manufactory
Scheibe-Alsbach VEB)

N

STATE'S PORCELAIN
MANUFACTORY/
STATE'S PORCELAIN
MANUFACTORY
MEISSEN VEB (KPM)
Meissen, Saxony, Germany
(E. Germany)
Porcelain. Blue underglaze
1875–present (1710–
present)

O

A. W. FR. KISTER
Scheibe-Alsbach,
Thuringia, Germany (E.
Germany)
Porcelain. Blue underglaze,
overglaze
ca.1887 (1838–present)
(Porcelain Manufactory
Sheibe-Alsbach VEB)

P

BRENNER & LIEBMANN/
EDUARD LIEBMANN
PORCELAIN FACTORY
KG
Schney, Bavaria, Germany
(W. Germany)
Porcelain. Blue underglaze,
impressed
ca.1887–ca.1923
(ca. 1780–1923)

A

A. W. FR. KISTER
  PORCELAIN
  MANUFACTORY
Scheibe-Alsbach,
  Thuringia, Germany (E.
  Germany)
Porcelain. Blue underglaze,
  overglaze
before 1900–1972 (1838–
  present)
(Porcelain Manufactory
  Scheibe-Alsbach VEB)

B

SAMSON & CO.
Paris, France
Replacements, copies. Blue
  underglaze
ca.1873–ca.1905 (1873–
  1957+)

C

CARL THIEME SAXONIAN
  PORCELAIN FACTORY
Potschappel, Saxony,
  Germany (E. Germany)
Porcelain
1888–1901 (1872–
  present)
(Saxonian Porcelain
  Manufactory Dresden
  VEB)

D

STATE'S PORCELAIN
  MANUFACTORY VEB
Meissen, Saxony, Germany
  (E. Germany)
Porcelain
1963+ (1919–present)

E

HACKEFORS
  PORCELAINS AB
Linkoping, Sweden
Porcelain
1929–1957 (1929–
  present)
(Upsala-Ekeby Group)

F

STATE'S PORCELAIN
  MANUFACTORY VEB
Meissen, Saxony, Germany
  (E. Germany)
Porcelain
ca.1972–present (1919–
  present)

G

CARL SCHUMANN
  PORCELAIN FACTORY
Arzberg, Bavaria, Germany
  (W. Germany)
Porcelain
ca.1896 (1881–present)

H

BOURDOIS & BLOCH/
  ACHILLE BLOCH
Paris, France
Porcelain. Blue underglaze
ca.1890–1948 (1887–
  present)
(Porcelaine de Paris)

I

FREDERICK CHRISTIAN
  GREINER & SONS
Rauenstein, Thuringia,
  Germany (E. Germany)
Porcelain. Blue underglaze
ca.1894–ca.1936
  (ca.1860–1936)

J

RUSKIN POTTERY
Smethwick, nr. Birmingham,
  England
Earthenware. Painted,
  incised
ca.1898+ (1898–1935)

K

ATLAN CERAMIC ART
  CLUB
Chicago, IL, U.S.A.
Ceramics
ca.1900 (1893–1921)

L

DUMMLER & BREIDEN
Hohr-Grenzhausen,
  Palatinate, Germany (W.
  Germany)
Stoneware
current (1883–present)

M

CHRISTIAN NONNE
Volkstedt, Thuringia,
  Germany (E. Germany)
Porcelain. Blue underglaze
1767–1800 (1762–
  present)
(various names & owners,
  now Oldest Volkstedt
  Porcelain Manufactory
  VEB)

N

RICHARD ECKERT & CO.
  PORCELAIN FACTORY
  VOLKSTEDT
Volkstedt, Thuringia,
  Germany (E. Germany)
Porcelain. Blue underglaze
1894–1918 (1894–
  present)
(various names & owners,
  now Oldest Volkstedt
  Porcelain Manufactory
  VEB)

O

TRIEBNER, ENS &
  ECKERT/RICHARD
  ECKERT & CO.
  PORCELAIN FACTORY
  VOLKSTEDT
Volkstedt, Thuringia,
  Germany (E. Germany)
Porcelain. Blue underglaze
1886–1894+ (1877–
  present)
(various names & owners,
  now Oldest Volkstedt
  Porcelain Manufactory
  VEB)

P

RYE POTTERY
Rye, Sussex, England
Pottery. Incised
ca.1920–1939 (1869–
  present)

A

JOHANN SELTMANN
Vohenstrauss, Bavaria,
Germany (W. Germany)
Porcelain
ca.1901+ (1901–present)

B

R S W
RYE

RYE POTTERY
Rye, Sussex, England
Pottery. Incised
ca.1869–ca.1920 (1869–
present)

C

CYBIS PORCELAINS
Trenton, NJ, U.S.A.
Porcelain
1942–1950 (ca.1939–
present)

D

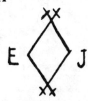
COPELAND

W. T. COPELAND (&
SONS LTD.)
Stoke, Staffordshire,
England
Porcelain, parian,
earthenware. Printed
ca.1847–1951 (1847–
present)
(Royal Worcester Spode
Ltd.)

E

COPELAND

W. T. COPELAND (&
SONS LTD.)
Stoke, Staffordshire,
England
Porcelain, parian,
earthenware. Printed
1851–1885 (1847–
present)
(Royal Worcester Spode
Ltd.)

F

Sevres

SÈVRES
Sèvres, France
Porcelain. Blue, variations
in wording, year indicated
1824–1828 (1756–
present)

G

D K F

DORNHEIM, KOCH &
FISCHER
Grafenroda, Thuringia,
Germany (E. Germany)
Porcelain. Blue
after 1880–ca.1938 (1880–
1938)

H

E   J

E. JACQUEMIN
Fontainebleau, France
Porcelain. Blue
ca.1862+ (ca.1862–1866)

I

J   P

JACOB & MARDOCHÉE
PETIT
Fontainebleau, France
Porcelain. Blue underglaze,
incised
1830–1862 (1830–1862)

J

CHARLES-JEAN
AVISSEAU
Tours, France
Faience, hard paste
porcelain. Painted,
incised
1842–ca.1861 (1842–
ca.1899)

K

SAMSON & CO.
Paris, France
Sèvres reproductions &
terra-cotta
1927–1941+ (1873–
1957+)

L

SÈVRES (VINCENNES)
Sèvres, France
Porcelain (see page 271)
1777 (date mark, see page
249) (1756–present)

M

OSCAR SCHALLER & CO.
Schwarzenbach, Bavaria,
Germany (W. Germany)
Porcelain. Green
underglaze
ca.1892–ca.1918 (1882–
present)
(member of Wedgwood
Group)

N

STONE WARE
DAVID METHVEN & SONS

DAVID METHVEN & SONS
Kirkaldy, Fifeshire, Scotland
Earthenware
ca.1883–1903 (ca.1850–
ca.1930)

O

STONE WARE
B &B

BATES & BENNETT
Cobridge, Staffordshire,
England
Stoneware. Printed
ca.1868–1895 (1868–
1895)

P

MISCELLANEOUS

A *Dresden* CARL THIEME SAXONIAN PORCELAIN FACTORY Potschappel, Saxony, Germany (E. Germany) Porcelain. Blue underglaze, overglaze 1903 + (1872–present) (Saxonian Porcelain Manufactory Dresden VEB)	**B** DUNN, BENNETT & CO. (LTD.) Burslem, Staffordshire, England Earthenware. Printed, variations in wording 1875–1907 (1875–·1964 +)	**C** BURGESS & LEIGH Burslem & Stoke, Staffordshire, England Earthenware. Printed 1930 + (1862–present)	**D** DELLA ROBBIA CO. LTD. Birkenhead, Cheshire, England Earthenware, tiles, plaques. Incised, initial above is decorator ca.1894–1901 (1894–1901)
E ALTENKUNSTADT PORCELAIN FACTORY Altenkunstadt, Bavaria, Germany (W. Germany) Earthenware, porcelain. Blue underglaze, black overglaze 1933–ca.1960 (1933–present)	**F**  T. & R. BOOTE, LTD. Burslem, Staffordshire, England Earthenware, parian, tiles. Printed 1890–1906 (1842–1964 +)	**G** W. T. COPELAND (& SONS, LTD.) Stoke, Staffordshire, England Porcelain, earthenware, parian. Printed ca.1894–1910 (1847–present) (Royal Worcester Spode, Ltd.)	**H** FURNIVALS LTD. Cobridge, Staffordshire, England Earthenware ca.1905–1913 (1890–1964 +)
I MADE IN U.S.A. EDWIN M. KNOWLES CHINA CO. East Liverpool, OH, U.S.A. Semivitreous dinnerware 1910–1948 (1900–1963)	**J**  PORCELAINE DE PARIS Paris, France Porcelair ca.1963	**K**  RÖRSTRAND AB Lidkoping, Sweden Porcelain 1930 + (1726–present)	**L** A. E. GRAY & CO. LTD. Stoke, Staffordshire, England Earthenware. Printed, variations in wording 1934–1961 (ca.1912–present) (Portmeirion Potteries, Ltd.)
M POWELL & BISHOP/ POWELL, BISHOP & STONIER/BISHOP & STONIER Hanley, Staffordshire, England Porcelain, earthenware 1876–1936 (1876–1939)	**N** HAAGSCHE PLATEELBAKKERY Rozenburg, Holland Porcelain 1909 + (ca.1883–ca.1915)	**O**  J. B. OWENS POTTERY Zanesville, OH, U.S.A. Art pottery 1885 + (1885–1929)	**P**  HOMER LAUGHLIN CHINA CO. East Liverpool, OH, U.S.A. Semivitreous dinnerware ca.1960 (1877–present)

A

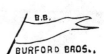

LIMOGES CHINA CO.
Sebring, OH, U.S.A.
Semivitreous dinnerware
1939–ca.1950 (1900–
1955)
(American Limoges China
Co.)

B

BARNY, RIGONI, LANGLE
Limoges, France
Porcelain
1894+ (1894–1902)

C

AMERICAN POTTERY
MANUFACTURING CO.
Jersey City, NJ, U.S.A.
Bone china. Printed, black
underglaze
1833–1840 (1829–1892)

D

BURFORD BROS.
East Liverpool, OH, U.S.A.
Ironstone
1881–1904 (1879–1904)

E

HARROP & BURGESS/
THOMAS BURGESS
Hanley, Staffordshire,
England
Earthenware. Printed,
impressed
1894–1917 (1894–1917)

F

J. H. WEATHERBY &
SONS (LTD.)
Hanley, Staffordshire,
England
Earthenware. Printed,
variations in wording
1892–present (1891–
present)

G

UNION POTTERIES CO.
East Liverpool, OH, U.S.A.
Ironstone
1894–1905 (1894–1905)

H

H. SCHMIDT PORCELAIN
FACTORY
Freiwaldau, Silesia,
Germany (Gozdnica,
Poland)
Hard paste porcelain. Blue
underglaze
ca.1894–1923 (1894–
1923)

I

VERNON KILNS
Vernon, CA, U.S.A.
Dinnerware
ca.1953–1954 (1912–
1958)

J

JOHNSON BROS. LTD.
Hanley, Staffordshire,
England
Earthenware, ironstone
current (1883–present)
(member of Wedgwood
Group)

K

ROYAL CHINA CO.
Sebring, OH, U.S.A.
Semivitreous dinnerware
ca.1970 (1933–present)

L

HOMER LAUGHLIN CHINA
CO.
East Liverpool, OH, U.S.A.
Semivitreous ware
ca.1957 (1877–present)

M

PLANKENHAMMER
PORCELAIN FACTORY
Plankenhammer, Bavaria,
Germany (W. Germany)
Hard paste porcelain
ca.1920–ca.1978 (1908–
ca.1978)

N

STATE PORCELAIN
FACTORY M. W.
LOMONOSSOW
LENINGRAD
Leningrad, U.S.S.R.
Hard paste porcelain
1917+ (1917–present)

O

FISCHER & MEIG
Pirkenhammer, Bohemia
(Brezova,
Czechoslovakia)
Porcelain. Green
underglaze
1875–1887 (1857–1918)

P

EPIAG
Pirkenhammer, Bohemia
(Brezova,
Czechoslovakia)
Porcelain. Green
underglaze, variations in
wording
1910–1945 (1920–
1945+)

A

.FRIEDRICH KAESTNER
Oberhohndorf, Saxony,
  Germany (E. Germany)
Porcelain
ca.1884–ca.1929 (1883–
  1972)

B

METZLER & ORTLOFF
Ilmenau, Thuringia,
  Germany (E. Germany)
Porcelain
ca.1887 (1875–present)
(Art Porcelain VEB)

C

MOSANIC POTTERY MAX
  EMANUEL & CO.
Mitterteich, Bavaria,
  Germany (W. Germany)
Hard paste porcelain
ca.1897–1918 (ca.1882–
  present)
(Mitterteich Porcelain
  Factory AG)

D

THEODORE HAVILAND
Limoges, France
Undecorated porcelain
1920–1936 (1892–
  present)
(Haviland SA)

E

HOMER LAUGHLIN CHINA
  CO.
East Liverpool, OH, U.S.A.
Ironstone. Impressed
1886+ (1877–present)

F

MIDDLE LANE POTTERY/
  BROUWER POTTERY
East Hampton &
  Westhampton, NY, U.S.A.
Art pottery
1894+ (1894–1946)

G

Many English factories
  used the "Staffordshire
  Knot" as a mark. Various
  initials and names were
  used. Some of these
  factories are listed on
  page 268.

H

CAMARK POTTERY CO.
Camden, AR, U.S.A.
Art pottery
current (ca.1927–present)

I

LEIGH POTTERY
Alliance, OH, U.S.A.
Semivitreous ware
1926–1931 (1926–1931)

J

SEBRING POTTERY CO.
East Liverpool & Sebring,
  OH, U.S.A.
Semivitreous ware.
  Variations in wording
ca.1925–ca.1942 (1887–
  1948)

K

JOHNSON CHINA CO.
East Liverpool, OH, U.S.A.
Semivitreous dinnerware
1931–1936 (1931–1936)

L

WELLSVILLE CHINA CO.
East Liverpool, OH, U.S.A.
Vitreous ware
ca.1958 (1902–1969)

M

METLOX POTTERIES
Manhattan Beach, CA,
  U.S.A.
Dinnerware
current (1935–present)

N

STERLING CHINA CO.
Wellsville, OH, U.S.A. &
  Puerto Rico
Vitreous ware
1951–1976 (1917–
  present)

O

FUKAGAWA
Arita, Japan
Ceramics, porcelain.
  Imprinted, variations in
  wording
current (1880–present)

P

CHUGAI CHINA
Japan
Porcelain
1945–1952

A

SOCIETA CERAMICA
ITALIANA
Laveno, Italy
Earthenware, porcelain
20th century (1856–
present)

B

SALEM CHINA CO.
Salem, OH, U.S.A.
Porcelain
ca.1970 (1898–1967)

C

MT. FUJIYAMA NIPPON
Japan
Porcelain. Blue
ca.1900 (1890–1921)

D

JONROTH STUDIOS
Japan
Porcelain. Turquoise
ca.1900 (ca.1894–1921)

E

PURINTON POTTERY
Shippenville, PA, U.S.A.
Semivitreous ware
1941–1959 (1941–1959)

F

BRUSH POTTERY
Roseville, OH, U.S.A.
Pottery
1907–1908, 1965–1972
(1907–1908, 1925–
present)

G

SABIN INDUSTRIES, INC.
McKeesport, PA, U.S.A.
Ceramics
1970 + (1946–present)

H

HOMER LAUGHLIN CHINA
CO.
East Liverpool, OH, U.S.A.
Semivitreous dinnerware
ca.1965 (1877–present)

I

LIMOGES CHINA CO./
AMERICAN LIMOGES
CHINA CO.
East Liverpool, OH, U.S.A.
Semivitreous dinnerware
1935–1945 (1900–1955)

J

ROYAL CHINA CO.
Sebring, OH, U.S.A.
Semivitreous dinnerware
1934–1955 (1933–
present)

K

JAMES H. BAUM
Wellsville, OH, U.S.A.
Ironstone dinnerware
1888–1896 (1888–1896)

L

H. A. WAIN & SONS LTD.
Longton & Stoke,
Staffordshire, England
Porcelain, earthenware
current (1946–present)

M

NATIONAL POTTERIES,
INC.
Cleveland, OH, U.S.A.
Pottery, importer
1970 + (1938–present)

N

CERAMIC ART CO.
Trenton, NJ, U.S.A.
Porcelain. Painted, violet,
green, gold, black
1894–1906 (1889–
present)
(Lenox, Inc.)

O

BELLEEK

LENOX, INC.
Trenton, NJ, U.S.A.
Belleek. Stamped, green
1906–1924 (1906–
present)

P

HOMER LAUGHLIN CHINA
CO.
East Liverpool, OH, U.S.A.
Semivitreous dinnerware
ca.1935–1955 (1877–
present)

A

PEARL CHINA CO.
East Liverpool, OH, U.S.A.
Pottery
current (1930s–present)

B

G. L. ASHWORTH & BROS.
Hanley, Staffordshire,
England
Ironstone. Printed
1957 + (1784–present)
(member of Wedgwood
Group)

C

NEW ENGLAND POTTERY
CO.
Boston, MA, U.S.A.
Semiporcelain. Black
underglaze
1888 + (1854–1914)

D

STERLING CHINA CO.
Wellsville, OH, U.S.A.
Semivitreous ware. Quality
stamp
ca.1940 (1917–present)

E

ROYAL CHINA CO.
Sebring, OH, U.S.A.
Semivitreous dinnerware
ca.1940–ca.1950 (1933–
present)

F

SYRACUSE CHINA CORP.
Syracuse, NY, U.S.A.
Porcelain
1935 + (1871–present)
(various names & owners)

G

PADEN CITY POTTERY
CO.
Paden City, WV, U.S.A.
Semiporcelain dinnerware
1940 + (1914–1963)

H

WEST END POTTERY CO.
East Liverpool, OH, U.S.A.
Ironstone
1904 + (1893–1938)

I

KUZNETSOV FACTORY
Moscow, U.S.S.R.
Porcelain
1937 + (1810–present)

J

ROYAL PORCELAIN
MANUFACTORY
Meissen, Saxony, Germany
(E. Germany)
Porcelain. Impressed
1850 + (1710–present)
(State's Porcelain
Manufactory Meissen
VEB)

K

MOSANIC POTTERY
MAX EMANUEL & CO.
Mitterteich, Bavaria,
Germany (W. Germany)
Pink souvenir ware
ca.1900 (ca.1882–present)
(Mitterteich Porcelain
Factory AG)

L

RIDGWAYS
Hanley, Staffordshire,
England
Earthenware. Printed
1912 + (1879–present)
(Royal Doulton Tableware
Ltd.)

M

CANONSBURG POTTERY
CO.
Canonsburg, PA, U.S.A.
Semiporcelain
1970 + (1900–1978)

N

O

J. & M. P. BELL
Glasgow, Scotland
Earthenware, parian.
Impressed, printed
1881 + (1842–1928)

P

EBELING & REUSS CO.
Devon & Philadelphia, PA,
U.S.A.
Importer's mark
1900 + (1866–present)

A

FRANZ MANKA
Altrohlau, Bohemia (Stara
Role, Czechoslovakia)
Hard paste porcelain
1936–1945 (1833–1945)

B

TRESSEMANES & VOGT
Limoges, France
Porcelain
1891–1907 (1883–
present)
(Porcelain Raynaud & Co.)

C

COLONIAL CO.
East Liverpool, OH, U.S.A.
Semivitreous ware
1903–1929 (1903–1929)

D

SEBRING POTTERY CO.
East Liverpool & Sebring,
OH, U.S.A.
Hotel ware
1900–ca.1925 (1887–
1948)

E

WALDSASSEN
PORCELAIN FACTORY
Waldsassen, Bavaria,
Germany (W. Germany)
Collector plates
1968–present (1866–
present)

F

CASTLETON CHINA, INC.
New Castle, PA, U.S.A.
Porcelain
1940+ (1940–present)
(Anchor Hocking)

G

CASTLETON CHINA, INC.
New Castle, PA, U.S.A.
Porcelain
1940+ (1940–present)
(Anchor Hocking)

H

ROLAND VUICHON
Chantilly, France
Porcelain
1959+ (1944–1959+)

I

HORNSEA POTTERY CO.
LTD.
Hornsea, Yorkshire,
England
Earthenware. Printed,
impressed
1951+ (ca.1951–present)

J

BLACK FOREST
EARTHENWARE
FACTORY
Hornberg, Badenia,
Germany (W. Germany)
Earthenware.
1906+ (ca.1906–present)
(Duravit-Hornberg, Sanitary
Ceramic Work)

K

SHIELD

L

The shield or "beehive" was
used by many 18th-,
19th-, & 20th-century
makers. See page 269

M

C. M. HUTSCHEN-
REUTHER PORCELAIN
FACTORY
Hohenberg, Bavaria,
Germany (W. Germany)
Porcelain. Blue underglaze
1879+ (1814–present)
(Hutschenreuther AG)

N

B. BLOCH & CO.
Eichwald, Bohemia (Dubi,
Czechoslovakia)
Pottery. Blue underglaze
ca.1900+ (1871–1945)

O

ARNART IMPORTS
New York, NY, U.S.A.
Porcelain importer
1957–1981+ (1957–
present)

P

AUGARTEN PORCELAIN
FACTORY, VIENNA
Vienna, Austria
Decorative porcelain,
figurines. Blue
1923–present (1923–
present)

A

ERDMANN
SCHLEGELMILCH
PORCELAIN FACTORY
Suhl, Thuringia, Germany
(W. Germany)
Porcelain
1900–1938 (1881–1938)

B

ADOLPHE PORQUIER
Quimper, France
Pottery
1898–1904 (1809–
present)
(Société Nouvelle des
Faïenceries de Quimper
HB Henriot)

C

LANGENTHAL
PORCELAIN FACTORY
AG
Langenthal, Bern,
Switzerland
Tableware
1900 + (1906–present)

D

JULIUS DIETL PORCELAIN
FACTORY, KALTENHOF
Kaltenhof, Bohemia
(Oblanov,
Czechoslovakia)
Porcelain
1918–1939 (1900–
ca.1945)

E

MEISSEN STOVE &
PORCELAIN FACTORY
Meissen, Saxony, Germany
(E. Germany)
Tiles, household porcelain
after 1872–ca.1930 (1863–
1945)

F

ZSOLNAY
Budapest, Hungary
Porcelain, pottery
1800 + (1862–present)

G

CARL THIEME SAXONIAN
PORCELAIN FACTORY
Potschappel, Saxony,
Germany (E. Germany)
Porcelain
1905 + (1872–present)
(Saxonian Porcelain
Manufactory Dresden
VEB)

H

PRINCE-ELECTORAL
PORCELAIN
MANUFACTORY
Nymphenburg, Bavaria,
Germany (W. Germany)
Porcelain. Impressed
1754–1921 + (1753–
present)
(Albert Bäuml State's
Porcelain Manufactory
Nymphenburg)

I

HANS NEUERER
Oberkotzau, Bavaria,
Germany (W. Germany)
Porcelain. Green
underglaze
1943 + (1943–present)
(Electroporcelain Factory
Hans Neuerer)

J

J. S. MAIER & CO.
Poschetzau, Bohemia
(Bozicany,
Czechoslovakia)
Porcelain
ca.1939–1945 (1890–
ca.1945)

K

KERAMOS
Vienna, Austria
Decorative earthenware
1945 + (1920–present)

L

THREE STAR CO.
Crooksville, OH, U.S.A.
Ironstone
ca.1900–1910 (1897–
1929)

M

BROWN-WESTHEAD,
MOORE & CO.
Hanley, Staffordshire,
England
Earthenware, porcelain.
Printed
1884 + (1862–present)
(various names and
owners, now member of
Wedgwood Group)

N

BURGESS & LEIGH
Middleport, Staffordshire,
England
Earthenware. Printed
1880–1912 (1862–
present)

O

GODWIN & HEWITT
Hereford, England
Tiles. Printed, impressed
1889–1910 (1889–1910)

P

LIMOGES
THEODORE
HAVILAND
FRANCE

THEODORE HAVILAND &
CO.
Limoges, France
Porcelain. Green
underglaze
1920 + (1892–present)
(Haviland SA)

A

BURGAU PORCELAIN
   MANUFACTORY
Burgau, Thuringia,
   Germany (E. Germany)
Porcelain
1901–1929 (1901–1929)

B

ROYAL SAXE
   CORPORATION
New York, NY, U.S.A.
Porcelain
1952–1970 (1952–1970)

C

GIUSEPPI TAGLIARIOL
   (TAY BIRDS)
Monza, Italy
Bird sculptures
1952 + (1952–present)

D

FISCHER & MIEG
Pirkenhammer, Bohemia
   (Brezova,
   Czechoslovakia)
Porcelain
ca.1887–1918 (1857–
   1918)

E

WACHTERSBACH
   EARTHENWARE
   FACTORY
Schlierbach, Hesse,
   Germany (W. Germany)
Earthenware. Black or blue
1900–1907 (1832–
   present)

F

BURFORD BROS.
East Liverpool, OH, U.S.A.
Ironstone
1881–1904 (1879–1904)

G

BAWO & DOTTER
Fischern, Bohemia (Rybare,
   Czechoslovakia) & New
   York, NY, U.S.A.
Porcelain, earthenware. Red
   overglaze
1884–ca.1914 (1883–
   ca.1914)

H

NEW YORK &
   RUDOLSTADT
   POTTERY (ROYAL
   RUDOLSTADT)/
   NATHAN STRAUS &
   SONS
Rudolstadt, Thuringia,
   Germany (E. Germany)
   & New York, NY, U.S.A.
Porcelain
1904–1924 + (1882–
   1932)

I

KERAMOS
Vienna, Austria
Earthenware, porcelain
1945 + (1920–present)

J

LETTIN
   PORCELAINWORK VEB
Lettin, Saxony, Germany (E.
   Germany)
Porcelain
ca.1954–present (ca.1953–
   present)

K

VILLEROY & BOCH
Mettlach, Saar, Germany
   (W. Germany)
Earthenware. Impressed
ca.1836–ca.1850 (1813–
   present)
(various names, owners, &
   locations)

L

MALING POTTERY
Newcastle upon Tyne,
   Northumberland,
   England
Pottery. Printed
ca.1930–1955 (1762–
   1963)

M

ROYAL DEVON
Providence, RI, U.S.A.
Collector plates
(made by Gorham for
   Hamilton Collection)
1975–1982 (1975–1982)

N

NEW YORK &
   RUDOLSTADT
   POTTERY (ROYAL
   RUDOLSTADT)/
   NATHAN STRAUS &
   SONS
Rudolstadt, Thuringia,
   Germany (E. Germany)
   & New York, NY, U.S.A.
Porcelain
ca.1906–1924 + (1882–
   1932)

O

SCHUMANN &
   SCHREIDER
Schwarzenhammer,
   Bavaria, Germany (W.
   Germany)
Porcelain
1905 + (1905–present)

P

SCHRAMBERGER
   MAJOLICA FACTORY
Schramberg, Wurttemberg,
   Germany (W. Germany)
Majolica, stoneware,
   porcelain
1918 + (1820–1918 +)

A

STENINGE CERAMIC AB
Stockholm, Sweden
Porcelain
1932–1937 (1700–
1975+)

B

Combined shield mark
used by both United
States and English firms.
See page 268.

C

SAMUEL BARKER & SON
Nr. Rotherham, Yorkshire,
England
Earthenware
1850+ (1834–1893)

D

HEWITT & LEADBEATER
Longton, Staffordshire,
England
Willoware. Printed
1907–1919 (1907–1919)

E

BOURNE & LEIGH (LTD.)
Burslem, Staffordshire,
England
Earthenware. Printed
1912+ (1892–1941)

F

AXE VALE POTTERY
(DEVON), LTD.
Seaton, Devon, England
Hand-painted earthenware.
Printed
1959–present (1959–
present)

G

W. BAKER & CO. LTD.
Fenton, Staffordshire,
England
Earthenware. Printed
1893+ (1839–1932)

H

BLAIR & CO.
Longton, Staffordshire,
England
Porcelain. Printed
1900+ (ca.1880–1930)

I

BOVEY POTTERY CO.
LTD.
Bovey Tracey, Devon,
England
Earthenware. Printed,
impressed
1949–1956 (1894–1957)

J

CARL SCHUMANN
Arzberg, Bavaria, Germany
(W. Germany)
Porcelain
1896+ (1881–present)

K

 (n

GEORGE GRAINGER &
CO.
Worcester, England
Porcelain, parian,
semiporcelain. Printed
ca.1870–1879 (ca.1839–
present)
(Royal Worcester Spode
Ltd.)

L

NEW HALL POTTERY CO.
LTD.
Hanley, Staffordshire,
England
Earthenware. Printed
ca.1930–1951 (1899–
1956)

M

OHIO VALLEY CHINA CO.
Wheeling, WV, U.S.A.
Hard paste porcelain
1887–1893+ (ca.1887–
1893)

N

KERR & BINNS
Worcester, England
Porcelain. Printed
ca.1854–1862 (ca.1751–
present)
(Royal Worcester Spode
Ltd.)

O

WEDGWOOD & CO.
Tunstall, Staffordshire.
England
Earthenware, stone china.
Printed
1957+ (1860–present)
(member of Wedgwood
Group)

P

McNICOL-SMITH CO.
East Liverpool, OH, U.S.A.
Semivitreous tableware
ca.1895–1907 (1889–
1907)

A

STETSON CHINA CO.
Lincoln, IL, U.S.A.
Porcelain. Backstamp
1946+ (1919–1965)

B

NATIONAL CHINA CO.
East Liverpool, OH, U.S.A.
Semivitreous hotel ware
1911–ca.1924 (1899–
1929)

C

UNITED STATES
POTTERY CO.
Wellsville, OH, U.S.A.
Semivitreous porcelain
1899–1901, 1907–
ca.1920 (1898–1932)

D

C. & E. CARSTENS
PORCELAIN FACTORY
BLANKENHAIN
Blankenhain, Thuringia,
Germany (E. Germany)
Hard paste porcelain
1918–1945 (ca.1918–
present)
(Weimar Porcelain)

E

BENEDIKT HASSLACHER
Altrohlau, Bohemia (Stara
Role, Czechoslovakia)
Porcelain. Embossed
1813–1823 (1813–
1945+)
(various names & owners)

F

POTTER'S CO-
OPERATIVE CO.
East Liverpool, OH, U.S.A.
Vitreous hotel ware
ca.1896 (1882–1925)

G

EDWARD MARSHALL
BOEHM
Malvern Link,
Worcestershire, England
Porcelain
1975+ (1950–present)

H

A. B. JONES & SONS
(LTD.)
Longton, Staffordshire,
England
Porcelain, earthenware.
Printed
1900–1913 (1900–
present)
(Royal Grafton Bone China)

I

HYALYN PORCELAIN
Zanesville, OH, U.S.A.
Porcelain
ca.1960 (ca.1940–present)
(Hyalyn Cosco)

J

LOW ART TILE WORKS
Chelsea, MA, U.S.A.
Tile
1878–1907 (1877–1907)

K

GEORGE GRAINGER &
CO.
Worcester, England
Porcelain, parian,
semiporcelain. Printed
ca.1889–1902 (ca.1839–
present)
(Royal Worcester Spode
Ltd.)

L

T. G. GREEN & CO. (LTD.)
Nr. Burton-on-Trent,
Derbyshire, England
Earthenware, stoneware.
Printed
1892+ (ca.1864–present)

M

JOHN & WILLIAM
RIDGWAY
Hanley, Staffordshire,
England
Earthenware, porcelain.
Printed, impressed
ca.1814–1830 (1814–
present)
(Royal Doulton Tableware
Ltd.)

N

JOHN & WILLIAM
RIDGWAY
Hanley, Staffordshire,
England
Earthenware, porcelain,
various pattern names
ca.1814–1830 (1814–
present)
(Royal Doulton Tableware
Ltd.)

O

ANDRÉ GIRAUD,
BROUSSEAU & CO.
Limoges, France
Porcelain
1959+ (1935–1974+)

P

LIMOGES CHINA CO.
Sebring, OH, U.S.A.
Semivitreous dinnerware
1936–ca.1950 (1900–
1955)
(American Limoges China
Co.)

A

CARL SCHUMANN
PORCELAIN FACTORY
Arzberg, Bavaria, Germany
(W. Germany)
Porcelain. Green, blue
underglaze
1918+ (1881–present)

B

EICHHORN & BANDORF
Elgersburg, Saxony,
Germany (E. Germany)
Porcelain
1895–1905 (1886–1919)

C

GUÉRIN-POUYAT-ÉLITE
LTD.
Limoges, France
Porcelain
1896–1900 (1870–
present)
(various names)

D

J. POPPAUER
Franz, Austria
Earthenware, porcelain
ca.1884–1885 (ca.1884–
1885)

E

LANCASTER & SONS
(LTD.)
Hanley, Staffordshire,
England
Earthenware. Printed
1906+ (1900–1944)

F

LIPPERT & HAAS
Schlaggenwald, Bohemia
(Horni Slavkov,
Czechoslovakia)
Porcelain. Impressed
1830–1846 (ca.1808–
1945+)

G

MYOTT, SON & CO.
Cobridge, Staffordshire.
England
Earthenware
1930+ (1875–present)
(Myott-Meakin, Ltd.)

H

PICKARD CHINA CO
Antioch, IL, U.S.A.
Porcelain. Gold
1925–1938 (1893–
present)
(Pickard, Inc.)

I

VILLEROY & BOCH
Dresden, Saxony, Germany
(E. Germany)
Earthenware
ca.1887–ca.1945 (1813–
present)
(various names, owners, &
locations)

J

CO-OPERATIVE
WHOLESALE SOCIETY,
LTD.
Longton, Staffordshire,
England
Earthenware. Printed
ca.1950–1960+ (1922–
1964+)

K

DOULTON & CO.
Burslem, Staffordshire,
England
Marqueterie. Printed,
impressed, variations in
wording
1887–ca.1906 (1853–
present)
(Royal Doulton Tableware
Ltd.)

L

BROWNHILLS POTTERY
CO.
Tunstall, Staffordshire,
England
Earthenware, Printed
ca.1880–1896 (1872–
1896)

M

D. F. HAYNES & CO.
(CHESAPEAKE
POTTERY CO.)
Baltimore, MD, U.S.A.
Semivitreous china
1882–1884 (1881–1914)

N

AMERICAN CHINAWARE
CORP.
East Liverpool, OH, U.S.A.
Dinnerware
1929–1931 (1929–1931)

O

WOOD & BARKER LTD.
Burslem, Staffordshire,
England
Earthenware
1897–1903 (1897–1903)

P

PEMBERTON & OAKES
Santa Barbara, CA, U.S.A.
Porcelain
current (1977–present)

A

EAST LIVERPOOL
POTTERIES CO.
East Liverpool, OH, U.S.A.
Semivitreous ware
1901–ca.1907 (1901–
1933)

B

CARL SCHUMANN
PORCELAIN FACTORY
Arzberg, Bavaria, Germany
(W. Germany)
Porcelain
(1881–present)

C

WACHTERSBACH
EARTHENWARE
FACTORY
Schierbach, Hesse,
Germany (W. Germany)
Earthenware. Various colors
1903–1921 (1832–
present)

D

EDWARD MARSHALL
BOEHM
Trenton, NJ, U.S.A.
Limited editions
1958–1970 (1950–
present)

E

MUELLER MOSAIC TILE
CO.
Trenton, NJ, U.S.A.
Pottery, tile
(1909–1938)

F

JAMES MACINTYRE & CO.
(LTD.)
Burslem, Staffordshire,
England
Earthenware. Printed,
brown
1898–ca.1904 (ca.1860–
ca.1928)

G

CHARLES AHRENFELDT
Limoges, France
Hard paste porcelain
(1859–1969)

H

D. E. McNICOL POTTERY
CO.
East Liverpool, OH, U.S.A.
Vitreous ware
1930–1954 (1892–1954)

I

PALISSY

ENGLAND

ALBERT & JONES
(LONGTON) LTD.
Longton, Staffordshire,
England
Earthenware. Printed,
impressed
ca.1908–1936 (1905–
1946)

J

ROWLAND & MARSELLUS
CO.
Longton, Staffordshire,
England
United States importer's
mark
1860+–1900+ (1860–
1900+)
(believed to be British
Anchor Pottery Co.)

K

Shelley

ENGLAND

SHELLEY POTTERIES
LTD.
Longton, Staffordshire,
England
Porcelain. Printed
ca.1925–1940 (1925–
present)
(Royal Doulton Tableware
Ltd.)

L

F. THOMAS PORCELAIN
FACTORY
Marktredwitz, Bavaria,
Germany (W. Germany)
Porcelain. Green
underglaze
1908+ (1908–present)
(Rosenthal Glass &
Porcelain AG

M

SAMPSON BRIDGWOOD
& SON
Longton, Staffordshire,
England
Earthenware, porcelain
1885+ (ca.1805–present)

N

D. E. McNICOL POTTERY
CO.
East Liverpool, OH, U.S.A.
Ironstone tableware
1892–ca.1910 (1892–
1954)

O

JOHN EDWARDS (& CO.)
Fenton, Staffordshire,
England
Porcelain, earthenware.
Printed
ca.1880–1900 (1847–
1900)

P

ONONDAGA POTTERY
CO.
Syracuse, NY, U.S.A.
White granite ware
1874–1893 (1871–
present)
(Syracuse China Co.)

A

FRENCH SAXON CHINA CO.
Sebring, OH, U.S.A.
Semivitreous tableware
1935–1964 (1935–present)
(Royal China Co.)

B

VILLEROY & BOCH
Mettlach, Saar, Germany (W. Germany)
Earthenware. Stamped 1874–present (1813–present)
(various names, owners, & locations)

C

BAREUTHER & CO. PORCELAIN FACTORY WALDSASSEN AG
Waldsassen, Bavaria, Germany (W. Germany)
Porcelain
current (1866–present)

D

ETRURIA POTTERY (OTT & BREWER)
Trenton, NJ, U.S.A.
Pottery
(1863–1894)

E

KNOWLES, TAYLOR & KNOWLES
East Liverpool, OH, U.S.A.
Belleek
1889 + (1870–1929)

F

KNOWLES, TAYLOR & KNOWLES
East Liverpool, OH, U.S.A.
Graniteware
ca.1890–ca.1907 (1870–1929)

G

COXON & CO.
Trenton, NJ, U.S.A.
White granite & cream-colored ware. Black underglaze
(1863–ca.1884)

H

SQUARE, RECTANGLE & OTHER GEOMETRIC SHAPES

I

JOSEF HOFFMANN
Vienna, Austria
Pottery
ca.1920 (ca.1905–1932)

J

EDUARD JOSEF WIMMER
Vienna, Austria
Pottery. Impressed
ca.1920 (ca.1905–1932)

K

ROBINEAU POTTERY
Syracuse, NY, U.S.A.
Porcelain, stoneware
ca.1910 (1901–1928)

L

BERNARD LEACH
St. Ives, Cornwall, England
Studio pottery
1921 + (1921–1964 +)

M

GLADDING, MCBEAN & CO.
Los Angeles, CA, U.S.A.
Franciscan dinnerware
1938–1939 (1875–present)
(member of Wedgwood Group)

N

KANDERN POTTERY WORKS
Kandern, Badenia, Germany (W. Germany)
Earthenware, pottery
ca.1915 (ca.1888–present)

O

KANDERN POTTERY WORKS
Kandern, Badenia, Germany (W. Germany)
Earthenware, pottery. Incised
ca.1895–1913 (ca.1888–present)

P

R. WOLFINGER PORCELAIN FACTORY WEINGARTEN
Weingarten, Badenia, Germany (W. Germany)
Porcelain
ca.1903–1922 (1882–1922)

A

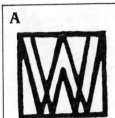

VIENNA WORKSHOPS
(WIENER WERKSTÄTTE)
Vienna, Austria
Porcelain, earthenware
ca.1913–1923 + (1905–
1932)

B

WILLIAM ADAMS & SONS
LTD.
Tunstall & Stoke,
Staffordshire, England
Earthenware. Printed
1896 + (1769–present)
(member of Wedgwood
Group)

C

W. T. COPELAND (&
SONS LTD.)
Stoke, Staffordshire,
England
Porcelain, parian,
earthenware. Printed
ca.1920 (1847–present)
(Royal Worcester Spode
Ltd.)

D

DOULTON & CO.
Lambeth, London, England
Persian ware. Printed,
impressed
ca.1920–1936 (1853–
present)
(Royal Doulton Tableware
Ltd.)

E

HALL CHINA CO.
East Liverpool, OH, U.S.A.
Vitrified household cooking
ware
ca.1950–ca.1955 (1903–
present)

F

GEORGE GRAINGER (&
CO.)
Worcester, England
Semiporcelain, parian
ca.1860–1889 (ca.1839–
present)
(Royal Worcester Spode
Ltd.)

G

HALL CHINA CO.
East Liverpool, OH, U.S.A.
Dinnerware. Stamped
ca.1932–1963 (1903–
present)

H

HARKER POTTERY CO.
East Liverpool, OH, U.S.A.
Semivitreous dinnerware
1955–ca.1960 (1890–
1972)

I

HUTSCHENREUTHER
ARZBERG
BAVARIA GERMANY

C. M. HUTSCHEN-
REUTHER PORCELAIN
FACTORY
Arzberg, Bavaria, Germany
(W. Germany)
Porcelain. Green
underglaze
1969 + (1814–present)
(Hutschenreuther AG)

J

KIRKHAM
POTTERY
MADE IN ENGLAND

KIRKHAMS, LTD.
Stoke, Staffordshire,
England
Earthenware. Printed
ca.1946–1961 (1946–
present)
(Portmeiron Potteries, Ltd.)

K

KUNSTWERKSTÄTTE
WILHELMSFELD

W. GOEBEL
Rodental, Bavaria, Germany
(W. Germany)
Porcelain, earthenware,
figurines. Overglaze
ca.1919 (1871–present)

L

KERAFINA PORCELAIN
FACTORY GMBH
Marktredwitz, Bavaria,
Germany (W. Germany)
Porcelain. Overglaze
1950–1981 + (1950–
present)

M

ERNST WAHLISS
ALEXANDRA
PORCELAIN WORKS
Turn-Teplitz, Bohemia
(Trnovany,
Czechoslovakia)
Porcelain, faience
ca.1912–ca.1921 (1894–
1934)

N

JOSIAH SPODE
Stoke, Staffordshire,
England
Stone china, earthenware,
porcelain. Printed
ca.1805–1830 (ca.1762–
present)
(Royal Worcester Spode
Ltd.)

O

W. T. COPELAND (&
SONS LTD.)
Stoke, Staffordshire,
England
Porcelain, parian,
earthenware. Printed
1875–1890 (1847–
present)
(Royal Worcester Spode
Ltd.)

P

STETSON CHINA CO.
Lincoln, IL, U.S.A.
Semiporcelain dinnerware.
Backstamp
1950 + (1919–1965)

A

WILLIAM DE MORGAN
Chelsea, London, England
Earthenware
1872–1881 (ca.1072–
1911)

B

WATCOMBE
TORQUAY
MADE IN
ENGLAND

ROYAL ALLER VALE &
WATCOMBE POTTERY
CO.
Torquay, Devon, England
Earthenware. Impressed
ca.1920–ca.1927(ca.1901–
1962)

C

ZELL

F. J, LEN7 & BURQER
Zell on Harmersbach,
Badenia, Germany (W.
Germany)
Earthenware
ca.1808–1819 (1784–
present)
(various names & owners,
Georg Schmider United
Zell Ceramic Factories)

D

PILKINGTON'S TILE &
POTTERY CO. LTD.
Clifton Junction,
Lancashire, England
Earthenware. Printed,
impressed
1904–1914 (1893–
present)
(Pilkington's Tiles Ltd.)

E

BOURNE & LEIGH LTD.
Burslem, Staffordshire,
England
Earthenware. Printed
1930s (1892–1941)

F

E. BRAIN & CO., LTD.

E. BRAIN & CO. LTD.
Fenton, Staffordshire,
England
Porcelain. Printed
1905+ (1903–present)
(member of Wedgwood
Group)

G

FRIEDRICH
GOLDSCHEIDER
VIENNA
MANUFACTORY
Vienna, Austria
Faience, porcelain
ca.1885–ca.1910 (1885–
present)
(various names)

H

WILLIAM DE MORGAN
Chelsea (London),
England
Earthenware, tiles, vases.
Impressed
1882–1888 (1872–1911)

I

VAN BRIGGLE POTTERY
Colorado Springs, CO,
U.S.A.
Art pottery. Incised
1901–1949, 1965+ (1900–
present)

J

AULT

WILLIAM AULT
Swadlincote, Staffordshire,
England
Earthenware. Impressed,
molded
ca.1887–1923 (1887–
1923)

K

CALIFORNIA FAIENCE
Berkeley, CA, U.S.A.
Art pottery, tiles. Incised
1920+ (1916–ca.1930)

L

DENBY TABLEWARE
Denby, Derbyshire,
England
Stoneware
ca.1972 (1809–present)

M

A. E. JONES/PALISSY
POTTERY, LTD.
Longton, Staffordshire,
England
Earthenware. Printed
1937–1946+ (1905–
present)
(Royal Worcester Spode
Ltd.)

N

REGINALD FAIRFAX
WELLS
Kent, London, & Sussex,
England
Studio pottery, stoneware.
Impressed, incised
ca.1918–1951 (ca.1909–
ca.1951)

O

TRESSEMANES & VOGT/
GUSTAV VOGT/
MARTIAL RAYNAUD
Limoges, France
Porcelain
1892–1917+ (1883–
present)

P

PORTHEIM & SONS
Chodau, Bohemia (Chodov,
Czechoslovakia)
Porcelain. Impressed
ca.1850–ca.1870 (1850–
1872)

A

VOLKMAR CERAMIC CO.
Brooklyn, NY, U.S.A.
Art tiles, mugs, plaques.
  Impressed, incised
  ca.1895 (1895 +)
  (various names &
  locations)

B

W. De Morgan

WILLIAM DE MORGAN
Chelsea & Fulham,
  London, England
Earthenware, tiles, vases
ca.1882–1888 (ca.1872–
  1911)

C

WELLER

WELLER POTTERY
Zanesville, OH, U.S.A.
Art pottery. Raised
ca.1910 (1882–1948)

D

EDUARD JOSEF WIMMER
Vienna, Austria
Ceramics. Impressed
1905 + (ca.1905–1932)

E

FULPER

FULPER POTTERY
Flemington, NJ, U.S.A.
Art pottery, dolls' heads
1910–1929 (1899–1935)

F

FULPER POTTERY
Flemington, NJ, U.S.A.
Art pottery, dolls' heads.
  Embossed
1922–1928 (1899–1935)

G

HERTWIG & CO.
  PORCELAIN FACTORY
Katzhutte, Thuringia,
  Germany (E. Germany)
Earthenware
ca.1932–1945 (1864–
  1945)

H

AMERICAN TERRA COTTA
  & CERAMIC CO.
Terra Cotta & Chicago, IL,
  U.S.A.
Art pottery. Stamped,
  impressed
1895–1922 (1886–1930)

I

VALENTIEN POTTERY
San Diego, CA, U.S.A.
Art pottery. Impressed
ca.1911–ca.1915
  (ca.1911–ca.1915)

J

ABINGDON POTTERY
  (ABINGDON SANITARY
  MANUFACTURING CO.)
Abingdon, IL, U.S.A.
Art pottery
1934–1950 (1934–1950)

K

A. E. HULL POTTERY CO.
Crooksville, OH, U.S.A.
Earthenware, stoneware.
  Impressed
1910–1935 (1905–1950,
  1952–present)
  (Hull Pottery)

L

HEINZL & CO.
Granesau, Bohemia
  (Chranisov,
  Czechoslovakia)
Ceramics
1924–1939 (1924–1945)

M

SOUTHERN POTTERIES
  (BLUE RIDGE CHINA
  CO.)
Erwin, TN, U.S.A.
Dinnerware
1920 + (1918–1957)

N

KOPPELSDORF UNITED
  PORCELAINWORKS
  VEB
Koppelsdorf, Germany
  (E. Germany)
Porcelain
1954 + (1945–present)
  (Electroceramics Works
  Sonneberg VEB)

O

PEARL POTTERY CO.
Hanley, Staffordshire,
  England
Earthenware. Printed,
  impressed
1894–1912 (1894–1936)

P

ROWLAND & MARSELLUS
  CO.
Longton, Staffordshire,
  England
Porcelain
United States importer's
  mark
1860–1900 + (1860–
  1900 +)
  (believed to be British
  Anchor Pottery Co.)

A

WILLIAM BLOOR
East Liverpool, OH, U.S.A.
Parian. Raised
1861–1862 (1860–1862)

B

English registry mark. See
pages 238–240 for
complete explanation.

C

LESME
Limoges, France
Porcelain, majolica. Raised
1852–ca.1881 (1852–
ca.1881)

D

NEW ENGLAND POTTERY
CO.
Boston, MA, U.S.A.
Porcelain
1883–1886 (1854–1914)

E

PHILADELPHIA CITY
POTTERY (J. E.
JEFFORDS)
Philadelphia, PA, U.S.A.
Earthenware, majolica
ca.1868 (1868–ca.1915)

F

BLYTH PORCELAIN CO.
LTD.
Longton, Staffordshire,
England
Porcelain. Printed,
impressed
ca.1925–1935 (ca.1905–
1935)

G

EDWIN BENNETT
POTTERY CO.
Baltimore, MD, U.S.A.
Earthenware, porcelain
1896+ (1856–1936)

H

A. T. FINNEY & SONS
LTD.
Longton & Stoke,
Staffordshire, England
Bone china
current (1947–present)

I

ROYAL CHINA CO.
Sebring, OH, U.S.A.
Dinnerware
ca.1934–ca.1960 (1933–
present)

J

EDWIN BENNETT
POTTERY CO.
Baltimore, MD, U.S.A.
Porcelain
ca.1886 (1856–1936)

K

MAYER CHINA CO.
Beaver Falls, PA, U.S.A.
Ironstone
1881–1891 (1881–
present)

L

PFALTZGRAFF CO.
York, PA, U.S.A.
Stoneware
1940+ (1811–present)

M

CORNING GLASS WORKS
Corning, NY, U.S.A.
Pyroceram (ceramic-like
glass)
1962+ (1868–present)

N

GLADDING, McBEAN &
CO./INTERPACE CORP.
Los Angeles, CA, U.S.A.
Franciscan dinnerware
1963–1964 (1875–
present)
(various owners & names,
now member of
Wedgwood Group)

O

HIBEL STUDIO
Staffelstein, Bavaria,
Germany (W. Germany)
Porcelain
1979+ (1979–present)

P

EDWIN M. KNOWLES
CHINA CO.
East Liverpool, OH, U.S.A.
Porcelain, dinnerware
1953+ (1900–1963)

A

LUCIE RIE
London, England
Studio pottery. Impressed
ca.1938–present (ca.1938–
present)

B

W. B. SIMPSON & SONS
London, England
Painted tiles. Impressed
1878+ (1873–1964+)

C

SÈVRES
Sèvres, France
Porcelain. Red & brown
overglaze, various dates
1902–1941 (1756–
present)

D

IROQUOIS CHINA CO.
Syracuse, NY, U.S.A.
Porcelain
1946+ (1905–1969)

E

HALL CHINA CO.
East Liverpool, OH, U.S.A.
Dinnerware
1969–1980+ (1903–
present)

F

NAPCOWARE

NATIONAL POTTERIES,
INC.
Cleveland, OH, U.S.A.
Pottery distributors
1938–present (1938–
present)

G

SÈVRES
Sèvres, France
Porcelain. Printed,
impressed, relief molded,
various dates
1897+ (1756–present)
(see pages 248–250)

H

ARABIA
HELSINGFORS

ARABIA PORCELAIN
FACTORY
Helsingfors (Helsinki),
Finland
Porcelain. Stamped
1880–1890 (1874–
present)
(Upsala-Ekeby Group)

I

August Nowotny & C
ALTROHLAU
Karlsbad.

AUGUST NOWOTNY
Altrohlau, Bohemia (Stara
Role, Czechoslovakia)
Faience, earthenware,
porcelain. Impressed
1838–1884 (1823–
1945+)
(various names & owners)

J

CARTER
STABLER
ADAMS
POOLE
ENGLAND

CARTER, STABLER &
ADAMS LTD.
Poole, Dorset, England
Earthenware. Impressed,
printed
1921–1925 (1921–
present)
(Poole Pottery Ltd.)

K

FENTON
STONE WORKS

G. M. & C. J. MASON
Lans Delph, Staffordshire,
England
Ironstone. Transfer-printed
with pattern number
1824+ (1813–present)
(member of Wedgwood
Group)

L

Fr. Goldscheider
WIEN

FRIEDRICH
GOLDSCHEIDER
VIENNA
MANUFACTORY
Vienna, Austria
Faience, porcelain. Printed,
impressed
1885–1897 (1885–
present)
(various names)

M

HAVILAND
DEPOSÉ

HAVILAND BROS. & CO./
HAVILAND & CO.
Limoges, France
Porcelain. Relief
1855–1865 (1852–
present)
(Haviland SA)

N

ENGLAND
1760
LEEDS
1878
FIRST REPRODUCED
BY MASONS 1932

G. L. ASHWORTH & BROS.
Hanley, Staffordshire,
England
Earthenware, ironstone.
Printed
1932+ (1784–present)
(member of Wedgwood
Group)

O

MEHUN
C.P.
& Co.
FRANCE

CHARLES PILLIVUYT
Mehun-sur-Yevre, France
Porcelain, faience
1854+ (1854+)

P

POOLE
ENGLAND

CARTER, STABLER &
ADAMS LTD.
Poole, Dorset, England
Earthenware. Impressed,
printed
1921+ (1921–present)
(Poole Pottery Ltd.)

A

UTZCHNEIDER & CO.
Sarreguemines, France
Porcelain, transfer-printed
wares, majolica
before 1890 (ca.1770–
present)

B

ABINGDON POTTERY
(ABINGDON SANITARY
MANUFACTORY CO.)
Abingdon, IL, U.S.A.
Art pottery
1940 + (1934–1950)

C

DOULTON & CO.
Lambeth, London, England
Earthenware, stoneware.
Impressed
ca.1881–1912 (1853–
present)
(Royal Doulton Tableware
Ltd.)

D

WORCESTER ROYAL
PORCELAIN CO. LTD.
Worcester, England
Porcelain
current (1862–present)
(Royal Worcester Spode
Ltd.)

E

UNITED STATES
POTTERY CO.
Bennington, VT, U.S.A.
Marbleized ware. Impressed
ca.1852–1858 (1793–
1858)

F

ROBERT HERON (& SON)
(FIFE POTTERY)
Sinclairtown, Kirkcaldy,
Scotland
Earthenware, Rockingham-
type ware
ca.1880–1929 (1850–
1929)

G

THOMAS DEAN (& SON)
(LTD.)
Tunstall, Staffordshire,
England
Earthenware. Printed
1937–1947 (1789–1947)

H

UNION PORCELAIN
WORKS
Greenpoint, NY, U.S.A.
Porcelain. Red, printed
ca.1879 (1865–1904)

I

FREIBERG PORCELAIN
FACTORY
Freiberg, Saxony, Germany
(E. Germany)
ca.1914–ca.1954 (1906–
present)
(Porcelain Combine Colditz
VEB)

J

WILLIAM STAITE MURRAY
Rotherhithe, Surrey,
England
Studio-type pottery. Printed
1919–1940 (ca.1915–
1940)

K

NORAH BRADEN
St. Ives & Coleshill,
Wiltshire, England
Studio-type pottery.
Impressed
1924–1936 (1924–1936)

L

HULL-HOUSE KILNS
Chicago, IL, U.S.A.
Ceramics
1927–ca.1940 (1927–
ca.1940)

M

CASTLETON CHINA, INC.
New Castle, PA, U.S.A.
Porcelain
(1940–present)
(Anchor Hocking)

N

WILLETS
MANUFACTURING CO.
Trenton, NJ, U.S.A.
Porcelain
1879–1909 (1879–1962)

O

FRIEDRICH
GOLDSCHEIDER VIENNA
MANUFACTORY
Vienna, Austria
Earthenware, porcelain,
faience, terra-cotta.
Printed, impressed
1930 + (1885–present)
(various names)

P

CHESTER POTTERY
Phoenixville, PA, U.S.A.
Pottery
ca.1894–1897 (1894–
1897)

A

KEYSTONE

CHINA

KEYSTONE CHINA CO.
East Liverpool, OH, U.S.A.
Semivitreous dinnerware
1952–1954 (ca.1946–
1954)

B

VODREY & BROTHERS
POTTERY CO.
East Liverpool, OH, U.S.A.
Ironstone hotel ware
1876–1896 (ca.1857–
1928)

C

JACKSON VITRIFIED
CHINA CO.
Falls Creek, PA, U.S.A.
Semivitreous ware
ca.1930 (1917–present)
(Jackson China Co.)

D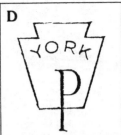

PFALTZGRAFF CO.
York, PA, U.S.A.
Stoneware
1940 + (1811–present)

E

STAR
&
SUN

F

HAAGSCHE
PLATEELBAKKERY
Rozenburg, Holland
Ceramics
ca.1913 (ca.1883–ca.1915)

G

LATRILLE BROTHERS
Limoges, France
Porcelain
ca.1900 (1899–1908)

H

STAR POTTERY
Possil Park, Glasgow,
Scotland
Earthenware, stoneware.
Printed, impressed
1880–1907 (1880–1907)

I

HEWITT & LEADBEATER
Longton, Staffordshire,
England
Porcelain, parian
ca.1907–1919 (1907–
1919)

J

SCHOENAU &
HOFFMEISTER
PORCELAIN FACTORY
BURGGRUB
Burggrub, Bavaria,
Germany (W. Germany)
Porcelain
1909–1952 (1909–1952)

K

GLOBE POTTERY CO.
East Liverpool, OH, U.S.A.
Ironstone
ca.1896 (1888–1901,
1907–1912)

L

STERN PORCELAIN
MANUFACTORY/
E. LEBER & SON
Tiefenfurt, Silesia, Germany
(Parowa, Poland)
Porcelain
ca.1920–ca.1933 (1914–
1933)

M

TRENTON POTTERY CO.
Trenton, NJ, U.S.A.
Pottery. Variations in
wording
1892 + (1853–1902 +)

N

ROBERT HAVILAND & LE
TANNEUR
Limoges, France
Hard paste porcelain
1937–1948 (1926–
present)
(various names, now Robert
Haviland & C. Parlon)

O

CHATHAM

C. C. THOMPSON
POTTERY CO.
East Liverpool, OH, U.S.A.
Semivitreous tableware
ca.1927–1938 (1868–
1938)

P

HEINRICH BAENSCH
Lettin, Saxony, Germany (E.
Germany)
Hard paste porcelain
1900–1930 (1858–1930)
(Lettin Porcelainwork VEB)

A

ILMENAU PORCELAIN
FACTORY AG
Ilmenau, Thuringia,
Germany (E. Germany)
Porcelain. Blue, green
ca.1905–ca.1938 (1777–
present)
(various names, now
Henneberg Porcelain
VEB)

B

REINHOLD MERKELBACH
Hohr-Grenzhausen,
Palatinate, Germany (W.
Germany)
Steins
ca.1895+ (1845–present)

C

P. DONATH SILESIAN
PORCELAIN FACTORY/
SILESIAN PORCELAIN
FACTORY
TIEFENFÜRTH
Tiefenfurth, Silesia,
Germany (Parowa,
Poland)
Porcelain
ca.1896–1919 (ca.1890–
1919)

D

MADE IN JAPAN
OCCUPIED
——————
Japan
Porcelain
1947–1952

E

AMPHORA WORK
REISSNER
Turn-Teplitz, Bohemia
(Trnovany,
Czechoslovakia)
Porcelain, earthenware
1892–1905 (1892–
1945+)
(various names,
nationalized in 1945)

F

TOOTH & AULT
Nr. Burton-on-Trent,
Staffordshire, England
Earthenware
1884–1887 (1883–
present)
(Tooth & Co. Ltd.)

G

A. B. JONES & SONS
(LTD.)
Longton, Staffordshire,
England
Porcelain, earthenware.
Printed
ca.1935+ (1900–present)
(Royal Grafton Bone China)

H

RISING SUN NIPPON
Japan
Porcelain. Blue
1890–1921

I

LINDNER PORCELAIN
FACTORY KG
Kups, Bavaria, Germany
(W. Germany)
Porcelain
1948–1981+ (1932–
present)

J

J. & G. MEAKIN (LTD.)
Hanley, Staffordshire,
England
Earthenware, ironstone.
Printed
1912+ (1851–present)
(member of Wedgwood
Group)

K

HERMAN SCHOLZ
SUCCESSOR
Tiefenbach, Bohemia
(Hluboka,
Czechoslovakia)
Porcelain
ca.1912–ca.1945
(ca.1912–ca.1945)

L

NEW MILFORD POTTERY
CO./WANNOPEE
POTTERY CO.
New Milford, CT, U.S.A.
Porcelain. Impressed
1886+ (1886–1903)

M

LA SOLANA POTTERIES
Scottsdale & Mesa, AZ,
U.S.A.
Earthenware
1954+ (1954–present)

N

MÜHLBACH PORCELAIN
FACTORY
Bruchmühlbach, Palatinate,
Germany (W. Germany)
Porcelain
1951–ca.1970 (1951–
present)
(Winterling Group)

O

TRIANGLE
&
HEART

P

DUX PORCELAIN
MANUFACTORY
Dux, Bohemia (Duchcov,
Czechoslovakia)
Porcelain
ca.1918–1945 (1860–
present)
(Duchcov Porcelain)

A

SIMON PETER GERZ
Hohr-Grenzhausen,
Palatinate, Germany (W.
Germany)
Ceramics
ca. 1910 (1862–present)

B

VIENNA ART CERAMIC
FACTORY/FOSTER &
CO./VIENNA ART
CERAMIC WORKSHOP
Vienna, Austria
Earthenware, porcelain
1906 + (1899–1940)

C

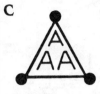

ARABIA PORCELAIN
FACTORY
Helsingfors (Helsinki),
Finland
Earthenware, porcelain
1897–1907 (1874–
present)
(Upsala-Ekeby Group)

D

FAÏENCERIE DE LA
GRANDE MAISON
(HUBAUDIÈRE)
Quimper, France
Faience
1898 + (1773–present)
(Société Nouvelle des
Faïenceries de Quimper
HB Henriot)

E

MOSA PORCELAIN &
BRICK FACTORY
Maastricht, Holland
Porcelain
ca.1900 (1883–present)
(Mosa Porcelain & Tile
Factory)

F

SÈVRES
Sèvres, France
Porcelain. Printed,
impressed, relief molded,
date varies, see page 248
1900 + (1756–present)

G

DUX PORCELAIN
MANUFACTORY
Dux, Bohemia (Duchov,
Czechoslovakia)
Porcelain. Raised
1900–1918 (1860–
present)
(Duchov Porcelain)

H

WEDGWOOD & CO.
Tunstall, Staffordshire,
England
Earthenware, stone china
1936 + (1860–present)
(member of Wedgwood
Group)

I

ADOLF BAUER
Magdeburg-Buckau,
Prussia, Germany (E.
Germany)
Earthenware
ca.1894–1907 (1806–
1907 +)

J

NARDON & LAFARGE
Limoges, France
Porcelain
1941–1963 (1941–1963)
(Lafarge Porcelain)

K

GRANIT
Budapest, Hungary
Faience
1922 + (1922–1981 +)

L

HALCYON ART POTTERY
Halcyon, CA, U.S.A.
Art pottery. Impressed
1910–1913 (1910–1913,
1931–1932)

M

SÈVRES
Sèvres, France
Porcelain. Various dates,
see page 248
1900–1902 (1756–
present)

N

MARTIN & NEPHEW/
CHARLES MARTIN/
MARTIN & DUCHES
Limoges, France
Porcelain
1912–1935 (1903–1935)

O

C. T. MALING/C. T.
MALING & SONS
Newcastle upon Tyne,
Northumberland,
England
Earthenware. Printed,
impressed
1875–ca.1908 (1859–
1963)

P

PINDER, BOURNE & CO.
Burslem, Staffordshire,
England
Earthenware
1862–1882 (1862–
present)
(Royal Doulton Tableware
Ltd.)

A

UTZCHNEIDER
Sarreguemines, France
Faience
1935+ (ca.1770–present)

B

NELSON McCOY
POTTERY
Roseville, OH, U.S.A.
Pottery
1972–present (1848–
present)
(Lancaster Colony Corp.)

C

ROSENTHAL GLASS &
PORCELAIN AG
Selb, Bavaria, Germany (W.
Germany)
Porcelain
1961+ (1879–present)

D

GLIDDEN POTTERY CO.
Alfred, NY, U.S.A.
Dinnerware
1954+ (ca.1947–ca.1957)

E

SWEDEN

STENINGE CERAMIC AB
Stockholm, Sweden
Ceramics
1937–1964 (1700–
1975+)

F

JULIUS DIETL PORCELAIN
FACTORY KALTENHOF
Kaltenhof, Bohemia
(Oblanov,
Czechoslovakia)
Porcelain
1918–1939 (1900–
ca.1945)

G

FIRST BAYREUTH
PORCELAIN FACTORY
"WALKÜRE" SIEGMUND
PAUL MEYER GMBH
Bayreuth, Bavaria, Germany
(W. Germany)
Porcelain
1928+ (1920–present)

H

Porzellanfabrik. Aich
Menzl & C°

MENZL & CO. PORCELAIN
FACTORY AICH
Aich, Bohemia (Doubi,
Czechoslovakia)
Porcelain. Impressed, blue,
green underglaze
1918–1922 (1918–1922)

I

KAHLA PORCELAIN
FACTORY BRANCH
HERMSDORF-
KLOSTERLAUSNTZ
Hermsdorf, Thuringia,
Germany (E. Germany)
Porcelain. Variations in
wording
ca.1923–present (1890–
present)
(various names, now
Hermsdorf Ceramic
Works Combine VEB)

J

DAI NIPPON
Nagoya, Japan
Porcelain
(1891–1921)

K

D. F. HAYNES & CO.
(CHESAPEAKE
POTTERY)
Baltimore, MD, U.S.A.
Semiporcelain, majolica
1882–1884 (1881–1914)

L

FIGER & CO. PORCELAIN
FACTORY
FRAUENTHAL
Frauenthal, Austria
Hard paste porcelain.
Variations in wording
ca.1930–present (ca.1930–
present)
(various names)

M

LONHUDA

WELLER POTTERY/
DENVER CHINA &
POTTERY CO.
Zanesville, OH/Denver, CO,
U.S.A.
Faience
1894–1895/ca.1900–1905
(1882–1948/1901–1905)

N

BAEHR & PROESCHILD
Ohrdruf, Thuringia,
Germany (E. Germany)
Porcelain
ca.1919–ca.1940 (1870–
ca.1940)

O

UNITED PORCELAIN
FACTORIES
MEIERHOFEN
Meierhofen, Bohemia
(Dvory, Czechoslovakia)
Porcelain
1925–1939 (ca.1925–
ca.1939)

P

SCHAUBACH-KUNST
LICHTE-WALLENDORF
VEB
Wallendorf, Thuringia,
Germany (E. Germany)
Porcelain
1958–1959 (1953–
present)
(various names, now Lichte
Decorative
Porcelainworks VEB)

INITIALS & WORDS

A

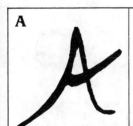

PETER G. ARNOLD
Leatherhead, Surrey,
England
Studio pottery. Painted
1958+ (1958–1964+)

B

EDUARD KICK
Amberg, Bavaria, Germany
(W. Germany)
Porcelain
1850–ca.1880 (1850–
1910)

C

ALAN BROUGH
London, England (Devon,
England)
Studio pottery. Painted
1946+ (1946–1964+)

D

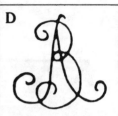

BAUSCHER BROS.
PORCELAIN FACTORY
WEIDEN
Weiden, Bavaria, Germany
(W. Germany)
Porcelain
1881+ (1881–present)

E

ASHBY POTTER'S GUILD
Woodville, Derbyshire,
England
Earthenware
ca.1909 (1909–1922)

F

C. E. & F. ARNOLDI
Elgersburg, Saxony,
Germany (E. Germany)
Porcelain
ca.1912–1962 (1808–
ca.1962)

G

AUGUSTE DELAHERCHE
Armentieres, France
Porcelain, stoneware
1896+ (1894–ca.1940)

H

AUGUSTE DELAHERCHE
Armentieres, France
Porcelain, stoneware.
Impressed
ca.1900 (1894–ca.1940)

I

A.E.HULL

A. E. HULL POTTERY CO.
Crooksville, OH, U.S.A.
Kitchenware, art pottery
1930s (1905–present)
(Hull Pottery)

J

A.E.T. C°

AMERICAN ENCAUSTIC
TILING CO.
Zanesville, OH, U.S.A.
Tile
ca.1893 (1875–1935)

K

JOS. ANT. HUSSL
Schwaz, Austria
Earthenware
1801–1883+ (1801–
1883+)

L

AMSTELHOEK
Ornwal, Holland
Ceramics. Printed
ca.1900 (ca.1894–1912)

M

ALBERT JACOB
THEWALT
Hohr-Grenzhausen,
Germany (W. Germany)
Steins
1920–1930 (1893–
present)

N

ALLANDER

ALLANDER POTTERY
Milngavie, Glasgow,
Scotland
Studio pottery. Incised,
painted
1904–1908 (1904–1908)

O

AM

JOHANN MOEHLING
Aich, Bohemia (Doubi,
Czechoslovakia)
Porcelain
1849–1860 (1849–1933)

P

SAMSON & CO.
Paris, France
Porcelain
1885+ (1873–1957+)

A

AUGUST NOWOTNY
Altrohlau, Bohemia (Stara
Role, Czechoslovakia)
Faience, earthenware,
porcelain. Impressed
ca.1850 (1823–1945+)
(various names & owners)

B

AREQUIPA POTTERY
Fairfax, CA, U.S.A.
Art pottery
1911–1918 (1911–1918)

C

AYLESFORD PRIORY
POTTERY
Aylesford, England
Stoneware. Impressed
1955+ (1955–1962)

D

WILLIAM AULT/AULT
POTTERIES LTD.
Swadlincote, Staffordshire,
England
Earthenware. Printed,
impressed,
1887–1923, 1937–1964+
(1887–1923/1937–
1964+)

E

ADOLPHE PORQUIER
Quimper, France
Faience
1897–1904 (1809–
present)
(Société Nouvelle des
Faïenceries de Quimper
HB Henriot)

F

ROYAL PORCELAIN
FACTORY
Meissen, Saxony, Germany
(E. Germany)
Porcelain. Mark for
Augustus Rex, often
copied
ca.1723–ca.1736 (1710–
present)
(State's Porcelain
Manufactory Meissen
VEB) (see page 270)

G

HELENA WOLFSOHN
Dresden, Germany (E.
Germany)
Decorator's mark. Blue
ca.1850–1881 (1848–
ca.1949) (see page 270)

H

ROBINEAU POTTERY
Syracuse, NY, U.S.A.
Art pottery, porcelain
1910+ (1901–1928)

I

AUGUST SAELTZER
Eisenach, Germany
Pottery
ca.1858 (1858+)

J

ALAN CAIGER-SMITH
Aldermaston, Berks,
England
Pottery. Incised, painted
1955–1964+ (1955–
1964+)

K

A. CARL ANGER
Aich, Bohemia (Doubi,
Czechoslovakia)
Porcelain. Impressed
1862–1901 (1849–1933)

L

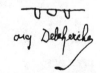

ALCOCK, LINDLEY &
BLOORE (LTD.)
Hanley, Staffordshire,
England
Earthenware. Printed,
impressed
1919+ (1919–present)
(Allied English Potteries)

M

ADAMS
ESTB^D 1657
TUNSTALL,
ENGLAND

WILLIAM ADAMS & SONS
LTD.
Tunstall & Stoke,
Staffordshire, England
Jasperware. Impressed
1896+ (1769–present)
(member of Wedgwood
Group)

N

MADE IN
Adderley Ware
ENGLAND
PORCELAINE MODERNE

ADDERLEYS LTD.
Longton, Staffordshire,
England
Porcelain, earthenware
1929–1947 (1906–
present)
(Royal Doulton Tableware
Ltd.)

O

A H & Co
V
FRANCE

ALFRED HACHE & CO.
Mehun-sur-Yevre, France
Porcelain
ca.1903 (1845–1931+)
(used by various factories)

P

aug Delaherche

AUGUSTE DELAHERCHE
Armentieres, France
Porcelain, stoneware
1896+ (1894–ca.1940)

A  **Aich** JOHANN MOEHLING Aich, Bohemia (Doubi, Czechoslovakia) Porcelain. Impressed 1849–1860 (1849–1933)	**B** **A &** **Bavaria** **K** ALBOTH & KAISER Kronach, Bavaria, Germany (W. Germany) Porcelain 1922–1927 (1872–present) (Kaiser Porcelain)	**C** **ALBERT PICK CO., Inc.** **CHICAGO ILLINOIS** **Mc NICOL CHINA** **1933** D. E. McNICOL POTTERY CO. Clarksburg, WV, U.S.A. Yellowware, Rockingham, ironstone ca.1935 (1892–1954)	**D** **ALBERT . PILLIVUYT** **A FOËCY (CHER)** **DEPÔT 61 rue PO SSOMMIÈRE** **A PARIS .** PILLIVUYT & CO. Foecy, France Porcelain. Green 1883–1893 (1830–present)
E **ALBERT POTTERIES LD** **BURSLEM** **MADE IN ENGLAND** ALBERT POTTERIES LTD. Burslem, Staffordshire, England Earthenware. Printed, impressed 1946–1954 (1946–1954)	**F** **ALLER VALE** ALLER VALE Newton Abbot, Devon, England Earthenware ca.1887–ca.1901 (1887–1901)	**G** **ALFRED MEAKIN** **M IRONSTONE** **ENGLAND** J. & G. MEAKIN (LTD.) Hanley, Staffordshire, England Ironstone current (1851–present) (member of Wedgwood Group)	**H** **ALOX®** H. F. COORS CO. Inglewood, CA, U.S.A. Porcelain, hotel ware ca.1980 (1925–present)
I **AMERICAN GIRL** SMITH-PHILLIPS CHINA CO. East Liverpool, OH, U.S.A. Semivitreous dinnerware ca.1904–ca.1920 (1901–1929)	**J** **AMERICAN LIMOGES** **SEBRING OHIO** LIMOGES CHINA CO. East Liverpool, OH, U.S.A. Semivitreous dinnerware ca.1950 (1900–1955) (American Limoges China Co.)	**K** **AMERICAN TERRA COTTA** AMERICAN TERRA COTTA & CERAMIC CO. Terra Cotta & Chicago, IL, U.S.A. Terra-cotta 1888–1929 (1886–1930)	**L** **AMPHORA** **HOLLAND** AMPHORA Oegstgeest-lez-Leiden, Holland Pottery. Painted 1900 + (ca.1900–ca.1920)
M **Amstel** – – – – – – Amstel, Holland Hard paste porcelain. Black ca.1800 (1784–1820)	**N** **ANDREA GALVANI** **PORDENONE.** GIUSEPPE CARLO GALVANI Pordenone, Italy Creamware 1860–1874 (ca.1823–ca.1883)	**O**  **ANNA PERENNA** ANNA PERENNA, INC. New York, NY, U.S.A. Porcelain importer current (1977–present)	**P** **P&F** **France** PILLIVUYT & CO. Foecy, France Porcelain ca.1900–ca.1920 (1830–present)

A

A.P
FRANCE

PILLIVUYT & CO.
Foecy, Paris, & Mehun,
France
Porcelain
1893–1900 (1830–
present)

B

APOMA

HANNS GRAF
Sonthofen, Bavaria,
Germany (W. Germany)
Ceramics, porcelain
decorating. Blue
1951–1964 (1951–
present)

C

ARABIA

ARABIA PORCELAIN
FACTORY
Helsingfors (Helsinki),
Finland
Porcelain. Stamped
1874–1930 (1874–
present)
(Upsala-Ekeby Group)

D

Arcadian
China

ARKINSTALL & SONS
(LTD.)
Stoke, Staffordshire,
England
Porcelain
1904–ca.1920 (1904–
1924)

E

Arklow
HONEY STONE
MADE IN IRELAND

ARKLOW POTTERY LTD.
Arklow, Co. Wicklow,
Ireland
Earthenware
current (1934–present)

F

ARTHUR
WOOD
ENGLAND

ARTHUR WOOD & SON
LTD.
Longport & Stoke,
Staffordshire, England
Earthenware
current (1904–present)

G

Arzberg
CHINA

ARZBERG PORCELAIN
FACTORY
Arzberg, Bavaria, Germany
(W. Germany)
Porcelain. Green
underglaze
1970–present (1890–
present)
(various names & owners,
now Hutschenreuther
AG)

H

Atla
BONE
CHINA
ENGLAND

GRIMWADES LTD.
Stoke, Staffordshire,
England
Bone china. Printed
ca.1934–1939 (1900–
present)
(Royal Winton Pottery)

I

AUGUSTE
DELAHERCHE

AUGUSTE DELAHERCHE
Paris & Armentieres,
France
Stoneware, porcelain.
Impressed
ca.1894–1940 (1894–
ca.1940)

J

August Rieber Starke

JOSEF RIEBER & CO.
PORCELAIN FACTORY AG
Metterteich, Bavaria,
Germany (W. Germany)
Porcelain
ca.1936 (1918–ca.1978)

K

Aultcliff
MADE IN
ENGLAND

AULT & TUNNICLIFFE
LTD.
Swadlincote, Staffordshire,
England
Earthenware. Printed,
impressed
1923–1937 (1923–1937)

L

aurelian
WELLER

WELLER POTTERY
Zanesville, OH, U.S.A.
Pottery. Incised
1895–1915 (1882–1948)

M

AVON

AVON POTTERY
Cincinnati, OH, U.S.A.
Pottery. Impressed
1886–1888 (1886–1888)

N

AYNSLEY
ENGLAND

AYNSLEY CHINA LTD.
Stoke, Staffordshire,
England
Porcelain
current (1864–present)
(Waterford Glass Ltd.)

O

AZUREAN

ROSEVILLE POTTERY CO.
Zanesville, OH, U.S.A.
Pottery. Impressed
1900 + (1892–1954)

P

B.

FRANZ LANG
Budau, Bohemia (Budov,
Czechoslovakia)
Earthenware, porcelain.
Blue underglaze
1831–ca.1860 (1825–
1860)

A

BOHEMIA CERAMIC
WORKS
Neurohlau, Bohemia (Nova
Role, Czechoslovakia)
Porcelain
ca.1941–1945 (1921–
1945)

B

WILLIAM BRUNT
POTTERY CO.
East Liverpool, OH, U.S.A.
Ironstone
1892–1911 (1848–1911)
(various names)

C

BURMANTOFTS
Leeds, Yorkshire, England
Pottery. Impressed
1880–1904 (1882–1904)

D

BRITANNIA CHINA CO.
Longton, Staffordshire,
England
Porcelain. Printed,
impressed
1904–1906 (1895–1906)

E

BOOTHS
Tunstall, Staffordshire,
England
Earthenware reproductions
of Worcester
1905+ (1891–present)
(Royal Doulton Tableware
Ltd.)

F

BOCH & BUSCHMANN
Mettlach, Saar, Germany
(W. Germany)
Earthenware. Impressed,
printed
1813–1825 (1813–
present)
(Villeroy & Boch)

G

WILLIAM COENRAD
BROUWER
Gouda & Leierdorp,
Holland
Ceramics. Incised
1898–1901 (ca.1898–
1933)

H

B-C
WILTON.

INTERNATIONAL
POTTERY CO.
Trenton, NJ, U.S.A.
Semiporcelain
1900+ (1860–1940+)

I

B. & G.

BING & GRONDAHL
Copenhagen, Denmark
Porcelain, earthenware
1895+ (1853–present)

J

HERTHA BUCHER
Vienna, Austria
Pottery. Incised
1920+ (1920–ca.1940)

K

KATHARINE PLEYDELL-
BOUVERIE
Kilmington Manor,
Wiltshire, England
Studio pottery, stoneware.
Incised, seal, stamped
1946+ (1925–present)

L

BURGESS & LEIGH
Burslem, Staffordshire,
England
Earthenware. Impressed,
printed
1862+ (1862–present)

M

BERNARD MOORE
Stoke, Staffordshire,
England
Earthenware, porcelain.
Painted
1905–1915 (1905–1915)

N

C. J. C. BAILEY
Fulham Pottery, London,
England
Stoneware, terra-cotta,
porcelain. Incised
1864–1889 (1864–1889)

O

B & Co.
LIMOGES
FRANCE

L. BERNARDAUD & CO.
Limoges & Paris, France
Porcelain. Printed
1925+ (1905–present)

P

BAKER & Cº
"ART ENGLAND
MODERNE"

W. BAKER & CO. LTD.
Fenton, Staffordshire,
England
Earthenware. Printed
ca.1893 (1839–1932)

A

BAKERITE
OVEN-TESTED
MADE IN U.S.A.
WARRANTED
22 K. GOLD

HARKER POTTERY CO.
East Liverpool, OH, U.S.A.
Semivitreous ovenware
ca.1935–1950 (1890–
1972)

B

Balmoral
BY
Crown
Clarence
England

CO-OPERATIVE
WHOLESALE SOCIETY
LTD.
Longton, Staffordshire,
England
Earthenware. Printed
1962+ (1946–1964+)

C

BARKER BROS.
LTD
LONGTON,
STAFFS,
ENGLAND

BARKER BROS. LTD.
Longton, Staffordshire,
England
Porcelain, earthenware.
Printed, various pattern
names
1937+ (1876–1964+)

D

BARON
N.DEVON

BARON'S POTTERY
Barnstaple, Devon, England
Earthenware. Impressed
ca.1905–ca.1938 (1899–
1939)

E

BARR FLIGHT & BARR
Royal Porcelain Works
WORCESTER
London House
No 1 Coventry Street

WORCESTER
PORCELAINS
Worcester, England
Porcelain. Printed
1807–1813 (ca.1751–
present)
(Royal Worcester Spode
Ltd.)

F

BASIL MATTHEWS

BASIL MATTHEWS
Wolverhampton,
Staffordshire, England
Porcelain, earthenware.
Printed, painted
1946–present (1946–
present)

G

BAUER POTTERY
LOS ANGELES

BAUER POTTERY
Los Angeles, CA, U.S.A.
Earthenware, pottery
ca.1934–1942 (1905–
ca.1958)

H

HB Cie
Choisy le Roy

HAUTIN & BOULANGER
Choisy-le-Roi, France
Earthenware, porcelain
ca.1836 (1804–1974+)

I

BERNARDAUD
LIMOGES
France

L. BERNARDAUD & CO.
Limoges, France
Porcelain
1905–1929 (1905–
present)

J

BERNARD
MOORE

BERNARD MOORE
Stoke, Staffordshire,
England
Earthenware, porcelain.
Printed, painted
1905–1915 (1905–1915)

K

BENGT BERGLUND

BENGT BERGLUND
(GUSTAFSBERG
PORCELAIN FACTORY)
Gustafsberg, Sweden
Stoneware
1960+ (1825–present)

L

BESWICK
ENGLAND

JOHN BESWICK LTD.
Longton, Staffordshire,
England
Earthenware
ca.1946–present (1936–
present)
(Royal Doulton Tableware
Ltd.)

M

Beswick
Ware.
MADE IN
ENGLAND

JOHN BESWICK LTD.
Longton, Staffordshire,
England
Earthenware. Printed
ca.1936 (1936–present)
(Royal Doulton Tableware
Ltd.)

N

Blair
decorated
by hand

BLAIR CERAMICS, INC.
Ozark, MO, U.S.A.
Dinnerware
ca.1946–1950s (1946–
1950s)

O

BLOCK

BLOCK CHINA CO.
Cameron, WV, U.S.A.
Porcelain. Backstamp
ca.1960 (ca.1930–present)

P

Blue Ridge
Hand Painted
Underglaze
Southern Potteries, Inc
MADE IN U. S. A.

SOUTHERN POTTERIES
Erwin, TN, U.S.A.
Dinnerware
ca.1930 (1917–1957)

A

BOVEY POTTERY CO.
LTD.
Bovey Tracey, Devon,
England
Earthenware. Printed
ca.1954–1957 (1894–
1957)

B

*Bochet Buschmann
a Mettlach*

BOCH & BUSCHMANN
Mettlach, Saar, Germany
(W. Germany)
Earthenware. Incised
1813–1825 (1813–
present)
(Villeroy & Boch)

C

Boehm

EDWARD MARSHALL
BOEHM
Malvern, England &
Trenton, NJ, U.S.A.
Porcelain. Variations in
wording
1954–present (1950–
present)

D

Böttgersteinzeug

– – – – – –
Meissen, Germany (E.
Germany)
Stoneware. Incised
1919+

E

BOURNE
DENBY
ENGLAND

JOSEPH BOURNE & SON
LTD.
Denby, Derbyshire,
England
Stoneware. Impressed,
printed
1930+ (ca.1809–present)
(Denby Tableware)

F

Bramfield Ware

JAMES PEARSON LTD.
Brampton, Derbyshire,
England
Stoneware
1920+ (19th century–
1939)

G

*Branksome
Ceramics
England*

BRANKSOME CERAMICS
Bournemouth, Hampshire,
England
Earthenware, stoneware.
Printed, variations in
wording
ca.1945–1956 (1945–
present)
(E. Baggaley Ltd.)

H

BRAUCKMAN
ART
POTTERY

GRAND FEU ART
POTTERY
Los Angeles, CA, U.S.A.
Art pottery. Impressed
ca.1916 (1912–1916+)

I

BRAUNTON
POTTERY
DEVON

BRAUNTON POTTERY
CO. LTD.
Braunton, Nr. Devon,
England
Earthenware. Printed,
impressed
ca.1947 (1910–1972)

J

Brentleigh
Ware
STAFFORDSHIRE
ENGLAND

HOWARD POTTERY CO.
LTD.
Shelton, Staffordshire,
England
Earthenware. Printed
1950+ (1925–1964+)

K

BREWER
*Longpark
Torquay*

BREWER BROTHERS
Longpark, Torquay,
England
Earthenware, terra-cotta.
Underglaze, scratched
ca.1895–ca.1905 (1883–
1957)

L

"Broadhurst"
ENGLAND
HAND PAINTED
UNDERGLAZE
FAST COLOUR

JAMES BROADHURST &
SONS LTD.
Fenton, Staffordshire,
England
Earthenware. Printed
current (1862–present)

M

Brock
OF CALIFORNIA

B. J. BROCK & CO.
Lawndale, CA, U.S.A.
Dinnerware
ca.1950–1955 (ca.1950–
1955)

N

BROOME

DAYTON PORCELAIN
WORKS
Dayton, OH, U.S.A.
Art pottery
1880–1882 (1880–1882)

O

Brouwer

MIDDLE LANE POTTERY
East Hampton, NY, U.S.A.
Artware
ca.1900 (1894–1946)

P

BRUNT
ART WARE

WILLIAM BRUNT
POTTERY CO.
East Liverpool, OH, U.S.A.
Semivitreous tableware,
ironstone
1892–1911 (1848–1911)
(various names)

A

Brusché

BRUSCHÉ CERAMICS
Whittier, CA, U.S.A.
Dinnerware
ca.1950 (ca.1950)

B

BRUSH USA

BRUSH POTTERY
Roseville, OH, U.S.A.
Florist ware, cookie jars
1938–1965 (1907–1908,
1925–present)

C

BUFFALO CHINA

BUFFALO POTTERY CO.
Buffalo, NY, U.S.A.
Pottery, porcelain
ca.1930 (1901–present)
(Buffalo China, Inc.)

D

"Burcraft"

BURGESS BROS
MADE IN ENGLAND.

BURGESS BROS.
Longton, Staffordshire,
England
Earthenware. Printed
1922–1939 (1922–1939)

E

Burford Bros

BURFORD BROS.
East Liverpool, OH, U.S.A.
Ironstone toiletware
ca.1890 (1879–1904)

F

Burleigh

STAFFORDSHIRE
ENGLAND

BURGESS & LEIGH
Stoke, Staffordshire,
England
Earthenware
current (1862–present)

G

**BURMANTOFTS
FAIENCE**

BURMANTOFTS
Leeds, Yorkshire, England
Art pottery. Incised
1882–1904 (1882–1904)

H

BURTON
WARE

BRETBY STONEWARE
CO. LTD.
Burton-on-Trent,
Staffordshire, England
Stoneware
current (ca.1953–present)

I

CARSTENS-UFFRECHT
Haldensleben, Prussia,
Germany (E. Germany)
Earthenware
1929–1945 (ca.1875–
present)
(Haldensleben
Earthenwareworks VEB)

J

CHARLES AHRENFELDT
& SON
New York, NY, U.S.A.
Porcelain importer
ca.1900 (1859–1969)

K

CARL AUVERA
Arzberg, Bavaria, Germany
(W. Germany)
Earthenware, faience,
porcelain
1884+ (1839–present)
(Hutschenreuther AG)

L

CAMBRIDGE ART
POTTERY
Cambridge, OH, U.S.A.
Faience
before 1904 (1895–1909)

M

CHARLES BONE A.R.C.A.
Brighton, Sussex, England
Studio-type pottery,
stoneware. Incised,
painted
1952+ (1952–1964+)

N

C.F

CHRISTIAN FISCHER
Pirkenhammer, Bohemia
(Brezova,
Czechoslovakia)
Porcelain, figurines.
Impressed
1846–1857 (1803–1945)
(various names & owners)

O

CHARLES FORD
Hanley, Staffordshire,
England
Porcelain. Impressed,
printed
1874–1904 (1874–1904)

P

**C F H
G D M
FRANCE**

CHARLES FIELD
HAVILAND
Limoges, France
Porcelain
1870–1882 (1870–
present)

A

CERAMICS HISPANIA
Manises, Spain
Utility ware, majolica
ca.1941 (1941–1981+)

B

NEW YORK CITY
POTTERY
New York, NY, U.S.A.
Majolica, parian, cream-
colored ware, white
granite
ca.1853 (1853–1888)

C

CHELSEA KERAMIC ART
WORKS
Chelsea, MA, U.S.A.
Art pottery
1872–1889 (1866–1940)

D

MICHAEL CASSON
Prestwood,
Buckinghamshire,
England
Earthenware, stoneware.
Impressed, painted
1953–1955 (1953–
1964+)

E

MICHAEL AMBROSE
CARDEW
Wenford Bridge, Cornwall,
England
Studio-type pottery.
Impressed
1926+ (1926–present)

F

CLEMENT MASSIER
Vallauris, France
Pottery. Painted.
ca.1883 (1883+)

G

CN

NEWCOMB POTTERY
New Orleans, LA, U.S.A.
Art pottery
1896–1945 (1886–1945)

H

CAMILLE NAUDOT & CO.
Paris, France
Porcelain. Printed
1904–1919 (1900–
1919+)

I

C.P.CO.
LTD.

CHESTER POTTERY
Phoenixville, PA, U.S.A.
Semigranite ware
1894–1897 (1894–1897)

J

CHESSELL POTTERY
(IOW) LTD.
Chessell, Isle of Wight,
England
Porcelain
current (1978–present)

K

CMIELOW PORCELAIN &
CERAMIC FACTORY
Cmielow, Poland
Porcelain
1842+ (1789–1930+)

L

CARTER, STABLER &
ADAMS
Poole, Dorset, England
Earthenware. Impressed
1921+ (1921–present)
(Poole Pottery Ltd.)

M

CAMILLE THARAUD
Limoges France
Porcelain. Underglaze
1922+ (1919–1968)

N

VOLKMAR POTTERY
Corona, NY, U.S.A.
Art pottery. Incised
1879–1888 (1875–
ca.1911)
(various names &
locations)

O

CHARLES VYSE
Chelsea, London, England
Pottery. Painted, various
dates
1928+ (1919–1963)

P

KLOSTER VEILSDORF
PORCELAIN FACTORY
Kloster Veilsdorf, Thuringia,
Germany (E. Germany)
Porcelain. Blue underglaze
before 1945 (1760–
present)

A

CLEWELL WARE
Canton, OH, U.S.A.
Bronzed pottery. Incised
1902–1955 (1902–1955)

B

C. AHRENFELDT
LIMOGES

CHARLES AHRENFELDT
Limoges, France
Porcelain
1859–1915 (1859–1969)

C

California
Porcelain

CALIFORNIA FAIENCE
Berkeley, CA, U.S.A.
Art pottery
1922+ (1916–ca.1930)

D

Calyx Ware
Reg. Trade Mark

WILLIAM ADAMS & SONS
LTD.
Tunstall & Stoke,
Staffordshire, England
Earthenware, basalt, jasper,
parian. Printed,
impressed
ca.1972 (1769–present)
(member of Wedgwood
Group)

E

CANTON
CHINA

STEUBENVILLE POTTERY
CO.
Steubenville, OH, U.S.A.
White granite
ca.1904 (1879–ca.1960)

F

Carefree
TRUE CHINA ✳
ↄ SYRACUSE

SYRACUSE CHINA CORP.
Syracuse, NY, U.S.A.
Pottery, white granite,
semivitreous porcelain
1972+ (1871–present)
(various names & owners)

G

Caribe
CHINA

STERLING CHINA CO.
Wellsville, OH, U.S.A. &
Puerto Rico
Dinnerware. Stamped
1947–1948 (1917–
present)

H

CARL KNOLL
CARLSBAD

CARL KNOLL
Fischern, Bohemia (Rybare.
Czechoslovakia)
Porcelain. Impressed
1848–1868 (1848–1945)

I

Carlton Ware
MADE IN ENGLAND
"TRADE MARK"

WILTSHAW & ROBINSON
(LTD.)/CARLTON WARE
LTD.
Stoke, Staffordshire,
England
Earthenware. Printed,
variations in wording
ca.1925–present (1890–
present)

J

Carter
poole

CARTER & CO. LTD.
Poole, Dorset, England
Earthenware, art pottery,
tiles. Printed, impressed,
incised
1902–1907 (1873–
present)
(Poole Pottery Ltd.)

K

THE CARTWRIGHT BROS. CO

CARTWRIGHT BROS. CO.
East Liverpool, OH, U.S.A.
Semivitreous dinnerware
ca.1919 (1880–1927)

L

Cat-Tail
by
CONTINENTAL KILNS

CONTINENTAL KILNS
Chester, WV, U.S.A.
Semivitreous dinnerware
1944–1954 (1944–1954)

M

Catalina

CATALINA POTTERY/
GLADDING, McBEAN &
CO.
Santa Catalina, CA, U.S.A.
Catalina dinnerware
ca.1930–1937 (1875–
present)
(member of Wedgwood
Group)

N

CAULDON
England

CAULDON LTD.
Hanley, Staffordshire,
England
Porcelain, earthenware
1905–1920 (1905–
present)
(member of Wedgwood
Group)

O

Cavitt-Shaw
DIVISION
W. S. GEORGE

W. S. GEORGE CO.
Kittanig, PA, U.S.A.
Dinnerware
1934+ (1880–1959)

P

Cazin.

CHARLES CAZIN
London, England
Stoneware. Incised
ca.1871–1874 (1871–
1874)

A

Dale

COALPORT PORCELAIN
  WORKS
Coalport, Shropshire,
  England
Porcelain
1810–1825 (ca.1795–
  present)
(member of Wedgwood
  Group)

B

CERAMITE
R
REVOL S^tUZE

GUSTAVE REVOL
Saint-Uze, France
Porcelain
1953 + (1800–1960 +)

C

Chamberlain's

CHAMBERLAIN & CO.
Worcester, England
Porcelain. Impressed,
  printed
ca.1847–1850 (ca.1786–
  present)
(Royal Worcester Spode
  Ltd.)

D

C.H. BRANNAM LTD
MADE IN ENGLAND

C. H. BRANNAM
Barnstaple, Devon, England
Earthenware. Impressed
after 1914 (1879–present)

E

CHELSEA KERAMIC
ART WORKS
ROBERTSON & SONS.

CHELSEA KERAMIC ART
  WORKS
Chelsea, MA, U.S.A.
Art pottery, terra-cotta,
  faience
ca.1875–1880 (1866–
  1940)

F

CHICAGO TERRACOTTA
WORKS, 1876

CHICAGO TERRA–COTTA
  WORKS
Chicago, IL, U.S.A.
Terra-cotta. Impressed
1876 + (1866–ca.1880)

G

Chodau

GEITNER & STIERBA
Chodau, Bohemia (Chodor,
  Czechoslovakia)
Earthenware, porcelain.
  Impressed
1845–ca.1850 (1810–
  1945 +)
(various names & owners)

H

Chr Dresser

LINTHORPE POTTERY
Middlesbrough, Yorkshire
  England
Earthenware. Incised,
  impressed, painted
ca.1879–1889 (1879–
  1889)

I

Clarice Cliff
NEWPORT POTTERY
ENGLAND

NEWPORT POTTERY CO.
Burslem, Staffordshire,
  England
Earthenware. Printed
1938–1966 (1920–
  present)
(member of Wedgwood
  Group)

J

CLASSIC

CHARLES L. DWENGER
New York, NY, U.S.A.
Porcelain importer
1912 + (ca.1895–1917 +)

K

CLASSIC
SATIN

EDWIN M. KNOWLES
CHINA CO.
East Liverpool, OH, U.S.A.
Semivitreous dinnerware
1934 + (1900–1963)

L

Clement-Massier
Golfe-Juan. AM

JEROME & DELPHIN
Vallauris, France
Art pottery
1917 + (1917–?)

M

CLIFF
ENGLAND

J. DIMMOCK & CO.
Hanley, Staffordshire,
  England
Earthenware. Printed
ca.1878–1904 (1862–
  1904)

N

CLIFTON
POTTERY
NEWARK, N.J.

CLIFTON ART POTTERY
Newark, NJ, U.S.A.
Art pottery
1905–1911 (1905–1911)

O

CLINCHFIELD
S.P.I.

SOUTHERN POTTERIES
Erwin, TN, U.S.A.
Dinnerware
1917–1923 (1917–1957)

P

LIO

STEUBENVILLE POTTERY
CO.
Steubenville, OH, U.S.A.
White granite,
  semiporcelain
1904 + (1879–ca.1960)

A *Coalbrookdale by Coalport*

COALPORT PORCELAIN
  WORKS
Coalport, Shropshire,
  England
Porcelain. Painted
ca.1805–1815 (ca.1795–
  present)
(member of Wedgwood
  Group)

B *Coalport.*

COALPORT PORCELAIN
  WORKS
Coalport, Shropshire,
  England
Porcelain. Blue underglaze
1810–1825 (ca.1795–
  present)
(member of Wedgwood
  Group)

C Colclough
GENUINE
BONE CHINA
MADE IN ENGLAND

COLCLOUGH CHINA LTD
Longton, Staffordshire,
  England
Porcelain. Printed
ca.1945–1948 (1937–
  present)
(Royal Doulton Tableware
  Ltd.)

D COLDRVM

REGINALD WELLS
Chelsea, London, England
Pottery. Impressed
ca.1909 (1909–1951)

E COLLINGWOOD
MADE IN
ENGLAND

COLLINGWOOD BROS.
  (LTD.)
Longton, Staffordshire,
  England
Porcelain. Printed
1924–1930 (1887–1957)

F *Columbus*

EAST END POTTERY CO.
East Liverpool, OH, U.S.A.
Ironstone, semivitreous
  ware
1894–1901,1903–1907
  (1894–1901,1903–
  1907)

G COORS
U.S.A.

COORS PORCELAIN
Inglewood, CA, U.S.A.
Hotel porcelain, tile
ca.1900–ca.1930 (1925–
  present)

H COPELAND
& GARRETT

COPELAND & GARRETT
Stoke, Staffordshire,
  England
Porcelain, earthenware,
  parian. Printed,
  impressed
1833–1847 (1833–
  present)
(Royal Worcester Spode
  Ltd.)

I Copeland late Spode

SPODE
Stoke, Staffordshire,
  England
Porcelain, earthenware,
  stone china. Impressed,
  printed
1867 + (ca.1762–present)
(various names, Royal
  Worcester Spode Ltd.)

J CORNS
CHINA
WELLSVILLE. O

CORNS CHINA CO.
Wellsville, OH, U.S.A.
Semivitreous kitchenware
1928–1932 (1928–1932)

K CORONATION POTTERY
COMPANY LTD.
B
MADE IN ENGLAND

CORONATION POTTERY
  CO.
Stoke, Staffordshire,
  England
Earthenware. Printed,
  impressed
ca.1947–1954 (1903–
  1954)

L CORONET

GEORGE BORGFELDT &
  CO.
New York, NY, U.S.A.
Importer
1902 + (1881–ca.1976)

M *Coronet*
U.S.A.

A. E. HULL POTTERY CO.
Crooksville, OH, U.S.A.
Dinnerware
1960 + (1905–1950,1952–
  present)
(Hull Pottery)

N *Coultry*

COULTRY POTTERY
Cincinnati, OH, U.S.A.
Yellowware, cream-colored
  pottery. Incised
ca.1880 (1859–ca.1882)

O COWAN
RG

COWAN POTTERY
Cleveland & Rocky River,
  OH, U.S.A.
Art pottery, porcelain
1913–1917 (1912–1931)

P CRAFTSMAN
DINNERWARE
USA

HOMER LAUGHLIN CHINA
  CO.
East Liverpool, OH, U.S.A.
Semivitreous dinnerware
ca.1939 (1877–present)

A

CREATIVE
WORLD
Ⓒ/W

VENETO FLAIR
Treviso, Italy
Earthenware
current (ca.1946–present)

B

CREIL

SAINT-CRICQ-CAZEAUX/
LeBOEUF & MILLIET
Creil et Montereau, France
Faience, stoneware,
porcelain. Green
underglaze
1794–1895 (1794–1895)

C

CRONIN CHINA
MINERVA
O.

CRONIN CHINA CO.
Minerva, OH, U.S.A.
Semiporcelain
1940+ (1934–1956)

D

CROOKSVILLE
CHINA CO.

CROOKSVILLE CHINA CO.
Crooksville, OH, U.S.A.
Semiporcelain
ca.1940 (1902–ca.1960)

E

Crown Devon

CROWN DEVON LTD.
Staffordshire, England
Porcelain
1972+ (1879–present)

F

CROWN HOTEL
WARE

CROWN POTTERY CO.
Evansville, IN, U.S.A.
Majolica, ironstone
ca.1891 (1891–1962)

G

STAFFORDSHIRE
CROWN MADE
CLARENCE IN
ENGLAND

CO-OPERATIVE
WHOLESALE SOCIETY
LTD.
Longton, Staffordshire,
England
Earthenware. Printed
1946+ (1946–1964+)

H

CROWN POTTERIES CO.
MADE
IN U.S.A.
EVANSVILLE, IND.

CROWN POTTERY CO.
Evansville, IN, U.S.A.
Majolica, ironstone
ca.1891 (1891–1962)

I

THARAUD
Limoges France

CAMILLE THARAUD
Limoges, France
Porcelain
1928+ (1919–1968)

J

Cybis

CYBIS PORCELAINS
Trenton, NJ, U.S.A.
Figurines, tableware
1952–1966 (ca.1939–
present)

K

Cyclop

FRANZ ANTON MEHLEM
EARTHENWARE
FACTORY
Bonn, Rhineland, Germany
(W. Germany)
Earthenware, porcelain,
figurines
1900–1920 (1836–1920)

L

DENBY TABLEWARE
Derby, England
Stoneware
current (1809–present)

M

DB

DORA BARRETT
Harpenden, Hertfordshire,
England
Stoneware, terra-cotta.
Incised
1938+ (1938–1964+)

N

DB

DORA MAY BILLINGTON
London, England
Ceramics
1920+ (1912–before
1964)

O

D. & C.

ERNST DORFNER & CO.
Hirschau, Bavaria, Germany
(W. Germany)
Porcelain
1887–ca.1919 (1850–
ca.1919)

P

D
C

DELAN COOKSON
West Bridgford,
Nottinghamshire,
England
Studio-type pottery.
Impressed
1961–1964+ (1958–
1964+)

A

D & Co
FRANCE

R. DELINIERES & CO.
Limoges, France
Porcelain
1879–1900 (1879–
present)
(Bernardaud & Co.)

B

GREEN DENE POTTERY
East Horsley, Surrey,
England
Studio pottery. Impressed,
painted
1953–1964+ (1953–
1964+)

C

N. DICKINSON
Worthing, Sussex, England
Studio-type pottery
1948+ (1948–1964+)

D

DEACON POTTERY
London, England
Studio pottery. Impressed
1952–1958 (1952–1958)

E

TAXILE DOAT
Sèvres, France, & United
States
Sculptor, pâte-sur-pâte.
Incised (see page 216A)
1875–1905,1909–1911
(1851–ca.1940)

F

DALLAS

DALLAS POTTERY
Cincinnati, OH, U.S.A.
Cream-colored, stone china
1856–1882 (1856–
ca.1882)

G

Dalpayrat.

ADRIEN DALPAYRAT
Bourg-la-Reine, France
Porcelain, pottery,
stoneware. Incised,
impressed
ca.1900 (1876–1905+)

H

Danesby Ware

JOSEPH BOURNE & SON
LTD.
Denby, Derbyshire,
England
Stoneware. Impressed,
printed
1930+ (ca.1809–present)
(Denby Tableware)

I

D. BECKLEY
Isle of Wight, Hampshire,
England
Pottery. Printed, impressed
1959+ (1958–1964+)

J

D.E.McNicol

D. E. McNICOL POTTERY
CO.
East Liverpool, OH, U.S.A.
Semivitreous dinnerware
ca.1915–1929 (1892–
1954)

K

DENVER
C & P Co

DENVER CHINA &
POTTERY CO.
Denver, CO, U.S.A.
Art pottery
1901–1905 (1901–1905)

L

DENVER

DENVER CHINA &
POTTERY CO.
Denver, CO, U.S.A.
Stoneware, art pottery
1901–1905 (1901–1905)

M

Devon Ware

ROYAL LONGPARK
POTTERY CO. (ART)
LTD.
Longpark, Torquoy,
England
Art pottery. Incised
ca.1900 (1883–1957)

N

DEVONMOOR

DEVONMOOR ART
POTTERY
Newton Abbot, Devon,
England
Earthenware. Impressed,
printed
1922+ (1913–1914,1922–
1964+)

O

DEWEY
E.E.P.CO

EAST END POTTERY CO.
East Liverpool, OH, U.S.A.
Whiteware
1894–1901/1903–1907
(1894–1901, 1903–
1907)

P

DIANA

GEO. BORGFELDT & CO.
New York, NY, U.S.A.
Importer
1926+ (1881–ca.1976)

A

DICKENS WARE
WELLER

WELLER POTTERY
Zanesville, OH, U.S.A.
Art pottery, kitchenware
1897–1910 (1882–1948)

B

D.M.
FULHAM

FULHAM POTTERY &
CHEAVIN FILTER CO.
LTD.
London, England
Pottery
ca.1900 (1889–present)

C

Doric Bone China
MADE IN ENGLAND

DORIC CHINA
Longton, Staffordshire,
England
Porcelain. Printed
1934–1935 (1924–1935)

D

Dorothy Ann
STOKE ON TRENT
ENGLAND

DOROTHY ANN FLORAL
CHINA
Stoke, Staffordshire,
England
Bone china
current (ca.1964–present)

E

Dorset

CROWN DORSET
POTTERY
Poole, England
Art pottery. Incised
ca.1920 (ca.1900–1937)

F

DOULTON
LAMBETH

DOULTON & CO.
Burslem, Staffordshire,
England
Stoneware. Impressed,
printed
ca.1858–ca.1910 (1853–
present)
(Royal Doulton Tableware
Ltd.)

G

DOULTON
& SLATERS
PATENT

DOULTON & CO.
Burslem, Staffordshire,
England
Earthenware, stoneware.
Impressed
ca.1886–1914 (1853–
present)
(Royal Doulton Tableware
Ltd.)

H

DRESDEN
HOTEL CHINA.

POTTER'S CO-
OPERATIVE CO.
East Liverpool, OH, U.S.A.
Hotel ware
ca.1892 (1882–1925)

I

THE
DURALINE
HOTEL WARE
CO LTD
SUPER VITRIFIED
made in
ENGLAND

DURALINE HOTEL
WARE
Tunstall & Stoke,
Staffordshire, England
Hotel ware
current (1908–present)

J

DuranT

DURANT KILNS
Bedford Village, NY, U.S.A.
Art pottery. Incised
1911–1929 (1911–1930)

K

ℰ

ELTON POTTERY
Clevedon, Somerset,
England
Art pottery. Painted
1883+ (ca.1875–1930)

L

EBD

E. J. D. BODLEY
Burslem, Staffordshire,
England
Porcelain, earthenware.
Printed, impressed
1875–1892 (1875–1892)

M

EMB

E. M. BLENSDORF
Bruton, Somerset, England
Studio-type pottery. Incised,
painted
1950+ (ca.1950–1964+)

N

ETIENNE MOREAU–
NELATON
La Tournelle, France
Pottery. Incised
ca.1905 (1898–ca.1927)

O

E.M.K.
C.CO.

EDWIN M. KNOWLES
CHINA CO.
East Liverpool, OH, U.S.A.
Semivitreous ware
ca.1905 (1900–1963)

P

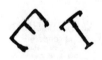

ERNST TEICHERT GMBH
Meissen, Saxony, Germany
(E. Germany)
Tiles, porcelain. Blue
underglaze
1885+ (1872–1945+)
(nationalized in 1945)

A

UNIVERSITY CITY
POTTERY
University City, MO, U.S.A.
Art pottery. Impressed,
Imprinted
1910–1915 (1910–1915)

B

EAST LIVERPOOL
POTTERIES CO.

EAST LIVERPOOL
POTTERIES CO.
East Liverpool, OH, U.S.A.
Semivitreous dinnerware
ca.1907–ca.1925 (1901–
1933)

C

E. BENNETT
1896.
POTTERY Co

EDWIN BENNETT
POTTERY
Baltimore, MD, U.S.A.
Belleek, pottery
1895 + (1856–1936)

D

Decoeur

EMILE DECOEUR
Fontenay-aux-Roses, Seine
& Sèvres, France
Porcelain, stoneware.
Incised
ca.1900–ca.1948
(ca.1900–ca.1948)

E

Edelstein

BAVARIA

EDELSTEIN PORCELAIN
FACTORY
Kups, Bavaria, Germany
(W. Germany)
Porcelain, figurines. Green
underglaze
1931 + (1890–present)

F

THE
EDWIN M. KNOWLES

EDWIN M. KNOWLES
CHINA CO.
East Liverpool, OH, U.S.A.
Semivitreous dinnerware
ca.1925–ca.1931 (1900–
1963)

G

EGERSUNDS
FAYANCEFABRIK

EGERSUND POTTERY
FACTORY
Egersunds, Norway
Faience
1872 + (1847–present)
(Porsgrund Porcelain
Factory)

H

E. H. Elton
Clevedon,

ELTON POTTERY
Clevedon, Somerset,
England
Earthenware. Various dates
1881 + (ca.1875–1930)

I

E. H. S. C. CO.
S.V.
CHINA

E. H. SEBRING CHINA CO.
East Liverpool, OH, U.S.A.
Semivitreous tableware
1908–1929 (ca.1908–
1929)

J

E.H.S.
S.V.
CHINA

E. H. SEBRING CHINA CO.
East Liverpool, OH, U.S.A.
Semivitreous tableware
1908–1929 (ca.1908–
1929)

K

EL CAMINO
CHINA
MADE IN U S A
California Ware

GLADDING, McBEAN &
CO.
Los Angeles, CA, U.S.A.
Franciscan dinnerware
ca.1934 (1875–present)
(member of Wedgwood
Group)

L

ÉLITE
L
FRANCE

BAWO & DOTTER/ÉLITE
New York, NY, U.S.A./
Limoges, France
Porcelain. Stamped green
1900 + (1883–ca.1914)

M

EST. 1875

Elizabethan
STAFFORDSHIRE
Hand Decorated
FINE BONE CHINA
ENGLAND

ELIZABETHAN FINE
BONE CHINA
Longton & Stoke,
Staffordshire, England
Porcelain
current (ca.1964–present)

N

E. L. P. CO.
WACO, CHINA.

EAST LIVERPOOL
POTTERY CO.
East Liverpool, OH, U.S.A.
Semivitreous dinnerware
1896–1901 (1894–1901)

O

Elton

SIR EDMUND ELTON
Clevedon, Somerset,
England
Earthenware
1879–1930 (1879–1930)

P

E Lycett

EDWARD LYCETT
Greenpoint, NY, & Atlanta,
GA, U.S.A.
Porcelain
ca.1900 (1884–1909)

A	B	C	D
Emile Gallé à Nancy	**EMPIRE** ENGLAND SHELTON IVORY	ENGLISH *Aristocrat Florals* BONE CHINA	**Enterprise Pottery Co**
EMILE GALLÉ Nancy, France Faience, pottery, dinnerware ca.1874–1904 (ca.1874–1904)	EMPIRE PORCELAIN CO. Stoke, Staffordshire, England Earthenware. Impressed, printed ca.1940–ca.1950 (1896–1964+)	ARISTOCRAT FLORALS & FANCIES Longton, Staffordshire, England Bone china, floral fancies. Printed 1958+ (1958–present) (member of Wedgwood Group)	ENTERPRISE POTTERY CO. Trenton, NJ, U.S.A. Sanitary ware ca.1880 (1879–1916)

E	F	G	H
EPIAG	**ℰPIC**	*Epicure* OVENPROOF HOMER LAUGHLIN U·S·A	*Erdmann Schlegelmilch* 1861 *Prussia*
EPIAG BRANCH ALTROHLAU Altrohlau, Bohemia (Stara Role, Czechoslovakia) Porcelain 1920–1939 (1920–1945+)	JOSEPH BOURNE & SON LTD. Denby, Derbyshire, England Stoneware. Impressed. printed 1930+ (ca.1809–present) (Denby Tableware)	HOMER LAUGHLIN CHINA CO. East Liverpool, OH, U.S.A. Ovenware ca.1946–ca.1960 (1877–present)	ERDMANN SCHLEGELMILCH (R. S. PRUSSIA) Suhl, Thuringia, Germany (E. Germany) Porcelain 1891+ (1881–1938)

I	J	K	L
ERNEST CARRIÈRE	*Vernon* CALIFORNIA	*E Schlegelmilch Germany*	**ETRUSCAN**
ERNEST CARRIÈRE Sèvres, France Ceramics. Incised ca.1908 (ca.1890–ca.1908)	VERNON KILNS Vernon, CA, U.S.A. Porcelain 1930s (1912–1958)	ERDMANN SCHLEGELMILCH (R. S. PRUSSIA) Suhl, Thuringia, Germany (E. Germany) Porcelain. Green 1891+ (1881–1938)	GRIFFEN, SMITH & HILL Phoenixville, PA, U.S.A. Majolica ca.1879 (1878–1889)

M	N	O	P
EUGENIA	*Eureka*	*Eva Zeisel* Fine STONEWARE from MONMOUTH	E. &W. BENNETT CANTON AVENUE BALTIMORE MD.
AMERICAN CHINA CO. Toronto, OH, U.S.A. Semiporcelain, white granite ca.1897 (1894–1910)	C. C. THOMPSON POTTERY CO. East Liverpool, OH, U.S.A. Ironstone ware ca.1915 (1868–1938)	WESTERN STONEWARE CO. Monmouth, IL, U.S.A. Stoneware, Rockingham ca.1930 (1906–1975)	BENNETT POTTERY Baltimore, MD, U.S.A. Majolica, parian ca.1850 (1846–1856)

A

F

DUCAL BRUNSWICK
PORCELAIN
MANUFACTORY/
FURSTENBERG
PORCELAIN FACTORY
Furstenberg, Brunswick,
Germany (W. Germany)
Porcelain. Blue underglaze
ca.1850–1894 (1747–
present)
(various names & owners)

B

MATHILDE FLOGL
Vienna, Austria
Ceramics. Incised
ca.1916 (1916–1935)

C

WORCESTER
PORCELAINS (FLIGHT,
BARR & BARR)
Worcester, England
Porcelain, earthenware,
parian
ca.1813–1840 (ca.1751–
present)
(Royal Worcester Spode
Ltd.)

D

f.c

FRANCIS GLANVILLE
COOPER
Sheffield, Yorkshire,
England
Studio–type pottery.
Incised, impressed,
painted
1945 + (1945–1964 +)

E

FH

WILLIAM FISHLEY
HOLLAND
Clevedon, Somerset,
England
Earthenware. Incised
1921 + (ca.1921–1964 +)

F

HUGO F. KIRSCH
Vienna, Austria
Porcelain, stoneware.
Incised, painted
ca.1910 (1906–1961)

G

F. H. R.

Los Angeles

ROBERTSON POTTERY
Los Angeles, CA, U.S.A.
Art pottery. Impressed
ca.1940 (1934–1952)

H

F&M

FISCHER & MIEG
Pirkenhammer, Bohemia
(Brezova,
Czechoslovakia)
Porcelain. Impressed
1857–1875 (1857–1918)

I

FMCo

FAIENCE
MANUFACTURING CO.
Greenpoint, NY, U.S.A.
Art pottery. Incised
1880–1892 (1880–1892)

J

FAIENCE
MANUFACTURING CO.
Greenpoint, NY, U.S.A.
Art pottery
1884–1890 (1880–1892)

K

F&R

FISCHER &
REICHENBACH
Pirkenhammer, Bohemia
(Brezova,
Czechoslovakia)
Porcelain. Impressed
1811–1846 (1811–1846)

L

FRACKELTON POTTERY
Milwaukee, WI, U.S.A.
Art pottery. Incised
1902–1910 (1902–
ca.1910)

M

NEWPORT POTTERY CO.
Burslem, Staffordshire,
England
Earthenware. Printed
1938 + (1920–present)
(member of Wedgwood
Group)

N

BLANCHARD BROS.
Limoges, France
Porcelain
ca.1900 (1890–1908)

O

F. C. CO.

FRENCH CHINA CO.
East Liverpool, OH, U.S.A.
Semivitreous ware
ca.1916–1929 (ca.1900–
present)
(Royal China Co.)

P

FERMANAGH
POTTERY

DAVID McBIRNEY & CO.
(BELLEEK POTTERY)
Belleek, Co. Fermanagh,
Ireland
Porcelain. Impressed,
printed
1863–1880 (1863–
present)

A	B	C	D
fiesta H·L·Cº USA HOMER LAUGHLIN CHINA CO. East Liverpool, OH, U.S.A. Semivitreous dinnerware 1936–1973 (1877–present)	*F. Legrand & Cᵗᵉ* *Limoges* **FRANCE** LEGRAND & CO. Limoges, France Porcelain ca.1924–1944 (1924–1962 +)	*Flight Barr & Barr* WORCESTER PORCELAINS Worcester, England Porcelain, earthenware, parian ca.1813–1840 (ca.1751–present) (Royal Worcester Spode Ltd.)	FLORALINE NELSON McCOY POTTERY Roseville, OH, U.S.A. Florist ware ca.1935 (1848–present) (Lancaster Colony Corp.)
E	**F**	**G**	**H**
Florence STANDARD POTTERY CO. East Liverpool, OH, U.S.A. Semivitreous dinnerware ca.1910-ca.1925 (1886–1927)	*flögl* MATHILDE FLOGL Vienna, Austria Ceramics. Incised ca.1916 (1916–1935)	**FOLEY** ENGLISH BONE CHINA PAINTED BY HAND E. BRAIN & CO. LTD. Fenton, Staffordshire, England Porcelain 1936 + (1903–present) (member of Wedgwood Group)	FRANCISCAN + + + WARE MADE IN U.S.A. GLADDING, McBEAN & CO. Los Angeles, CA, U.S.A. Franciscan dinnerware 1938–1939 (1875–present) (member of Wedgwood Group)
I	**J**	**K**	**L**
F.R.G. ——— LIMOGES FRANCE RENÉ FRUGIER Limoges, France Hard paste porcelain 1900 + (1900–present) (Haviland SA)	*Fujiyama* ROSEVILLE POTTERY CO. Zanesville, OH, U.S.A. Art pottery, dinnerware. Black ink stamped ca.1906 (1892–1954)	*G.* FRIEDRICH EGIDIUS HENNEBERG Gotha, Thuringia, Germany (E. Germany) Porcelain. Blue underglaze, blue, red, yellow overglaze 1805–1834 (1757–1927) (various names & owners)	*G.* GREINER'S WIDOW & LEERS Gera, Thuringia, Germany (E. Germany) Porcelain. Blue underglaze 1804–ca.1840 (1779–1840 +)
M	**N**	**O**	**P**
EB GUNDRUN BAUDISCHE-WITTKE Hallstadt, Austria Ceramics. Incised, printed ca.1926 (1926–1943 +)	*GDA* **FRANCE** GÉRARD, DUFRAISSEIX & ABBOT (G.D.A.) Limoges, France Porcelain 1937 + (1902–present)	*G.H.&C.* G. H. & E. E. CHAMPION Rustington, Sussex, England Studio pottery 1947 + (1947–1981 +)	*GM* AGNES BENSON Ruislip, Middlesex, England Studio-type pottery 1959 + (1951–1964 +)

A

FR. PFEFFER
Gotha, Thuringia, Germany
(E. Germany)
Faience, porcelain
1900 + (1892–ca.1945)

B

G.P. Co.

GREENWOOD POTTERY
Trenton, NJ, U.S.A.
Graniteware, vitrified
porcelain
ca.1904 (1868–ca.1933)
(various names)

C

GR

WALRICH POTTERY
Berkeley, CA, U.S.A.
Art pottery
ca.1922 (1922–ca.1930)

D

GS

GEORGES SERRE
Sèvres, France
Stoneware. Incised
1923 + (1922–1956)

E

Gallé

EMILE GALLÉ
Nancy, France
Ceramics. Painted,
impressed, variations
1900 + (ca.1874–1904)

F

G. BOYER & LIMOGES Cº
FRANCE

GEORGES BOYER
Limoges, France
Porcelain
ca.1936 (1936–1953)

G

Gefle
SWEDEN

GEFLE
PORCELAINWORKS
Gavle, Sweden
Faience, porcelain
1972 + (1850–present)

H

Cemmo

HEINRICH & CO.
Selb, Bavaria, Germany
(W. Germany)
Porcelain
1949 + (1896–present)
(Villeroy & Boch)

I

GEO. E. OHR
BILOXI, MISS.

BILOXI ART POTTERY
(GEORGE OHR)
Biloxi, MS, U.S.A.
Pottery
ca.1883 (1883–1906)

J

G.E.Ohr

BILOXI ART POTTERY
(GEORGE OHR)
Biloxi, MS, U.S.A.
Pottery. Incised by hand
1899–1906 (1883–1906)

K

George
Clews & Cºld
STAFFORDSHIRE
ENGLAND

GEORGE CLEWS & CO.
Tunstall, Staffordshire,
England
Earthenware. Printed
1947–1961 (1906–1961)

L

*George Grainger
Royal China Works
Worcester.*

GEORGE GRAINGER (&
CO.)
Worcester, England
Porcelain, parian,
semiporcelain. Painted,
printed
ca.1839–1860 (ca.1839–
present)
(Royal Worcester Spode
Ltd.)

M

GEORGE MORLEY'S
MAJOLICA.
EAST LIVERPOOL, O.

GEORGE MORLEY &
SONS
East Liverpool, OH, U.S.A.
Ironstone, majolica
1884–1891 (1884–1900)

N

G.Holland

GEORGE FISHLEY
HOLLAND
Clevedon, Somerset,
England
Earthenware. Printed,
painted, impressed
1955 + (1955–1964 +)

O

Gibsons
• HAND
PAINTED
• ENGLAND•

GIBSON & SONS
Burslem, Staffordshire,
England
Earthenware
1940 + (1885–1972 +)

P

Gille *H.* front
à Paris

GILLE JEUNE
Paris, France
Porcelain
ca.1832 (1832–1868)

A	B	C	D
GINORI	**GLASGOW CHINA** **VITRIFIED** **TRENTON.N J**	**Made by** **Globe Pottery Co** **E. L. O.**	**GMUNDNER KERAMIK AUSTRIA**
SOCIETÀ CERAMICA RICHARD Milan, Italy Porcelain 1868–1903 (1735– present) (Richard-Ginori)	GLASGOW POTTERY (JOHN MOSES & CO.) Trenton, NJ, U.S.A. Semiporcelain 1904 + (1839–1906)	GLOBE POTTERY CO. East Liverpool, OH, U.S.A. Semivitreous ware ca.1898 (1881–1901, 1907–1912)	GMUNDNER KERAMIK Gmunden, Austria Art pottery. Painted, impressed 1909–1922 (1909–1922)

E	F	G	H
Goebel	**Goebel**	**Goedewaagen**	**Goldscheider**
W. GOEBEL Rodental, Bavaria, Germany (W. Germany) Figurines, pottery. Printed 1979–present (1871– present)	W. GOEBEL (HUMMEL) Rodental, Bavaria, Germany (W. Germany) Figurines, pottery. Blue underglaze, Goebel with stylized bee 1972–1979 (1871–present)	GOEDEWAAGEN POTTERY Gouda, Holland Pottery ca.1902 (1749–present)	FRIEDRICH GOLDSCHEIDER VIENNA MANUFACTORY Vienna, Austria Earthenware, porcelain, faience, terra-cotta 1937–ca.1941 (1885– present) (various names)

I	J	K	L
Goldscheider	**Gonder Originals**	**GOODWIN'S HOTEL CHINA**	**GRAND FEU POTTERY** **L. A., CAL.**
GOLDSCHEIDER POTTERY LTD. Hanley, Staffordshire, England Bone china figures. Printed 1946–1959 (1946–1959)	GONDER CERAMIC ART CO. Zanesville, OH, U.S.A. Vitrified porcelain 1941–1957 (1941–1957)	GOODWIN POTTERY CO. East Liverpool, OH, U.S.A. Ironstone, semivitreous hotel ware 1893–ca.1906 (1844– 1853,1863–1865,1872– 1913)	GRAND FEU ART POTTERY Los Angeles, CA, U.S.A. Art pottery. Impressed ca.1912 (1912–1916 +)

M	N	O	P
GREENWOOD CHINA TRENTON,N.J.	**Grès Keramis**	**GRIMWADES ENGLAND**	**GRIMWADES Potteries England**
GREENWOOD POTTERY Trenton, NJ, U.S.A. Ironstone ca.1904 (1868–ca.1933) (various names)	BOCH FRÈRES Hainault, Belgium/ Septfontaines, Luxembourg Art pottery. Printed, impressed ca.1900 (1841–present)	GRIMWADES LTD. Stoke, Staffordshire, England Earthenware, majolica, jet 1930 + (1900–present) (Royal Winton Pottery)	GRIMWADES LTD. Stoke, Staffordshire, England Earthenware, majolica, jet 1911 + (1900–present) (Royal Winton Pottery)

A

GRUEBY

GRUEBY FAIENCE CO.
Boston, MA, U.S.A.
Semiporcelain, art pottery.
Impressed
1897–1911 (1897–1911)

B

The Guernsey Pottery

GUERNSEY POTTERY
LTD.
Guernsey, Channel Islands,
England
Red majolica ware, studio
pottery, earthenware
current (ca.1964–present)

C

Gustafsberg

GUSTAFSBERG
Gustafsberg, Sweden
Semiporcelain, faience,
earthenware
ca.1895–1900 (1825–
present)

D

Chr. Dresser

CHRISTOPHER DRESSER
England
Designer
ca.1850 (1847–1890s,

E

Gwent Ware

C. H. BRANNAM
Barnstaple, Devon, England
Earthenware
1880+ (1879–present)

F

RUSSIAN IMPERIAL
PORCELAIN FACTORY
St. Petersburg, Russia
(Leningrad, U.S.S.R.)
Porcelain
1894–1917 (1744–
1917+) (see page 248)

G

H&Cº

HAVILAND & CO.
Limoges, France
Porcelain. Red, black, green
1879+ (1864–present)
(Haviland SA)

H

H&Cº.

HEINRICH & CO.
Selb, Bavaria, Germany (W.
Germany)
Porcelain
1911+ (1896–present)
(Villeroy & Boch)

I

FAÏENCERIE DE LA
GRANDE MAISON
(HUBAUDIÈRE)
Quimper, France
Faience
1882+ (1773–present)
(Société Nouvelle des
Faïenceries de Quimper
HB Henriot)

J

HOMER LAUGHLIN CHINA
CO.
East Liverpool, OH, U.S.A.
Porcelain
1926–present (1877–
present)

K

PETER HOLDSWORTH
Ramsburg, Wiltshire,
England
Earthenware, stoneware.
Impressed, printed
1945+ (1945–1964+)

L

HALCYON ART POTTERY
Halcyon, CA, U.S.A.
Art pottery. Incised
1931–1932 (1910–
1913.1931–1932)

M

ROBERTSON ART TILE
CO.
Morrisville, PA, U.S.A.
Art pottery
1890+ (1890–present)

N

C M. HUTSCHEN-
REUTHER
PORCELAIN
FACTORY
Hohenberg, Bavaria,
Germany (W. Germany)
Porcelain
1882+ (1814–present)
(Hutschenreuther AG)

O

HENRIOT QUIMPER
(DUMAINE)
Quimper, France
Pottery
1904+ (1773–present)
(Société Nouvelle des
Faïenceries de Quimper
HB Henriot)

P

HAWLEY, WEBBERLY &
CO.
Longton, Staffordshire,
England
Earthenware, majolica.
Printed
1895–1902 (1895–1902)

A	B	C	D
HACA-БATEH. BATENIN PORCELAIN MFG. St. Petersburg, Russia (Leningrad, U.S.S.R.) Porcelain 1812–1839 (1812–1839)	*Hadley* WORCESTER ROYAL PORCELAIN CO. LTD. Worcester, England Artist's mark. Incised, impressed ca.1875–1894 (1862–present) (Royal Worcester Spode Ltd.)	 HAEGER POTTERIES Dundee, IL, U.S.A. Pottery, dinnerware ca.1971 (1914–present)	**HAËL** HAEL WORKSHOPS FOR ARTISTIC CERAMICS Marwitz, Prussia, Germany (E. Germany) Ceramics ca.1929–1934 (ca.1927–present) (State's Art Dealership of GDR Workshop for Ceramics)

E	F	G	H
Haidinger RUDOLF & EUGEN HAIDINGER Elbogen, Bohemia (Loket, Czechoslovakia) Porcelain, figurines ca.1815–1873 (1815–1945) (various names & owners)	**HALCYON CALIF.** HALCYON ART POTTERY Halcyon, CA, U.S.A. Art pottery. Impressed 1910–1913 (1910–1913,1931–1932)	**HALL CHINA** HALL CHINA CO. East Liverpool, OH, U.S.A. Vitrified porcelain 1936–1970+ (1903–present)	**HALLCRAFT** *Eva Zeisel* MADE IN U.S.A. BY HALL CHINA CO. HALL CHINA CO. East Liverpool, OH, U.S.A. Whiteware, dinnerware 1950+ (1903–present)

I	J	K	L
HAMPSHIRE POTTERY HAMPSHIRE POTTERY (J. S. TAFT) Keene, NH, U.S.A. Stoneware, majolica, art pottery. Red 1904+ (1871–1923)	*Harkerware* HARKER POTTERY CO. East Liverpool, OH, U.S.A. Semivitreous ware 1954–ca.1965 (1890–1972)	**HARLEQUIN MADE IN U.S.A** HALL CHINA CO. East Liverpool, OH, U.S.A. Vitrified dinnerware ca.1945 (1903–present)	HARTLEY GREENS & Co. LEEDS • POTTERY HARTLEY, GREENS & CO. Leeds, Yorkshire, England Earthenware. Impressed ca.1781–1820 (ca.1781–1820)

M	N	O	P
HAVILAND ALUMINITE FRUGIER LIMOGES FRANCE HAVILAND SA Limoges, France Porcelain 1964+ (1941–present)	HAVILAND BAVARIA JOHANN HAVILAND Waldershof, Bavaria, Germany (W. Germany) Porcelain. Green underglaze 1910–1924 (1907–present) (various names, now Rosenthal Glass & Porcelain AG)	**HAVILAND & Cº** HAVILAND & CO. Limoges, France Porcelain ca.1876 (1864–present) (Haviland SA)	**HAVILAND & Cº LIMOGES** HAVILAND & CO. Limoges, France Porcelain 1889–1905+ (1864–present) (Haviland SA)

A	B	C	D
HAVILAND & Cº **LIMOGES** HAVILAND SA Limoges, France Porcelain 1941 + (1941–present)	*Haviland & Cº* *Limoges* HAVILAND & CO. Limoges, France Porcelain. Red 1876–1930 (1864– present) (Haviland SA)	**HAVILAND** **FRANCE** HAVILAND & CO. Limoges, France Porcelain 1889–1905 + (1864– present) (Haviland SA)	**HAVILAND** **FRANCE** HAVILAND SA Limoges, France Porcelain 1941 + (1941–present)

E	F	G	H
Haviland France HAVILAND & CO. Limoges, France Whiteware 1893–1930, ca.1941– 1962 (1864–present) (Haviland SA)	*Haviland* France ESTABLISHED 1842 HAVILAND SA Limoges, France Porcelain current (1941–present)	*Haviland* France Limoges HAVILAND SA Limoges, France Porcelain current (1941–present)	*Haviland's* *Chantilly* HAVILAND & CO. Limoges, France Porcelain. Red, green 1948–1953 (1864– present) (Haviland SA)

I	J	K	L
HB QUIMPER LES FAÏENCERIES DE QUIMPER Quimper, France Faïence 1972–1984 (1685– present) (Société Nouvelle des Faïenceries de Quimper HB Henriot)	**HEATH** HEATH CERAMICS Sausalito, CA, U.S.A. Dinnerware, tile 1941 + (1941–1963 +)	**ARMORLITE** **HEATH** **ENGLAND** J. E. HEATH, LTD. Stoke, Staffordshire, England Vitrified hotel ware current (1951–present)	**Heinrich** FRANZ HEINRICH Selb, Bavaria, Germany (W. Germany) Porcelain 1911 + (1896–present)

M	N	O	P
HELE CROSS **POTTERY** **TORQUAY** TORQUAY TERRA-COTTA CO. Torquay, Devon, England Art pottery. Stamped ca.1912–1918 (1875– 1940) (various names)	HENRI ARDANT & Cᵛ HENRI ARDANT & CO. Limoges, France Porcelain. Unglazed ca.1854 (1854–1884)	**HENRI** **DEUX** J. B. OWENS POTTERY Zanesville, OH, U.S.A. Art pottery, dinnerware 1900 + (1885–1929)	*HENRIOT* *QUIMPER* HENRIOT QUIMPER (DUMAINE) Quimper, France Faïence 1922 + (1773–present) (Société Nouvelle des Faïenceries de Quimper HB Henriot)

A

HEU: BACH

HEUBACH BROS.
Lichte, Thuringia, Germany
  (E. Germany)
Porcelain. Green, black
1904 + (1822–present)
(various names and
  owners, now United
  Decorative
  Porcelainworks Lichte
  VEB)

B

H.M. EXETER

HART & MOIST POTTERY
Exeter, England
Art pottery. Impressed
ca.1900–ca.1934 (1894–
  ca.1935)

C

HOMER JAUGHLIN

HOMER LAUGHLIN CHINA
CO.
East Liverpool, OH, U.S.A.
Semivitreous ware
ca.1970–1980 (1877–
  present)

D

HONITON POTTERY
DEVON ENGLAND

HONITON POTTERY LTD.
Honiton, Devon, England
Earthenware
current (1881–present)

E

HORNBERG

HORN BROS.
Hornberg, Badenia,
  Germany (W. Germany)
Earthenware. Impressed
ca.1830–ca.1860 (1817–
  present)
(Durairt-Hornberg, Sanitary
  Ceramic Work)

F

Hull
U.S.A.

HULL POTTERY CO.
Crooksville, OH, U.S.A.
Dinnerware
ca.1950 (1905–1950,
  1952–present)

G

Hywood
BY
Niloak

NILOAK POTTERY
Benton, AR, U.S.A.
Art pottery, florist ware
ca.1930 (1909–1944)

H

Imperial
U.S.A.

HULL POTTERY CO.
Crooksville, OH, U.S.A.
Dinnerware, art pottery
1960 + (1905–1950, 1952–
  present)

I

Intaglio
A BEN SEIBEL DESIGN
GENUINE CHINA
by Iroquois

IROQUOIS CHINA CO.
Syracuse, NY, U.S.A.
Hotel ware, dinnerware
ca.1946 (1905–1969)

J

INTERNATIONAL CHINA
TRENTON N.J.

INTERNATIONAL
POTTERY CO.
Trenton, NJ, U.S.A.
Semiporcelain
1860–1868 (1860–
  1940 +)

K

iron [❋] mountain

IRON MOUNTAIN
Laurel Bloomery, TN,
  U.S.A.
Stoneware
ca.1968 (1965–present)

L

IROQUOIS
CASUAL CHINA
by Russel Wright

IROQUOIS CHINA CO.
Syracuse, NY, U.S.A.
Semiporcelain
1950 + (1905–1969)

M

IVORA · Gouda
Holland

IVORA
Gouda, Holland
Porcelain
ca.1895–1910 (ca.1895–
  1910)

N

JOSEF BOCK PORCELAIN
MANUFACTORY
VIENNA
Vienna, Austria
Porcelain. Impressed,
  printed
ca.1893–ca.1933 (1879–
  1960)

O

& Ⴔ Co
CLIFF ENGLAND

J. DIMMOCK & CO.
Hanley, Staffordshire,
  England
Earthenware
1878–1904 (1862–1904)

P

J.&G.
MEAKIN
ENGLAND

J. & G. MEAKIN (LTD.)
Hanley, Staffordshire,
  England
Earthenware, ironstone.
  Impressed, printed
ca.1962 (1851–present)
(member of Wedgwood
  Group)

A

GEORGE JONES (&
   SONS LTD.)
Stoke, Staffordshire,
   England
Porcelain. Relief, impressed,
   printed
ca.1861–1873 (1861–
   1951)

B

JAMES HADLEY & SONS
   (LTD.)
Worcester, England
Porcelain, earthenware,
   terra-cotta. Printed
1896–1897 (1896–1905)

C

LOW ART TILE CO.
Chelsea, MA, U.S.A.
Art tiles. Impressed
1881–1885 (1877–1907)

D

JACOB PETIT
Fontainebleau, France
Porcelain. Painted blue
ca.1830–1862 (ca.1830–
   1862)

E

ASHBY POTTERS GUILD
Woodville, Derbyshire,
   England
Earthenware
ca.1909 (1909–1922)

F

J Z & Co

JACOB ZEIDLER & CO.
Selb, Bavaria, Germany (W.
   Germany)
Porcelain. Impressed
after 1866–ca.1879 (1866–
   1917)

G

WILHELM JAGER
   PORCELAIN FACTORY
Eisenberg, Thuringia,
   Germany (E. Germany)
Porcelain
after 1900 (1868–present)
(United Porcelainworks
   Eisenberg VEB)

H

STUDIO
J.&G MEAKIN
ENGLAND

J. & G. MEAKIN (LTD.)
Hanley, Staffordshire,
   England
Earthenware, ironstone.
Printed, impressed
current (1851–present)
(member of Wedgwood
   Group)

I

JEAN HAVILAND
Limoges, France
Porcelain
1957 + (1957–present)

J

Jersey
Pottery
C.I.

JERSEY POTTERY LTD.
Gorey Village, Jersey,
   Channel Islands
Earthenware. Painted
1946 + (1946–present)

K

JEWEL
C.P.Co.

CROWN POTTERY CO.
Evansville, IN, U.S.A.
Dinnerware
1891 + (1891–1962)

L

J.F. LENZ
ZELL

JAKOB FERDINAND LENZ
   & BURGER
Zell on Harmersbach,
   Badenia, Germany (W.
   Germany)
Earthenware
ca.1809–1819
   (1794–present)
(various names & owners,
   Georg Schmidt United
   Zell Ceramic Factory)

M

J.Fryer&Son,
Tunstall,
England

J. FRYER & SON
Tunstall, Staffordshire,
   England
Earthenware. Printed
1945 + (1945–present)
(J. Fryer Ltd.)

N

J.Massier fils

JEROME MASSIER
Vallauris, France
Studio pottery. Painted
ca.1908 (1908+)

O

JOHANN HAVILAND/
   WALDERSHOF
   PORCELAIN FACTORY
   AG
Waldershof, Bavaria,
   Germany (W. Germany)
Porcelain. Green underglaze,
   green, red overglaze
1912–1936 (1907–present)
(various names, now
   Rosenthal Glass &
   Porcelain AG)

P

John Ridgway

JOHN RIDGWAY (& CO.)
Hanley, Staffordshire,
   England
Porcelain, earthenware.
Printed, impressed
ca.1830–1841 (ca.1830–
   present)
(Royal Doulton Tableware
   Ltd.)

A

Johnson's **E. LIVERPOO U.S.A**

JOHNSON CHINA CO.
East Liverpool, OH, U.S.A.
Semivitreous dinnerware
1931–1936 (1931–1936)

B

Joseph Chéret

JOSEPH CHERET
Nice, France
Porcelain
1887–1894 (1887–1894)

C

J .P / L / FRANCE

LA CERAMIQUE (JEAN POUYAT)
Limoges, France
Porcelain, dinnerware
1905 + (1883–present)
(Guerin-Pouyat-Elite)

D

J.S.T.&CO.
KEENE.NH.

HAMPSHIRE POTTERY
(J. S. TAFT)
Keene, NH, U.S.A.
Art pottery. Impressed
1883 + (1871–1923)

E

K

UPPER FRANCONIAN
PORCELAIN FACTORY
(OHNEMÜLLER & ULRICH)
Kups, Bavaria, Germany
(W. Germany)
Porcelain
1896–ca.1919 (1890–1919)

F

KB

KATHERINE PLEYDELL-BOUVERIE
Kilmington Manor, Wiltshire, England
Studio potter, stoneware.
Incised
1925 + (1925–present)

G

WILLIAM KIRKBY & CO.
Fenton, Staffordshire, England
Porcelain, earthenware.
Impressed, printed
1879–1885 (1879–1885)

H

 KPF

CARL KRISTER
PORCELAIN FACTORY
Waldenburg, Silesia, Germany (Walbrzych, Poland)
Porcelain. Green, blue underglaze
1903 + (1831–present)
(Rosenthal Glass & Porcelain AG)

I

K.P.M

ROYAL PORCELAIN MANUFACTORY
Meissen, Saxony, Germany (E. Germany)
Porcelain. Blue underglaze, often copied by later factories
1756 + (1710–present)
(State's Porcelain Manufactory Meissen VEB)

J

K.P.M.

KRISTER PORCELAIN MANUFACTORY
Waldenburg, Silesia, Germany (Walbrzych, Poland)
Porcelain. Green, blue underglaze
1885 + (1831–present)
(Rosenthal Glass & Porcelain AG)

K

KPM / W

KRISTER PORCELAIN MANUFACTORY
Waldenburg, Silesia, Germany (Walbrzych, Poland)
Porcelain. Green, blue underglaze
ca.1896–ca.1906 (1831–present)
(Rosenthal Glass & Porcelain AG)

L

K & S

KURLBAUM & SCHWARTZ
Philadelphia, PA, U.S.A.
Porcelain. Impressed
1851–1855 (ca.1851–1855)

M

K.T.& K. / S —— V

KNOWLES, TAYLOR & KNOWLES
East Liverpool, OH, U.S.A.
Semivitreous dinnerware
ca.1925 (1870–1929)

N

VKE

KARL ENS PORCELAIN FACTORY
Volkstedt, Thuringia, Germany (E. Germany)
Porcelain
1900 + (1898–present)
(Underglaze Porcelain Factory VEB)

O

K / WPM

KRISTER PORCELAIN MANUFACTORY
Waldenburg, Silesia, Germany (Walbrzych, Poland)
Porcelain. Green, blue underglaze
1896–1906 (1831–present)
(Rosenthal Glass & Porcelain AG)

P

Kaiser-Porzellan

HEINRICH & CO.
Selb, Bavaria, Germany (W. Germany)
Porcelain
1911–ca.1918 (1896–present)
(Villeroy & Boch)

A

KeraDea

KERA DEA
Laveno, Italy
Earthenware
20th century (1856–
present)

B

KERAMIS
MADEinBELGIUM

BOCH FRÈRES
La Louvlère, Belgium
Ceramics
1914+ (1841–present)

C

KERN COLLECTIBLES
Stillwater, MN, U.S.A.
Collector plates
current (1969–present)

D

KEYSTONE WARE
FINE
EARTHENWARE
HANLEY
STAFFORDSHIRE
ENGLAND

KEYSTONE POTTERY
LTD.
Hanley, Staffordshire,
England
Earthenware
current (1964–present)

E

KEZONTA

CINCINNATI ART
POTTERY
Cincinnati, OH, U.S.A.
Porcelain. Red, impressed
ca.1886 (1879–1891)

F

*KG
Lunéville*

KELLER & GUÉRIN
Lunéville, France
Porcelain. Printed,
impressed
ca.1889 (ca.1788–1890+)

G

Klentsch.

JOSEF MAYER
Klentsch (Klenci),
Czechoslovakia
Porcelain. Impressed
ca.1835–1865+ (1835–
1889)

H

Knowles

EDWIN M. KNOWLES
CHINA CO.
East Liverpool, OH, U.S.A.
Semivitreous dinnerware
1955–1957 (1900–1963)

I

KODAU

J. HUTTNER & CO.
Chodau, Bohemia (Chodov,
Czechoslovakia)
Porcelain. Impressed
1834–1845 (1834–1845)

J

KOKUS
CHINA

SEBRING POTTERY CO.
East Liverpool, OH, U.S.A.
Ironstone
ca.1895 (1887–1948)

K

KP
REPRO
ENGLAND

KEYSTONE POTTERY
LTD.
Hanley, Staffordshire,
England
Earthenware
current (1964–present)

L

Kraft
INC
MADE EXPRESSLY FOR
KRAFT INC
BY
THE HALL CHINA CO.
MADE IN U S A

HALL CHINA CO.
East Liverpool, OH, U.S.A.
Vitrified crocks for cheese
ca.1937–present (1903–
present)

M

Krister

KRISTER PORCELAIN
MANUFACTORY
Landstuhl, Palatinate,
Germany (W. Germany)
Porcelain
1952+ (1950–present)
(Rosenthal Glass &
Porcelain AG)

N

KW
WIEN

CERAMIC WORKSHOP
CO-OPERATIVE
SOCIETY (KERAMISCHE
WERKGENOSSEN-
SCHAFT)
Vienna, Austria
Art pottery. Impressed
ca.1911–1920 (1911–
1920)

O

L

LANGENTHAL
PORCELAIN FACTORY
AG
Langenthal, Bern,
Switzerland
Tableware, hotel & fancy
ware
1906+ (1906–present)

P

LD

DAVID LEACH
Bovey Tracey, Devon,
England
Studio pottery, stoneware,
porcelain. Impressed
1956+ (ca.1956–present)

A LJ JOHN LEACH Langport, Somerset, England Studio-type pottery. Impressed before 1958 (1950– 1980+)	**B** L.M & Cie LEBOEUF & MILLIET Creil, France Soft paste porcelain. Green underglaze, impressed ca.1841–ca.1863 (1841– 1895)	**C** LM^cL LOSANTI (MARY LOUISE McLAUGHLIN) Cincinnati, OH, U.S.A. Porcelain. Incised 1898+ (1876–1939)	**D** ΦL NEW MILFORD POTTERY CO./WANNOPEE POTTERY CO. New Milford, CT, U.S.A. Whiteware, creamware, porcelain 1886+ (1886–1903)
E ◁P LUBTHEEN PORCELAIN FACTORY Lubtheen, Mecklenburg, Germany (E. Germany) Porcelain 1933–ca.1945 (1933– ca.1945)	**F** L. P.& CIE L. PARANT (LA PÉPINIÈRE) Limoges, France Porcelain 1863–1868 (1843–1939)	**G** tc TIFFANY POTTERY Corona, NY, U.S.A. Pottery. Incised 1904+ (1898–ca.1920)	**H** Lele DAISON POTTERY Torquay, Devon, England Porcelain. Incised ca.1922–ca.1925 (ca. 1922–ca.1932)
I LaBelle. China. WHEELING POTTERY CO. Wheeling, WV, U.S.A. Semiporcelain 1893+ (1879–ca.1910)	**J** LACHENAL EDMOND LACHENAL Paris & Chatillon-sous- Bagneaux, France Faience, stoneware. Painted 1880+ (1880–ca.1930)	**K** La Française Porcelain FRENCH CHINA CO. East Liverpool, OH, U.S.A. Semivitreous ware ca.1900–ca.1916 (ca.1900–present) (Royal China Co.)	**L** **LAKE'S CORNISH POTTERY TRURO** W. H. LAKE & SON (LTD.) Truro, Cornwall, England Earthenware. Printed, impressed current (1872–present)
M LAKEWARE COWAN POTTERY Cleveland & Rocky River, OH, U.S.A. Artware 1927–1931 (1912–1931)	**N** Lambeth Pottery DOULTON &WATTS HIGH STREET LAMBETH DOULTON & WATTS Lambeth, London, England Stoneware, terra-cotta. Impressed, molded, incised ca.1827–1858 (ca.1815– present) (various names & locations, Royal Doulton Tableware Ltd.)	**O** La Porcelaine Théodore Haviland Limoges THÉODORE HAVILAND Limoges, France Porcelain 1925+ (1892–present) (Haviland SA)	**P** Lauder Barum ALEXANDER LAUDER (LAUDER & SMITH) Barnstaple (& Pottington), Devon, England Earthenware. Incised, painted 1876–1914 (1876–1914)

A	B	C	D
L.BERNARDAUD&C°. LIMOGES	L.C.T. Tiffany Pottery	LEEDS & POTTERY	Legrand Limoges FRANCE
BERNARDAUD & CO. Limoges, France Porcelain. Printed red 1900–1929 (1929–present)	TIFFANY POTTERY Corona, NY, U.S.A. Art pottery 1904 + (1898–ca.1920)	HARTLEY, GREENS & CO. Leeds, Yorkshire, England Earthenware. Impressed ca.1781–1820 (ca.1781–1820)	LEGRAND & CO. Limoges, France Porcelain ca.1924–1926 (1924–1962 +)

E	F	G	H
LELAND.	LENOX	TRADE "LETTUCE LEAF" MARK	LIMOGES A.F FRANCE
C. C. THOMPSON POTTERY CO. East Liverpool, OH, U.S.A. Rockingham, yellowware ca.1890 (1868–1938)	LENOX, INC. Trenton, NJ, U.S.A. Dinnerware, tableware current (1906–present)	WANNOPEE POTTERY CO. New Milford, CT, U.S.A. Porcelain. Imprinted 1901 + (1892–1903)	ANDRÉ FRANÇOIS Limoges, France Porcelain 1919–1934 (1919–1934)

I	J	K	L
LIMOGES B & C i? FRANCE	LIMOGES CHINA L. C. CO.	LIMOGES J.P. L. FRANCE	LIMOGES ELTé FRANCE
H. A. BALLEROY BROS. Limoges, France Porcelain ca.1889 (1908–1937)	LIMOGES CHINA CO. East Liverpool, OH, U.S.A. Semivitreous dinnerware ca.1910–ca.1930 (1900–1955) (American Limoges China Co.)	GUÉRIN-POUYAT-ÉLITE LTD. Limoges, France Porcelain 1905 + (1870–present) (various names)	L. TEXERAUD Limoges, France Porcelain 1929 + (ca.1929 +)

M	N	O	P
LIMOGES MG FRANCE	LIMOGES PL FRANCE	LIMOGES P♦P FRANCE	LIMOGES S FRANCE
MAVALEIX & GRANGER Limoges, France Porcelain ca.1920–1938 (ca.1920–1938)	PORCELAINE LIMOUSINE Limoges, France Porcelain 1926 + (1905–1939)	PAROUTAUD FRÈRES LaSeynie, Limoges, France Porcelain ca.1903 (ca.1903–ca.1919)	SERPAUT Limoges, France Porcelain 1923–1930 (1919–present)

A

LIMOGES ·U·S·A· CHINA CO·

LIMOGES CHINA CO.
East Liverpool, OH, U.S.A.
Semivitreous dinnerware
1910–ca.1930 (1900–
1955)
(American Limoges China
Co.)

B

LIMOGES {W.G & C.} FRANCE

GUÉRIN-POUYAT-ÉLITE
LTD.
Limoges, France
Porcelain
1901 + (1870–present)
(various names)

C

THE
LINCOLN CHINA CO
SEBRING,
OHIO
U. S. A.

LIMOGES CHINA CO.
East Liverpool, OH, U.S.A.
Semivitreous dinnerware
ca.1950 (1900–1955)
(American Limoges China
Co.)

D

LINTHORPE

LINTHORPE POTTERY
Middlesbrough, Yorkshire,
England
Earthenware. Impressed
ca.1879–1889 (1879–
1889)

E

LLADRO
MADE
IN SPAIN

LLADRÓ
Tabernes Blanques, Spain
Porcelain, figurines.
Impressed
1964 + (1951–present)

F

LLADRO

LLADRÓ
Tabernes Blanques, Spain
Porcelain, figurines. Dark
blue
1965–present (1951–
present)

G

Longpark Torquay

ROYAL LONGPARK
POTTERY CO. (ART)
LTD.
Longpark & Torquay,
Devon, England
Art pottery
ca.1914–ca.1923 (1883–
1957)

H

LONGPARK
TORQUAY

LONGPARK POTTERY CO.
LTD.
Longpark & Torquay,
Devon, England
Earthenware. Black, rubber-
stamped
ca.1918–ca.1925 (1883–
1957)

I

LONHUDA

LONHUDA POTTERY CO.
Steubenville, OH, U.S.A.
Faience. Impressed
1892 + (1892–ca.1894)

J

Lore

HEINRICH WINTERLING
PORCELAIN FACTORY
Marktleuther, Bavaria,
Germany (W. Germany)
Porcelain
1934 + (1903–present)

K

Losanti

LOSANTI (MARY LOUISE
McLAUGHLIN)
Cincinnati, OH, U.S.A.
Porcelain. Impressed,
painted blue
ca.1899–1906 (1876–
1939)

L

Lotus

ROSEVILLE POTTERY CO.
Zanesville, OH, U.S.A.
Art pottery. Raised
1950s (1892–1954)

M

LOUWELSA
WELLER

WELLER POTTERY
Zanesville, OH, U.S.A.
Art pottery, kitchenware
1895–1918 (1882–1948)

N

LOY-NEL-ART
McCOY

J. W. McCOY CO.
Zanesville, OH, U.S.A.
Art pottery, commercial
ware. Impressed
1906 + (1899–present)
(Brush Pottery Co.)

O

T.S.&T.
Lu-RAY
PASTELS
U.S.A

TAYLOR, SMITH &
TAYLOR
East Liverpool, OH, U.S.A.
Semiporcelain, porcelain,
white granite
late 1930s–early 1950s
(1901–present)
(Anchor Hocking)

P

M

E. & A. MULLER
Schwarza-Saale, Thuringia,
Germany (E. Germany)
Porcelain, figurines. Blue
underglaze, overglaze
1890 + (1890–ca.1945)

A

VOIGT & HOLAND
Unterweissbach, Thuringia,
Germany (E. Germany)
Pottery
1884+ (1884–1887)

B

MINTON
Stoke, Staffordshire,
England
Bone china
ca.1800–1830 (1793–
present)
(Royal Doulton Tableware
Ltd.)

C

FRIEDRICH CARL MULLER
Stutzerbach, Thuringia,
Germany (E. Germany)
Porcelain
1887–ca.1922 (1830–
1922)

D

MICHAEL CASSON
Prestwood,
Buckinghamshire,
England
Earthenware, stoneware.
Impressed
1955+ (1953–1964+)

E

MOREAU AÎNÉ & CO.
Limoges, France
Porcelain
1880+ (1880–1882+)

F

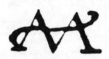

ANGELO MINGHETTI &
SON
Bologna, Italy
Reproductions of Italian
Renaissance majolica
(1849+)

G

FRANZ ANTON MEHLEM
EARTHENWARE
FACTORY
Bonn, Rhineland, Germany
(W. Germany)
Earthenware
1881–1920 (1836–1920)

H

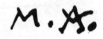

MICHEL AARON
Chantilly, France
Utility ware, porcelain. Blue
underglaze
1845–1870 (1845–1870)

I

M. B.

MANSFIELD BROS.
Woodville & Church
Gresley, Burton-on-Trent,
Staffordshire, England
Earthenware, tile.
Impressed
1890+ (ca.1890–1957+)

J

VILLEROY & BOCH
Mettlach, Saar, Germany
(W. Germany)
Porcelain, earthenware
1842+ (1813–present)
(various names, owners, &
locations)

K

C. E. & F. ARNOLDI
Elgersburg, Saxony,
Germany (E. Germany)
Porcelain
1912+ (1808–ca.1962)

L

NELSON McCOY
POTTERY
Roseville, OH, U.S.A.
Stoneware, earthenware
1934–ca.1940 (1848–
present)
(Lancaster Colony Corp.)

M

MAYER & ELLIOTT
Longport, Staffordshire,
England
Earthenware. Printed,
impressed
1858–1861 (1858–1861)

N

FORTUNÉ DE
MONESTROL
Rungis, France
Reproductions of Italian
lusterware
(ca.1853+)

O

M. E. BULMER
Burill, Yorkshire, England
Studio-type pottery. Incised,
painted
1956–1960 (1956–1960)

P

MF

MORITZ FISCHER
Herend, Hungary
Porcelain. Painted blue
19th century (1839–
1948+)

A

MG

MARTIN BROS.
Lubau, Bohemia (Hlubany, Czechoslovakia)
Porcelain
after 1847–ca.1918 (1874–ca.1918)

B

MgH

BUCKFAST ABBEY POTTERY
Buckfast, Devon, England
Studio-type pottery. Incised, impressed
1952+ (1952–1964+)

C

KOLO MOSER
Vienna, Austria
Ceramics. Incised, painted
(ca.1899 (ca.1899–ca.1918)

D

MARZOLF & CO.
Montreuil, France
Porcelain
(1885–1980+)

E

LOSANTI (MARY LOUISE McLAUGHLIN)
Cincinnati, OH, U.S.A.
Porcelain, pottery.
Impressed, painted blue
(1876–1939)

F

MEKUS & MOEST PORCELAIN FACTORY
Turn-Teplitz, Bohemia (Trnovany, Czechoslovakia)
Porcelain·
after 1892–ca.1912 (1892–ca.1912)

G

McNEAL & CO.
Longton, Staffordshire, England
Earthenware. Printed
1894–1906 (1894–1906)

H

BRUSH-McCOY POTTERY CO.
Roseville, OH, U.S.A.
Pottery. Various patterns, probably blurred MC mark
ca. 1911–1925 (1911–present)
(Brush Pottery)

I

MP

MOUNTAINSIDE ART POTTERY
Mountainside, NJ, U.S.A.
Stoneware, artware
ca.1938 (1929–ca.1940)

J

MP

R. DODD
Henfield, Sussex, England
Studio-type pottery.
Impressed
1961+ (1961–1964+)

K

MIIR
FRANCE

MARTIAL REDON & CO.
Limoges, France
Porcelain
1890+ (1882–1896)
(also used by Porcelaine Limousine until 1938)

L

Magie

ROSENTHAL PORCELAIN AG
Selb, Bavaria, Germany (W. Germany)
Tableware, porcelain, earthenware
1951+ (1879–present)
(Rosenthal Glass & Porcelain AG)

M

MADE IN OCCUPIED JAPAN

At the end of World War II Allied occupation forces remained in Japan.· All ceramics exported from Japan from 1945 to 1952 were marked with the words "Occupied Japan."

N

MADE IN SCOTLAND
BY
WEST HIGHLAND POTTERY
CO..LTD.
DUNOON   ARGYLL

WEST HIGHLAND POTTERY CO. LTD.
Dunoon, Argyll, Scotland
Earthenware
current (after 1964–present)

O

M.A.Hadley

M. A. HADLEY POTTERY
Louisville, KY, U.S.A.
Dinnerware, ornamental pieces
(1939–present)

P

HOMER LAUGHLIN CHINA CO.
East Liverpool, OH, U.S.A.
Semivitreous dinnerware
ca.1914 (1877–present)

A

MALING POTTERY
Newcastle upon Tyne,
Northumberland,
England
Porcelain. Impressed
ca.1817–1853 (1762–
1963)

B

MALING POTTERY
Newcastle upon Tyne,
Northumberland,
England
Porcelain. Printed
ca.1945–1955 (1762–
1963)

C

W. MANNL PORCELAIN
FACTORY
KRUMMENNAAB
Krummennaab, Germany
(W. Germany)
Porcelain
ca.1917–1931 (1879–
1931)

D

Manufactured
by Jos Hemphill
Philad—

TUCKER CHINA CO.
Philadelphia, PA, U.S.A.
Porcelain
1832 + (1825–1838)

E

MANUFACTURE DE
PORCELAINE DE CHANTILLY

MANUFACTURE DE
PORCELAINE DE
CHANTILLY
Chantilly, France
Porcelain
1944 + (1944 +)

F

STOCKTON ART
POTTERY
Stockton, CA, U.S.A.
Terra-cotta. Slip beneath
glaze
(1895–1902)

G

MARKHAM POTTERY
Ann Arbor, MI & National
City, CA, U.S.A.
Art pottery. Incised
(1905–1921)

H

BONE CHINA
Made in England

ROYAL GRAFTON BONE
CHINA
Longton, Staffordshire,
England
Bone china, tableware,
giftware
current (1900–present)

I

GALLUBA & HOFMANN
Ilmenau, Thuringia,
Germany (E. Germany)
Porcelain
1905–ca.1927 (1888–
1927)

J

MARTIN BROS.
Fulham & Southall,
London, England
Studio-type stoneware
1900 + (1873–1914)

K

MARY WRIGHT

BAUER

BAUER POTTERY
Los Angeles, CA, U.S.A.
Artware
(1905–ca.1958)

L

MASON

WILLIAM MASON
Lane Delph, Staffordshire,
England
Earthenware. Impressed
ca.1811–1822 (ca.1811–
1824)
(member of Wedgwood
Group)

M

MASON'S
CAMBRIAN ARGIL

G. M. & C. J. MASON
Lane Delph, Staffordshire,
England
Ironstone. Impressed,
transfer-printed, blue
ca.1819–1920 (1813–
present)
(member of Wedgwood
Group)

N

MASON'S PATENT
IRONSTONE CHINA

G. M. & C. J. MASON
Lane Delph, Staffordshire,
England
Ironstone. Impressed
ca.1813–1825 (1813–
present)
(member of Wedgwood
Group)

O

MASON'S
PATENT IRONSTONE
HOTEL WARE
ENGLAND
EST. 1780

MASON'S IRONSTONE
CHINA LTD.
Hanley, Staffordshire,
England
Earthenware
current (1813–present)
(member of Wedgwood
Group)

P

MAW & CO.

BROSELEY

MAW & CO.
Broseley, Shropshire,
England
Tiles, art pottery
1851 + (ca.1850–1964 +)

A

Mayer China®
C BY INTERPACE

MAYER CHINA
Beaver Falls, PA, U.S.A.
Hotel ware
after 1964–1979 (1881–
present)

B

MᶜCoy

NELSON McCOY
POTTERY
Roseville, OH, U.S.A.
Stoneware, earthenware
1940–1966 (1848–
present)
(Lancaster Colony Corp.)

C

M
CHINA
L

MADDOCK POTTERY
Trenton, NJ, U.S.A.
Yellowware, Rockingham,
porcelain
ca.1900 (1893–ca.1929)

D

MᶜNICOL CHINA

D. E. McNICOL POTTERY
CO.
East Liverpool, OH, U.S.A.
Vitreous institutional ware
ca.1935–ca.1950 (1892–
1954)

E

Meissen

STATE'S PORCELAIN
MANUFACTORY VEB
Meissen, Saxony, Germany
(E. Germany)
Porcelain. Blue
1972+ (1919–present)

F

Melba Ware
H. WAIN & SONS LTD.
MELBA WORKS
LONGTON
STOKE-ON-TRENT
MADE IN ENGLAND

H. A. WAIN & SONS LTD.
Longton & Stoke,
Staffordshire, England
Porcelain
current (1946–present)

G

Mettlacher
Hartsteingut

VILLEROY & BOCH
Mettlach, Saar, Germany
(W. Germany)
Earthenware. Incised
before 1836–ca.1850
(1813–present)
(various names, owners, &
locations)

H

M F^nes
LIMOGES
MADE IN FRANCE

L. MICHELAUD
Limoges, France
Porcelain
after 1918 (1908–1952+)

I

Midwinter
FINE TABLEWARE
STAFFORDSHIRE   ENGLAND

MIDWINTER
Burslem, Staffordshire,
England
Earthenware, stoneware
current (ca.1910–present)

J

M.J.Hummel
GERMANY

W. GOEBEL (HUMMEL)
Rodental, Bavaria, Germany
(W. Germany)
Porcelain, earthenware,
figurines
1949–1973+ (1871–
present)

K

mikasa ⊕·

MIKASA
Secaucus, NJ, U.S.A.
Porcelain, dinnerware
current (ca.1953–present)
(most porcelains made in
Japan)

L

MINTON
LTD.

MINTON
Stoke, Staffordshire,
England
Earthenware. Printed
ca.1900–1908 (1793–
present)
(Royal Doulton Tableware
Ltd.)

M

MINTONS
Art-Pottery
STUDIO
Kensington
Gore

MINTON
Stoke, Staffordshire,
England
Earthenware. Printed
1871–1875 (1793–
present)
(Royal Doulton Tableware
Ltd.)

N

MITTERTEICH
BAVARIA

MITTERTEICH
PORCELAIN FACTORY
AG
Mitterteich, Bavaria,
Germany (W. Germany)
Porcelain
after 1945 (1918–present)

O

MYOTT MEAKIN
ENGLAND

MYOTT-MEAKIN
Hanley & Stoke,
Staffordshire, England
Earthenware
current (ca.1982–present)

P

Modell von
Th.Rosenthal

PHILIP ROSENTHAL & CO.
Selb, Bavaria, Germany (W.
Germany)
Porcelain, earthenware.
Printed
ca. 1897–ca.1939 (1879–
present)
(Rosenthal Glass &
Porcelain AG)

A

OVEN TO TABLE
HANDCRAFTED
MOIRA
MADE IN ENGLAND
STONEWARE

MOIRA POTTERY CO.
LTD.
Burton-on-Trent,
Staffordshire, England
Brownware, stoneware
current (ca.1922–present)

B

MOORCROFT

W. MOORCROFT (LTD.)
Burslem, Staffordshire,
England
Earthenware. Printed,
impressed, variations in
wording
1913–present (1913–
present)

C

W. MOORCROFT (LTD.)
Burslem, Staffordshire,
England
Earthenware
1919+ (1913–present)

D

MORAVIAN

MORAVIAN POTTERY &
TILE WORKS
Doylestown, PA, U.S.A.
Tiles. Stamped
ca.1904 (1897–ca.1963)

E

MORGAN
BELLEEK
AZURE

MORGAN BELLEEK
Canton, OH, U.S.A.
Ceramics
1928+ (1924–1934)

F

MORLEY & CO.
MAJOLICA
WELLSVILLE, O.

MORLEY & CO.
Wellsville, OH, U.S.A.
Ironstone, majolica
1879–1884 (1878–1891)

G

MORTLOCK

ROCKINGHAM WORKS
Nr. Swinton, Yorkshire,
England
Porcelain. Impressed
1826+ (ca.1745–1842)

H

Mosanic

MOSAIC POTTERY MAX
EMANUEL & CO./
MITTERTEICH
PORCELAIN FACTORY
AG
Mitterteich, Bavaria,
Germany (W. Germany)
Porcelain
ca.1895–after 1928
(ca.1882–present)

I

M.R.C."
LIMOGES

MIANTRÉ, RAYNAUD &
CO.
Limoges, France
Porcelain
1929+ (1924–1934)

J

MUNCIE

MUNCIE POTTERY
Muncie, IN, U.S.A.
Pottery. Incised
1922+ (1922–1938)

K

The
MUSEUM COLLECTION
Iroquois China Company, Syracuse, N.Y. U.S.A.

IROQUOIS CHINA CO.
Syracuse, NY, U.S.A.
Dinnerware, hotel ware
1950+ (1905–1969)

L

IRONSTONE WARE BY
MYOTT
ENGLAND

MYOTT-MEAKIN
Hanley, Staffordshire,
England
Earthenware, tableware
current (ca.1982–present)

M

Altrohlau
M.Z.

MORITZ ZDEKAUER
Altrohlau, Bohemia, (Stara
Role, Czechoslovakia)
Porcelain
1884–ca.1909 (1884–
1945+)
(nationalized in 1945)

N

GOTTLOB NATHUSIUS
Althaldensleben, Prussia,
Germany (E. Germany)
Porcelain. Blue underglaze
1826–ca.1860 (1826–
ca.1860)

O

BARONI GIOVANNI
Nove, Italy
Faience, porcelain
1802–1825 (1728–1835)

P

CHESTER NICODEMUS
Columbus, OH, U.S.A.
Vitrified ware
1971+ (1935–present)

A  NORAH BRADEN St. Ives, England Studio-type pottery. Impressed, incised 1924–1936 (1924–1936)	**B** **N.G.F.** W. VON NEUBERG Giesshubel, Bohemia (Struzna, Czechoslovakia) Porcelain. Impressed 1846–ca.1892 (1803– 1945) (various names & owners)	**C** **NM** **U. S. A.** NELSON McCOY POTTERY Roseville, OH, U.S.A. Dinnerware, steins, artware ca.1935 (1848–present) (Lancaster Colony Corp.)	**D** **ND** **NEUTETTAU** NEW PORCELAIN FACTORY TETTAU Tettau, Bavaria, Germany (W. Germany) Porcelain. Green underglaze, gold overglaze 1935–1948 (1904– present) (Porcelain Factory Gerold & Co.)
E **NPS** FRANZ PRAUSE Niedersalzbrunn, Silesia, Germany (Szczawienko, Poland) Porcelain 1910 + (1894–1936)	**F** **NS** **SWEDEN** NITTSJO EARTHENWARE FACTORY AB Rattirk, Sweden Earthenware 1934 + (1847–present)	**G** **N.V** NICHOLAS VERGETTE London, England Studio potter, tiles. Painted, incised 1946 + (1946–1958)	**H** *Nantgarw* NANTGARW CHINA WORKS Nantgarw, Glamorgan, Wales Porcelain. Painted red (ca.1813–1814, 1817– 1822)
I OVEN **Nasco** PROOF GLADDING, McBEAN & CO. Los Angeles, CA, U.S.A. Franciscan dinnerware. Stamped 1934–1940 (1875– present) (member of Wedgwood Group)	**J** *Nashville Art Pottery* NASHVILLE ART POTTERY Nashville, TN, U.S.A. Earthenware, artware. Incised 1883 + (1883–1888 +)	**K** *Nassau* MERCER POTTERY CO. Trenton, NJ, U.S.A. White granite, semiporcelain. Backstamp before 1904 (1868– ca.1937)	**L** *nast* NAST Paris, France Porcelain. Red, gold 1785–1817 (1783–1835)
M **HLC** **NAUTILUS** **MADE IN U.S.A.** HOMER LAUGHLIN CHINA CO. East Liverpool, OH, U.S.A. Semivitreous dinnerware ca.1935–ca.1950 (1877– present)	**N** NAUTILUS **M** PORCELAIN NAUTILUS PORCELAIN CO. Glasgow, Scotland Porcelain, parian 1903–1913 (1896–1913)	**O** **N. C. Co.** **S — V** **HOTEL.** NATIONAL CHINA CO. East Liverpool, OH, U.S.A. Semivitreous ware 1899–1929 (1899–1929)	**P** **Nelson McCoy** NELSON McCOY POTTERY Roseville, OH, U.S.A. Dinnerware, steins, artware current (1848–present) (Lancaster Colony Corp.)

A

NEUMARK

ANTON FISCHER
Neumark, Bohemia
(Vseruby,
Czechoslovakia)
Earthenware
ca.1833–1870 + (1832–
ca.1905)

B

NEWCOMB COLLEGE

NEWCOMB POTTERY
New Orleans, LA, U.S.A.
Art pottery
1895–1910 (1886–1945)

C

NEW ERA
W.B.P.CO.

WILLIAM BRUNT
POTTERY CO.
East Liverpool, OH, U.S.A.
Semivitreous dinnerware
1892–1911 (1848–1911)
(various names)

D

New Hall

NEW HALL PORCELAIN
WORKS
Hanley, Staffordshire,
England
Porcelain. Painted red
ca.1800 (1781–1835)

E

NICODEMUS

CHESTER NICODEMUS
Columbus, OH, U.S.A.
Vitrified ware
1971 + (1935–present)

F

NILOAK

NILOAK POTTERY
Benton, AR, U.S.A.
Artware. Impressed
1910 + (1909–1944)

G

Nittsjö
SWEDEN

NITTSJO EARTHENWARE
FACTORY AB
Rattirk, Sweden
Earthenware
1947 + (1847–present)

H

N.o. art Pottery

NEW ORLEANS ART
POTTERY
New Orleans, LA, U.S.A.
Art pottery. Incised
ca.1888 (1888–1889)

I

NORITAKE
NIPPON

NORITAKE
Nagoya, Japan
Porcelain. Green, blue,
magenta
1890–1921 (1904–
present)

J

NORSE POTTERY
Edgerton, WI, & Rockford,
IL, U.S.A.
Art pottery. Impressed
1903–1913 (1903–1913)

K

NORTHWESTERN
TERRA COTTA
CHICAGO

NORTHWESTERN TERRA
COTTA CO.
Chicago, IL, U.S.A.
Artware, terra-cotta
1888 + (1888–1956)

L

NORWETA

NORTHWESTERN TERRA
COTTA CO.
Chicago, IL, U.S.A.
Artware, terra-cotta
ca.1907–ca.1920 (1888–
1956)

M

Nove
✳

NOVE
Nove, Italy
Faience, porcelain. Gold
19th century (1728–1835)

N

NOWOTNY
ALTROHLAU

AUGUST NOWOTNY
Altrohlau, Bohemia (Stara
Role, Czechoslovakia)
Faience, earthenware,
porcelain. Impressed
1823–1884 (1813–
1945 +)
(various names & owners)

O

O/1911

OVERBECK POTTERY
Cambridge City, IN, U.S.A.
Art pottery. Various dates
1911 + (1911–1955)

P

O.& B.

ETRURIA POTTERY (OTT
& BREWER)
Trenton, NJ, U.S.A.
Parian, semiporcelain,
porcelain
ca.1886 (1863–1894)

A	B	C	D
 J. B. OWENS POTTERY Zanesville, OH, U.S.A. Art pottery before 1906 (1885–1929)	OVERBECK POTTERY Cambridge City, IN, U.S.A. Artware 1911–1936 (1911–1955)	 OSCAR SCHLEGELMILCH Langewiesen, Thuringia, Germany (E. Germany) Porcelain 1896 + (1892–present) (Porcelain Combine Colditz VEB)	 ADRIEN DALPAYRAT Bourg-la-Reine, France Stoneware 1889–1905 + (1876– 1905 +)

E	F	G	H
O. V. OHIO VALLEY CHINA CO. Wheeling, WV, U.S.A. Porcelain 1887 + (ca.1887–1893)	**OAKWOOD** CAMBRIDGE ART POTTERY Cambridge, OH, U.S.A. Faience, brown-glazed ware before 1904 (1895–1909)	*Old Foley* JAMES KENT LTD. STAFFORDSHIRE ENGLAND JAMES KENT, LTD. Stoke, Staffordshire, England Earthenware current (1897–present)	OLD ROSE EDWIN M. KNOWLES CHINA CO. East Liverpool, OH, U.S.A. Semivitreous ware 1929 + (1900–1963)

I	J	K	L
O.MILET Sèvres OPTAT MILET Sèvres, France Decorator. Painted ca.1876 (1862–1879)	Opaque China B and C BRIDGWOOD & CLARKE Burslem, Staffordshire, England Earthenware. Printed 1857–1864 (1857–1864)	WILLETS MANUFACTURING CO. Trenton, NJ, U.S.A. White graniteware. Impressed, applied in color ca.1884 (1879–1962)	O.P.CO SYRACUSE CHINA ONONDAGA POTTERY CO. Syracuse, NY, U.S.A. Semiporcelain 1886–1898 (1871– present) (Syracuse China Co.)

M	N	O	P
ORIENT MORGAN BELLECK Canton, OH, U.S.A. Pottery, porcelain 1928 (1923–ca.1934)	ORLEANS ZS & Co. BAVARIA ZEH, SCHERZER & CO. Rehau, Bavaria, Germany (W. Germany) Porcelain. Green underglaze 1880 + (1880–present)	OSSO CERAMICS EDWARD MARSHALL BOEHM Trenton, NJ, U.S.A. Porcelain, figurines 1950–1951 (1950– present)	OWENS J. B. OWENS POTTERY Zanesville, OH, U.S.A. Art pottery 1901 + (1885–1929)

A

OWENSART

J. B. OWENS POTTERY
Zanesville, OH, U.S.A.
Art pottery
1906+ (1885–1929)

B

P

POHL BROS. PORCELAIN
FACTORY
Schmiedeberg, Silesia,
Germany (Kowary,
Poland)
Porcelain
1871–1932 (1869–1945)

C

P

PILKINGTON'S TILE &
POTTERY CO. LTD.
Clifton Junction,
Lancashire, England
Earthenware. Incised,
various style letters
ca.1897–1904 (1893–
present)
(Pilkington's Tiles Ltd.)

D

P

SARGADELOS
Sargadelos, Spain
Earthenware
1835–1842 (1804–1875)

E

PIGORY
Chantilly, France
Porcelain
Faience. Blue
ca.1803 (ca.1803–1812)

F

P

K. KRIEGL & CO.
Prague, Bohemia (Praha,
Czechoslovakia)
Earthenware, porcelain.
Impressed
1835–1910 (1835–1910)

G

P

HUBEL & CO.
Prague, Bohemia (Praha,
Czechoslovakia)
Earthenware. Red overglaze
ca.1800–1835 (1800–
1835)

H

P

HUBEL & CO.
Prague, Bohemia (Praha,
Czechoslovakia)
Earthenware. Impressed
ca.1800–1835 (1800–
1835)

I

K. KRIEGL & CO.
Prague, Bohemia (Praha,
Czechoslovakia)
Earthenware, porcelain.
Impressed
1835–1910 (1835–1910)

J

P

WALTER STEPHEN
Skyland & Arden, NC,
U.S.A.
Art pottery. Incised
1920–1961 (1901–
1961+)

K

!

DAGOBERT PECHE
Vienna, Austria
Porcelain. Incised, painted
1910+ (ca.1910–1923)

L

PILKINGTON'S TILE &
POTTERY CO. LTD.
Clifton Junction,
Lancashire, England
Earthenware. Printed,
impressed
ca.1904–1914 (1893–
present)
(Pilkington's Tiles Ltd.)

M

PEGGY CHERNIAVSKY
London, England
Pottery. Impressed, painted
1951–1954 (1951–
1964+)

N

PAF

ARNO FISCHER
PORCELAIN FACTORY
Ilmenau, Thuringia,
Germany (E. Germany)
Porcelain, figurines.
Impressed
after 1907 (1907–1952+)
(Ilmenau Decorative
Promotional, Porcelain
Factory VEB)

O

ELOURY-PORQUIER
Quimper, France
Faience
ca.1840 (1733–present)
(Société Nouvelle des
Faïenceries de Quimper
HB Henriot)

P

PFEFFER BROS.
Gotha, Thuringia, Germany
(E. Germany)
Porcelain
1900+ (1892–1900+)

A

TRIEBNER, ENS &
ECKERT
Volkstedt, Thuringia,
Germany (E. Germany)
Porcelain, figurines
1884–1894 (1877–
present)
(various names & owners,
now Oldest Volkstedt
Porcelain Manufactory
VEB)

B

H. HUTSCHENREUTHER
Probstzella, Thuringia,
Germany (E. Germany)
Porcelain, figurines
ca.1886–ca.1952 (1886–
present)
(Porcelain Combine Kahla
VEB)

C

CARL THIEME SAXONIAN
PORCELAIN FACTORY
Potschappel, Saxony,
Germany (E. Germany)
Porcelain, figurines
1914+ (1872–present)
(Saxonian Porcelain
Manufactory Dresden
VEB)

D

STADTLENGSFELD
PORCELAIN FACTORY
Stadtlengsfeld, Thuringia,
Germany (E. Germany)
Porcelain
1904–ca.1908 (1889–
present)
(Stadtlengsfeld
Porcelainwork VEB)

E

MICHAEL POWOLNY
Vienna, Austria
Ceramics. Painted,
impressed
1894+ (1894–ca.1905)

F

MICHAEL POWOLNY
Vienna, Austria
Ceramics. Painted,
impressed
1894+ (1894–ca.1905)

G

ZETTLITZ KAOLIN
WORKS PORCELAIN
FACTORY
MERKELSGRUN
Merkelsgrun, Bohemia
(Merklin, Czechoslovakia)
Porcelain
1918–1939 (1871–1945)
(various names & owners)

H

PAULINE THOMPSON
East Hendred, Berkshire,
England
Studio-type pottery. Incised,
painted
1950+ (1950–1964+)

I

PN

PORCELAIN FACTORY
NEUMUNSTER
Neumunster, Schleswig-
Holstein, Germany (W.
Germany)
Porcelain
1897+ (1897+)

J

PROBSTZELLA
PORCELAIN FACTORY
VEB
Probstzella, Thuringia,
Germany (E. Germany)
Porcelain
1954–1968 (1886–
present)
(Porcelain Combine Kahla
VEB)

K

PORTLAND POTTERY
LTD.
Cobridge, Staffordshire,
England
Earthenware
1946+ (1946–1953)

L

ROOKWOOD POTTERY
Cincinnati, OH, U.S.A.
Pottery. One flame added
for each year until 1900
(see page 245)
1886–1900 (1880–1967)
(name, molds purchased
by Arthur J. Townley,
Michigan Center, MI, 1982)

M

ROOKWOOD POTTERY
Cincinnati, OH, U.S.A.
Pottery. Roman numeral
added for last two digits
of year (see page 245)
1901+ (1880–1967)
(name, molds purchased
by Arthur J. Townley,
Michigan Center, MI, 1982)

N

YELLOWSANDS
POTTERY/BEMBRIDGE
POTTERY
Bembridge, Isle of Wight,
England
Studio pottery. Painted
1927–1932/1949–1961
(1927–1932/1949–
1961)

O

•ᗡᎱᎩ•

PAUL RAUSCHERT
Huttengrund, Thuringia,
Germany (E. Germany)
Porcelain
(1898–1945)

P

P·R·P

PAUL REVERE POTTERY
Boston & Brighton, MA,
U.S.A.
Pottery. Painted
1908+ (1906–1942)

A

STEINWIESSEN
  PORCELAIN FACTORY
Steinwiessen, Bavaria,
  Germany (W. Germany)
Porcelain
1910–1965 (1910–
  present)
(Eduard Harter)

B

P&S

PORTHEIM & SONS
Chodau, Bohemia (Chodov,
  Czechoslovakia)
Earthenware, porcelain.
  Impressed
ca.1860–ca.1870 (1850–
  1872)

C

STADTLENGSFELD
  PORCELAIN FACTORY
Stadtlengsfeld, Thuringia,
  Germany (E. Germany)
Porcelain
1909–ca.1945 (1889–
  present)
(Stadtlengsfeld
  Porcelainwork VEB)

D

WALRICH POTTERY
Berkeley, CA, U.S.A.
Artware, earthenware,
  porcelain
1922 + (1922–ca.1930)

E

ASHBY POTTER'S GUILD
Woodville, Derbyshire,
  England
Earthenware
ca.1909 (1909–1922)

F

PERCY BROWN
Middlesex, England
Studio potter
1947 + (1938–1964 +)

G

Palme

JOSEF PALME
Shelten, Bohemia (Novy
  Bor, Czechoslovakia)
Earthenware, porcelain.
  Impressed
1829–1851 (1829–1851)

H

Papoco

PADEN CITY POTTERY
  CO.
Paden City, WV, U.S.A.
Semiporcelain, dinnerware
ca.1940 (1914–1963)

I

PARAGON
FINE BONE CHINA
ENGLAND REGD.

PARAGON CHINA (CO.)
  LTD.
Stoke, Staffordshire,
  England
Bone china
current (1920–present)
(Royal Doulton Tableware
  Ltd.)

J

Paris
S. C. M. & Co.

GEORGE C. MURPHY
  POTTERY CO.
East Liverpool, OH, U.S.A.
Semivitreous, ironstone
  ware
1897–1901 (1897–1901,
  1903–1904)

K

Parkhall
Fine Bone
China
England

HEALACRAFT CHINA LTD.
Longton & Stoke,
  Staffordshire, England
Bone china
current (1980–present)

L

Parmos

CREIDLITZ PORCELAIN
  FACTORY
Creidlitz, Bavaria, Germany
  (W. Germany)
Porcelain
1930 + (1903–present)

M

PATENT IRONSTONE CHINA
WARRANTED

C. J. MASON & CO.
Lane Delph, Staffordshire,
  England
Ironstone. Blue underglaze
ca.1829–1835 (1813–
  present)
(member of Wedgwood
  Group)

N

PAULINE
POTTERY

PAULINE POTTERY
Chicago, IL, & Edgerton,
  WI, U.S.A.
Art pottery
1883 + (1883–1893)

O

EMPIRE
PORCELAIN
COMPANY
Staffordshire
England

EMPIRE PORCELAIN CO.
Stoke, Staffordshire,
  England
Earthenware
1960s (1896–1964 +)

P

Pennsbury
Pottery

PENNSBURY POTTERY
Morrisville, PA, U.S.A.
Pottery, porcelain
ca.1951 (ca.1951–1971)

A	B	C	D
PEORIA ILLINOIS	*PEWABIC DETROIT*	**PFALTZGRAFF**	**PFALTZGRAFF** COPYRIGHT U S A
PEORIA POTTERY CO. Peoria, IL, U.S.A. Yellowware, whiteware ca.1880 (1873–1902)	PEWABIC POTTERY Detroit, MI, U.S.A. Art pottery. Impressed ca.1920 (1903–present)	PFALTZGRAFF CO. York, PA, U.S.A. Redware, stoneware 1960–1970 (1811–present)	PFALTZGRAFF CO. York, PA, U.S.A. Stoneware 1980+ (1811–present)

E	F	G	H
Phillips Aller	Phoenix POttery	*Picasso*	*Pickard*
PHILLIPS POTTERY Newton Abbot, Devon, England Earthenware. Incised ca.1881–ca.1887(ca.1881–1887)	PHOENIX POTTERY, KAOLIN & FIRE BRICK CO. Phoenixville, PA, U.S.A. Rockingham ware, yellowware ca.1867 (1867–1872)	PABLO PICASSO Vallauris, France Dinnerware 1946+ (1946–1973)	PICKARD, INC. Antioch, IL, U.S.A. Porcelain current (1893–present)

I	J	K	L
P.L.Dagoty & E.Honoré a Paris.	*ESPAIN*	**P.L.** **LIMOGES** **FRANCE**	**PML** **LIMOGES** **(FRANCE)**
FABRIQUE DE L'IMPÉRATRICE Paris, France Porcelain. Stenciled red 1816–1820 (1785–1865)	LLADRÓ Tabernes Blanques, Spain Porcelain, stoneware. Impressed 1962+ (1951–present)	PORCELAINE LIMOUSINE Limoges, France Porcelain 1931+ (1905–1939)	MERLIN-LEMAS Limoges, France Porcelain 1926+ (1926–?)

M	N	O	P
POILLON woodbridge N.J	**POOLE** **ENGLAND**	*Pope Gosser*	*POPE-GOSSER* CHINA MADE IN U.S.A.
POILLON POTTERY Woodbridge, NJ, U.S.A. Art pottery. Incised (1901–1928)	CARTER, STABLER & ADAMS LTD. Poole, Dorset, England Earthenware (1921–present) (Poole Pottery Ltd.)	POPE-GOSSER CHINA CO. Coshocton, OH, U.S.A. Dinnerware 1931+ (1902–1958)	POPE-GOSSER CHINA CO. Coshocton, OH, U.S.A. Porcelain, dinnerware 1930s (1902–1958)

A

Poppytrail

POTTERY

METLOX POTTERY
Manhattan Beach, CA,
U.S.A.
Dinnerware
ca.1980 (1935–present)

B

PORCELAINE DURE

Georges Boyer

LIMOGES - FRANCE

GEORGES BOYER
Limoges, France
Porcelain
(1936–1953)

C

PORCELAINE
G. Labesse
LIMOGES
Made in France

GOUMOT-LABESSE
Limoges, France
Porcelain
(1955–1977)

D

PORCELAINE
HAVILAND

HAVILAND & CO.
Limoges, France
Porcelain
1889–1926+ (1864–
present)
(Haviland SA)

E

PORCELAINE
HAVILAND
FRANCE

HAVILAND & CO.
Limoges, France
Porcelain
1889–1941+ (1864–
present)
(Haviland SA)

F

Porcelaine Mousseline

T✴H

Limoges FRANCE

THÉODORE HAVILAND
Limoges, France
Porcelain
1894+ (1892–present)
(Haviland SA)

G

Porcelaine

Theo. Haviland

Limoges FRANCE

THÉODORE HAVILAND
Limoges, France
Porcelain
1893+ (1892–present)
(Haviland SA)

H

PORCELAINES
HA BALLEROY FRÈRES
LIMOGES

H. A. BALLEROY BROS.
Limoges, France
Decorator's mark
1912+ (1908–1937)

I

PORZELLAN
Apel
BAVARIA

ARNO APEL
Ebersdorf, Bavaria,
Germany (W. Germany)
Porcelain. Gold overglaze
1954–1957 (1954–1974)

J

*Porzellanfabrik Arzberg
Arzberg (Bayern)*

ARZBERG PORCELAIN
FACTORY
Arzberg, Bavaria, Germany
(W. Germany)
Porcelain. Green
underglaze
1930–1947 (1890–
present)
(various names & owners,
now Hutschenreuther
AG)

K

fitted by . Doulton &Co

DOULTON & CO.
Burslem, Staffordshire,
England
Earthenware, stoneware
before 1939 (1853–
present)
(Royal Doulton Tableware
Ltd.)

L

POTTERS
Co-OPERATIVE Co.

POTTER'S CO-
OPERATIVE CO.
East Liverpool, OH, U.S.A.
Semivitreous tableware
ca.1915 (1882–1925)

M

POXON
LOS ANGELES

POXON CHINA CO.
Vernon, CA, U.S.A.
Tiles, dinnerware.
Embossed
(1912–1931)

N

Prag

K. KRIEGL & CO.
Prague, Bohemia (Praha,
Czechoslovakia)
Porcelain
1835–1910 (1835–1910)

O

Prag

HUBEL & CO.
Prague, Bohemia (Praha,
Czechoslovakia)
Earthenware. Impressed
ca.1800–1835 (1800–
1835)

P

PT
germany

TIRSCHENREUTH
PORCELAIN FACTORY
Tirschenreuth, Bavaria,
Germany (W. Germany)
Porcelain, figurines
1969–present (1838–
present)
(Hutschenreuther AG)

A	B	C	D
PUEBLO MADE IN U.S.A. POTTERY	PURITAN L.C.C.Co.	*Purinton* SLIP WARE	PURITAN W.E.P.CO. E.L.O.
GLADDING, McBEAN & CO. Los Angeles, CA, U.S.A. Franciscan dinnerware 1940 + (1875–present) (member of Wedgwood Group)	LIMOGES CHINA CO. East Liverpool, OH, U.S.A. Semivitreous dinnerware ca.1925–ca.1935 (1900–1955) (American Limoges China Co.)	PURINTON POTTERY Shippenville, PA, U.S.A. Slipware 1941 + (1941–1959)	WEST END POTTERY CO. East Liverpool, OH, U.S.A. Semivitreous ware ca.1915 (1893–1938)

E	F	G	H
	Q.M.D.		R
FAÏENCERIE DE LA GRANDE MAISON (HUBAUDIÈRE) Quimper, France Faience 1810 + (1773–present) (Société Nouvelle des Faïenceries de Quimper HB Henriot)	GLASGOW POTTERY (JOHN MOSES & CO.) Trenton, NJ, U.S.A. Crockery. Stamped ca.1899 (1859–1906)	JOHANN HEINRICH KOCH Regensburg, Bavaria, Germany (W. Germany) Earthenware. Impressed 1805–1816 (1805–1867) (various names & owners)	GREINER & HOLZAPFEL Volkstedt, Thuringia, Germany (E. Germany) Porcelain. Blue underglaze ca.1804–ca.1815 (1759–present) (various names & owners, now Oldest Volkstedt Porcelain Manufactory VEB)

I	J	K	L

RHEINSBERG PORCELAIN FACTORY Rheinsberg, Prussia, Germany (E. Germany) Earthenware 1954 + (1901–present)	RÖRSTRAND AB Lidkoping, Sweden Porcelain, faience 1938 + (1726–present)	FAÏENCERIE DE LA GRANDE MAISON (HUBAUDIÈRE) Quimper, France Faience 1920 + (1773–present) (Société Nouvelle des Faïenceries de Quimper HB Henriot)	ISIDORE DE RUDDER Brussels, Belgium Masks, statues, tiles. Incised 1900 + (1900–1943)

M	N	O	P
	R/A	A R C P	R & C
ROBINEAU POTTERY Syracuse, NY, U.S.A. Artware ca.1901 (1901–1928)	THOMAS RECKNAGEL Alexandrinenthal, Bavaria, Germany (W. Germany) Porcelain 1907 + (1886–1934)	ROBLIN ART POTTERY San Francisco, CA, U.S.A. Art pottery. Impressed 1898–1906 (1899–1906)	RISLER & CO. Freiberg, Badenia, Germany (W. Germany) Porcelain ca.1870–ca.1880 (1847–1927)

A **RF&H** RICHTER, FENKL & HAHN Chodau, Bohemia (Chodov, Czechoslovakia) Porcelain 1883+ (1883–1945)	**B** *RFH* RICHTER, FENKL & HAHN Chodau, Bohemia (Chodov, Czechoslovakia) Porcelain 1900+ (1883–1945)	**C**  LOWE, RATCLIFFE & CO. Longton, Staffordshire, England Earthenware. Printed impressed 1882–1892 (1882–1892)	**D** RMG REINHOLD MERKELBACH Hohr-Grenzhausen, Palatinate, Germany (W. Germany) Steins 1964–1968 (1845–present)
E RMR G. ROBRECHT Mildeneichen, Bohemia (Luzec, Czechoslovakia) Porcelain before 1920 (1869–ca.1927)	**F** **RPM** ROBERT PERSCH PORCELAIN FACTORIES MILDENEICHEN & RASPENAU Mildeneichen, Bohemia (Luzec, Czechoslovakia) Porcelain 1869–ca.1905 (1869–ca.1927)	**G** R.R.P. Co. USA ROBINSON RANSBOTTOM Roseville, OH, U.S.A. Pottery ca.1920–present (1900–present)	**H** R U.S.A. ROSEVILLE POTTERY CO. Zanesville, OH, U.S.A. Art pottery 1935–1954 (1892–1954)
I RV ROSEVILLE POTTERY CO. Zanesville, OH, U.S.A. Dinnerware, kitchenware. Stamped, black, blue, green ca.1914–ca.1930 (1892–1954)	**J** R VEB EARTHENWARE FACTORY VEB Rheinsberg, Prussia, Germany (E. Germany) Earthenware ca.1952–1957 (1901–present)	**K** RADFORD JASPER A. RADFORD POTTERY Tiffin & Zanesville, OH, & Clarksburg, WV, U.S.A. Art pottery. Impressed 1896+ (1896–1912)	**L** *RADURA.* A. RADFORD POTTERY Tiffin & Zanesville, OH, & Clarksburg, WV, U.S.A. Art pottery 1896+ (1896–1912)
M *Raleigh* UNITED STATES POTTERY CO. East Liverpool, OH, U.S.A. Semivitreous ware 1899–1901 (1898–1932)	**N** "RAM" RAM Arnhem, Holland Pottery. Painted 1923+ (1923–1930+)	**O** raymor by Roseville U.S.A. OVENPROOF PAT. PEND. ROSEVILLE POTTERY CO. Zanesville, OH, U.S.A. Art pottery 1950s (1892–1954)	**P** R&Cº LIMOGES FRANCE RAYNAUD & CO. Limoges, France Porcelain 1928+ (1911–present)

A

CHR. CARSTENS
Rheinsberg, Prussia,
Germany (E. Germany)
Earthenware
ca.1901–1945 (1901–
present)
(Rheinsberg Earthenware
Factory VEB)

B

R. DELINIERES & CO.
Limoges, France
Porcelain
ca.1879 (1879–present)
(Bernardaud & Co.)

C

RED WING STONEWARE
CO.
Red Wing, MN, U.S.A.
Stoneware
1878–1892 (1878–1967)

D

HULL POTTERY CO.
Crooksville, OH, U.S.A.
Dinnerware, artware
ca.1952–ca.1960 (1905–
1950,1952–present)

E

CROWN POTTERIES CO.
Evansville, IN, U.S.A.
Dinnerware, semiporcelain
1904+ (1902–1962)

F

REGINA ART POTTERY
Gouda, Holland
Pottery
1898–1910 (1898–
1970+)

G

HOLLAND & GREEN
Longton, Staffordshire,
England
Earthenware, ironstone.
Impressed, printed
1853–1882 (1853–1882)

H

REINHOLD MERKELBACH
Hohr-Grenzhausen,
Palatinate, Germany (W.
Germany)
Steins, stoneware.
Impressed
1925–1945 (1845–
present)

I

REINHOLD
SCHLEGELMILCH
Tillowitz, Silesia, Germany
(Tulovice, Poland)
Porcelain, figurines
1891+ (1869–ca.1938)

J

GEO. BORGFELDT & CO.
New York, NY, U.S.A.
Importer
1915+ (1881–ca.1976)

K

ROGER GUÉRIN
Bouffioulx, Belgium
Art pottery. Incised
1900+ (ca.1900–?)

L

RHEAD POTTERY
Santa Barbara, CA, U.S.A.
Art pottery
ca.1913 (1913–1917)

M

OSCAR SCHALLER & CO.
SUCCESSOR
Kirchenlamitz, Bavaria,
Germany (W. Germany)
Porcelain
1935+ (1918–present)
(Winterling Group)

N

Gouda, Holland
Polychrome pottery.
Painted
1850+ (ca.1850–?)

O

RIBES
Limoges, France
Ceramics
1891+

P

SOCIETÀ CERAMICA
RICHARD
Milan, Italy
Porcelain, faience
ca.1883 (1735–present)
(Richard-Ginori)

A

Rieber
MITTERTEICH

JOSEF RIEBER & CO.
PORCELAIN FACTORY
AG
Mitterteich, Bavaria,
Germany (W. Germany)
Porcelain
1938+ (1918–ca.1978)

B

RINGTONS
LIMITED.

TEA MERCHANTS

NEWCASTLE UPON TYNE

C. T. MALING & SONS
Newcastle upon Tyne,
Northumberland,
England
Tea caddy
ca.1930–1955 (1890–
1963)

C

RIVIERA
Casuals

by
U.S.A.

STERLING CHINA
East Liverpool, OH, U.S.A.
Vitreous ware
1951–1976 (1917–
present)

D

HANDCRAFTED IN CARIBE

STERLING CHINA
(Probably for Haviland, New
York)
East Liverpool, OH, U.S.A.
Porcelain
ca. 1972 (1917–present)

E

R
Los Angeles

ROBERTSON POTTERY
Los Angeles & Hollywood,
CA, U.S.A.
Stoneware, artware.
Imprinted, incised
1934+ (1934–1952)

F

R·MERKELBACH
GRENZHAUSEN

REINHOLD MERKELBACH
Hohr-Grenzhausen,
Palatinate, Germany (W.
Germany)
Steins, stoneware.
Impressed
ca.1910 (1845–present)

G

ROBERT
HAVILAND
LIMOGES

ROBERT HAVILAND
Limoges, France
Porcelain
1924+ (1864–present)
(Haviland SA)

H

*Robertson
Hollywood*

ROBERTSON POTTERY
Los Angeles & Hollywood,
CA, U.S.A.
Artware. Impressed
1934+ (1934–1952)

I

Robj

Paris

ROBJ
Paris, France
Porcelain dealer
ca.1920 (1920–1931,
1964+)

J

ROCKET

WILLIAM BRUNT
POTTERY CO.
East Liverpool, OH, U.S.A.
Ironstone
1877–1911 (1848–1911)
(various names)

K

Rock Pottery.
Edgerton.Wis.

EDGERTON POTTERY
Edgerton, WI, U.S.A.
Artware. Incised
1894+ (1894–1901)

L

ROCKINGHAM

ROCKINGHAM WORKS
Swinton, Yorkshire,
England
Earthenware
ca.1806–ca.1842
(ca.1745–1842)

M

ROCKINGHAM

JOSIAH WEDGWOOD &
SONS LTD.
Burslem, Staffordshire,
England
Rockingham ware
ca.1840 (ca.1759–present)
(member of Wedgwood
Group)

N

Rockingham

JOSIAH SPODE/
COPELAND &
GARRETT
Stoke, Staffordshire,
England
Rockingham ware
ca.1826 (ca.1762–present)
(Royal Worcester Spode
Ltd.)

O

Rockingham
Harker
U.S.A.

HARKER POTTERY CO.
East Liverpool, OH, U.S.A.
Rockingham ware
ca.1965 (1890–1972)

P

ROHLAU

BENEDIKT HASSLACHER
Altrohlau, Bohemia (Stara
Role, Czechoslovakia)
Earthenware. Impressed
1813–1823 (1813–
1945+)
(various names & owners)

A

ROMA

EDWIN M. KNOWLES
CHINA CO.
East Liverpool, OH, U.S.A.
Semivitreous dinnerware
1929 + (1900–1963)

B

ROOKWOOD
1882

ROOKWOOD POTTERY
Cincinnati, OH, U.S.A.
Dinnerware. Impressed,
date varies
1882 + (1880–1967)
(name, molds purchased
by Arthur J. Townley,
Michigan Center, MI, 1982)

C

ROOKWOOD POTTERY
Cincinnati, OH, U.S.A.
Dinnerware. Impressed
ca.1881 (1880–1967)
(name, molds purchased
by Arthur J. Townley,
Michigan Center, MI, 1982)

D

RÖRSTRAND

RÖRSTRAND PORCELAIN
FACTORY
Lidkoping, Sweden
Porcelain, faience.
Impressed
ca.1790–ca.1800 (1726–
present)
(Rörstrand AB)

E

Rörstrand

RÖRSTRAND AB
Lidkoping, Sweden
Porcelain, faience
1940 + (1726–present)

F

Rörstrand
SWEDEN

RÖRSTRAND AB
Lidkoping, Sweden
Porcelain, faience
current (1726–present)

G

ROSEATE PORCELAIN
BIRKS RAWLINS & CO.
STOKE·ON·TRENT

BIRKS, RAWLINS & CO.
Stoke, Staffordshire,
England
Porcelain
1917 + (1900–1933)

H

Roseville

ROSEVILLE POTTERY CO.
Zanesville, OH, U.S.A.
Stoneware. Impressed
ca.1930 (1892–1957)

I

ROYAL
BARUM WARE

C. H. BRANNAM
Barnstaple, Devon, England
Redware, terra-cotta
current (1879–present)

J

ROYAL CHINA
WARRANTED
22 KT. GOLD

ROYAL CHINA CO.
Sebring, OH, U.S.A.
Semivitreous dinnerware
ca.1940–ca.1950 (1933–
present)

K

Royal Crown Derby
ENGLAND

DERBY PORCELAIN
WORKS
Derby, England
Porcelain
current (ca.1750–present)
(Royal Doulton Tableware
Ltd.)

L

ROYAL
DOULTON
FLAMBÉ

DOULTON & CO.
Burslem, Staffordshire,
England
Earthenware, porcelain
1900 + (1853–present)
(Royal Doulton Tableware
Ltd.)

M

Royal Dresden China

STATE'S PORCELAIN
MANUFACTORY/
STATE'S PORCELAIN
MANUFACTORY
MEISSEN VEB
Meissen, Saxony, Germany
(E. Germany)
Porcelain. Blue
1938–present (1919–
present)

N

ROYAL ESSEX ART
POTTERY WORKS

EDWARD BINGHAM
Castle Hedingham, Essex,
England
Earthenware. Incised
ca.1901 (1864–1901)

O

ROYAL *Mayfair*
BONE
CHINA
ENGLAND
1938–41

CHAPMANS LONGTON
LTD.
Longton, Staffordshire,
England
Porcelain. Printed
1938–1941 (1916–
1964 +)

P

"Royal"
OVEN SERVE
Guaranteed
100% ovenproof

ROYAL CHINA CO.
Sebring, OH, U.S.A.
Ovenware
1938–1951 (1933–
present)

A

royal●sentinel
CHINA MADE IN U.S.A. BY SHENANGO

SHENANGO CHINA CO.
New Castle, PA, U.S.A.
Porcelain
after 1950 (1901–present)
(Anchor Hocking)

B

ROYAL
STAFFORDSHIRE
LIBERTY
J.&G. MEAKIN
ENGLAND

J. & G. MEAKIN (LTD.)
Stoke, Staffordshire,
England
Earthenware
current (1851–present)
(member of Wedgwood
Group)

C

ROYAL
TORQUAY
POTTERY
ENGLAND

ROYAL ALLER VALE &
WATCOMBE POTTERY
CO.
Torquay, Devon, England
Earthenware. Impressed,
printed
1901 + (ca.1901–1962)

D

Royal
V. & B.

VODREY & BROTHERS
POTTERY CO.
East Liverpool, OH, U.S.A.
Ironstone
1876–1896 (ca.1857–
1928)

E

Royal
Winton
MADE IN
ENGLAND

GRIMWADES LTD.
Stoke, Staffordshire,
England
Earthenware, majolica, jet.
Printed
1951 + (1900–present)
(Royal Winton Pottery)

F

ROYAL WORCESTER SPODE

ROYAL WORCESTER
SPODE LTD.
Worcester, England
Porcelain, earthenware.
Printed
1976–present (ca.1751–
present)

G

Rozenburg
Den Haag

ROZENBURG
The Hague, Holland
Earthenware. Painted
ca.1890 (1885–1914 +)

H

ROZANE
RPCo

ROSEVILLE POTTERY CO.
Zanesville, OH, U.S.A.
Dinnerware, artware.
Impressed
before 1905 (1892–1954)

I

R R P C o
ROSEVILLE, O
U.S.A.

ROBINSON
RANSBOTTOM
Roseville, OH, U.S.A.
Stoneware, kitchenware
ca.1920–present (1900–
present)

J

RS
Tillowitz

REINHOLD
SCHLEGELMILCH (R. S.
TILLOWITZ)
Tillowitz, Silesia (Tulovice,
Poland)
Porcelain. Green
ca.1932–ca.1938 (1869–
ca.1938)

K

Rubel
& Company

PURINTON POTTERY
Shippenville, PA, U.S.A.
Slipware
1941 + (1941–1959)

L

R U K O

A. RADFORD POTTERY
Tiffin & Zanesville, OH, &
Clarksburg, WV, U.S.A.
Artware
1896 + (1896–1912)

M

RumRill

RED WING POTTERY
Red Wing, MN, U.S.A.
Kitchenware
1933–1938 (1878–1967)

N

RUSKIN POTTERY

RUSKIN POTTERY
Smethwick, nr.
Birmingham, England
Earthenware. Impressed
1904 + (1898–1935)

O

Russel Wright
BAUER

BAUER POTTERY
Los Angeles, CA, U.S.A.
Artware
ca.1945 (1905–ca.1958)

P

Russel Wright
by
Knowles

EDWIN M. KNOWLES
CHINA CO.
East Liverpool, OH, U.S.A.
Semivitreous dinnerware
ca.1956 (1900–1963)

A

Russel Wright
MFG. BY
STEUBENVILLE

STEUBENVILLE POTTERY
CO.
Steubenville, OH, U.S.A.
Dinnerware
1939 + (1879–ca.1960)

B

R. WALLACE MARTIN
SOUTHALL

MARTIN BROS.
Fulham, London, England
Stoneware. Incised,
impressed
1900 + (1873–1914)

C

RW Martin & Brothers
London & Southall

MARTIN BROS.
Southall, London, England
Stoneware
1882–1914 (1873–1914)

D

RYE
POTTERY
ENGLAND

RYE POTTERY LTD.
Rye, Sussex, England
Earthenware, stoneware
current (1869–present)

E

J. G. PAULUS/LUISE
GREINER/LIPPERT &
HAAS
Schlaggenwald, Bohemia,
(Horni Slavkov,
Czechoslovakia)
Porcelain. Blue underglaze
1793–1812 (1792–
1945 +)
(various names & owners)

F

SARGADELOS
Sargadelos, Spain
Earthenware
1804–1829 (1804–1875)

G

AUGUST HAAS
Schlaggenwald, Bohemia
(Horni Slavkov,
Czechoslovakia)
Porcelain. Impressed
1847–1867 (1792–
1945 +)
(various names & owners)

H

MAX LAEUGER
(KANDERN POTTERY)
Kander, Badenia, Germany
(W. Germany)
Pottery
1908 + (ca.1888–present)

I

LIPPERT & HAAS
Schlaggenwald, Bohemia
(Horni Slavkov,
Czechoslovakia)
Porcelain. Blue, gold, red
overglaze
1810–1820 (ca.1808–
1945 +)

J

G. GREINER & CO.
Schauberg, Bavaria,
Germany (W. Germany)
Porcelain. Blue underglaze
1894–1927 (1815–
present)
(various names and
owners, now Richard S.
Rosler)

K

LIPPERT & HAAS
Schlaggenwald, Bohemia
(Horni Slavkov,
Czechoslovakia)
Porcelain. Blue underglaze
1815–1832 (ca.1808–
1945 +)

L

SLAMA & CO.
Vienna, Austria
Ceramics
1955–present (1868–
present)

M

SCHEIBE-ALSBACH
PORCELAIN
MANUFACTORY VEB
Scheibe-Alsbach,
Thuringia, Germany (E.
Germany)
Porcelain
1972 + (1838–present)
(United Decorative
Porcelainworks Lichte
VEB)

N

A. W. FR. KISTER
Scheibe-Alsbach,
Thuringia, Germany (E.
Germany)
Porcelain
ca.1900–1972 (1838–
present)
(United Decorative
Porcelainworks Lichte
VEB)

O

SHAWSHEEN POTTERY
Billerica, MA, & Mason City,
IA, U.S.A.
Art pottery. Imprinted,
incised
1906 + (1906–ca.1972)

P

S:t

ST. ERIKS
EARTHENWARE
FACTORY AB
Upsala, Sweden
Porcelain.
1929–1937 (ca.1880–
1937)

A

PORCELAINE LIMOUSINE
Limoges, France
Porcelain
1931+ (1905–1939)

B

MAXIMILIEN-JOSEPH
BETTIGNIES
Saint-Amand-les-Eaux,
France
Porcelain
ca.1817–1880 (ca.1817–
1880)

C

S.E.G.

PAUL REVERE POTTERY
(Saturday Evening Girls)
Boston & Brighton, MA,
U.S.A.
Art pottery. Painted
1906+ (1906–1942)

D

ERIC & MEIRA STOCKL
London, England
Studio pottery, stoneware.
Painted, incised
1961+ (1956–1964+)

E

S.E.T.
CO.

STAR ENCAUSTIC TILE
CO.
Pittsburgh, PA, U.S.A.
Tile. Impressed
ca.1900 (1882–ca.1914)

F

S & G

SCHILLER & GERBING
Bodenbach, Bohemia
(Podmokly,
Czechoslovakia)
Earthenware, stoneware
after 1829–ca.1885 (1829–
1905+)

G

FASOLD & STAUCH
Bock-Wallendorf,
Thuringia, Germany (E.
Germany)
Porcelain
1914–ca.1972 (1903–
1972)

H

JOSEPH SCHACHTEL
Charlottenbrunn, Silesia,
Germany (Zofiowka,
Poland)
Porcelain
after 1900–1919 (1859–
1919)

I

SHAWSHEEN POTTERY
Billerica, MA, & Mason City,
IA, U.S.A.
Art pottery. Imprinted,
incised
1906+ (1906–ca.1972)

J

JOSEF PALME
Schelten, Bohemia (Novy
Bor, Czechoslovakia)
Earthenware, porcelain.
Impressed, blue
underglaze
1829–1851 (1829–1851)

K

SCHUTZMEISTER &
QUENDT
Gotha, Thuringia, Germany
(E. Germany)
Dolls' heads
1899–ca.1927 (1889–
1927+)

L

LEROSEY
Paris, France
Porcelain
ca.1885 (1867–1889+)

M

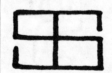

AMPHORA WORK
REISSNER
Turn-Teplitz, Bohemia
(Trnovany,
Czechoslovakia)
Porcelain, earthenware
1892+ (1892–1945+)
(various names,
nationalized in 1945)

N

SAMSON & CO.
Paris, France
Porcelain
1941–1957 (1873–
1957+)

O

STROBEL & WILKEN
New York, NY, U.S.A.
Importer's mark
after 1886+ (1864–
1925+)

P

JAMES SADLER & SONS
LTD.
Burslem & Stoke,
Staffordshire, England
Earthenware
current (ca.1899–present)

A	B	C	D
S A L A M I N A *Designed by* *Rockwell Kent* **VERNON KILNS** Made in U.S.A. VERNON KILNS Vernon, CA, U.S.A. Dinnerware, artware 1938–1940 (1912–1958)	*Salem* SALEM CHINA CO. Salem, OH, U.S.A. Dinnerware ca.1960 (1898–1967)	*Samford Ware* SAMUEL FORD & CO. Burslem, Staffordshire, England Earthenware. Printed ca.1936–1939 (1898– 1939)	SAMSON BROS. & CO. American Art Clay Works Est'd 1892 Edgerton, Wis. AMERICAN/EDGERTON ART CLAY WORKS Edgerton, WI, U.S.A. Art pottery 1892–1895 (1892–1899, 1902–1903)

E	F	G	H
Santa Anita **Ware** MADE IN CALIFORNIA SANTA ANITA POTTERY Los Angeles, CA, U.S.A. Dinnerware 1948+ (1948–ca.1957)	*Santa Rosa* **L. A. POTTERIES** **CALIFORNIA** LOS ANGELES POTTERIES Lynwood, CA, U.S.A. Dinnerware 1948+ (1948–ca.1954)	*Sara-Lee* SARA LEE MALLORY Cleveland, OH, U.S.A. Studio potter 1920–1950 (1920– present)	*Sarreguemines & Cie* UTZCHNEIDER & CO. Sarreguemines, France Pottery ca.1900 (ca.1770–present)

I	J	K	L
Savona ANTONIO FOLCO Savona, Italy Creamware ca.1856 (1856+)	**SAXON CHINA** SAXON CHINA CO. East Liverpool, OH, U.S.A. Ironstone, dinnerware 1911–ca.1920 (1911– 1929)	Schaubachkunst W. GOEBEL Rodental, Bavaria, Germany (W. Germany) Earthenware, figurines. Blue ca.1953–1954 (1871– present)	*Schlaggenwald* LIPPERT & HAAS Schlaggenwald, Bohemia (Horni Slavkov, Czechoslovakia) 1830–1846 (ca.1808– 1945+)

M	N	O	P
Schmid SCHMID Boston, MA, U.S.A. Porcelain importer current (1930s–present)	*schoëlcher* SCHOELCHER Paris, France Utilitarian ware. Red, gold 1806+ (ca.1806–1834)	**SCHOONHOVEN HOLLAND** N. V. POTTERY SCHOONHOVEN Gouda, Holland Delftware, pipes, decorated ware ca.1900 (1749–present)	*SCHOONHOVEN HOLLAND* *X* N. V. POTTERY SCHOONHOVEN Gouda, Holland Delftware, pipes, decorated ware ca.1900 (1749–present)

A

CLAYWARE FACTORY
SCHWANDORF
Schwandorf, Bavaria,
Germany (W. Germany)
Earthenware, stoneware
1955–ca.1972 (1865–
present)
(Hutschenreuther Keramag
GMBH)

B

SEBRING POTTERY CO.
East Liverpool, OH, U.S.A.
White granite
1890–ca.1905 (1887–
1948)

C

SEBRING POTTERY CO.
East Liverpool & Sebring,
OH, U.S.A.
Semivitreous ware
ca.1925–ca.1943 (1887–
1948)

D

STEUBENVILLE POTTERY
CO.
Steubenville, OH, U.S.A.
Semivitreous porcelain
ca.1904 (1879–ca.1960)

E

ERDMANN
SCHLEGELMILCH (E.S.
PRUSSIA)
Suhl, Thuringia, Germany
(E. Germany)
Porcelain
after 1900–ca.1938 (1881–
1938)

F

Serapis

ERNEST WAHLISS
ALEXANDRA
PORCELAIN WORKS
Turn-Teplitz, Bohemia
(Trnovany,
Czechoslovakia)
Porcelain, faience
1911–ca.1921 (1894–
1934)

G

SÈVRES
Sèvres, France
Hard & soft paste porcelain.
Green, black, light blue
1941 + (1756–present)

H

SÈVRES
HOTEL CHINA

SEVRES CHINA CO.
East Liverpool, OH, U.S.A.
Hotel porcelain
1900–1908 (1900–1908)

I

SEVRES
MANUFACTURE
NATIONALE
FRANCE

SÈVRES
Sèvres, France
Hard & soft paste porcelain.
Green, black, brown
1928–1940 (1756–
present)

J

Shawnee
U.S.A.

SHAWNEE POTTERY
Zanesville, OH, U.S.A.
Art pottery
1937 + (1936–1961)

K

Shelley
CHINA
ENGLAND

SHELLEY POTTERIES LTD.
Longton, Staffordshire,
England
Porcelain
1930–1932 (1925– present)
(Royal Doulton Tableware
Ltd.)

L

Shelley
ENGLISH FINE BONE CHINA

SHELLEY POTTERIES
LTD.
Longton, Staffordshire,
England
Porcelain
ca.1973 (1925–present)
(Royal Doulton Tableware
Ltd.)

M

Shelton Ivory

EMPIRE PORCELAIN CO.
Stoke, Staffordshire,
England
Earthenware. Printed,
impressed
1930s (1896–1964 +)

N

Shenandoah
PASTELS
MADE IN U.S.A.

PADEN CITY POTTERY
Paden City, WV, U.S.A.
Semiporcelain, dinnerware
ca.1940 (1914–1963)

O

SICARDO
WELLER.

WELLER POTTERY
Zanesville, OH, U.S.A.
Art pottery
1902–1907 (1882–1948)

P

Silhouette ®
FINE CHINA
by SYRACUSE
MADE IN U.S.A

SYRACUSE CHINA CORP.
Syracuse, NY, U.S.A.
Dinnerware
ca.1972 (1871–present)

A	B	C	D
SILVER SPRINGS, FLA.	*SLP* **LIMOGES** **FRANCE**	*SMITH PHILLIPS* *SEMI PORCELAIN*	*Solian ware* **SIMPSONS (POTTERS) LTD.** **COBRIDGE ENGLAND.**
SILVER SPRINGS, FLORIDA Silver Springs, FL, U.S.A. Art pottery. Backstamp ca.1938 (ca.1924–present)	SOCIÉTÉ LIMOUSINE DE PORCELAINE Limoges, France Porcelain 1950+ (1947–1961+)	SMITH-PHILLIPS CHINA CO. East Liverpool, OH, U.S.A. Semivitreous tableware 1903+ (1901–1929)	SIMPSONS (POTTERS) LTD. Cobridge, Staffordshire, England Earthenware. Printed 1944+ (1944–present)

E	F	G	H
S. P. CO. **S—V** **SEBRING, O.**	**Spode**	**Spode** **ENGLAND**	**SPODE & COPELAND,**
SEBRING POTTERY CO. East Liverpool & Sebring, OH, U.S.A. Semivitreous tableware ca.1925 (1887–1948)	JOSIAH SPODE Stoke, Staffordshire, England Earthenware. Painted 1790–1827 (ca.1762–present) (Royal Worcester Spode Ltd.)	SPODE Stoke, Staffordshire, England Porcelain, earthenware, bone china. Printed ca.1970–present (ca. 1762–present) (Royal Worcester Spode Ltd.)	SPODE Stoke, Staffordshire, England Porcelain, earthenware 1812–1823, 1826–1833 (ca.1762–present) (Royal Worcester Spode Ltd.)

I	J	K	L
SPODE **BONE CHINA** **ENGLAND**	**SPODE** **COPELAND CHINA** **ENGLAND**	**SPODES** **NEW STONE**	**THE** **Standard** **MADE IN U.S.A.**
W. T. COPELAND (& SONS LTD.) Stoke, Staffordshire, England Porcelain, earthenware, parian ca.1950–1960+ (1847–present) (Royal Worcester Spode Ltd.)	SPODE Stoke, Staffordshire, England Porcelain, earthenware. ca.1940–1956 (ca.1762–present) (Royal Worcester Spode Ltd.)	SPODE Stoke, Staffordshire, England Porcelain, earthenware ca.1822–1933+ (ca.1762–present) (Royal Worcester Spode Ltd.)	STANDARD POTTERY CO. East Liverpool, OH, U.S.A. Semivitreous ware ca.1910–1927 (1886–1927)

M	N	O	P
Stangl POTTERY	*Sté* *Porcelainière* *Limoges France*	**STERLING CHINA** *by* *Russel Wright*	**STERLING CHINA**
STANGL POTTERY Trenton, NJ, U.S.A. Dinnerware 1930 (1805–1978) (various names, Stangl name first used in 1926)	SOCIÉTÉ PORCELAINIÈRE Limoges, France Porcelain, tableware 1929+ (ca.1926–present)	STERLING CHINA CO. East Liverpool, OH, U.S.A. Vitreous dinnerware ca.1949 (1917–present)	STERLING CHINA CO. East Liverpool, OH, U.S.A. Vitreous dinnerware ca.1920–1972 (1917–present)

A

By
Steubenville
U. S. A.

STEUBENVILLE POTTERY
CO.
Steubenville, OH, U.S.A.
Dinnerware
ca.1960–1978 (1879–
ca.1960)
(molds and mark
purchased by
Canonsburg Pottery,
Canonsburg, PA, and
used until 1978)

B

STONE CHINA,
WARRANTED.

MARYLAND POTTERY
Baltimore, MD, U.S.A.
White granite, porcelain
1887–1890 (1879–1914)

C

Stonehenge
EVEN TO TABLE WARE, DISHWASHER SAFE
Midwinter®
MADE IN ENGLAND
O

MIDWINTER
Burslem & Stoke,
Staffordshire, England
Earthenware, stoneware
current (ca.1910–present)

D

Susie Cooper

SUSIE COOPER POTTERY
(LTD.)
Burslem, Staffordshire,
England
Earthenware, porcelain.
Printed
1930 + (ca.1930–1964 +)

E

Susie Cooper
*
BONE CHINA
ENGLAND

SUSIE COOPER CHINA
LTD.
Longton & Burslem,
Staffordshire, England
Bone china. Printed
1950 + (ca.1950–1961 +)

F

A
SUSIE COOPER
PRODUCTION
CROWN WORKS
BURSLEM
ENGLAND
Susie Cooper

SUSIE COOPER POTTERY
(LTD.)
Burslem, Staffordshire,
England
Earthenware, porcelain.
Printed
1932 + (ca.1930–1964 +)

G

Sussex Ware, Rye

RYE POTTERY
Rye, Sussex, England
Pottery. Incised
late 19th century (1869–
present)

H

SYRACUSE
1111
1871 *China*

SYRACUSE CHINA CORP.
Syracuse, NY, U.S.A.
Porcelain, dinnerware
after 1966 (1871–present)
(various names & owners)

I

SZEILER
ENGLAND

SZEILER STUDIO, LTD.
Burslem & Stoke,
Staffordshire, England
Earthenware
current (ca.1951–present)

J

$\mathcal{T}.$

SCHMIDT & GREINER/
F. KLAUS/SONTAG &
BIRKNER
Tettau, Bavaria, Germany
(W. Germany)
Porcelain. Blue underglaze
1794–ca.1885 (1794–
present)
(Royally Privileged Porcelain
Factory Tettau GMBH)

K

LONGTON

THOMAS CONE LTD.
Longton, Staffordshire,
England
Earthenware. Printed
1912–1935 (1892–
present)
(Staffordshire Potteries)

L

KENNETH QUICK
St. Ives, Cornwall, England
Studio-type pottery.
Impressed, incised
ca.1955–1960 (1945–
1963)

M

THÉODORE HAVILAND
Limoges, France
Porcelain
ca.1892 (1892–present)
(Haviland SA)

N

FD

THÉODORE DECK
Paris, France
Faience, porcelain
1859–ca.1891 (1859–
1891)

O

RUSKIN POTTERY (W.
HOWSON TAYLOR)
Smethwick, Nr.
Birmingham, England
Earthenware. Painted,
incised
1898 + (1898–1935)

P

T. J. WHEATLEY & CO.
Cincinnati, OH, U.S.A.
Art pottery. Incised
1879–1882 (1879–1882)

A

T.P.M.

CARL HANS TUPPACK
Tiefenfurth, Silesia,
  Germany (Parowa,
  Poland)
Porcelain
after 1919–1935 (1919–
  1935)

B

VILLEROY & BOCH
Schramberg, Wurttemberg,
  Germany (W. Germany)
Porcelain, earthenware,
  majolica
1902–1912 (1813–
  present)
(various names, owners, &
  locations)

C

GRAND FEU ART
  POTTERY
Los Angeles, CA, U.S.A.
Art pottery. Impressed
1912+ (1912–1916+)

D

TORQUAY TERRA-COTTA
  CO.
Torquay, Devon, England
Terra-cotta. Impressed,
  printed
1875–1909 (1875–1940)
(various names)

E

TEPLITZ TECHNICAL
  SCHOOL
Teplitz, Bohemia (Teplice,
  Czechoslovakia)
Ceramics. Impressed
ca.1897 (1897+)

F

Tannawa

FRANZ JOSEF MAYER
Tannawa, Bohemia
  (Zdanov, Czechoslovakia)
Porcelain. Impressed
1840–1872 (1813–1872)

G

TAYLOR, LEE & SMITH
East Liverpool, OH, U.S.A.
Semivitreous ware
1900–1901 (1899–1901)

H

TAYLOR, SMITH &
  TAYLOR
East Liverpool, OH, U.S.A.
Ironstone
ca.1970 (1901–present)
(Anchor Hocking)

I

T. A. McNICOL POTTERY
  CO.
East Liverpool, OH, U.S.A.
Semivitreous dinnerware
ca.1924 (1913–1929)

J

TECO

AMERICAN TERRA COTTA
  & CERAMIC CO.
Terra Cotta & Chicago, IL,
  U.S.A.
Artware, terra-cotta
ca.1901–ca.1922 (1886–
  1930)

K

LENOX, INC.
Trenton, NJ, U.S.A.
Porcelain
1970+ (1906–present)

L

TERRHEA

CAMBRIDGE ART
  POTTERY
Cambridge, OH, U.S.A.
Brown-glazed
ca.1900 (1895–1909)

M

THARAUD
Limoges, France
Porcelain
1977+ (ca.1920–1977+)

N

THÉODORE DECK
Paris, France
Faience, porcelain
(1859–1891)

O

THÉODORE HAVILAND
Limoges, France
Porcelain
1893+ (1892–present)
(Haviland SA)

P

THÉODORE HAVILAND
Limoges, France
Porcelain
1925+ (1892–present)
(Haviland SA)

A

THEO. HAVILAND
PORCELAINE
FRANCE

THÉODORE HAVILAND
Limoges, France
Porcelain
1895+ (1892–present)
(Haviland SA)

B

[THERA]

A. RADFORD POTTERY
Tiffin & Zanesville, OH, &
Clarksburg, WV, U.S.A.
Art pottery
ca.1900 (1896–1912)

C

Thomas
China Co.

THOMAS CHINA CO.
East Liverpool, OH, U.S.A.
Semivitreous tableware
1902–1905 (1900–1905)

D

Thomas
GERMANY

ROSENTHAL GLASS &
PORCELAIN AG
Selb, Bavaria, Germany
(W. Germany)
Porcelain, earthenware,
figurines
1957–present (1879–
present)

E

THOMPSON
GLENWOOD.

C. C. THOMPSON
POTTERY CO.
East Liverpool, OH, U.S.A.
Semivitreous tableware
ca.1920 (1868–1938)

F

TH OM
PS ON
MADISON

C. C. THOMPSON
POTTERY CO.
East Liverpool, OH, U.S.A.
Semivitreous tableware
ca.1916–1938 (1868–
1938)

G

TINET
32
Rue du Bac

TINET
Montreuil-sous-Bois,
France
Porcelain
1815+ (1815–1873)

H

J.J.Wheatley

T. J. WHEATLEY & CO.
Cincinnati, OH, U.S.A.
Faience. Incised
ca.1879 (1879–1882)

I

Tokay
U.S.A.

HULL POTTERY CO.
Crooksville, OH, U.S.A.
Art pottery, dinnerware
1958+ (1905–1950; 1952–
present)

J

Jomaszów

MICHAEL MEZER
Tomaszow, Poland
Porcelain. Black
1805+ (ca.1805–1810)

K

Tor Vale

TOR VALE POTTERY
Torquay, Devon, England
Pottery. Painted black
ca.1923 (ca.1913–ca.1924)

L

Toreas

LUDWIG WESSEL
Bonn, Rhineland, Germany
(W. Germany)
Earthenware, porcelain
1903+ (1825–present)
(Wessel Ceramic Works
AG)

M

TORMOHUN
WARE

ROYAL TORMOHUN
POTTERY CO.
Longpark & Torquay,
Devon, England
Pottery. Impressed
ca.1910 (1883–1957)

N

TORQUAY
POTTERY

TORQUAY TERRA-COTTA
CO.
Torquay, Devon, England
Pottery. Painted
ca.1910–1924 (1875–
1940)
(various names)

O

T. P. Co.
CHINA

TRENTON POTTERY CO.
Trenton, NJ, U.S.A.
White granite. Painted black
1865–1870 (1853–
1902+)

P

TREND
OVEN TO TABLEWARE
J&G Meakin
ENGLAND

J. & G. MEAKIN (LTD.)
Stoke, Staffordshire,
England
Earthenware
current (1851–present)
(member of Wedgwood
Group)

A

TRENLE
CHINA

TRENLE CHINA CO.
East Liverpool, OH, U.S.A.
Vitrified hotel porcelain
1917–1937 (1909–
ca.1942)

B

TRENT

TRENT TILE CO.
Trenton, NJ, U.S.A.
Tiles
1882 + (1882–1938)

C

TRENTON CHINA CO.
TRENTON, N.J.

TRENTON CHINA CO.
Trenton, NJ, U.S.A.
Vitrified porcelain.
Impressed
1859 + (1859–1891)

D

THE TRENTON POTTERIES CO
HOTEL CHINA

TRENTON POTTERIES
CO.
Trenton, NJ, U.S.A.
Hotel porcelain
1896 + (1892–1960)

E

TRENTON POTTERIES CO
TRENTON, NEW JERSEY.
U S A

TRENTON POTTERIES
CO.
Trenton, NJ, U.S.A.
Sanitary ware, pottery
ca.1900 (1892–1960)

F

TRIANON
WARE
BRITISH ANCHOR
ENGLAND
EST. 1884

BRITISH ANCHOR
POTTERY CO. LTD.
Longton, Staffordshire,
England
Earthenware. Printed,
impressed
1961 + (1884–1964 +)

G

TRILBY
J. M. & S. CO.

GLASGOW POTTERY
(JOHN MOSES & CO.)
Trenton, NJ, U.S.A.
White granite
ca.1863 (1859–1906)

H

Triptis
A.-G.

TRIPTIS AG
Triptis, Thuringia, Germany
(E. Germany)
Porcelain
ca.1913–1945 (1881–
present)
(Porcelain Combine Kahla
VEB)

I

CHINA

TAYLOR, SMITH &
TAYLOR
East Liverpool, OH, U.S.A.
Semivitreous ware
1908–ca.1915 (1901–
present)
(Anchor Hocking)

J

T.S.&T.
DURABLE EDGE

TAYLOR, SMITH &
TAYLOR
East Liverpool, OH, U.S.A.
Semivitreous ware
ca.1960 (1901–present)
(Anchor Hocking)

K

Tucker & Hulme
China Manufacturers
Philadelphia
1828

TUCKER & HULME
Philadelphia, PA, U.S.A.
Porcelain. Painted
1828 + (1825–1838)

L

T&G
HANLEY

URIAH THOMAS & CO.
Hanley, Staffordshire,
England
Earthenware, majolica.
Printed, impressed
1888–1905 (1888–1905)

M

TUDOR
ROSE

HOMER LAUGHLIN CHINA
CO.
East Liverpool, OH, U.S.A.
Semivitreous ware
ca.1943 (1877–present)

N

TURADA
WELLER

WELLER POTTERY
Zanesville, OH, U.S.A.
Art pottery
1897–1898 (1882–1948)

O

Turner's-Patent.

JOHN TURNER
Longton, Staffordshire,
England
Earthenware. Painted
1800–1805 (ca.1762–
1806)

P

1910

UNIVERSITY CITY
POTTERY
University City, MO, U.S.A.
Earthenware, porcelain.
Impressed, year varies
1910–1915 (1910–1915)

A U·C 19☐14 UNIVERSITY CITY POTTERY University City, MO, U.S.A. Art pottery. Impressed, various dates and potters (see page 170E) 1910–1915 (1910–1915)	**B** U. & C. J. UFFRECHT & CO. Haldensleben, Prussia, Germany (E. Germany) Earthenware after 1887–ca.1895 (1855– 1924)	**C**  M. UTZCHNEIDER Sarreguemines, France Porcelain ca.1862–ca.1868 (ca.1770–present)	**D** UP UNIVERSITY CITY POTTERY University City, MO, U.S.A. Art pottery. Impressed, imprinted 1910–1915 (1910–1915)
E U DALWITZ FRANZ URFUSS Dallwitz, Bohemia (Dalovice, Czechoslovakia) Earthenware, porcelain. Impressed 1855–1875 (1804– 1945+) (various names)	**F** UL LIMOGES FRANCE UNION LIMOUSINE Limoges, France Porcelain 1929–1943 (1908– 1979+)	**G** Ulm J J. J. SCHMIDT Ulm, Wurttemberg, Germany (W. Germany) Figurines 1827–1833 (1827–1833)	**H**  Kleindembach UNION PORCELAIN MANUFACTORY Kleindembach, Thuringia, Germany (E. Germany) Porcelain 1919–1927 (1905–1927)
I UNION CO-OPERATIVE POTTERY CO. East Liverpool, OH, U.S.A. Ironstone tableware. Various pattern names 1894–1905 (1894–1905)	**J** UNITY FREIBERG PORCELAIN FACTORY Freiberg, Saxony, Germany (E. Germany) Porcelain 1926–1945 (1906– present) (Porcelain Combine Colditz VEB)	**K** UPCHURCH UPCHURCH POTTERY Rainham, Kent, England Earthenware 1913–1961 (1913–1961)	**L** U – S – E – T – W INDIANAPOLIS. IND. UNITED STATES ENCAUSTIC TILE CO. Indianapolis, IN, U.S.A. Tile ca.1893 (1877–ca.1934)
M U.S. - Zone Germany Added to marks for some German factories 1946–1948. See page 234.	**N** VOLKMAR POTTERY/ VOLKMAR KILNS Tremont & Corona, NY, U.S.A. Art pottery, tile. Relief, incised 1904+ (1875–ca.1911) (various names & locations)	**O** NICHOLAS VERGETTE London, England Studio-type pottery, tile 1946+ (1946–1958)	**P** W. GOEBEL (HUMMEL) Rodenthal, Bavaria, Germany (W. Germany) Earthenware. Incised, underglazed black, blue, green, magenta, incised bee or full bee mark 1950–1955 (1871– present)

A  W. GOEBEL (HUMMEL) Rodenthal, Bavaria, Germany (W. Germany) Earthenware. Black, blue underglaze, small bee mark 1956 (1871–present)	**B**  W. GOEBEL (HUMMEL) Rodenthal, Bavaria, Germany (W. Germany) Earthenware. Black, blue underglaze, high bee mark 1957 (1871–present)	**C**  W. GOEBEL (HUMMEL) Rodenthal, Bavaria, Germany (W. Germany) Earthenware. Black, blue underglaze, low bee or baby bee mark 1958 (1871–present)	**D** W. GOEBEL (HUMMEL) Rodenthal, Bavaria, Germany (W. Germany) Earthenware. Black or blue underglaze, vee bee mark 1959 (1871–present)
E W. GOEBEL (HUMMEL) Rodenthal, Bavaria, Germany (W. Germany) Earthenware. Black, blue underglaze, new bee or stylized bee mark 1960–1972 (1871– present)	**F** VISTA ALEGRE Oporto, Portugal Porcelain 1824–present (1824– present)	**G** VILLEROY & BOCH Mettlach, Saar, Germany (W. Germany) Earthenware, figurines. Incised ca.1885–1895 (1813– present) (various names, owners, & locations)	**H**  VILLEROY & BOCH Mettlach, Saar, Germany (W. Germany) Earthenware, figurines. Blue stamped, painted ca.1890–1910 (1813– present) (various names, owners, & locations)
I VILLEROY & BOCH Mettlach, Saar, Germany (W. Germany) Earthenware. Blue ca.1885–1900 (1813– present) (various names, owners, & locations)	**J**  VEUVE LANGLOIS Bayeux, France Porcelain. Green 1830–ca.1881 (1810– 1951)	**K** VEUVE LANGLOIS Bayeux, France Porcelain. Blue, red 1830–ca.1847 (1810– 1951)	**L** J. N. VAN RECUM & HEIRS Grunstadt, Palatinate, Germany (W. Germany) Faience ca.1800–1812 (1799– present) (H. Kalau Von Hofe Earthenware Factory Grunstadt)
M  NICOLAS VILLEROY Wallerfangen, Saar, Germany (W. Germany) Earthenware, faience. Impressed 1789–1836 (1789–1931)	**N** VANCE/AVON FAIENCE Tiltonville, OH, & Wheeling, WV, U.S.A. Art pottery. Imprinted, impressed ca.1900 (1880–1908)	**O** NICOLAS VILLEROY Wallerfangen, Saar, Germany (W. Germany) Earthenware. Impressed 1789–1836 (1789–1931)	**P**  W. GOEBEL (HUMMEL) Rodenthal, Bavaria, Germany (W. Germany) Earthenware. Three-line mark 1968–1979 (1871– present)

A	B	C	D
Vᵉ LANGLOIS BAYEUX	↱ERNON CHINA VERNON, CAL.	VERNON KILNS CALIFORNIA MADE IN U.S.A.	Vernon ware ING DINNERWARE
VEUVE LANGLOIS Bayeux, France Porcelain. Blue, red 1830–ca.1847 (1810–1951)	POXON CHINA CO./ VERNON KILNS Vernon, CA, U.S.A. Dinnerware 1912+ (1912–1958)	VERNON KILNS Los Angeles, CA, U.S.A. Dinnerware 1931+ (1912–1958)	VERNON KILNS/METLOX POTTERIES Vernon, CA, U.S.A. Dinnerware, figurines 1956–1960+ (1912–1958/1935–present)

E	F	G	H
CALIFORNIA Vernonware	VERUS PORCELAIN	Victoria Porelite	Vieux Saxe
VERNON KILNS Los Angeles, CA, U.S.A. Dinnerware 1945–1958 (1912–1958)	OLIVER CHINA CO. Sebring, OH, U.S.A. Porcelain 1899–ca.1908 (1899–ca.1908)	VICTORIA PORCELAIN FACTORY Altrohlau, Bohemia (Stara Role, Czechoslovakia) Earthenware. Stamped before 1945 (1883–1945)	STATE'S PORCELAIN MANUFACTORY VEB Meissen, Saxony, Germany (E. Germany) Porcelain. Blue 1940–present (1919–present)

I	J	K	L
VIGILANT. J. M. & S. CO.	↱VIGNAUD	VIGNAUD LIMOGES	FINE CHINA BY VILETTA U.S.A.
GLASGOW POTTERY (JOHN MOSES & CO.) Trenton, NJ, U.S.A. White granite, cream-colored ware ca.1895 (1859–1906)	PIERRE VIGNAUD (JAMAULT & VIGNAUD) Paris, France Art porcelain ca.1963 (1963+)	A. VIGNAUD Limoges, France Porcelain ca.1920 (1912–1980+) (part of Bernardaud in 1970)	VILETTA Houston, TX, U.S.A. Porcelain current (1959–present)

M	N	O	P
Villeroy & Boch.	VITRYWARE	LIMOGES	VODREY S---V CHINA
VILLEROY & BOCH Mettlach, Saar, Germany (W. Germany) Earthenware, figurines. Incised 1836–1855 (1813–present) (various names, owners & locations)	MOIRA POTTERY CO. LTD. Burton-on-Trent, Staffordshire, England Brown ware, stoneware current (ca.1922–present)	A. VIGNAUD Limoges, France Porcelain 1920+ (1911–1980+) (part of Bernardaud in 1970)	VODREY POTTERY CO. East Liverpool, OH, U.S.A. Semivitreous tableware ca.1905–1928 (1896–1928)

A	B	C	D
VOGUE MODERNE BY **H. AYNSLEY & CO. ENGLAND** H. AYNSLEY & CO. (LTD.) Longton, Staffordshire, England Earthenware. Printed, impressed 1955 + (1873–present) (subsidiary of Waterford)	**VOHANN** VOHANN OF CALIFORNIA Capistrano Beach, CA, U.S.A. Kitchenware, ceramics 1950 + (1950–present)	*Volkmar.* VOLKMAR KILNS Metuchen, NJ, U.S.A. Pottery, tile 1900 + (1895–ca.1911) (various names & locations)	VOLKMAR VOLKMAR POTTERY Tremont & Corona, NY, U.S.A. Art pottery. Raised letters 1895 + (1875–ca.1911) (various names & locations)

E	F	G	H
VOLKMAR & CORY VOLKMAR & CORY Tremont & Corona, NY, U.S.A. Art pottery ca.1895–1896 (1895–1896) (various names & locations)	**VOLKMAR KILNS,** METUCHEN, N.J. VOLKMAR KILNS Metuchen, NJ, U.S.A. Pottery, tile 1903 + (1895–ca.1911) (various names & locations)	 WATCOMBE POTTERY CO. Torquay, Devon, England Terra-cotta. Impressed ca. 1875–ca. 1883 (1870–1962)	 HEUBACH, KAMPFE & SONTAG Wallendorf, Thuringia, Germany (E. Germany) Porcelain 1887–1896 (1763–present) (United Decorative Porcelainworks Lichte VEB)

I	J	K	L
  HARDTMUTH Budweis, Bohemia (Budejoirce, Czechoslovakia) Porcelain, earthenware after 1846 (1790–1905 +)	 TUCKER & HULME Philadelphia, PA, U.S.A. Porcelain. Impressed 1825 + (1825–1838)	 WORCESTER ROYAL PORCELAIN CO. LTD. Worcester, England Bone china current (1862–present) (Royal Worcester Spode Ltd.)	 KAMPFE & HEUBACH Wallendorf, Thuringia, Germany (E. Germany) Porcelain 1896–ca.1920 (1763–present) (United Decorative Porcelainworks Lichte VEB)

M	N	O	P
W HAMMANN FAMILY Wallendorf, Thuringia, Germany (E. Germany) Porcelain. Blue underglaze 1787–ca.1833 (1763–present) (United Decorative Porcelainworks Lichte VEB)	VK VIENNA CERAMICS Vienna, Austria Earthenware, porcelain ca.1912 (1905–1912)	*cjj* HAMMANN FAMILY Wallendorf, Thuringia, Germany (E. Germany) Porcelain. Blue underglaze 1787–1833 (1763– present) (United Decorative Porcelainworks Lichte VEB)	W WARDLE & CO. (LTD.) Hanley, Staffordshire, England Earthenware, parian, majolica. Printed ca.1885–1890 (1871–1935)

A

WIENERBERGER
WORKSHOP SCHOOL
FOR CERAMICS
Vienna, Austria
Ceramics. Impressed
1919+ (1919–1932+)

B

WILLIAM B. DALTON
London, England
Stoneware, porcelain.
Incised, painted
1900+ (1900–1941+)

C

_WB_

FRIEDRICH THOMIN
Wunsiedel, Bavaria,
Germany (W. Germany)
Porcelain
early 19th century

D

W.B.

WILLIAM BROWNFIELD (&
SON)
Cobridge, Staffordshire,
England
Earthenware, porcelain
1850–1871 (1850–1891)

E

WILLIAM BARNES
Swinton, Manchester,
England
Studio-type pottery. Incised,
painted
1945+ (1945–1964+)

F

WILLIAM BROWNFIELD (&
SON)
Cobridge, Staffordshire,
England
Earthenware, porcelain
1871–1891 (1850–1891)

G

FASOLD & STAUCH
Bock-Wallendorf,
Thuringia, Germany
(E. Germany)
Porcelain
1962–ca.1972 (1903–
1972)

H

_W. G._

WILHELM GERIKE & CO.
Althaldensleben, Prussia,
Germany (E. Germany)
Earthenware
1896–1921 (ca.1896–
1921)

I

WGS
ENGLAND

WILLIAM GILL (& SONS)
Yorkshire, Castleford,
England
Earthenware. Printed
1880+ (1880–1932)

J

_yW_

J. F. WALFORD
Crownborough, Sussex, &
Redhill, Surrey, England
Studio-type pottery.
Impressed
1948+ (1948–1964+)

K

W J W

WALLEY POTTERY
West Sterling, MA, U.S.A.
Art pottery. Impressed
1898+ (1898–1919)

L

WEISS, KUHNERT & CO.
Grafenthal, Thuringia,
Germany (E. Germany)
Porcelain, figurines
ca.1956–1972 (1891–
present)
(Utility Porcelain VEB)

M

WAGNER & APEL
Lippelsdorf, Thuringia,
Germany (E. Germany)
Porcelain, figurines
before 1945 (1877–
present)
(Porcelain Figurines VEB)

N

W. MOORCROFT (LTD.)
Burslem, Staffordshire,
England
Earthenware. Painted
1945+ (1913–present)

O

_WN_

WILLIAM NEWLAND
Prestwood,
Buckinghamshire,
England
Studio-type pottery.
Painted, incised
1948+ (1948–1964+)
(various dates)

P

hoH

WILLIAM FISHLEY
HOLLAND
Clevedon, Somerset,
England
Earthenware
1921+ (ca.1921–1964+)

A
 	
WR
 	
WILLIAM RUSCOE
Stoke, Staffordshire, &
  Exeter, Devon, England
Pottery. Incised, painted
1920 + (ca.1920–1964 +)
	B
	
	M. W. REUTTER
	Denkendorf, Wurttemberg,
	  Germany (W. Germany)
	Porcelain
	1948–present (1948–
	  present)
		C
		
		W.S.& S.
		
		W. SCHILLER & SONS
		Bodenbach, Bohemia
		  (Podmokly,
		  Czechoslovakia)
		Porcelain, earthenware.
		  Impressed
		1895 + (1829–1895 +)
			D
			
			W
			
			BARNHOUSE POTTERY
			Brockweir, Monmouth,
			  Wales
			Studio-type pottery.
			  Impressed
			1946 + (1946–1951)

E
 	
W
 	
WICK WORKS AG
Grenzhausen, Palatinate,
  Germany (W. Germany)
Stoneware. Impressed
1960–present (1872–
  present)
	F
	
	WENCK & ZITZMANN
	Kups, Bavaria, Germany
	  (W. Germany)
	Porcelain
	1882 + (1882 +)
		G
		
		Wachtersbach
		
		WACHTERSBACH
		EARTHENWARE
		FACTORY
		Schlierbach, Hesse,
		  Germany (W. Germany)
		Earthenware. Impressed
		1832–1853 (1832–
		  present)
			H
			
			WACO, CHINA
			
			EAST LIVERPOOL
			POTTERY CO.
			East Liverpool, OH, U.S.A.
			Semivitreous dinnerware
			1896–1901 (1894–1901)

I
 	
WADE
ENGLAND
 	
WADE HEATH & CO. LTD.
Burslem & Stoke,
  Staffordshire, England
Earthenware
current (1927–present)
	J
	
	WAECHTERSBACH
	
	WACHTERSBACH
	EARTHENWARE
	FACTORY
	Schlierbach, Hesse,
	  Germany (W. Germany)
	Earthenware. Blue
	1852–1883 (1832–
	  present)
		K
		
		Walker China VITRIFIED
		
		WALKER CHINA CO.
		Bedford, OH, U.S.A.
		Vitreous porcelain,
		  tableware
		current (1923–present)
			L
			
			WALLENDORF
			
			WALLENDORF
			PORCELAIN FACTORY
			VEB
			Wallendorf, Thuringia,
			  Germany (E. Germany)
			Porcelain
			1959 + (1960–present)
			(United Decorative
			  Porcelainworks Lichte
			  VEB)

M WALRICH Berkeley, Cal WALRICH POTTERY Berkeley, CA, U.S.A. Art pottery. Impressed ca.1922 (1922–ca.1930)	**N** **WANNOPEE** WANNOPEE POTTERY CO. New Milford, CT, U.S.A. Porcelain. Impressed, molded ca.1900 (1892–1903)	**O** **WARWICK** **SEMI** **PORCELAIN** WARWICK CHINA CO. Wheeling, WV, U.S.A. Semiporcelain 1893–1898 (1887–1951)	**P** WARWICK CHINA WARWICK CHINA CO. Wheeling, WV, U.S.A. Semiporcelain 1893–1898 (1887–1951)

A	B	C	D
WARWICK WHEELING SAMPSON, HANCOCK & SONS Staffordshire, England Pottery, various patterns 1891–1935 (1858–1937)	**WARWICK S.H. & S.** WARWICK CHINA CO. Wheeling, WV, U.S.A. Semiporcelain ca.1900 (1887–1951)	**WATCOMBE TORQUAY** WATCOMBE POTTERY (EVANS & CO.) Torquay, Devon, England Terra-cotta. Glazed, printed 1880–1901 (1870–1962)	**WBACH** WACHTERSBACH EARTHENWARE FACTORY Schlierbach, Hesse, Germany (W. Germany) Earthenware. Black, blue 1872–1880 (1832–present)

E	F	G	H
W BLOOR WILLIAM BLOOR East Liverpool, OH, & Trenton, NJ, U.S.A. Ironstone 1861–1862 (1860–1862)	**WEDG** — — — — — Frain, Czechoslovakia Porcelain ca.1820	**Wedgwood** JOSIAH WEDGWOOD Burslem, Etruria, & Barlaston, Staffordshire, England Earthenware, basalt, jasper, porcelain, parian, majolica. Impressed, (lower case mark) 1780–1795 (ca.1759–present) (member of Wedgwood Group)	**WEDGWOOD** JOSIAH WEDGWOOD Burslem, Etruria, & Barlaston, Staffordshire, England Earthenware, jasper, bone china, majolica. Impressed, printed, (upper case mark) 1769–present (ca.1759–present) (member of Wedgwood Group)

I	J	K	L
WEDGWOOD A GIUSEPPE CARLO GALVANI Pordenone, Italy Creamware 1845–1850 (ca.1823–ca.1883)	**WEDGWOOD & BENTLEY** JOSIAH WEDGWOOD Burslem, Etruria, & Barlaston, Staffordshire, England Earthenware, basalt, jasper, porcelain, parian, majolica 1768–1780 (ca.1759–present) (member of Wedgwood Group)	**WEDGWOOD & CO.** RALPH WEDGWOOD (& CO.)/PODMORE, WALKER & CO./ WEDGWOOD & CO. Burslem & Tunstall, Staffordshire, England Creamware, earthenware ca.1796–1801/ca.1834–present (1766–1837/ ca.1834–present) (member of Wedgwood Group)	**WEDGWOOD ETRURIA** JOSIAH WEDGWOOD Etruria & Barlaston, Staffordshire, England Earthenware, basalt, jasper, porcelain, parian, majolica 1840–1845 (ca.1759–present) (member of Wedgwood Group)

M	N	O	P
West Germany Added to many marks after 1949. See page 234	C. & E. CARSTENS PORCELAIN FACTORY BLANKENHAIN Blankenhain, Thuringia, Germany (E. Germany) Porcelain 1933–ca.1975 (ca.1918–present) (Weimar Porcelain)	**WELLER** WELLER POTTERY Zanesville, OH, U.S.A. Art pottery ca.1900 –ca.1925 (1882–1948)	**Weller Pottery** WELLER POTTERY Zanesville, OH, U.S.A. Art pottery ca.1928 (1882–1948)

A Weller Pottery Since 1872 WELLER POTTERY Zanesville, OH, U.S.A. Art pottery. Molded after 1935 (1882–1948)	**B** Weller Rhead Faience WELLER POTTERY Zanesville, OH, U.S.A. Art pottery ca.1903 (1882–1948)	**C** **WELLSVILLE CHINA CO.** WELLSVILLE CHINA CO. Wellsville, OH, U.S.A. Vitreous hotel ware 1933–ca.1960 (1902– 1969)	**D** Wemyss. ROBERT HERON (& SON) Sinclairtown, Kirkcaldy, Scotland Earthenware, Rockingham 1883–ca.1929 (1850– 1929)
E **W.E.P.CO. CHINA** WEST END POTTERY CO. East Liverpool, OH, U.S.A. Vitreous hotel ware ca.1893–1910 (1893– 1938)	**F** W F Holland WILLIAM FISHLEY HOLLAND Clevedon, Somerset, England Earthenware. Incised, signature 1921 + (ca.1921–1964 +)	**G** **THE WHEELING POTTERY CO** WHEELING POTTERY CO. Wheeling, WV, U.S.A. Semiporcelain, artware ca.1879 (1879–ca.1910)	**H** **W. H. GOSS COPYRIGHT** WILLIAM HENRY GOSS Stoke, Staffordshire, England Porcelain, parian, earthenware. Impressed, printed 1862 + (ca.1858–1944)
I **White Denver** WHITE POTTERY Denver, CO, U.S.A. Art pottery. Impressed, incised ca.1910 (1893–ca.1955)	**J** WHITE ROSE *carv-kraft* ◆ ◆ ◆ BY HARKER HARKER POTTERY CO. East Liverpool, OH, U.S.A. Semivitreous tableware ca.1950 (1890–1972)	**K** Wick Werke WICK WORKS AG Grenzhausen, Palatinate, Germany (W. Germany) Stoneware 1937–1960 (1872– present)	**L** **WIENER** JOHN & KARL HARTMUTH Budweis, Bohemia (Budejovice, Czechoslovakia) Earthenware, porcelain 1846 + (1790–1905 +)
M Wild Rose U·S·A HOMER LAUGHLIN CHINA CO. East Liverpool, OH, U.S.A. Semivitreous tableware ca.1949 (1877–present)	**N** William Ellis Tucker China Manufacturer Philadelphia 1828 TUCKER & HULME Philadelphia, PA, U.S.A. Porcelain. Painted, glaze, black ca.1828 (1825–1838)	**O** WILSHIRE EL CAMINO CHINA MADE IN U. S. A. GLADDING, McBEAN & CO. Los Angeles, CA, U.S.A. Franciscan ware 1942 + (1875–present) (member of Wedgwood Group)	**P** Winfield HANDCRAFT CHINA WINFIELD POTTERY Pasadena, CA, U.S.A. Semiporcelain ca.1940 (1937–1960)

A

W. K. C. Co.
Flometa

WARNER KEFFER CHINA
CO.
East Liverpool, OH, U.S.A.
Semivitreous tableware
1908–1911 (1908–1911)

B

Wm Dell
& Co
CINO

WM. DELL POTTERY
Cincinnati, OH, U.S.A.
Art pottery. Incised
ca.1890 (after 1887–1892)

C

Wm GUÉRIN & Cº
Limoges
FRANCE.

WILLIAM GUÉRIN
Limoges, France
Porcelain. Unglazed
ca.1900 (1877–1924 +)

D

W. Moorcroft

W. MOORCROFT LTD.
Burslem, Staffordshire,
England
Earthenware
ca.1919–1945 (1913–
present)

E

WOOD'S
WARE
Jasmine
ENGLAND

WOOD & SON(S) (LTD.)
Burslem, Staffordshire,
England
Hotel ware, tableware,
various pattern names
current (1865–present)

F

W.P.P.Co.
SEMI-PORCELAIN

PIONEER POTTERY CO.
Wellsville, OH, U.S.A.
Semiporcelain, tableware
1896–1900 (1884–1900)

G

W Jervis

ROSE VALLEY POTTERY
Rose Valley, PA, U.S.A.
Art pottery. Incised
1901–1905 (1901–1905)

H

W.S.GEORGE

W. S. GEORGE CO.
Kittanning, PA, U.S.A.
Semiporcelain, dinnerware
1930 + (1880–1959)

I

SONS
V&

H. M. WILLIAMSON &
SONS
Longton, Staffordshire,
England
Porcelain. Printed
1903 + (ca.1879–1941)

J

W.W.L.
DALWITZ

W. W. LORENZ
Dallwitz, Bohemia
(Dalovice,
Czechoslovakia)
Earthenware, figurines.
Impressed
1832–1850 (1804–
1945 +)
(various names & owners)

K

X J. Fouque

JOSEPH FOUQUE/JEAN-
FRANCOIS PELLOQUIN
Moustiers, France
Faience, tableware
ca.1800 (1749–1852)

L

Y.M.P.

YNYSMEDW POTTERY
Ynysmedw, Wales
Earthenware, stoneware,
terra-cotta. Impressed
1850 + (1840–1870 +)

M

REGINALD WELLS
Storrington, Sussex,
England
Studio-type pottery,
stoneware, figurines.
Incised
1910 + (1909–1951)

N

YEOMAN POTTERS
Yeomans Row, London
Pottery. Incised
ca.1915 (ca.1915–1919)

O

Z
• • •

————
Zurich, Switzerland
Porcelain, faience,
earthenware
1778 +

P

ZELL

JACOB FERDINAND LENZ
Zell on Harmersbach,
Badenia, Germany (W.
Germany)
Earthenware
ca.1819–ca.1869 (1794–
present)
(various names & owners,
Georg Schmider United
Zell Ceramic Factories)

A

Zenith Gouda Holland

ZENITH POTTERY
 FACTORY
Gouda, Holland
Delftware, pipes, decorated
 ware. Blue, white
1891 + (1749–present)

B

ZP

ZANEWARE
MADE IN USA

ZANE POTTERY
Zanesville, OH, U.S.A.
Pottery
(1920–1941)

C

Z. S. & CO.
BAVARIA

ZEH, SCHERZER & CO.
Rehau, Bavaria, Germany
 (W. Germany)
Porcelain
1880 + (1880–present)

D

ZSOLNAY
PÉCS

ZSOLNAY
Pecs, Hungary
Lusterware, art pottery
ca.1862–1900 (1862–
 present)

E

Z.W.PECS

ZSOLNAY
Pecs, Hungary
Lusterware, art pottery
ca.1862–1900 (1862–
 present)

SOME ADDITIONAL INFORMATION

THE VOCABULARY OF MARKS

This is a list of words and symbols that are often found in back-stamps. The dates given are guides, based on our observations of marks, or are the dates of events that created the terms or symbols. This is useful only to indicate the earliest date a term may appear; it does not tell how recently it may have been used.

COUNTRY NAMES

The McKinley Tariff Act of 1891 required that the name of the country where the ceramic was originally made must be printed on each piece. Sometimes country names were used as part of the mark before 1891; here are the dates of the earliest marks we have seen using the country name as part of the mark:

China	ca.1900
Czechoslovakia	1918
Danmark (Danish for Denmark)	ca.1850
Denmark	ca.1890
England	1880
Finland	1897
France	1867
Germany	1885
Hungary	1935
Japan	1921
Norge (Norwegian for Norway)	1911
Norway	1935
Portugal	1853
Sweden	1933
Switzerland	1906
United States of America	1935

WORDS FOUND IN MARKS

bone china—20th century
The English name for a special type of ceramic developed about 1800. The words "bone china" do not appear as part of a mark until about 1915.

©—1914–present
The copyright symbol used in the United States, indicating that a work has been registered with the U.S. Copyright Office. The earliest we have seen a © mark used is 1914.

cooking ware—ca.1923–present
A ceramic container that is suitable to use while cooking food. It can withstand oven temperatures and is appropriately shaped.

copyright—after 1858 to present, usually 20th century
The design or name or material is registered under the United States copyright laws. The earliest we have seen the whole word used is 1892.

copyright reserved—after 1876
A legal term used on English wares.

craze proof—ca.1960–1970
The glaze will not develop fine lines or cracks with normal wear.

Delft—If the word "delft" appears, the pottery probably dates from the 19th or 20th century
A tin-glazed earthenware, often blue and white, but other colors were also used.

Déposé—ca.1900
Déposé is the French word for "registered."

designed expressly for—ca.1927–present
Factories sometimes made special patterns for use by one special customer. These were often marked with the customer's name as well as the factory name.

detergent proof—ca.1944–present
The design will not wash off if dishwashing detergent is used.

dishwasher proof—after 1955
The dishes can safely be washed in a dishwasher. The heat of the water will not injure the decoration or ceramic.

East Germany—1949
Germany was divided into four occupation zones after World War II, from 1945 to 1949. The Russian zone became the German Democratic Republic, or East Germany.

fast color—ca.1960
The decorations will not fade.

freezer-oven-table—1960s and after
The dish can be put in the freezer, then directly into an oven until the contents are cooked, then used for table service.

Gesetzlich Geschützt (Ges. Gesch.)—after 1899
These are the German words for legally patented or registered.

handmade—ca.1962
The dishes are at least partially made by hand, not molded by machine.

hand-painted—England and the United States about 1935
The design is painted directly on the dish by an artist. Each dish is therefore slightly different. Hand-painted china was popular in the 1880–1910 period, when it was made by many women at home as a hobby. The words "hand-painted" as part of a mark were used in the 20th century.

incorporated—ca.1940
A legal designation for the formation of a corporation in the United States.

Limited (Ltd.)—after 1861
Part of English firm name that has a specific legal meaning concerning the formation of the company.

made expressly for, made exclusively for—ca.1927–present
A factory made the dishes with a special design used by one customer.

Made in—1887 and after
English law required imported wares to be marked with these words and the country name.

Made in Occupied Japan—1945–1952
The Allies occupied Japan after World War II and these words were used on exported goods.

microwave safe—after 1970
The ceramic is suitable for a microwave oven.

National Brotherhood of Operative Potters—1940–1955
United States Potters Union members were employed at the factory.

Nippon—1891–1921 as a country name, sometimes after 1891 as part of a company name
It is the Japanese name for Japan.

NRA and eagle symbol—1933–1936
The National Recovery Administration, United States, created by the National Industrial Recovery Act of 1933, helped to create jobs. The symbol was used on products the NRA supported.

oven proof—after 1933
The ceramic can be used for baking in an oven.

oven tested—ca.1935
The ceramic has been tested and is safe for use in an oven.

oven-to-table—1978–present
A ceramic designed to be used in the oven and as a serving dish.

patent applied for—1902–present
A patent application has been filed with the United States Patent Office.

patent pending—1940–present
A patent has been applied for in the United States but not yet granted.

patented—1900–current
A patent has been granted by the United States Patent Office.

permanent colours—ca.1960
Term used on English wares.

published by—ca.1830–1840
This term refers to the Sculpture Copyright Act of 1797 (amended in 1814) in England.

®—1949–present
This symbol is used to designate a legally registered design in the United States Patent and Trademark Office. Trademark registration began in 1881.

refrigerator ware—ca.1938–1952
These words were often stamped on sets of ice water pitchers and containers made for refrigerators and sold as part of the original equipment.

Reg. U.S. Pat. Off.—ca.1932–present
Registered United States Patent Office.

Reg., Rd, Registered, with a number—1884–present
The English designation that indicates a design or process has been registered. See page 239.

Registry mark, diamond shaped—1842–1883
The English designation that indicates a design or process has been registered. See page 238.

Royal—after 1850 (Royal Crown Derby, 1876; Royal Doulton, 1902; Royal Worcester, 1862)
The word "Royal" was used as part of many English marks.

semi-vitreous (s-v)—after 1901
A type of heavy ceramic popular for dinnerware.

trademark—after 1862, usually after 1875
This word was used on English pieces after the Trademark Act of 1862, used on United States wares after 1875.

22 carat—term used after 1930s
The gold trim is real, 22 carat gold.

underglaze—ca.1903–1945
The design is applied under the glaze.

Union Label—1930s
The dish was made by a factory in the United States with a unionized work force.

union made—1930s
A term used in the United States; dishes made by a company with union employees.

USPA approved glaze—1975
The United States Potters Association approved the glaze for safety, durability, etc.

U.S. patent—after 1900
The design or method is patented in the United States. This term may appear on wares made outside the United States also.

U.S. Zone, U.S. Zone Germany—1945–1949
The name of the United States–occupied section of Germany after World War II.

warranted—1890s, 1920s
There are three different uses of the term "warranted." In the United States it appears with the factory marks as a description of the company in the 1890s. It is part of the term "warranted 22 karat gold," meaning guaranteed to be real gold, in the 1920s. It appears as part of a company name on English wares in the 1890s.

West Germany—1949–present
At the end of World War II, Germany was divided into occupation zones. The United States, Britain, and France occupied these zones from 1945 to 1949. Then the three zones became the Federal Republic of Germany, or West Germany.

FOREIGN WORDS SOMETIMES FOUND IN MARKS

AG—Aktiengesellschaft; joint stock company (German)
aluminite—high-fired porcelain developed in 1900, used for oven-to-table cookware (French)
breveté—patented (French), used as early as 1820
Cie—company (French)
décoré à la main—hand-decorated (French)
décoré par—decorated by (French)
dep—**déposé;** registered (French)
deponiert—registered (German)
déposé—registered (French)
eingetragen muster—registered design (German)
eneret—monopoly or privilege, the same as patented (Danish)
fabrique par—manufactured by (French)
fayence—faience (German)
fils—son (French)
Firenze—Florence, Italy
flammefest—flame resistant (German)
flintporslin—creamware (Swedish)

Gebrüder (Gebr.)—brothers (German)
ges.—protected (German)
geschutzt—protected (German)
gesellschaft—corporation (German)
gesetzlich—by law or legally (German)
GMBH—Gesellschaft mit beschränkte Haftung; limited liability company (German)
grand feu—high temperature, name for a ceramic fired at a high temperature (French)
grès—stoneware (French)
hochfein—super fine (German)
hochfeine qualität—finest quality (German)
keramische—ceramic (German)
KG—Kommanditgesellschaft, limited partnership (German)
mikrowellen—microwave safe (German)
musterschutz—protected against copying (German)
plateelbakkery—pottery factory (Dutch)
porcelaine fabrique—porcelain factory (French)
porzellanfabrik—porcelain factory (German)
porzellanwerke—porcelain works (German)
registered—registered design or process (England)
SA—Société Anonyme (French), limited liability company
S.A.R.L.—Société Anonyme à Responsabilité Limitée, a limited liability company (French)
SAG—Sowjetische Aktiengesellschaft—Soviet joint stock company in Germany
S.G.D.G.—Sans Garantie du Gouvernement, without government guarantee (French)
sohn—son (German)
solidaire—jointly and separately liable (French)
steingutfabrik—stoneware company (German)
VEB—Volkseigner Betreib; Nationalized German Democratic Republic company, used after 1945 (German)
Venezia—Venice, Italy
veuve (vve)—widow (French)
VVB—Vereinigung Volkseigener Betriebe, Association of People's Own Enterprises (German)
werkstatte—workshop (German)
Wien—Vienna, Austria
Witwe (Wwe)—widow (German)

DATING SYSTEMS USED BY SPECIFIC FACTORIES

Dating systems were systems of numbers or symbols used by some factories to record the month and/or year a piece of pottery or porcelain was manufactured. Although not all factories employed such systems, many of the larger firms did, and we have included most of them here.

Much of the material contained in this book was obtained directly from the factory or manufacturer but in some cases we were obliged to turn to other sources. With the Russian system, we, of course, found it impossible to check with the existing factory to confirm our findings. With regard to other companies, even the factory records themselves were unclear, and thus we received conflicting information. Despite this, we have included information that each factory felt was most accurate.

In Selected Reading we have supplied a list of all the books and pamphlets we consulted for our research. If you wish to research the dating of a piece further, write directly to the manufacturer of your piece, or consult one of the books listed in our bibliography.

DOULTON & COMPANY

DOULTON & CO.
Burslem, Staffordshire, England
1853–present
(Royal Doulton Tableware Ltd.)

Impressed. Date added between 1872 and 1877; sometimes added between 1877 and 1887. Also a circular variation.

ca.1873–ca.1914 date was sometimes added in the center of this impressed or printed mark.

Impressed on Doulton Ware and some Lambeth faience ca.1876–1880.

Impressed or printed on Doulton Ware ca.1880–1902 (England added after 1891). Occasionally the date was added.

From 1913 to the 1930s, an impressed date-number system was used to indicate when the mold was made. The first numerals are the day, next the month, then the year. So, 4–3–29 means the fourth of March 1929. If two numbers were used, it indicates month and year. So, 10–27 means October 1927. This date number system was used with a variety of Royal Doulton backstamps.

Occasionally, after 1927, a printed number can be found to the right of the crown. Add 1927 to the number and it will give the date of manufacture. Thus, if you see "12" on the mark, add 1927 and you will see that the piece was made in 1939.

This material is based on information from *The Kovels' Illustrated Price Guide to Royal Doulton,* 2nd Edition, by Ralph and Terry Kovel (New York: Crown Publishers, Inc., 1984), and *The Doulton Lambeth Wares* by Desmond Eyles (Hutchinson Publishing Group Ltd., London, 1975).

ENGLISH REGISTRY MARKS

English registry marks are perhaps the most comprehensive and useful marks for dating any piece of English pottery and porcelain. Since 1842, English decorative art designs (including wood, glass, metal, and ceramic designs) were registered at the British patent office, but not every registered piece is marked.

To obtain more detailed information, write to one of the following addresses:

For pieces registered before 1909	For pieces registered after 1909
Public Record Office	Designs Registry
Ruskin Avenue	Patent Office
Kew, Richmond	Chancery Lane
Surrey, England	London WC2A 1LR England

The Public Record Office or Patent Office may charge a small fee.

Here are some notes to help date any piece that bears an English registry mark.

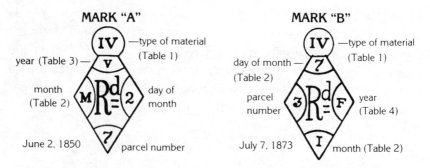

MARK "A"
IV —type of material (Table 1)
year (Table 3)— v
month (Table 2) M Rd =2 day of month
June 2, 1850 7 parcel number

MARK "B"
IV —type of material (Table 1)
day of month (Table 2)— 7
parcel number 3 Rd =F year (Table 4)
July 7, 1873 I month (Table 2)

A diamond-shaped registry mark was used between 1842 and 1883. The information within the diamond changed after 1867.

Mark "A" represents the mark used between 1842 and 1867; mark "B" represents the mark between 1868 and 1883. After 1884, the diamond-shaped marks were replaced by the letters Rd. No. (for registry number) — and numbers indicating the year the piece was registered (see Mark "C").

In Mark "A," the various letters and numbers indicate the following: the large "Rd" means "registered"; the Roman numeral in the circle at the top of the mark represents the type of material of which the piece is made (see Table 1); the Roman numeral in the top inside section of the diamond represents the year the piece was registered (see Table 3); the Arabic numeral on the right-hand section represents the *day of the month* the piece was registered; the Arabic numeral in the section at the bottom represents the *parcel number,* which is a code indicating the person or company who registered the piece; and the letter in the left-hand section represents the month the piece was registered (see Table 2). In other words, Mark "A" appeared on a piece of ceramics registered on June 2, 1850.

In Mark "B," the various letters and numbers reflect the following: the large "Rd" means *"registered";* the Roman numeral in the circle at the top of the mark represents the *type of material* from which the piece was made (see Table 1); the Arabic numeral in the top inside section of the diamond represents the *day of the month;* the letter at the right-hand section represents the *year* the piece was registered (see Table 4); the letter in the bottom segment represents the *month* the piece was registered (see Table 2); and the Arabic numeral at the left-hand side represents the parcel number. In other words, this mark appeared on a piece of ceramics registered on July 7, 1873.

TABLE 1	
Type of material or class	
I—metal	III—glass
II—wood	IV—ceramics

TABLE 2	
Month of the Year of Manufacture	
C—January	I—July
G—February	R—August
W—March	D—September
H—April	B—October
E—May	K—November
M—June	A—December

TABLE 3		
Year of Manufacture—1842–1867		
1842—X	1851—P	1860—Z
1843—H	1852—D	1861—R
1844—C	1853—Y	1862—O
1845—A	1854—J	1863—G
1846—I	1855—E	1864—N
1847—F	1856—L	1865—W
1848—U	1857—K	1866—Q
1849—S	1858—B	1867—T
1850—V	1859—M	

TABLE 4		
Year of Manufacture—1868–1883		
1868—X	1874—U	1879–Y
1869—H	1875—S	1880—J
1870—C	1876—V	1881—E
1871—A	1877—P	1882—L
1872—I	1878—D	1883—K
1873—F		

After 1883, the diamond marks were discontinued and a simpler marking system, consisting of the letters "Rd No" followed by a number, was instituted. This mark appears on decorative art (china, glass, metal, or wood) manufactured in England since 1884.

MARK "C"

Rd Nº 821265.

1884–present

Table 5: Design Registry Numbers—1884–1981 lists the English registry numbers by year. (For example, if a piece is marked with the number Rd. No. 821265, it was registered sometime in 1937.)

TABLE 5
Design Registry Numbers 1884–1981

Jan.	1884— 1	1916—653521	1949—856999
	1885— 20000	1917—658988	1950—860854
	1886— 40800	1918—662872	1951—863970
	1887— 64700	1919—666128	1952—866280
	1888— 91800	1920—673750	1953—869300
	1889—117800	1921—680147	1954—872531
	1890—142300	1922—687144	1955—876067
	1891—164000	1923—694999	1956—879282
	1892—186400	1924—702671	1957—882949
	1893—206100	1925—710165	1958—887079
	1894—225000	1926—718057	1959—891665
	1895—248200	1927—726330	1960—895000
	1896—268800	1928—734370	1961—899914
	1897—291400	1929—742725	1962—904638
Jan.	1898—311677	1930—751160	1963—909364
	1899—332200	1931—760583	1964—914536
	1900—351600	1932—769670	1965—919607
	1901—368186	1933—779292	1966—924510
	1902—385180	1934—789019	1967—929335
	1903—403200	1935—799097	1968—934515
	1904—424400	1936—808794	1969—939875
	1905—447800	1937—817293	1970—944932
	1906—471860	1938—825231	1971—950046
	1907—493900	1939—832610	1972—955342
	1908—518640	1940—837520	1973—960708
	1909—535170	1941—838590	1974—965185
Sep.	1909—548919	1942—839230	1975—969249
Oct.	1909—548920	1943—839980	1976—973838
Jan.	1911—575817	1944—841040	1977—978426
	1912—594195	1945—842670	1978—982815
	1913—612431	Jan. 1946—845550	1979—987910
	1914—630190	1947—849730	1980—993012
	1915—644935	1948—853260	1981—998302

Based on information supplied by the Patent Office, Chancery Lane, London.

GEORGE GRAINGER

GEORGE GRAINGER (& CO.)
Worcester, England
c.1839–1902

Date letters were used under the backstamp. The company was taken over by Worcester Royal Porcelain Co. Ltd. in 1889 and closed in 1902.

1891—A	1895—E	1899—I
1892—B	1896—F	1900—J
1893—C	1897—G	1901—K
1894—D	1898—H	1902—L

Based on information from *Royal Worcester Porcelain* by Henry Sandon (New York: Clarkson N. Potter, Inc., 1975).

HOMER LAUGHLIN

HOMER LAUGHLIN
East Liverpool, OH, U.S.A.
1877–present

STANDARD DATING SYSTEM

MONTH	YEAR	PLANT
1900–1909 Number 1–12	Single number	1, 2, or 3 numbers to designate an East Liverpool plant
1910–1919 Letter	One- or two-digit number	Letter (and number)
1920–1929 Number	One- or two-digit number	Letter (and number)
1930–1969 Letter	Two-digit number	Letter (and number)
1970+	Four-digit number	

1900–1909	1910–1919	1920–1929	1930–1969
❦	❦	❦	❦
HOMER LAUGHLIN	HOMER LAUGHLIN	HOMER LAUGHLIN	HOMER LAUGHLIN
371	D14N5	B34	A39R5
March 1907, Plant 1	April 1914, Plant 5	Feb. 1923, Plant 4	Jan. 1939, Plant 5

"BEST CHINA" DATING SYSTEM

Two letters were used. The first indicates the year, the second the month.

YEAR	JAN	FEB	MAR	APR	MAY	JUNE	JULY	AUG	SEPT	OCT	NOV	DEC
1960	—	—	—	—	AE	AF	AG	AH	AI	AJ	AK	AL
1961	BA	BB	BC	BD	BE	BF	BG	BH	BI	BJ	BK	BL
1962	CA	CB	CC	CD	CE	CF	CG	CH	CI	CJ	CK	CL
1963	DA	DB	DC	DD	DE	DF	DG	DH	DI	DJ	DK	DL
1964	EA	EB	EC	ED	EE	EF	EG	EH	EI	EJ	EK	EL
1965	FA	FB	FC	FD	FE	FF	FG	FH	FI	FJ	FK	FL
1966	GA	GB	GC	GD	GE	GF	GG	GH	GI	GJ	GK	GL
1967	HA	HB	HC	HD	HE	HF	HG	HH	HI	HJ	HK	HL
1968	IA	IB	IC	ID	IE	IF	IG	IH	II	IJ	IK	IL
1969	JA	JB	JC	JD	JE	JF	JG	JH	JI	JJ	JK	JL
1970	KA	KB	KC	KD	KE	KF	KG	KH	KI	KJ	KK	KL
1971	LA	LB	LC	LD	LE	LF	LG	LH	LI	LJ	LK	LL
1972	MA	MB	MC	MD	ME	MF	MG	MH	MI	MJ	MK	ML
1973	NA	NB	NC	ND	NE	NF	NG	NH	NI	NJ	NK	NL
1974	OA	OB	OC	OD	OE	OF	OG	OH	OI	OJ	OK	OL
1975	PA	PB	PC	PD	PE	PF	PG	PH	PI	PJ	PK	PL
1976	QA	QB	QC	QD	QE	QF	QG	QH	QI	QJ	QK	QL
1977	RA	RB	RC	RD	RE	RF	RG	RH	RI	RJ	RK	RL
1978	SA	SB	SC	SD	SE	SF	SG	SH	SI	SJ	SK	SL
1979	TA	TB	TC	TD	TE	TF	TG	TH	TI	TJ	TK	TL
1980	UA	UB	UC	UD	UE	UF	UG	UH	UI	UJ	UK	UL
1981	VA	VB	VC	VD	VE	VF	VG	VH	VI	VJ	VK	VL
1982	WA	WB	WC	WD	WE	WF	WG	WH	WI	WJ	WK	WL
1983	XA	XB	XC	XD	XE	XF	XG	XH	XI	XJ	XK	XL
1984	YA	YB	YC	YD	YE	YF	YG	YH	YI	YJ	YK	YL
1985	ZA	ZB	ZC	ZD	ZE	ZF	ZG	ZH	ZI	ZJ	ZK	ZL

Based on information supplied by Homer Laughlin China Company.

JOHN MEIR

JOHN MEIR & SON
Tunstall, Staffordshire, England
1837–1897

Sometimes the piece was marked with a backstamp and a double number: $\dfrac{10}{76}$ for October 1876.

MINTON

MINTON
Stoke, Staffordshire, England
1793–present
(Royal Doulton Tableware Ltd.)

A backstamp, an impressed letter for the month and a special year symbol, was used from 1842 to 1942. It was stamped near the factory mark.

Minton, July 1843

MONTH

J—January	E—May	S—September
F—February	I—June	O—October
M—March	H—July	N—November
A—April	Y—August	D—December

MINTON YEAR CYPHERS

1842	1843	1844	1845	1846	1847	1848	1849
1850	1851	1852	1853	1854	1855	1856	1857
1858	1859	1860	1861	1862	1863	1864	1865
1866	1867	1868	1869	1870	1871	1872	1873
1874	1875	1876	1877	1878	1879	1880	1881
1882	1883	1884	1885	1886	1887	1888	1889
1890	1891	1892	1893	1894	1895	1896	1897
1898	1899	1900	1901	1902	1903	1904	1905
1906	1907	1908	1909	1910	1911	1912	1913
1914	1915	1916	1917	1918	1919	1920	1921
1922	1923	1924	1925	1926	1927	1928	1929
1930	1931	1932	1933	1934	1935	1936	1937
	1938	1939	1940	1941	1942		

In 1943 a new dating system was started. The workman was indicated by a number. This number was followed by a two-digit number indicating the year. For example, 3—75 would mean the piece was made in 1975 by workman number 3.

PISGAH FOREST POTTERY

PISGAH FOREST POTTERY
Pisgah Forest, NC, U.S.A.
ca.1901–present

From 1926 on, the date was included in the impressed mark.

ROOKWOOD POTTERY

Rookwood Pottery
Cincinnati, OH, U.S.A.
1880–1967

The RP mark was used from 1886. One flame was added each year through 1900, making 14 flames. After 1900 a Roman numeral beneath the mark indicated the last two digits of the year.

1886

1887

1902

Based on information from *The Kovels' Collector's Guide to American Art Pottery* by Ralph and Terry Kovel (New York: Crown Publishers, Inc., 1974).

ROYAL CROWN DERBY

ROYAL CROWN DERBY
Derby, England
ca.1750–1848, ca.1878–present
(Royal Doulton Tableware Ltd.)

Cypher is printed below the mark:

  ca.1878–1890

  ca.1890–

ROYAL CROWN DERBY YEAR CYPHERS
(Correct to within one year)

1880	1881	1882	1883	1884	1885	1886	1887
1888	1889	1890	1891	1892	1893	1894	1895
1896	1897	1898	1899	1900	1901	1902	1903
1904	1905	1906	1907	1908	1909	1910	1911
1912	1913	1914	1915	1916	1917	1918	1919
1920	1921	1922	1923	1924	1925	1926	1927
1928	1929	1930	1931	1932	1933	1934	1935
		1936	1937	1938	1939		
				I	II		

The "V" mark of 1904 is accompanied by the word "England"; that of 1942, the words "Made in England." The "X" marks of 1901 and 1947 appear together with the words "Made in England." Roman numerals for each year begin in 1938.

Based on information from *Royal Crown Derby* by John Twitchett, F.R.S.A., and Betty Bailey, F.R.S.A. (New York: Clarkson N. Potter, Inc., 1976).

ROYAL DELFT

DE PORCELEYNE FLES (The Porcelain Bottle)
Delft, Holland
1653–present

From 1879 to the present an alphabetical year code has been used by Royal Delft. It is impressed on the bottom of the piece near the backstamp.

DATING SYSTEM

1879—A	1905—AA	1931—BA	1956—CA	1981—DA
1880—B	1906—AB	1932—BB	1957—CB	1982—DB
1881—C	1907—AC	1933—BC	1958—CC	1983—DC
1882—D	1908—AD	1934—BD	1959—CD	1984—DD
1883—E	1909—AE	1935—BE	1960—CE	
1884—F	1910—AF	1936—BF	1961—CF	
1885—G	1911—AG	1937—BG	1962—CG	
1886—H	1912—AH	1938—BH	1963—CH	
1887—I	1913—AI	1939—BI	1964—CI	
1888—J	1914—AJ	1940—BJ	1965—CJ	
1889—K	1915—AK	1941—BK	1966—CK	
1890—L	1916—AL	1942—BL	1967—CL	
1891—M	1917—AM	1943—BM	1968—CM	
1892—N	1918—AN	1944—BN	1969—CN	
1893—O	1919—AO	1945—BO	1970—CO	
1894—P	1920—AP	1946—BP	1971—CP	
1895—Q	1921—AQ	—BQ	—CQ	
1896—R	1922—AR	1947—BR	1972—CR	
1897—S	1923—AS	1948—BS	1973—CS	
1898—T	1924—AT	1949—BT	1974—CT	
1899—U	1925—AU	1950—BU	1975—CU	
1900—V	1926—AV	1951—BV	1976—CV	
1901—W	1927—AW	1952—BW	1977—CW	
1902—X	1928—AX	1953—BX	1978—CX	
1903—Y	1929—AY	1954—BY	1979—CY	
1904—Z	1930—AZ	1955—BZ	1980—CZ	

Delft
BF
1936

Based on information in an article by Violette Steinke, "Delving into Royal Delft" (*The Plate Collector,* March 1984).

RUSSIAN MARKS

Russian porcelains can be dated from the marks of the reigning czar.

marks of Paul I
1796–1801

marks of Alexander I
1801–1825

mark of Nicholas I
1825–1855

mark of Alexander II
1855–1881

mark of Alexander III
1881–1894

mark of Nicholas II
1894–1917

mark of Soviet regime
1917–present

SÈVRES PORCELAIN FACTORY

SÈVRES PORCELAIN FACTORY
Sèvres, France
1753–present

From 1753 to 1793 date letters were used with the following marks. The letters may be capital or small, either inside the ⚔ or beside it.

1753—A	1767—O	1781—DD
1754—B	1768—P	1782—EE
1755—C	1769—Q	1783—FF
1756—D	1770—R	1784—GG
1757—E	1771—S	1785—HH
1758—F	1772—T	1786—II
1759—G	1773—U	1787—JJ
1760—H	1774—V	1788—KK
1761—I	1775—X	1789—LL
1762—J	1776—Y	1790—MM
1763—K	1777—Z	1791—NN
1764—L	1778—AA	1792—OO
1765—M	1779—BB	1793—PP
1766—N	1780—CC	

1753   1773

Soft paste   Hard paste

QQ (1794) and RR (1795) have been found but are thought to be unauthorized. Date letter marks apparently were not used between 1795 and 1801.

The following date marks were used around the time of France's First Empire (1804–1815). The Roman numerals refer to the year of the Revolutionary Calendar, which began in 1793 with the year "I."

1801 (IX)—T_9	1810 —10
1802 (X)—X	1811 —oz
1803 (XI)—II	1812 —dz
1804 (XII)— ⹀	1813 —tz
1805 (XIII)— -II-	1814 —qz
1806 (XIV)— ∿	1815 —qn
1807 —7	1816 —sz
1808 —8	1817 —ds
1809 —9	

dz

1812

Each king, republic, or empire had a special mark.

Reign of Louis XVIII, 1814–1824
Backstamp mark with last two digits
of the year

1821–1822

Reign of Charles X, 1824–1830
Mark with last two digits of the year

1824   1825   1829–1830

Reign of Louis-Philippe, 1830–1848
Mark with last two digits of the year

1830

1834   1843–1845   1845–1848   1845–1848

Second Republic, 1848–1852
Last two digits of the year

1851

1849

Second Empire, 1852–1870
Last two digits of the year

Hard paste   Soft paste
1852   1854

Third Republic, 1871–1946

1871   1872   Stoneware   Porcelain
                  1900   1900

SYRACUSE CHINA CORPORATION

SYRACUSE CHINA CORPORATION
Syracuse, NY, U.S.A.
1871–present

SYRACUSE
iiii *China*

After 1966

DATING SYSTEM

Beginning in 1895, each piece was stamped with the year and month code.

1895 May to Dec.—1 thru 6	1914 Jan. to Dec.—25 thru 36
1896 Jan. to Dec.—9 thru 20	1915 Jan. to Dec.—37 thru 48
1897 Jan. to Dec.—21 thru 32	1916 Jan. to Dec.—49 thru 60
1898 Jan. to Dec.—33 thru 44	1917 Jan. to Dec.—61 thru 72
1899 Jan. to Dec.—45 thru 56	1918 Jan. to Dec.—73 thru 84
1900 Jan. to Dec.—57 thru 68	1919 Jan. to June—85 thru 90

1901 Jan. to Dec.—69 thru 80
1902 Jan. to Dec.—81 thru 92
1903 Jan.—93

July 1919 to Dec.—1 thru ◇9◇

1903 Feb.—94
1903 Mar.—95
1903 Apr.—96
1903 May—97
1903 June—98
1903 July, Aug., Sept.—99

1920—A	1925—F
1921—B	1926—G
1922—C	1927—H
1923—D	1928—I
1924—E	1929—J

Oct. 1903 thru Dec. 1911 has a circle around the numeral.

1930 Jan Fayette Plant—K-1
1930 Jan Court Plant—1-K

1903 Oct.— ①
1903 Nov.—2
1903 Dec.—3

Number with letters is month until Feb. 1960.

1904 Jan. to Dec.—4 thru 15	
1905 Jan. to Dec.—16 thru 27	
1906 Jan. to Dec.—28 thru 39	1930—K 1946—AA
1907 Jan. to Dec.—40 thru 51	1931—L 1947—BB
1908 Jan. to Dec.—52 thru 63	1932—M 1948—CC
1909 Jan. to Dec.—64 thru 75	1933—N 1949—DD
1910 Jan. to Dec.—76 thru 87	1934—O 1950—EE
1911 Jan. to Dec.—88 thru 99⃝	1935—P 1951—FF

1936—Q   1952—GG
1937—R   1953—HH
1938—S   1954—II
1939—T   1955—JJ
1940—U   1956—KK

Jan. 1912 thru June 1919 has a diamond around the numeral.

1941—V   1957—LL
1942—W   1958—MM
1943—X   1959—NN

1912 Jan. to Dec.—◇1◇ thru 12
1913 Jan. to Dec.—13 thru 24

1944—Y   1960
1945—Z   Jan.—OO

Month indicated by a series of dots Feb. 1960 thru June 1962.	Since 1975 one digit has been used to identify year of manufacture.
1960 Feb. to Dec.—89 (Dots) 1961 Jan. to Dec.—90 (Dots) 1962 Jan. to June—91 (Dots)	1975—4 A/L 1976—5 A/I

Letter with numbers is month from July 1962 on.	Beginning in 1976 code letters have been retained for two or more months in some cases.
July 1962 to Dec.—91 1963—92 A/L 1969—98 A/L 1964—93 A/L 1970—99 A/L 1965—94 A/L 1971—100 A/L 1966—95 A/L 1972—101 A/L 1967—96 A/L 1973—102 A/L 1968—97 A/L 1974—103 A/L	1977—5 I to 6 L 1978—6 L to 7 L 1979—7 L to 8 J 1980—9 A to 9 J 1981—9 J No longer used after 1981

Information provided by the Syracuse China Corporation, Syracuse, New York.

VAN BRIGGLE POTTERY

VAN BRIGGLE POTTERY
Colorado Springs, CO, U.S.A.
ca.1901—present

From 1900 to 1920, many pieces were dated with the four digits of the year.

WEDGWOOD

WEDGWOOD
Burslem, Barlaston, & Etruria, England
ca.1759—present
(Wedgwood Group)

Each piece of Wedgwood is marked with a backstamp. From 1860 to 1906, three capital letters were impressed—the first representing the month the piece was manufactured, the second the potter, and the third the year the piece was made. Thus, according to the dating system below, since cycle numbers are not part of the stamp, a stamp with the letters "LBS" could mean July 1864 or July 1890.

In 1907 the month code system was changed to a "3" or "4" for every month. Therefore, a backstamp of "3B S" indicates that a piece was manufactured in 1916.

After 1930, the month of manufacture was indicated by a number between 1 and 12 corresponding to the months of the year, the potter by a letter, and the year by two digits. Thus, a mark "6 P 50" means the piece was manufactured in June 1950.

English registry marks are also used (see page 238).

1860–1864	*Monthly marks*		1864–1906	*Monthly marks*	
J January	V July		J January	L July	
F February	W August		F February	W August	
M March	S September		R March	S September	
A April	O October		A April	O October	
Y May	N November		M May	N November	
T June	D December		T June	D December	

Year Marks 1860–1930

Cycle 2		Cycle 3		Cycle 4		Cycle 1		Cycle 2		Cycle 3	
1872	A	1898	A	1924	A			1885	N	1911	N
1873	B	1899	B	1925	B	1860	O	1886	O	1912	O
1874	C	1900	C	1926	C	1861	P	1887	P	1913	P
1875	D	1901	D	1927	D	1862	Q	1888	Q	1914	Q
1876	E	1902	E	1928	E	1863	R	1889	R	1915	R
1877	F	1903	F	1929	F	1864	S	1890	S	1916	S
1878	G	1904	G			1865	T	1891	T	1917	T
1879	H	1905	H			1866	U	1892	U	1918	U
1880	I	1906	I			1867	V	1893	V	1919	V
1881	J	1907	J			1868	W	1894	W	1920	W
1882	K	1908	K			1869	X	1895	X	1921	X
1883	L	1909	L			1870	Y	1896	Y	1922	Y
1884	M	1910	M			1871	Z	1897	Z	1923	Z

WORCESTER

WORCESTER
Worcester, England
1751–present
(Royal Worcester Spode Ltd.)

This table shows the date letter system used by Worcester since 1867. From 1867 to 1890, a letter was impressed below the mark; sometimes two numbers, representing the last two digits of the year, were used. Beginning in 1891, the words "Royal Worcester England" were written around the mark, but no letter was used in that year.

In 1892 a dot system was instituted and it became more elaborate over the years. In 1916 an asterisk was printed together with the dots; thus a piece of porcelain with just an asterisk was manufactured in 1916. From then on various symbols were used together with the dots to indicate the year of manufacture. (See chart.)

After 1956, transfer printed patterns (designs taken from old engraving plates) were marked with a "W" and new designs were marked with an "R." The dot system continued together with the letters "W" or "R" until 1963. After 1963, *new* patterns were marked with the four digits of the current year while *patterns taken from old engravings* continued to be marked with the "W" and dot system. After 1970, a circle was put around a dot for each subsequent year; thus a "W" together with twenty dots with two rings indicates 1972.

DATING TABLE

1867—A	1883—U	
1868—B	1884—V	
1869—C	1885—W	
1870—D	1886—X	
1871—E	1887—Y	
1872—G	1888—Z	
1873—H	1889—O	
1874—I	1890—a	1883
1875—K	1891—(New crown	
1876—L	and words "Royal	
1877—M	Worcester England")	
1878—N	1892—. 1 dot to left	
1879—P	of crown	
1880—R	1893—. . 2 dots, one	
1881—S	each side of crown	Note dot to left of
1882—T	1894—3 dots	crown

U

1883

1892

1895—4 dots
1896—5 dots
1897—6 dots
1898—7 dots
1899—8 dots
1900—9 dots
1901—10 dots
1902—11 dots
1903—12 dots
1904—13 dots
1905—14 dots
1906—15 dots
1907—16 dots
1908—17 dots
1909—18 dots
1910—19 dots
1911—20 dots
1912—21 dots
1913—22 dots
1914—23 dots
1915—24 dots
1916—* under the
circle (dots could
continue)
1917—* and 1 dot
1918—*. and 2 dots
1919—* and 3 dots
1920—* and 4 dots
1921—* and 5 dots
1922—* and 6 dots
1923—* and 7 dots
1924—* and 8 dots
1925—* and 9 dots
1926—* and 10 dots
1927—* and 11 dots
1928—□
1929—◇
1930—÷
1931—∞
1932—∞∞
1933—∞∞ and 1 dot
1934—∞∞ and 2 dots
1935—∞∞ and 3 dots
1936—∞∞ and 4 dots
1937—∞∞ and 5 dots
1938—∞∞ and 6 dots
1939—∞∞ and 7 dots

1940—∞∞ and 8 dots
1941—∞∞ and 9 dots
1942—∞∞ and 10 dots
1943—∞∞ and 11 dots
1944—∞∞ and 12 dots
1945—∞∞ and 13 dots
1946—∞∞ and 14 dots
1947—∞∞ and 15 dots
1948—∞∞ and 16 dots
1949—V
1950—W
1951—W.
1952—.W.
1953—.W. and 3 dots
1954—W and 4 dots
1955—W and 5 dots
1956—W and 6 dots
(or R and 6 dots etc.)
1957—W (or R) and 7 dots
1958—W (or R) and 8 dots
1959—W (or R) and 9 dots
1960—W (or R) and 10 dots
1961—W (or R) and 11 dots
1962—W (or R) and 12 dots
1963—W (or R) and 13 dots
1964—"W" and 14 dots
All new patterns, formerly
marked with "R," now marked
with the four digits of the date
stamped in full.
1965–"W" and 15 dots
or date in numerals
1966—"W" and 16 dots
or date in numerals
1967—"W" and 17 dots
or date in numerals
1968—"W" and 18 dots
or date in numerals
1969—"W" and 19 dots
or date in numerals
1970—"W" and 20 dots
or date in numerals
1971—"W" and 21 dots with
one dot encircled, or date in
numerals.
Etc.

1915
24 dots—6 on either
side of crown and
12 below words

1922
Star and 6 dots below
words Royal Worcester

1956
New patterns were
marked with an "R"

ADDITIONAL TIPS FOR
DATING POTTERY AND PORCELAIN

Here are some clues that help determine the age of a piece. To begin, study the shape of a mark printed on the bottom. The unicorn and lion, the shield mark, the knot, and the garter were all English marks that were popular from about 1806 to the present time. American makers liked to copy these marks and they used them at about the same time. Sometimes, American manufacturers changed the mark a little and used two lions or two unicorns.

If the name of a pattern of dish appears, such as Asiatic Pheasants, it was made after 1810. Elaborate scrolls, etc., were popular from 1820 to 1860.

Rectangular marks with heavy line initials were favored by the Wiener Werkstatte and other art pottery movements from 1900 to 1932; the design was copied by others. The "squared circle"—or perhaps it should be called the "round cornered square"—was a shape of mark favored during the 1950s and 1960s, when it was used by Edwin M. Knowles, Gladding, McBean, and others.

To some extent the prevailing school of design influenced the shape of the mark, so that the Oriental-looking marks with Chinese mandarins or pagodas often date from the Japonisme ideas of the 1880s, the very severe rectangular marks from the 1920s Art Deco period.

Although it was not uncommon for an artist to sign a piece with initials or even a name in the nineteenth century, the name was not a part of the factory mark until the twentieth century. Susie Cooper, Eva Zeisel, Russel Wright, Rockwell Kent, and others are names that denote the designer and the pattern. They are part of the company mark used as backstamps.

DATE YOUR DISHES FROM THE TOP

There are some design clues that can help date a dish. Colors moved in and out of fashion. There was a limited palette during the eighteenth century. Flow blue was popular from 1830 to the early

256

1900s and a gold sponged edging came into use with the blue by the late 1800s. Violets were popular flowers about 1910, then roses followed. Fish sets were the rage about 1910, portrait plates in the 1880s, and plain gold bands on white dishes became popular about 1876. The first calendar plate was made in the United States in 1906, although a few earlier English examples can be found. The first Christmas plate was made in Denmark in 1895. Kewpie dolls were introduced in 1912, Palmer Cox brownies in 1892.

POTTERY AND PORCELAIN "FAMILY TREES"

The making of ceramics has been a family business since the seventeenth century. Factories were passed from father to son, even to daughter, widow, or in-laws. With each change of management there was usually a change of name. In the twentieth century the ceramic industry went through a series of acquisitions and mergers. Often the old marks and names were kept and used by the new companies. Sometimes a ceramic factory in a specific location was sold to a series of firms. The name of the location of the kiln was used in old books and even today some companies refer to a branch in a specific city by the city name. All of this has led to confusion for the collector. While working on this book we had to trace the family trees of some of the major companies that are still making ceramics. Those lists are included here. Notice how the names are repeated for several generations.

The marks used by these companies are listed in the proper place in the main parts of this book. The name in parentheses at the bottom of the information about the mark refers to the present-day company that should have all the past history of the firm. We have been dismayed by the lack of record keeping. Often a new owner simply destroyed all the old records. One company was sold while we were tracing a family tree. By the time we had reached the new owners, a matter of a few weeks, the records were gone and we found our answers only through interviews with ex-employees, the local historical society, and the local library.

THE HAVILAND FAMILY

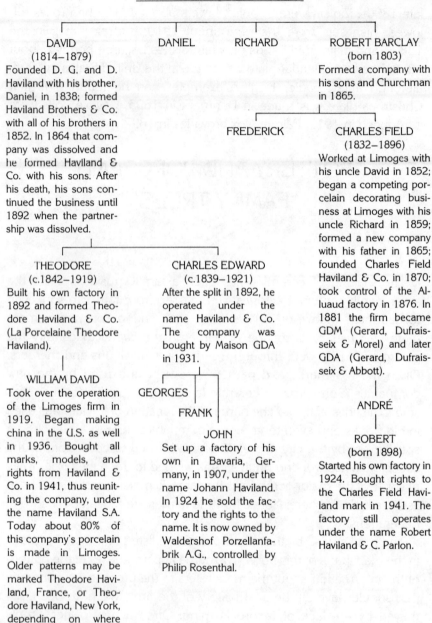

DAVID
(1814–1879)
Founded D. G. and D. Haviland with his brother, Daniel, in 1838; formed Haviland Brothers & Co. with all of his brothers in 1852. In 1864 that company was dissolved and he formed Haviland & Co. with his sons. After his death, his sons continued the business until 1892 when the partnership was dissolved.

DANIEL

RICHARD

ROBERT BARCLAY
(born 1803)
Formed a company with his sons and Churchman in 1865.

FREDERICK

CHARLES FIELD
(1832–1896)
Worked at Limoges with his uncle David in 1852; began a competing porcelain decorating business at Limoges with his uncle Richard in 1859; formed a new company with his father in 1865; founded Charles Field Haviland & Co. in 1870; took control of the Alluaud factory in 1876. In 1881 the firm became GDM (Gerard, Dufraisseix & Morel) and later GDA (Gerard, Dufraisseix & Abbott).

THEODORE
(c.1842–1919)
Built his own factory in 1892 and formed Theodore Haviland & Co. (La Porcelaine Theodore Haviland).

WILLIAM DAVID
Took over the operation of the Limoges firm in 1919. Began making china in the U.S. as well in 1936. Bought all marks, models, and rights from Haviland & Co. in 1941, thus reuniting the company, under the name Haviland S.A. Today about 80% of this company's porcelain is made in Limoges. Older patterns may be marked Theodore Haviland, France, or Theodore Haviland, New York, depending on where they were made. Patterns introduced in the last 20 or 30 years are marked Haviland Limoges France.

CHARLES EDWARD
(c.1839–1921)
After the split in 1892, he operated under the name Haviland & Co. The company was bought by Maison GDA in 1931.

GEORGES

FRANK

JOHN
Set up a factory of his own in Bavaria, Germany, in 1907, under the name Johann Haviland. In 1924 he sold the factory and the rights to the name. It is now owned by Waldershof Porzellanfabrik A.G., controlled by Philip Rosenthal.

ANDRÉ

ROBERT
(born 1898)
Started his own factory in 1924. Bought rights to the Charles Field Haviland mark in 1941. The factory still operates under the name Robert Haviland & C. Parlon.

THEODORE II —— FREDERICK

HAROLD —— CHRISTOPHER

HUTSCHENREUTHER AG

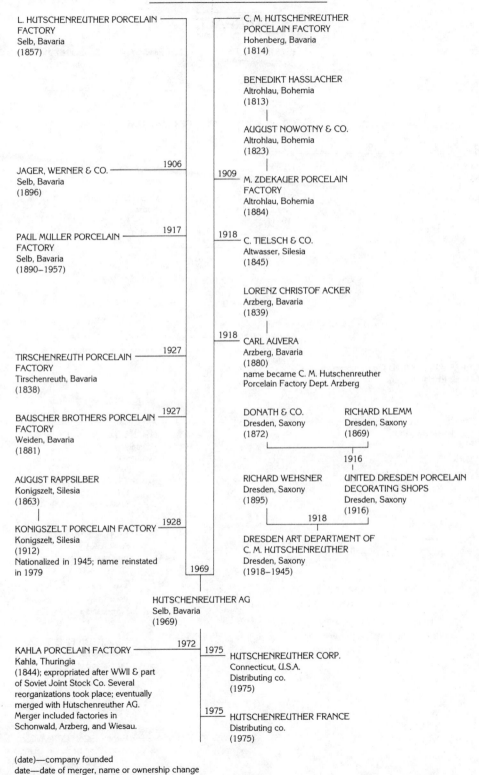

L. HUTSCHENREUTHER PORCELAIN
FACTORY
Selb, Bavaria
(1857)

C. M. HUTSCHENREUTHER
PORCELAIN FACTORY
Hohenberg, Bavaria
(1814)

BENEDIKT HASSLACHER
Altrohlau, Bohemia
(1813)

AUGUST NOWOTNY & CO.
Altrohlau, Bohemia
(1823)

JAGER, WERNER & CO. ——— 1906
Selb, Bavaria
(1896)

1909 —— M. ZDEKAUER PORCELAIN
FACTORY
Altrohlau, Bohemia
(1884)

PAUL MULLER PORCELAIN ——— 1917
FACTORY
Selb, Bavaria
(1890–1957)

1918 —— C. TIELSCH & CO.
Altwasser, Silesia
(1845)

LORENZ CHRISTOF ACKER
Arzberg, Bavaria
(1839)

1918 —— CARL AUVERA
Arzberg, Bavaria
(1880)
name became C. M. Hutschenreuther
Porcelain Factory Dept. Arzberg

TIRSCHENREUTH PORCELAIN ——— 1927
FACTORY
Tirschenreuth, Bavaria
(1838)

BAUSCHER BROTHERS PORCELAIN ——— 1927
FACTORY
Weiden, Bavaria
(1881)

DONATH & CO.   RICHARD KLEMM
Dresden, Saxony   Dresden, Saxony
(1872)   (1869)

1916

AUGUST RAPPSILBER
Konigszelt, Silesia
(1863)

RICHARD WEHSNER   UNITED DRESDEN PORCELAIN
Dresden, Saxony   DECORATING SHOPS
(1895)   Dresden, Saxony
                     (1916)

KONIGSZELT PORCELAIN FACTORY ——— 1928
Konigszelt, Silesia
(1912)
Nationalized in 1945; name reinstated
in 1979

1918

DRESDEN ART DEPARTMENT OF
C. M. HUTSCHENREUTHER
Dresden, Saxony
(1918–1945)

1969

HUTSCHENREUTHER AG
Selb, Bavaria
(1969)

KAHLA PORCELAIN FACTORY ——— 1972
Kahla, Thuringia
(1844); expropriated after WWII & part
of Soviet Joint Stock Co. Several
reorganizations took place; eventually
merged with Hutschenreuther AG.
Merger included factories in
Schonwald, Arzberg, and Wiesau.

1975 —— HUTSCHENREUTHER CORP.
Connecticut, U.S.A.
Distributing co.
(1975)

1975 —— HUTSCHENREUTHER FRANCE
Distributing co.
(1975)

(date)—company founded
date—date of merger, name or ownership change

INTERPACE

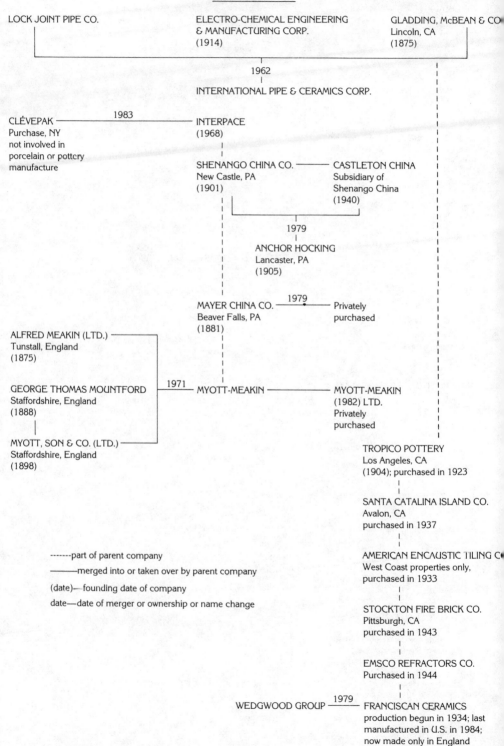

LOCK JOINT PIPE CO.

ELECTRO-CHEMICAL ENGINEERING
& MANUFACTURING CORP.
(1914)

GLADDING, McBEAN & CO
Lincoln, CA
(1875)

1962

INTERNATIONAL PIPE & CERAMICS CORP.

CLÉVEPAK
Purchase, NY
not involved in
porcelain or pottery
manufacture

1983

INTERPACE
(1968)

SHENANGO CHINA CO. ——— CASTLETON CHINA
New Castle, PA
(1901)

CASTLETON CHINA
Subsidiary of
Shenango China
(1940)

1979

ANCHOR HOCKING
Lancaster, PA
(1905)

MAYER CHINA CO. —1979— Privately
Beaver Falls, PA   purchased
(1881)

ALFRED MEAKIN (LTD.)
Tunstall, England
(1875)

GEORGE THOMAS MOUNTFORD
Staffordshire, England
(1888)

1971 — MYOTT-MEAKIN ——— MYOTT-MEAKIN
                                     (1982) LTD.
                                     Privately
                                     purchased

MYOTT, SON & CO. (LTD.)
Staffordshire, England
(1898)

TROPICO POTTERY
Los Angeles, CA
(1904); purchased in 1923

SANTA CATALINA ISLAND CO.
Avalon, CA
purchased in 1937

AMERICAN ENCAUSTIC TILING CO
West Coast properties only,
purchased in 1933

STOCKTON FIRE BRICK CO.
Pittsburgh, CA
purchased in 1943

EMSCO REFRACTORS CO.
Purchased in 1944

-------part of parent company

———merged into or taken over by parent company

(date)— founding date of company

date—date of merger or ownership or name change

WEDGWOOD GROUP —1979— FRANCISCAN CERAMICS
production begun in 1934; last
manufactured in U.S. in 1984;
now made only in England

QUIMPER

HB

HenRiot

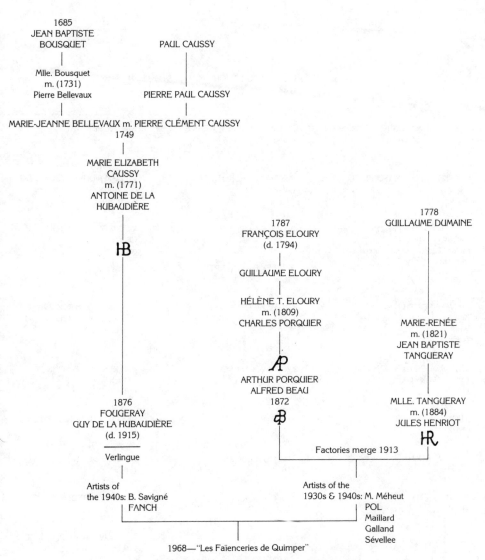

1685
JEAN BAPTISTE
BOUSQUET

PAUL CAUSSY

Mlle. Bousquet
m. (1731)
Pierre Bellevaux

PIERRE PAUL CAUSSY

MARIE-JEANNE BELLEVAUX m. PIERRE CLÉMENT CAUSSY
1749

MARIE ELIZABETH
CAUSSY
m. (1771)
ANTOINE DE LA
HUBAUDIÈRE

HB

1787
FRANÇOIS ELOURY
(d. 1794)

GUILLAUME ELOURY

HÉLÈNE T. ELOURY
m. (1809)
CHARLES PORQUIER

1778
GUILLAUME DUMAINE

MARIE-RENÉE
m. (1821)
JEAN BAPTISTE
TANGUERAY

AP

ARTHUR PORQUIER
ALFRED BEAU
1872

AB

1876
FOUGERAY
GUY DE LA HUBAUDIÈRE
(d. 1915)

MLLE. TANGUERAY
m. (1884)
JULES HENRIOT

HR

Factories merge 1913

Verlingue

Artists of
the 1940s: B. Savigné
FANCH

Artists of the
1930s & 1940s: M. Méheut
POL
Maillard
Galland
Sévellee

1968—"Les Faïenceries de Quimper"

1984—Société Nouvelle des Faïenceries de Quimper HB Henriot

Quimper Faience by Millicent S. Mali. Privately printed, 1979 (210 Spring St., East Greenwich, RI 02818). Reproduced with permission.

RIDGWAY, MASON, COALPORT

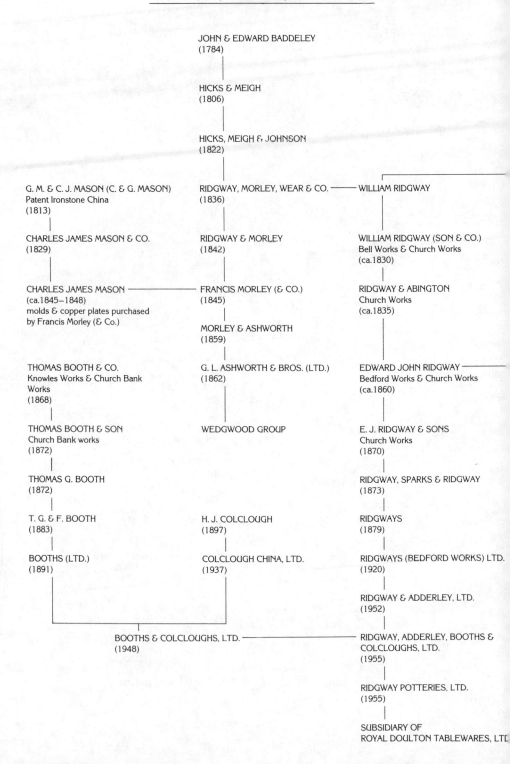

JOHN & EDWARD BADDELEY
(1784)

HICKS & MEIGH
(1806)

HICKS, MEIGH & JOHNSON
(1822)

G. M. & C. J. MASON (C. & G. MASON)
Patent Ironstone China
(1813)

CHARLES JAMES MASON & CO.
(1829)

CHARLES JAMES MASON
(ca.1845–1848)
molds & copper plates purchased
by Francis Morley (& Co.)

THOMAS BOOTH & CO.
Knowles Works & Church Bank
Works
(1868)

THOMAS BOOTH & SON
Church Bank works
(1872)

THOMAS G. BOOTH
(1872)

T. G. & F. BOOTH
(1883)

BOOTHS (LTD.)
(1891)

RIDGWAY, MORLEY, WEAR & CO. ——— WILLIAM RIDGWAY
(1836)

RIDGWAY & MORLEY
(1842)

FRANCIS MORLEY (& CO.)
(1845)

MORLEY & ASHWORTH
(1859)

G. L. ASHWORTH & BROS. (LTD.)
(1862)

WEDGWOOD GROUP

H. J. COLCLOUGH
(1897)

COLCLOUGH CHINA, LTD.
(1937)

WILLIAM RIDGWAY (SON & CO.)
Bell Works & Church Works
(ca.1830)

RIDGWAY & ABINGTON
Church Works
(ca.1835)

EDWARD JOHN RIDGWAY ———
Bedford Works & Church Works
(ca.1860)

E. J. RIDGWAY & SONS
Church Works
(1870)

RIDGWAY, SPARKS & RIDGWAY
(1873)

RIDGWAYS
(1879)

RIDGWAYS (BEDFORD WORKS) LTD.
(1920)

RIDGWAY & ADDERLEY, LTD.
(1952)

BOOTHS & COLCLOUGHS, LTD. ——————— RIDGWAY, ADDERLEY, BOOTHS &
(1948)   COLCLOUGHS, LTD.
                                                                      (1955)

RIDGWAY POTTERIES, LTD.
(1955)

SUBSIDIARY OF
ROYAL DOULTON TABLEWARES, LTD.

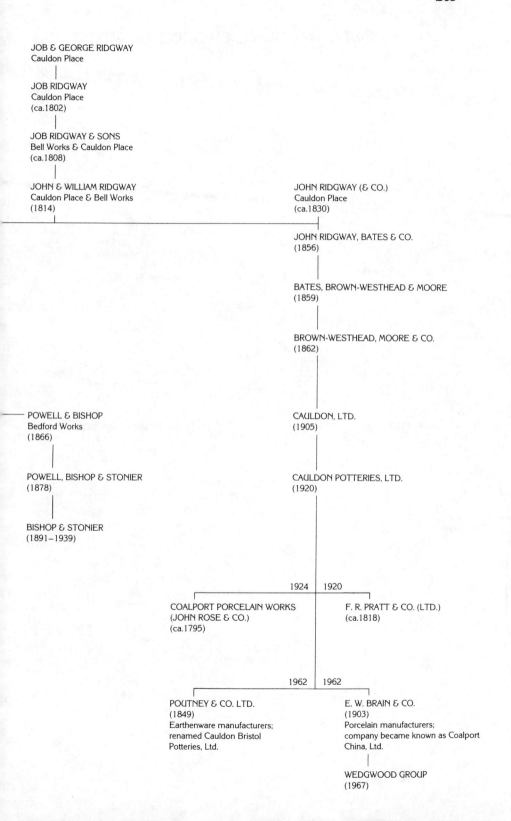

JOB & GEORGE RIDGWAY
Cauldon Place

JOB RIDGWAY
Cauldon Place
(ca.1802)

JOB RIDGWAY & SONS
Bell Works & Cauldon Place
(ca.1808)

JOHN & WILLIAM RIDGWAY
Cauldon Place & Bell Works
(1814)

JOHN RIDGWAY (& CO.)
Cauldon Place
(ca.1830)

JOHN RIDGWAY, BATES & CO.
(1856)

BATES, BROWN-WESTHEAD & MOORE
(1859)

BROWN-WESTHEAD, MOORE & CO.
(1862)

POWELL & BISHOP
Bedford Works
(1866)

CAULDON, LTD.
(1905)

POWELL, BISHOP & STONIER
(1878)

CAULDON POTTERIES, LTD.
(1920)

BISHOP & STONIER
(1891–1939)

1924 | 1920

COALPORT PORCELAIN WORKS
(JOHN ROSE & CO.)
(ca.1795)

F. R. PRATT & CO. (LTD.)
(ca.1818)

1962 | 1962

POUTNEY & CO. LTD.
(1849)
Earthenware manufacturers;
renamed Cauldon Bristol
Potteries, Ltd.

E. W. BRAIN & CO.
(1903)
Porcelain manufacturers;
company became known as Coalport
China, Ltd.

WEDGWOOD GROUP
(1967)

ROSENTHAL GLASS & PORCELAIN AG

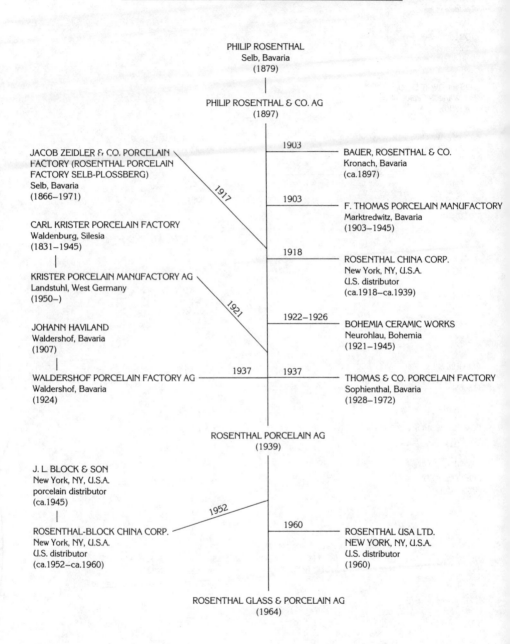

PHILIP ROSENTHAL
Selb, Bavaria
(1879)

PHILIP ROSENTHAL & CO. AG
(1897)

JACOB ZEIDLER & CO. PORCELAIN
FACTORY (ROSENTHAL PORCELAIN
FACTORY SELB-PLOSSBERG)
Selb, Bavaria
(1866–1971)

CARL KRISTER PORCELAIN FACTORY
Waldenburg, Silesia
(1831–1945)

KRISTER PORCELAIN MANUFACTORY AG
Landstuhl, West Germany
(1950–)

JOHANN HAVILAND
Waldershof, Bavaria
(1907)

WALDERSHOF PORCELAIN FACTORY AG
Waldershof, Bavaria
(1924)

1903

BAUER, ROSENTHAL & CO.
Kronach, Bavaria
(ca.1897)

1903

F. THOMAS PORCELAIN MANUFACTORY
Marktredwitz, Bavaria
(1903–1945)

1918

ROSENTHAL CHINA CORP.
New York, NY, U.S.A.
U.S. distributor
(ca.1918–ca.1939)

1922–1926

BOHEMIA CERAMIC WORKS
Neurohlau, Bohemia
(1921–1945)

1937   1937

THOMAS & CO. PORCELAIN FACTORY
Sophienthal, Bavaria
(1928–1972)

1917

1921

ROSENTHAL PORCELAIN AG
(1939)

J. L. BLOCK & SON
New York, NY, U.S.A.
porcelain distributor
(ca.1945)

ROSENTHAL-BLOCK CHINA CORP.
New York, NY, U.S.A.
U.S. distributor
(ca.1952–ca.1960)

1952

1960

ROSENTHAL USA LTD.
NEW YORK, NY, U.S.A.
U.S. distributor
(1960)

ROSENTHAL GLASS & PORCELAIN AG
(1964)

ROYAL DOULTON TABLEWARE LTD.

Companies that have become part of Royal Doulton Tableware Ltd., or whose successors have become part of it, include:

W. A. Adderley (& Co.)
Adderleys Ltd.
John Beswick (Ltd.)
Thomas Booth (& Co.) (& Son) (see Ridgways' chart)
T. G. & F. Booth (see Ridgways' chart)
Booths (Ltd.) (see Ridgways' chart)
Booths & Colcloughs Ltd. (see Ridgways' chart)
H. J. Colclough (see Ridgways' chart)
Colclough China Ltd. (see Ridgways' chart)
Crown Derby Porcelain
Derby Porcelain Works
Doulton & Co.
Doulton & Watts
Doulton Fine China
Dunn, Bennett & Co.
Eurolux
Minton
Mr. M. Nevvar
Paragon China (Co.) Ltd.
Pinder, Bourne & Co.
Queen Anne
Ridgway & Abington (see Ridgways' chart)
Ridgway & Adderley Ltd. (see Ridgways' chart)
Ridgway, Adderley Booths & Colcloughs Ltd. (see Ridgways' chart)
E. J. Ridgway (& Sons) (see Ridgways' chart)
William Ridgway (Son & Co.) (see Ridgways' chart)
Ridgway, Sparks & Ridgway (see Ridgways' chart)
Ridgways (see Ridgways' chart)
Royal Albert
Royal Crown Derby
Shelley Potteries Ltd.
Star China
Steelite

ROYAL WORCESTER SPODE LTD.

Companies that have become part of Royal Worcester Spode Ltd., or whose successors have become part of it, include:

Carlton Ware
Chamberlain & Co.
W. T. Copeland (& Sons Ltd.)
Copeland & Garrett
Hammersley & Co.
A. E. Jones
Kerr & Binns
Palissy Pottery Ltd.
Royal Worcester
Josiah Spode
Wiltshaw & Robinson (Ltd.)
Worcester Porcelains
Worcester Royal Porcelain Co. Ltd.

WEDGWOOD GROUP

Companies that have become part of the Wedgwood Group, or whose successors have become part of it, include:

William Adams & Sons (Potters) Ltd.
Aristocrat Florals & Fancies
G. L. Ashworth & Bros. (Mason's Ironstone) (see Ridgways' chart)
John & Edward Baddeley (see Ridgways' chart)
Bates, Brown-Westhead & Moore (see Ridgways' chart)
Cauldon Potteries Ltd. (see Ridgways' chart)
Coalport Porcelain Works (see Ridgways' chart)
Susie Cooper (Ltd.)
Crown Staffordshire
Franciscan Ceramics (see Interpace chart)
Hicks & Meigh (& Johnson) (see Ridgways' chart)
Johnson Brothers
Charles James Mason (& Co.) (see Ridgways' chart)
G. M. & C. J. Mason (see Ridgways' chart)

J. & G. Meakin
W. R. Midwinter Ltd.
Francis Morley (& Co.) (see Ridgways' chart)
Morley & Ashworth (see Ridgways' chart)
Newport Pottery Co.
F. R. Pratt & Co. (Ltd.) (see Ridgways' chart)
Precision Studios
John Ridgway (& Co.) (see Ridgways' chart)
John Ridgway, Bates & Co. (see Ridgways' chart)
Ridgway & Morley (see Ridgways' chart)
Ridgway, Morley, Wear & Co. (see Ridgways' chart)
Unicorn Tableware
Enoch Wedgwood
Josiah Wedgwood
Wedgwood Hotelware

MARKS USED BY MANY FACTORIES

Some symbols are more salable than others when used as part of a backstamp or trademark. In England, the Royal Arms symbols were used by many factories. In the United States, there were symbols that were similar to the English marks but more salable in the United States market. All of these marks are shown in the appropriate section of the book.

Below are three marks commonly used by many manufacturers together with a list of the names of some of the factories that used them. Most of the factories also included the company name or initials with the mark. Dates indicate the years the marks may have been used.

BRITISH ROYAL ARMS

Many companies in England, the United States, and Europe used the British Royal Arms or a close version as a backstamp. The arms included an oval central area with a lion on one side and a unicorn on the other. The oval shield was divided into quadrants after 1837. Before that time the shield had an extra oval or shield-shaped design in the center. From 1801 to 1814 the mark included a cap over the shield. From 1814 to 1837 the cap was changed to a crown. The marks used outside England often made minor changes. Many firms used two lions or two unicorns at the side of the oval. Some firms used human figures, birds, or other types of animals. Because the wares from England were considered the best available, it was good business to try to look British. Designs, shapes, and even the marks were deliberately misleading. A small printed mark, often blurred, could easily be misread.

The Royal Arms mark was so popular it was used by dozens of factories and it is impossible to give an all-inclusive listing here.

KNOT OR STAFFORDSHIRE KNOT

A pretzel-shaped mark that was really a representation of a knotted rope was used by many English makers. Often the maker's initials were included as part of the mark. Makers who used this mark include:

H. Aynsley & Co. (Ltd.), Longton,
England (1873–1932)

Bodley & Co., Burslem, England
(1865)

Edward F. Bodley & Son (New
Bridge Pottery), Burslem,
England (1883–1898)

George Frederick Bowers & Co.,
Tunstall, England (1842–
1868)

E. Brain & Co. Ltd., Fenton,
England (1903–1964+)

William Brownfield & Sons,
Cobridge, England (1850–
1891)

Burslem School of Art, Burslem,
England (1935–1941)

Hanley Porcelain Co., Hanley,
England (1892–1899)

Kensington Pottery Ltd., Hanley,
England (1922–present)

William Kent Ltd., Burslem,
England (1944–1962)

Arthur J. Mountford, Burslem,
England (1897–1901)

New Wharf Pottery, Burslem,
England (1878–1894)

George Phillips, Longport,
England (1834–1848)

Ridgway, Sparks & Ridgway,
Hanley, England (1873–1879)

Salt & Nixon Ltd., Longton,
England (1901–1934)

Smith & Binnall, Tunstall,
England (1879–1900)

Wellington Pottery Co., Hanley,
England (1899–1901)

Wilkinson & Wardle, Yorkshire,
England (1864–1866)

H. J. Wood Ltd., Burslem,
England (1884–1964+)

W. Wood & Co., Burslem,
England (1873–1932)

COMBINED SHIELD MARK USED BY BOTH UNITED STATES AND ENGLISH FIRMS

A strange mark combining the shields of the United States and England was used in the late nineteenth century by both English and American firms. It seems to have been used as part of a joint marketing arrangement. Some firms using this mark are listed here:

Edward Clarks & Co., Burslem,
England (ca.1865–1887)

International Pottery Co.,
Trenton, NJ, U.S.A. (1860–
1936)

Mercer Pottery Co., Trenton, NJ,
U.S.A. (1868–ca.1937)

New York City Pottery, New York,
NY, U.S.A. (1853–1888)

John Wyllie & Son, East
Liverpool, OH, U.S.A. (1874–
1891)

FAKES AND FORGERIES

If your dish is marked with any of the following marks, you may or may not have a piece with a forged mark. The marks we have included here are ones most often faked on new ceramics. Because the original marks and the later copies are hand-painted, each mark can vary slightly and be of little help in determining the age of the porcelain. All of these marks are listed in the correct section of this book, but beware. Even if your mark looks the same, it may be a copy. The most often forged nineteenth-century marks are the beehive, crossed swords, Augustus Rex mark, crown and N mark, and Sèvres date mark. These are explained here and also included in the main section of the book.

BEEHIVE OR BEEHIVE VIENNA MARK

The Imperial and Royal Porcelain Manufactory of Vienna used a version of the beehive mark from 1744 to 1864. The mark was an adaptation of the center of the coat-of-arms of the Hapsburg family. The hand-painted blue mark was often read upside down and became known as a "beehive." Many firms used variations of the mark, when deliberately trying to deceive the customer. Many small decorating firms added the blue beehive to other marks on a piece.

The original mark was almost always applied under the glaze; later copies were over the glaze. If you run a fingernail over the mark you can tell whether it is over or under the glaze. The original mark was always hand-painted and therefore slightly asymmetrical. If the mark appears to be printed, it is a later copy. If the mark appears with other printing and is positioned so that it resembles the beehive, it is a later copy.

Factories using a variation of the beehive mark include:

Ackerman & Fritze, Volkstedt, Germany (1908–present)

Phillip Aigner, Vienna, Austria (ca.1900)

Bourdois & Bloch, Paris, France (ca.1900)

Carl Knoll, Fischern, Bohemia (Rybare, Czechoslovakia) (1848–1945)

Langewiesen Factory (Oscar Schlegelmilch), Langewiesen, Germany (1892–present)

Edmé Samson, Paris, France (1845–1905)

Beehive, originally used by the Imperial and Royal Porcelain Manufactory of Vienna

CROSSED SWORDS

The crossed swords mark was first used at the Royal Porcelain Manufactory in Meissen, Germany, from about 1725. Variations of this mark are still being used by the factory. It has been copied by many other companies. An extensive list of these factories and facsimiles of the marks can be found in *The Book of Meissen* by Robert Rontgen (Exton, PA: Schiffer Publishing, Ltd., 1984).

Crossed swords mark originally used by the Meissen factory of Meissen, Germany

AUGUSTUS REX OR AR MARK

The Meissen Augustus Rex mark has been copied by many factories and decorators. Helene Wolfsohn of Dresden, Germany, used the mark until 1883, when the Royal Porcelain Manufactory in Meissen won a lawsuit that ordered Wolfsohn to stop. The AR mark was registered by the Meissen factory as a trademark in 1873 after it had been in use for many years. The mark is still being used.

AR mark, originally the mark for the reign of Augustus Rex for the Royal Porcelain Manufactory in Meissen, Germany

CROWN WITH N MARK

The letter N with a crown above it was the mark used from 1771 to 1821 by the Capo-di-Monte factory in Naples, Italy. The company closed and many of the molds were purchased by the Ginori factory in Doccia, Italy, which had started working in 1713. The crowned N mark is still in use. The original mark was hand-painted both over and under the glaze. Some German, French, Italian, and other companies have also used copies of this mark.

Crown with N mark, originally used by the Capo-di-Monte factory of Naples, Italy, and later of Buen Retiro, Spain

SÈVRES DATE MARK

The scrolled cartouche was used with a letter to designate the date of a piece of porcelain from the Sèvres Manufactory at Sèvres, France, from 1753. It has been copied on porcelains from England, Germany, France, and the United States, as well as other small factories. See page 249 for a complete description of the original mark.

Sèvres date mark, originally used by the Royal Factory at Sèvres, France

SELECTED READING
(Entries with asterisks are especially useful books.)

Andrews, Sandy. *Crested China: The History of Heraldic.* London: Spring-wood Books, Ltd., 1980. (English souvenir china.)

Baer, Winfried. *Berlin Porcelain.* Washington, D.C.: Smithsonian Institution Press, 1980.

*Barber, Edwin Atlee. *Marks of American Potters.* Reprint. Southampton, NY: Cracker Barrel Press, 1904.

Barr, Margaret; Miller, Donald; and Barr, Robert. *University of North Dakota Pottery, The Cable Years.* Privately printed, 1977 (Box 8044, Grand Forks, ND 58202).

Boehm Porcelain Objects of Art. Trenton, NJ: Edward Marshall Boehm, Inc., 1976.

Boger, Louise Ade. *Dictionary of World Pottery & Porcelain—From Prehistoric Times to the Present.* New York: Charles Scribner's Sons, 1971.

Bondhus, Sandra V. *Quimper Pottery: A French Folk Art Faience.* Privately printed, 1981 (P.O. Box 203, Watertown, CT 06795).

Bradford Book of Collector Plates. New York: Charles Winthrop & Sons, 1983. (Modern limited edition plates.)

Brand Name & Trademark Guide. Radnor, PA: Chilton Book Co., 1978.

Brand Name & Trademark Guide. Radnor, PA: Chilton Book Co., 1984.

Branin, M. Lelyn. *Early Potters and Potteries of Maine.* Middletown, CT: Wesleyan University Press, 1978.

Bulletin of the Buten Museum of Wedgwood, October 1952. Merion, PA: Buten Museum of Wedgwood.

Burnett, Fred Mark. *Evans Family Potters of Southeast Missouri.* Cape Girardeau, MO: Southeast Missouri State University, 1978.

Buxton, Virginia Hillway. *Roseville Pottery: For Love or Money.* Nashville, TN: Tymbre Hill, 1977.

Chandler, Ceil. *Made in Occupied Japan.* Privately printed (1832 Westheimer Rd., Houston, TX 77006).

China, Glass & Tablewares Red Book Directory. Clifton, NJ: Ebel-Doctorow Publications, 1972.

Chipman, Jack, and Stangler, Judy. *Complete Collectors Guide to Bauer Pottery.* Culver City, CA: California Spectrum, 1982.

Coates, Pamela. *Hull.* Privately printed, 1974 (5121 South Harlan, Indianapolis, IN 46227).

———. *The Real McCoy.* Cherry Hill, NJ: Reynolds Publishers, 1971. (McCoy Pottery.)

———. *The Real McCoy.* Vol. II. Des Moines, IA: Wallace-Homestead Book Co., 1974. (McCoy Pottery.)

Collectors Catalogue: Lladro. Carlstadt, NJ: Weil Ceramics & Glass, Inc., 1981.

Cox, Alwyn and Angela. *Rockingham Pottery & Porcelain 1745–1842.* London: Faber & Faber, 1983. (English Rockingham.)

Cross, A. J. *Pilkington's Royal Lancastrian Pottery & Tiles.* London: Richard Dennis, 1980.

Cunningham, Jo. *The Autumn Leaf Story.* Privately printed, 1976 (535 E. Normal, Springfield, MO 65807). (Autumn Leaf pattern wares, especially ceramics.)

————. *Collector's Encyclopedia of American Dinnerware.* Paducah, KY: Collector Books, 1982. (United States commercial dinnerwares 1920–1960.)

Cushion, J. P. *Handbook of Pottery & Porcelain Marks.* London: Faber & Faber, 1980.

————. *Pocket Book of French & Italian Ceramic Marks.* London: Victoria & Albert Museum, 1965.

————. *Pocket Book of German Ceramic Marks.* London: Victoria & Albert Museum, 1962.

Cybis. *Commemorative Catalog.* Trenton, NJ: Cybis, 1979.

Dahl-Jensen Porcelaensfabrik, Copenhagen Art Porcelain. Copenhagen: Dahl-Jensens Porcelaensfabrik. Company catalog. (Written in Danish.)

*d'Albis, Jean, and Romanet, Celeste. *La Porcelaine de Limoges.* Paris: Sous le Vent, 1980. (Porcelains from the city of Limoges, France, since the 1840s. Written in French.)

Danckert, Ludwig. *Directory of European Porcelain.* 4th ed. London: N.A.G. Press, Ltd., 1981.

Darling, Sharon S. *Chicago Ceramic & Glass: An Illustrated History from 1871 to 1933.* Chicago, IL: Chicago Historical Society, 1979.

de Plenival de Guillebon, Regine. *Porcelain of Paris 1770–1850.* New York: Walker and Co., 1972.

*Derwich, Jenny B., and Latos, Mary. *Dictionary Guide to United States Pottery & Porcelain (19th & 20th centuries).* Privately printed, 1984 (P.O. Box 674, Franklin, MI 48025). (History, no marks.)

Duke, Harvey. *Hall China: A Guide for Collectors.* Privately printed, 1977 (12135 N. State Rd., Otisville, MI 48463).

————. *Superior Quality Hall China: A Guide for Collectors.* Privately printed, 1977 (12135 N. State Rd., Otisville, MI 48463).

Eaglestone, Arthur A., and Lockett, T. A. *The Rockingham Pottery.* New rev. ed. Rutland, VT: Charles E. Tuttle Co., 1973. (United States Rockingham Pottery.)

Enge, Delleen. *Franciscan Ware.* Paducah, KY: Collector Books, 1981.

*Evans, Paul. *Art Pottery of the United States.* New York: Charles Scribner's Sons, 1974.

Eyles, Desmond. *The Doulton Lambeth Wares.* Totowa, NJ: Rowman and Littlefield, 1975.

Gaston, Mary Frank. *Collector's Encyclopedia of Flow Blue China.* Paducah, KY: Collector Books, 1983. (Primarily English flow blue dishes of the 19th century but pieces from other countries are included.)

Gaunt, William, and Clayton-Stamm, M.D.E. *William DeMorgan, Pre-Raphaelite Ceramics.* Greenwich, CT: New York Graphic Society, Ltd., 1971.

Gilhespy, F. Brayshaw. *Derby Porcelain.* New York: Archer House, Inc., 1961.

*Godden, Geoffrey A. *Encyclopedia of British Pottery & Porcelain Marks.* New York: Crown Publishers, 1964.

————. *Godden's Guide to Mason's China and the Ironstone Wares.* Suffolk, England: Antique Collectors' Club, 1980.

————. *Illustrated Guide to Mason's Patent Ironstone China.* New York: Praeger Publishers, 1971.

Gustavsberg 150 Years. Sthlm, Sweden: National Museum, 1975. (Written in Swedish.)

Haggar, Reginald, and Adams, Elizabeth. *Mason Porcelain & Ironstone 1796–1853.* London: Faber & Faber, 1977.

Haslam, Malcolm. *Marks & Monograms of the Modern Movement, 1875–1930.* New York: Charles Scribner's Sons, 1977. (One chapter of ceramic marks.)

Hawkins, Jennifer. *Poole Potteries.* London: Barrie & Jenkins, 1980.

Hayes, Barbara Jean. *Bauer: The California Pottery Rainbow.* Privately printed, 1975 (1629 W. Washington Blvd., Venice, CA 90291).

Hoffman, Donald C., Sr. *Why Not Warwick.* Privately printed, 1979 (P.O. Box 3162, Aurora, IL 60506). (United States, Warwick china.)

Hudgeons, Thomas E. III, ed. *Official 1983 Price Guide to Collector Plates.* Orlando, FL: House of Collectibles, 1983. (Modern limited edition plates.)

Huxford, Sharon and Bob. *Collectors Encyclopedia of Brush McCoy Pottery.* Paducah, KY: Collector Books, 1978.

————. *Collectors Encyclopedia of Fiesta.* Rev. 4th ed. Paducah, KY: Collector Books, 1981.

————. *Collectors Encyclopedia of McCoy Pottery.* Paducah, KY: Collector Books, 1978.

Jensen, Veryl M. *First International Book of Willow Ware.* Privately printed, 1975 (P.O. Box 601, Oakridge, OR 97463). (Primarily English and United States samples of dishes with the Willow pattern.)

Jervis, W. Percival. *A Book of Pottery Marks.* Philadelphia: Wright, ca.1897.

Kerr, Ann. *Steubenville Saga.* Privately printed, 1979 (P.O. Box 437, Sidney, OH 43565). (United States dinnerwares from Steubenville, Ohio, with emphasis on Russel Wright.)

Kirsner, Gary. *The Mettlach Book.* Cincinnati, OH: Seven Hills Books, 1983.

Klamkin, Marian. *Made in Occupied Japan: A Collector's Guide.* New York: Crown Publishers, Inc., 1976.

————. *White House China.* New York: Charles Scribner's Sons, 1972. (The dishes from many countries used in the White House since the days of George Washington.)

*Kovel, Ralph M. and Terry H. *Dictionary of Marks—Pottery and Porcelain*. New York: Crown Publishers, Inc., 1953.

*———. *The Kovels' Collector's Guide to American Art Pottery*. New York: Crown Publishers, Inc., 1974.

———. *The Kovels' Illustrated Price Guide to Depression Glass and American Dinnerware*. 2nd ed. New York: Crown Publishers, Inc., 1983. (Dinnerware from 1930 to 1960 era.)

———. *Kovels' Illustrated Price Guide to Royal Doulton*. 2nd ed. New York: Crown Publishers, Inc., 1984.

———. *Kovels' Know Your Antiques*. New York: Crown Publishers, Inc., 1981. (Various factory histories and marks.)

*———. *Kovels' Know Your Collectibles*. New York: Crown Publishers, Inc., 1981. (Various factory histories and marks used after 1875.)

Kybalová, Jana. *Ceramic Marks of the World*. London: Hamlyn Publishing Group Ltd., 1981.

*Lehner, Lois. *Complete Book of American Kitchen & Dinner Wares*. Des Moines, IA: Wallace-Homestead Book Co., 1980. (1930–1960 era.)

———. *Ohio Pottery & Glass Marks & Manufacturers*. Des Moines, IA: Wallace-Homestead Book Co., 1978.

Lima, Paul and Candy. *Enchantment of Hand-Painted Nippon*. Privately printed, 1971 (P.O. Box 517, Silverado, CA 92676). (Japanese wares of the 1890–1920 period.)

Loendorf, Gene. *Nippon, Hand-Painted China*. Privately printed, 1975 (Valley City, ND). (Japanese wares of the 1890–1920 period.)

Maling, 4 Tyneside Pottery. Tyne & Wear, England: Tyne & Wear County Council, 1981.

Mankowitz, Wolf. *Wedgwood*. New York: E. P. Dutton & Co., 1953.

Meyer, Florence E. *Colorful World of Nippon*. Des Moines, IA: Wallace-Homestead Book Co., 1971. (Japanese wares of the 1890–1920 period.)

Nelson, Maxine. *Versatile Vernon Kilns: An Illustrated Value Guide, Book II*. Paducah, KY: Collector Books, 1983.

Newbound, Betty and Bill. *Southern Potteries, Inc., Blue Ridge Dinnerware*. Paducah, KY: Collector Books, 1980.

*Ormerod, Dana E., and Gates, William C., Jr. *The East Liverpool, Ohio, Pottery District, Identification of Manufacturers and Marks*. Washington, D.C.: Society for Historical Archeology, 1982.

Palley, Reese. *The Porcelain Art of Edward Marshall Boehm*. New York: Harry N. Abrams, Inc., 1976.

Penkala, Maria. *European Porcelain*. Amsterdam: R. W. Haentjens, 1947.

———. *European Pottery*. Rutland, VT: Charles E. Tuttle, 1968.

Platt, Dorothy Pickard. *The Story of Pickard China*. Hanover, PA: Everybody's Press, 1970.

Postle, Kathleen R. *Overbeck*. Indianapolis: Indiana Historical Society, 1978.

The Pottery of Walter Stephen. Charlotte, NC: Mint Museum of History, 1978. (Pisgah pottery.)

Raines, Joan & Marvin. *A Guide to Royal Bayreuth Figurals.* Privately printed, 1973 (P.O. Box 275, New City, NY 10956).

*Random House Collector's Encyclopedia, Victoriana to Art Deco. New York: Random House, 1974. (History, no marks.)

Ray, Marcia. *Collectible Ceramics.* New York: Crown Publishers, Inc., 1974. (Emphasis on 19th- and 20th-century wares.)

Rebert, M. Charles. *American Majolica 1850–1900.* Des Moines, IA: Wallace-Homestead Book Co., 1981.

Reilly, Robin, and Savage, George. *The Dictionary of Wedgwood.* Suffolk, England: Antique Collectors' Club, 1980.

Roberts, Brenda. *Collector's Encyclopedia of Hull Pottery.* Paducah, KY: Collector Books, 1980.

Robinson, Dorothy. *Nippon Hand-Painted China.* Privately printed (West Rd., Box 567, Manchester, VT 05254). (Japanese wares of the 1890–1920 period.)

Robinson, Dorothy, and Feeny, Bill. *Official Price Guide to American Pottery & Porcelain.* Paducah, KY: Collector Books, 1980. (Trenton, NJ, wares.)

Rontgen, Robert E. *The Book of Meissen.* Exton, PA: Schiffer Publishing, Ltd., 1984.

*———. *Marks on German, Bohemian & Austrian Porcelain, 1710–Present.* Exton, PA: Schiffer Publishing, Ltd., 1981.

Royal Copenhagen. Copenhagen: Det Berlingske Bugtrykkeri, 1976.

Salley, Virginia Sutton and George H. *Royal Bayreuth China.* Privately printed, 1969 (P.O. Box 3305, Portland, ME 04104).

Sandon, Harry. *Royal Worcester Porcelain from 1862 to the Present Day.* New York: Clarkson N. Potter, Inc., 1973.

Savage, George, and Newman, Harold. *Illustrated Dictionary of Ceramics.* New York: Van Nostrand Reinhold Co., 1974.

Schlegelmilch, Clifford. *R. S. Prussia.* Privately printed, 1973 (P.O. Box 4322, Flint, MI 48504).

Schwartzman, Paulette. *Collector's Guide to European & American Art Pottery.* Paducah, KY: Collector Books, 1978. (Emphasis is on the 1875–1920 period.)

Stevenson, James R. *Antique Steins, A Collectors' Guide.* East Brunswick, NJ: Cornwall Books, 1982.

Stitt, Irene. *Japanese Ceramics of the Last 100 Years.* New York: Crown Publishers, Inc., 1974.

The Story of Minton. Stoke, England: Royal Doulton Tableware Ltd., 1976.

*The Tableware Reference Book. Surrey, England: International Trade Publications, Ltd., 1983.

Taburet, Marjatta. *La Faience de Quimper.* Paris: Sous le Vent, 1979. (Quimper pottery of France. Written in French.)

**Tardy. *Les Porcelaines Françaises.* England: Hilmarton Manor Press, 1978.

*———. *Poteries Faiences Françaises.* Vols. I–IV. Paris: Tardy, 1949, 1982. (French porcelain history. Written in French.)

Thomas, D. and E. Lloyd. *The Old Torquay Potteries, From Castle to Cottage.* London: Arthur H. Stockwell, Ltd., 1977.

Thomas, E. Lloyd. *Victorian Art Pottery.* London: Guildart, 1974.

Trademarks of the Jewelry & Kindred Trades. New York: Jewelers' Circular Publishing Co., 1915. (Reprinted by American Reprints Co., 111 West Dent, Ironton, MO 63650.)

25th Anniversary Edward Marshall Boehm Studio 1950 to 1975, Porcelain Objects of Art. Trenton, NJ: Edward Marshall Boehm, Inc., 1975.

Twitchett, John, and Bailey, Betty. *Royal Crown Derby.* New York: Clarkson N. Potter, Inc., 1976.

Van Patten, Joan F. *Collector's Encyclopedia of Nippon Porcelain.* Paducah, KY: Collector Books, 1979. (Japanese wares of the 1875–1920 period.)

———. *Collector's Encyclopedia of Nippon Porcelain.* 2nd Series. Paducah, KY: Collector Books, 1982. (Japanese wares of the 1875–1920 period.)

*Vingedal, S. E. *Porslinsmarken.* Stockholm: Forum, 1977. (Marks of European, especially Scandinavian ceramics. Written in Swedish.)

Watkins, Chris; Harvey, William; and Senft, Robert. *Shelley Potteries: The History and Production of a Staffordshire Family of Potters.* London: Barrie & Jenkins, 1980.

Weiss, Gustav. *The Book of Porcelain.* New York: Praeger Publishers, 1971.

Werke um 1900. Berlin: Kunstgewerbe Museum, 1966. (Catalog of exhibition of ceramics of 1900–1920. Written in German.)

Whiter, Leonard. *Spode.* New York: Praeger Publishers, 1970.

Worth, Veryl Marie. *Willow Pattern China.* Privately printed, 1979 (P.O. Box 601, Oakridge, OR 97463).

General Index

Entries are listed with page and letter indicating position on the page. The names of the factories using marks are listed in bold type. Words that appear in the actual mark are listed in regular type. The names of sections of the book are listed in capital letters.